Walter W. Skeat

The Tale of the Man of Lawe; The Pardoneres Tale; The Second Nonnes Tales; The Chanouns Yemannes Tale

Walter W. Skeat

The Tale of the Man of Lawe; The Pardoneres Tale; The Second Nonnes Tales; The Chanouns Yemannes Tale

ISBN/EAN: 9783744671613

Printed in Europe, USA, Canada, Australia, Japan

Cover: Foto ©Thomas Meinert / pixelio.de

More available books at **www.hansebooks.com**

Clarendon Press Series

CHAUCER

SKEAT

HENRY FROWDE, M.A.

PUBLISHER TO THE UNIVERSITY OF OXFORD

LONDON, EDINBURGH, AND NEW YORK

Clarendon Press Series

CHAUCER

THE TALE OF THE MAN OF LAWE
THE PARDONERES TALE
THE SECOND NONNES TALE
THE CHANOUNS YEMANNES TALE

FROM

THE CANTERBURY TALES

EDITED BY THE

REV. WALTER W. SKEAT

LITT.D., LL.D., D.C.L., PH.D.

Elrington and Bosworth Professor of Anglo-Saxon in the University of Cambridge

New Edition, Revised

Oxford

AT THE CLARENDON PRESS

M DCCC XCVII

Oxford
PRINTED AT THE CLARENDON PRESS
BY HORACE HART, M.A.
PRINTER TO THE UNIVERSITY
.

CONTENTS.

INTRODUCTION.

FOR remarks upon Grammatical Forms occurring in Chaucer, I must beg leave to refer the reader to the Introduction to Dr. Morris's edition of the Prologue, Knight's Tale, &c.; and to some further remarks in the Introduction to my edition of the Prioresses Tale, &c. (Clarendon Press Series), p. xlix.

Remarks upon the Metre and Versification will be found in the Introduction to the Prioresses Tale, p. liii.; followed by a Metrical Analysis of Part I. of the Squire's Tale, p. lxvi.

An account of the manner in which the text of the present edition has been formed will be found in the same volume, p. lxxiii. It may suffice to repeat here that the text follows, in general, the readings of the Ellesmere MS. (called ' E.' in the footnotes), with occasional variations from six others, viz. the Hengwrt, Cambridge, Corpus, Petworth, Lansdowne, and Harleian MSS., denoted respectively by the symbols Hn., C., Cp., Pt., Ln., and Hl. Of these, all but the Harleian MS. are printed in full in Mr. Furnivall's splendid Six-text Edition, published for the Chaucer Society; whilst MS. Hl. is substantially the same as the text in Wright's, Morris's and Bell's editions. The text of Tyrwhitt's edition comes near to that of the Ellesmere MS., and does not much differ from that in the present volume. As in ' The Prioresses Tale,' &c., the Grouping of the Tales and the numbering of the lines exactly correspond with those of the Six-text edition, for the purpose of convenience of reference. The Tales here chosen belong partly to Group B (see Introd. to Prior. Tale, p. xii.); partly to Group C; and partly to Groups G, H, and I. Group G, containing the Second Nun's Tale and the Canon's Yeoman's Tale, is printed here in full.

In my former Introduction, I endeavoured to explain all that
seemed necessary for a right understanding of the text. But I
have been reminded that I gave no explanation of the *titles* of
the various parts of the Groups, such as 'Man-of-Law Head-
link,' and the rest; and I have been asked to explain what a
'Head-link' means. The answer is, that all these titles are
copied exactly, for convenience, from Mr. Furnivall's Six-text
edition, and that they were adopted by him, in the first instance,
in order to show the exact condition in which the Canterbury
Tales have come down to us in the existing MSS. Thus, before
the Man of Law's Tale, we find, in reality, two introductory
passages. The latter of these is the real Prologue, ll. 99–133.
But it was necessary to find another name for the preliminary
dialogue in ll. 1–98. The name fixed upon by Mr. Furnivall was
a 'Link,' a term adopted in order so to name these connecting
dialogues as to indicate the connection between the Tales.
Thus the dialogue or Link connecting the Clerk's Tale with the
Merchant's Tale (Group E, ll. 1213-1244, in Prioresses Tale, &c.
pp. 100, 101) came to be called the 'Clerk-Merchant Link,' and
so in other cases. Hereupon there arose, however, a new difficulty.
The Tales are left in an imperfect state, in unconnected groups,
and there is nothing to show what Tale was intended to precede
that told by the Man of Law. The result is, that the passage now
under discussion, i.e. the first 98 lines of Group B, turns out to be
a 'Blank-Man of Law Link.' To avoid this awkward expression,
Mr. Furnivall determined to call it the 'Man-of-Law Head-
link,' that is to say, a passage *preceding* the Man of Law's Prologue, without anything to join it on to anything else. The
same explanation makes clear the meaning of The Squire Head-
link, Group F, ll. 1–8, a passage only eight lines long. Similarly,
at the end of the Man of Law's Tale, there is a passage (Group
B, ll. 1163-1190) which has a *double* title; viz. Man-of-Law End-
link, or Shipman's Prologue. Now for this double title there is
a special reason. No doubt the passage is, properly, the Shipman's Prologue, as it is rightly called in MS. Arch. Seld. B. 14.
But it is convenient to have the alternative title, because in some

MSS. it is wrongly called the Prologue of the Squire's Tale. The title Man-of-Law End-link expresses, therefore, that it is, in *any* case, a pendant or tag to the Man of Law's Tale, and that it must certainly *follow* that Tale, whatever other Tale it is to precede. These titles are, then, mere explanatory phrases, and are in all cases copied exactly from the Chaucer Society's Six-text edition. It is easy, by merely observing the names of these 'links,' to understand and to remember the exact extent to which the Tales were partially arranged by their author.

PRONUNCIATION.

There is yet one other matter on which I have been asked to say somewhat, viz. the Pronunciation of Chaucer's English. This matter I purposely left untouched until students should have become somewhat more familiar with the nature of the Metre and Versification, so far as that can be understood by using the modern pronunciation only. It is now, perhaps, high time to insist on the importance of making some attempt towards understanding, if only in a rough and approximate manner, the great changes that have occurred in our pronunciation since Chaucer's days, so that the beauty of his rhythm may not be marred by the application to it of that system of English pronunciation which is in use at the present day ; a system which might be applied to the reading of Dante or Boccaccio with the same fitness as to Chaucer, and with a very similar result as regards an approximation to the sounds with which the author was himself familiar.

On the subject of Pronunciation,. my guide is, as a matter of course, Mr. Alexander J. Ellis, whose standard work on Early English Pronunciation [1] is well-known, at any rate by name, to all

---

[1] On Early English Pronunciation, with especial reference to Shakspere and Chaucer. By Alexander J. Ellis, F.R.S., F.S.A., London, Trübner and Co. Parts I and II are dated 1869; Part III is dated 1870; Part IV is dated 1874, extending to p. 1432. The work will be completed in two more parts.

who have taken any interest in the matter. Mr. Ellis has treated
the question so carefully and fully that an attempt on my part
at giving a general notion of his results would be hardly fair to
him or satisfactory to the reader; but he has, fortunately, *himself*
drawn up a brief abstract of his results, which was printed as
Appendix A (pp. 253*—264*) in the second issue of the Aldine
edition of Chaucer, edited by Dr. Morris. It is here reprinted
by permission of the publishers, after revision by Mr. Ellis, for
the present work.

I also draw attention **to Mr.** Sweet's book on English Sounds,
with its full Word-lists and abundance of examples[1]. The results
there arrived at sufficiently agree with Mr. Ellis's, and fully **con-**
firm them in all that is material.

The pronunciation of English during the fourteenth century
differed materially from that now in use. The following is an
abstract of the conclusions at which Mr. Ellis has arrived respecting
the pronunciation probably in use among the highly educated
southern speakers for whom Chaucer wrote, and directions are
subjoined for modern readers who wish to imitate it.

A long = *ah*, as in father, *a*lms, *a*re; the usual continental
sound of long *a*. The present pronunciation of *a*, as *ai* in *wait*,
seems not to have become thoroughly established till the beginning
of the eighteenth century.

A short = *ăh*, the short sound of *ah*, not now used in received
English, but still common in the midland and northern provinces;
the usual continental sound of short *a*. The present very different pronunciation, as *a* in *cat*, agreeing with the sound in the
south-western and eastern counties, was not established till the
seventeenth century; those, however, to whom *ăh* is difficult may
use this *a* in *cat*.

AA, the same as A long.

---

[1] A History of English Sounds, from the earliest period, with full Word-
lists. By H. Sweet, M.A. Oxford; Clarendon Press, 1888. (Originally
published for the London Philological Society and the English Dialect
Society in 1864.)

AI = *ah'ee*, a diphthong consisting of *ah* pronounced briefly but with a stress, and gliding on to *ee* in one syllable; sometimes used now in *aye*, and in the second syllable of *Isaiah*, as distinct from the first; the German sound of *ai*, nearly the Italian *ahi!* and the French *aï*. Those who have a difficulty with this sound may use the ordinary pronoun I. The modern sound *ai*, as in *wait*, was not thoroughly established till the seventeenth century, although it began to make its appearance in the first half of the sixteenth. Almost all dialects treat this combination differently from long A. See EY.

AU = *ah'oo*, a diphthong consisting of *ah* pronounced briefly but with a stress, and gliding on to *oo* in one syllable: not used in modern English; the German *au*, nearly the Italian *au* in *Laura*, the French *aou*. Those who have a difficulty with this sound may use the ordinary *ou* in *house*. The modern sound of *au*, as in *Paul*, was not established till the seventeenth century.

AW, the same as AU.

AY, the same as AI.

B, as at present.

C = *k* before *a, o, u*, or any consonant, and = *s* before *e, i, y*. It was never called *sh*, as in the present sound of *vicious*, which then formed three syllables, *vi-ci-ous*.

CCH = *tch*, as in *fetch*.

CH = *ch*, as in *such, cheese*, and in Greek words occasionally *k*, as at present.

D, as at present.

E long = *ē* in *there*, *ai* in *pair*, *a* in *dare*; that is, as *ai* is now pronounced before *r*, or rather more broadly than before any other consonant, and without any tendency to taper into the sound of *ee*; the German *eh* long, nearly the French *è*, and Italian open *e*. Those who find this sound too difficult may say *ai* as in *ail*. The present use of the sound of *ee* in *eel* was not established till the beginning of the eighteenth century, although two sounds of *e* as in *mere, there*, were partially marked by *ee* and *ea* in the latter part of the sixteenth century, and *ea* very gradually changed to the sound of *ee* in the seventeenth. It is possible that a close and open sound of this letter, as in the Italian *e chiuso* and *e aperto* (which are allowed to rhyme), or the French *é* and *è* (which are not allowed to rhyme), may have existed, but as they were allowed to rhyme in Chaucer, they cannot be separated with certainty. Dickens's *Sai*-rey Gamp has the close sound, the usual *Sa*rah has the open sound.

E short = *e* in *met, pen, well*.

E final = *ë*, or short *e* lightly and obscurely pronounced, as the final *e* in the German *einë herrlichë gutë Gabë*; nearly like the present *a* in *idea* or final *er* when the *r* is not trilled. This sound was **always used** in prose, when the final *e* was the mark of some final vowel in older forms of the language, when it marked oblique cases, feminine genders, plurals, inflections of verbs, adverbs, &c. **But** in poetry it was regularly elided altogether before a following vowel, and before *he, his, him, hire* = her, *here* = their, *hem* = them, and occasionally before *hath, hadde, have, how, her, here* = here. It was never pronounced in *hire* = her, *here* = their, *oure* = our, *youre* = your; and was frequently omitted in *hadde* = had, *were, time, more*. It was occasionally, but rarely, omitted when necessary for the rhyme and metre, and for force of expression, in other positions, especially when it replaced an older vowel, or marked an oblique case, precisely as in modern German. As this pronunciation of the final *e* gradually fell out of use during the fifteenth century, when most of the MSS. of Chaucer now in existence were written, the final *e* is often incorrectly inserted and omitted in their orthography, and has to be omitted or restored from metric and other considerations. Practically the reader should always insert it when necessary for the metre, and never pronounce it as our final *y*, but always as above indicated.

EA, the same as long E, like *ea* in *break, great, to wear, to tear, bear*; seldom used except in the words *ease, please*. The modern sound of *ea*, as *ee* in *eel*, was not established till the eighteenth century.

EE, the same as long E, that is, as *e'e* in *e'er*; in frequent use. The combination *ee*, with its modern sound of *ee*, was not established till past the middle of the sixteenth century.

EI, the same as AI, with which it was constantly interchanged by the scribes, that is, nearly as the present pronoun I. The modern sound as *ee* belongs to the eighteenth century. See EY.

EO, the same as long E; seldom used except in the word *people*, often spelled *pepel*. The modern sound of *eo* as *ee*, dates from the sixteenth century.

ES final, the mark of the plural, was generally pronounced as *es* or *is*, even in those cases where the *e* is now omitted.

EU. There is much difficulty in arriving at a satisfactory conclusion respecting this combination, which is not frequent in rhymes. Very possibly it was = *ui* in the Scotch *puir*, the long sound of the French *u*, German *ü*, in all words of French origin. This became like our modern *ew* during the seventeenth century, and may be so pronounced by those to whom the French sound is too difficult. In words not of French origin, *eu* = *ai'oo*, a diphthong consisting of *ai* pronounced briefly, but with a stress, and gliding on to *oo* in one syllable, as in the Italian *Europa*. Neither sound is now used in received English, but both occur provincially. See EW.

EW, like EU, had possibly the sound of *ui* in the Scotch *puir*, or else *ai'oo*, precisely as EU. The following words, generally written with *ew* in Chaucer, seem to have the sound of *ui*, or French *u*; *blue, due, eschew, glue*, a *mew* for hawks, *remew, stew, sue*. The following, on the other hand, seem to have had the sound of *ai'oo*: *dronkelew, few, hew, hue, knew, new, rew* = row, *rue, spew, shrew, threw, true*.

EY, the same as AY, with which it is constantly interchanged by the scribe. The modern sound as *ee* belongs to the eighteenth century. AY, EY were possibly pronounced as *e* in *there* during the fifteenth century, in the north and west midland counties, and hence occasionally interchanged with long *e* in the orthography of some later or northern MSS. Modern dialects treat them as they do *ai* and not as they do the long *e*.

F = *f*, as at present.

G = *g* hard in all words not of French origin, and = *j* before *e*, *i*, in words of French origin. Sometimes G was *j* before other vowels in words where the *e* usually inserted was omitted by the scribe, just as at present in *judgment, gaol*.

GE final, or before *a, o*, in French words = *j*, but the *e* was sometimes omitted in writing.

GH = *kh*, the Scotch and German sound of *ch*, or *kh* as it is best written, produced by making the contact of the tongue with the soft palate for *k* so imperfect that a hissing sound can be heard. After *e, i*, the tongue was probably raised higher, so that *kh* approached to the sound of a hissed *y*; and after *o, u*, the lips were probably often rounded, giving the effect of the modern Scotch *quh*; the former sound fell into *y* and short *i*, the latter into *wh* and *f*, or into *oh, oo*. *Gh* may be conveniently always spoken like the German and Scotch *ch*, that is *kh*, but it will have to be occasionally omitted where written, and pronounced where not written, on account of the negligence of the scribes of the old MSS.[1], and it is very possible that the changes above indicated were already more or less in vogue, and that the poet availed himself of either use according as it suited his rhyme. This guttural is still in full force in Scotland and is even still heard in living use in England from a few old people.

H initial = *h*, just as at present; but it seems to have been generally omitted in unaccented *he, his, him, hire* = her, *here* = their[2], *hem* = them, and often in *hath, hadde, haue*, just as we still have *I've told 'em*; and in some French words, as *host, honour, honest*, &c. it was probably omitted as at present. H final represents a very faint sound of the guttural *kh* (see GH), into which it dwindled before it became entirely extinguished.

I long was not at all the modern sound of *I*. It was the lengthened sound of *i* in *still*, which was nearly but not quite *ee*; compare *still, steal*, in singing ' *Still* so gently o'er me *stealing*,' in which also the last syllables of *gently* and *stealing* are lengthened with the same vowel. Those who think they find it difficult to lengthen this vowel which, when short, is extremely common

---

[1] In the present edition these anomalies are avoided as much as possible.

[2] In the present edition, the *hire, here* of the MSS. is printed *hir, her*.

in English, but is not known in French and Italian[1], may say *ee*, as in *mien, mean,* but they will be quite wrong if they pronounce it as at present in *mine.*

I short = *i,* as in *pit, stiff, pin;* not as in French or Italian. Compare English *finny, fish,* with French *fini, fiche.*

I consonant = *j.*

I E, before a consonant in many MSS., but only in French words, was possibly the same as long E, with which it was often interchanged by the scribe. The modern sound of *ee* dates from the seventeenth century. I E final and unaccented as in *berie, merie,* must be pronounced as two syllables *i-ë,* the first probably as the short I just described, and the second as the final E already described. But I E final, then more often written Y E, has more frequently the accent on the I or Y, and then that letter was pronounced as Chaucer's long I, that is nearly as *ee.* Thus *melodie* (commonly written *melodye*) had nearly the same sound as it has in modern French songs when sung.

J = *j,* was not distinguished from I consonant in MSS.

K, as at present.

L, as at present.

L E final, probably as at present in *little* = *lit'l,* except when *ë* is inflectional.

L H (which does not occur in this edition) was the same as simple L. It was scarcely ever used, but in the thirteenth century it was probably a hissed *l,* not unlike (but not the same as) Welsh *ll.*

M, as at present.

N, as at present. There is no reason to suppose that it was nasalized in French words as in modern French. *An, on,* in French words were often written *aun, oun,* and were probably always sounded as these combinations in Chaucer's orthography, that is as *ah'oon, oon.*

---

[1] Extensive observation shows that the sound is still very common in English, even where the speaker thinks he says *ee* as in *three*; and even Italian singers involuntarily introduce it when trying to sing our *ee,* their *i,* on a low note.

NG had probably three values, as at present in *sing, singer, linger, change.* It is not possible to determine with certainty whether it was generally a simple *ng* as in *singer,* or an *ng* followed by *g,* as at present in *longer, linger, finger,* when medial or final, so that the modern custom alone can be followed.

O long was *oa* in *oar,* **boar,** *o* in *more,* that is a somewhat broader sound than *oa* in *moan, o* in *stone,* and with no tendency to **taper** into *oo.* It is still heard in the provinces, and is like the Italian open *o* or *o aperto;* approaching *au,* but not so broad. Those who find the sound difficult to pronounce may say *oh,* which was not established till the seventeenth century. It had also the sound of *oo,* generally in those words where it is still *oo,* as *prove, move,* or where it has become *u* in *but,* as *love, shove.* Just as E long and E E gave place to two sounds, written *ee* and *ea* in the latter part of the sixteenth century, as in modern *peer, pear,* so O long and O O gave place to two sounds, written *oo* and *oa* in the latter part of the sixteenth century, as in modern *boor, boar.* It is possible therefore that even as early as the fourteenth century, and perhaps still earlier, these changes were prepared by a division of both sounds into *close* (as in Italian **fede,** sète, avere, vendè, credeva, &c.; ombra, ondo, amore, amoroso, &c.) and *open* (as in Italian regola, predica, cedo, &c.; buono, uomo, oro, poco, &c.), nearly modern *ail, air, mole, more,* supposing *ail, mole,* not to have tapering vowels. Mr. Sweet has endeavoured to make these distinctions in his 'History of English Sounds,' but there is no evidence from rhymes, and dialectal investigations (as yet very incomplete) have so far failed to confirm the conclusion.

O short was *ŏa,* the short sound of the last, the regular sound of short *o* on the continent, very common in the provinces, but not so broad as the modern *o* in *got,* which was not established till the seventeenth century, but may be **used** for *ŏa* by those who find the proper **sound** too difficult. In a few words short O had also occasionally the sound of short *ŭ* in *bull, push, put;* where it replaced Anglo-Saxon *u,* and was pronounced *ŭ* in the sixteenth century. These **cases** correspond almost precisely to those in which it is now pronounced as *u* in *but,* as *sonne, wonder.*

OA does not seem to have been used in Chaucer. It was introduced for long *o* in the sixteenth century.

OE is very rarely used, chiefly in *poepel* for *people* and in *re-proeve* for *repreve*, to show the change of sound. It was the same as long **E**.

OI was perhaps generally *oo'ee*, a diphthong consisting of the sound of *oo* pronounced briefly, but with a stress, gliding on to *ee* in one syllable, as sailors pronounce *buoy*, almost as in *wooing*, or Italian *lui*, and very like French *oui*, as distinct from *ouï*. It may have occasionally had the sound of Chaucer's *o* short (open *o*, nearly *o* in *got*) followed by *ee*, nearly as modern *joy*.

OO, the same as long O, with which it is constantly interchanged. The modern sound of *oo* in *pool* dates from after the middle of the sixteenth century.

OU had three sounds: properly it was = modern *oo* long, as in *loud*, *hous*, called *lood*, *hoos*; occasionally it was used for *ŭ* in *bull*, as in *ous* [us], *outher*; and sometimes for the diphthong *oa'oo*, that is, the sound of long O gliding into modern *oo*, almost the same as in modern *soul*, except that the first sound was broader. The three cases may be distinguished pretty accurately thus:—OU was *oo*, where it is now pronounced as in *loud*; OU was *ŭ*, where it is now pronounced as in *double*; OU was *oa'oo* where it is now occasionally pronounced *oh'oo* as in *soul*.

OUGH must be considered as OU followed by GH. In *drought* it was *drŏŏkht*, in *plough* it was *plookh*; in *fought*, *bought*, where it has now the sound of *au*, it was probably *ŏä'oo-kh*, or nearly our modern tapering *oh* followed by *kh*; but, if the reader feels any difficulty, he may use the modern *ow* in *cow* followed by the guttural *kh*, as *fowkht*. Many modern dialects treat *ought* in this way.

OW was the same as OU, but was more commonly used when final.

OY was the same as OI.

P, as at present.

PH = *f*, as at present.

QU, as at present.

R as *r* in *ring, herring, carry;* always trilled, never as now in *car, serf, third, cord.* Hence it did not lengthen **or** alter the preceding vowel, **so** that *her* in *herd* must have the *r* as well trilled **as** in *herring,* nearly the same as now in Scotland and Ireland, but possibly not so strongly, when not preceding a vowel.

RE final, probably the same as ER, except when *ĕ* was inflectional.

RH, where it is found in MSS. of the period (it is not in this edition), **was** probably *r* **as** now, but a truly hissed *rh* occurs in some dialects.

S was more frequently a sharp *s* when final, than at present; thus *wys, was, is,* all had *s* sharp. But between two vowels, and when **the** final *es* had the *e* omitted after long vowels or voiced consonants, it was probably *z,* a letter which sometimes interchanged with *s,* but was rarely used. S was never *sh* or *zh* as at present, thus *vision* had three syllables, as *vi-si-oon.*

SCH was *sh,* as in *shall.*

SH sometimes used for SCH and pronounced as at present.

SSH, used occasionally for double SCH when the sound of *sh* followed **a short** vowel.

T, as at present, but final *-tion* was in two syllables, *-si-oon.*

TH had two sounds, as in *thin, then,* and there is no means of telling whether these sounds were distributed differently from what they now are, except that *with* probably rhymed to *smith.* They can therefore be pronounced as at present.

U long only occurred in French words, and probably always had the sound of Scotch *ui* in *puir,* or French *u,* German *ü,* a sound which remained nearly to the eighteenth century. Those who find this sound too difficult, may pronounce as the present long English *u* in *tune,* which was not considered to be the normal sound till the seventeenth century.

U short was generally short *ŭ,* as in *bull, pull,* the modern sound of *u* in *but* not having been established till the seventeenth century. Occasionally, however, it was used for short *i* or short *e,* precisely as in the modern *busy, bury;* these cases can generally be distinguished by seeing that they would be now so pronounced. Possibly the *u* then represented an ancient **sound of** **short** French *u*.

U consonant = *v*. In the MSS. *u* and *v* are confused as vowel or consonant, and *u* vowel initial is commonly **written *v*.**

V vowel, the same as U.

V consonant, the same as at present.

W vowel, used in diphthongs **as a** substitute **for** U, and some- times used absolutely for *oo*, as wde = *oodë*, herberw = *herberoo.*

W consonant, the same as at present.

WH, a blowing through the lips when in the position for *w*, something like a whistle; still generally pronounced in the north of England, but commonly confused with *w* in the south. To foreigners, when initial, it sounds *hŏŏ*, as in whan = *hŏŏăhn* nearly, but *whăhn* correctly. In Chaucer it often occurs final in place of GH (which see) when pronounced as the Scotch *quh.* It was the transition sound of GH from *kh* to the modern *f.*

WR was probably pronounced as an *r* with rounded lips, which produces the effect of a *w* and *r* sounded together, as in the French *roi.* Those who find a difficulty in speaking it thus, may pronounce *w'r*, with the faintest sound of a vowel between the *w* and *r*, almost *wĕreet'ë* for *write*, but not making an addi- tional syllable; such sounds are still heard provincially.

X was *ks*, as at present.

Y vowel, long and short, had precisely the same value as I long and short.

Y consonant was generally written with the same character as GH, which resembled *z* (ʒ), and may have had that sound of GH which resembled a hissed *y*. But probably it had become thoroughly *y* in Chaucer's time, and should be so pronounced.

Z = *z*, as now, and never *zh.*

The position of the accent was not always the same as at pre- sent. French words seem to have been pronounced with equal stress on all the syllables, as at present. Some English termina- tions, as *-and*, *-ing*, *-ly*, always had a considerable stress, even when a preceding syllable was accented.

If we adopt most of the easy modern English substitutes for

the difficult old sounds, as pointed out in the preceding table, but use *dh* for the flat sound of *th* in *thee*, *ŭ* for *u* in *bull*, *ui* as in Scotch for French *u*, and *ahy*, *ahw* for *ah'ee*, *ah'oo*, as described under AI, AW, mark the pronounced final *e* by *ë*, and indicate the accent, when it does not fall on the first syllable only, by ('), we may write the pronunciation of the first lines of the Canterbury Tales as follows. Observe that the first line begins with an accented syllable, without a precedent short syllable, as is not unfrequent in Chaucer.

Whan dhat Ah'preel' with 'is shoorĕs swoh:ē
Dhë drookht of March hath persed toh dhë rohtĕ,
And bahdhëd evree vahyn in swich lee'koor'
Of which ver'tui' enjen'dred is dhë floor ;
Whan Zefirŭs, aik, with 'is swaitë braithë
Enspee'red hath in evree holt and haithë
Dhë tendre kropës, and dhë yŭngë sŭnö
Hath in dhë ram 'is halfë koors irŭn'ë,
And smahlë foolës mahken melohdee'ë
Dhat slaipen al dhë nikht with ohpen ee'ë,—
Soh priketh 'em nah'tuir' in her kohraa'jës,
Dhan longen folk toh gohn on pilgrimaa'jës,
And palmerz for toh saiken strahwnjö strondës
Toh fernë halwëz kooth in sŭndree londës,
And spes'ialee', from evree sheerës endö
Of Engelond, to Kahwn'terber'ee dhahy wendö
Dhë hohlee blisfŭl marteer for toh saikö
Dhat hem hath holpen whan dhat dhahy wair saikö.
Beefel' dhat in dhat sai'zoon' on a dahy
At Soothwerk at dhë Tab'ard' as Ee lahy,
Redee toh wenden on mee pilgrimah'jö
Toh Kahwn'terber'ee with fŭl devoot' kohrah'jö,
At nikht was koom in'toh' dhat ostelree'ë
Well neen and twentee in a kŭmpanee'ë
Of sŭndree folk, bee ah'ven'tuir' ifal'ö
In fel'ahw'sheep', and pilgrimz wair dhahy allö,
Dhat tohwerd Kahwn'terber'ee wolden reedë.
Dhë chahmbrez and dhë stahb'lz wairen weedö
And wel wai wairen aized atë bestë.
And shortlee, whan dhë sŭnë was toh restö
Soh had Ee spohken with 'em evreech ohn,
Dhat Ee was of 'ér fel'ahw'sheep' anohn',
And mahdë forwerd airlee for toh reezö
Toh tahk oor wahy dhair as Ee yoo devee'zö.

It is proper to add that Mr. Ellis's results were chiefly obtained from a careful examination of the Harleian MS. (Hl.), the spelling of which does not altogether agree with that of the Ellesmere MS., here chiefly followed. The only result in which I do not feel full confidence is that which makes the sound of EY identical with that of AY. I look upon these rather as *permissible rimes* than as real ones, and should prefer to regard EY and EI as indicating the sound *ai'ee,* that is, a diphthong consisting of *e* long (=*ē* in *there,* or *ai* in *pair*) pronounced briefly but with a stress, and gliding on to *ee.* I do not find that they are interchanged by the scribe of the Ellesmere MS. in all cases, though they are so frequently. There are certain words, such as *deye,* to die, *tweye*[1], twain, *burgeys,* a burgess, *eighte,* eight, *queynte,* quaint, *receyue,* to receive, *pleye,* to play, &c. which seem to be spelt with *ey* rather than with *ay;* and, on the other hand, may be cited *daye,* a day, *paye,* to please, *arrayed,* arrayed, *nay,* nay, *may,* may, &c. which seem to be spelt with *ay* rather than with *ey.* I offer this criticism with diffidence, merely saying that I am unable as yet to see how words like A.S. *weg, plega, twegen,* should have passed in Middle English into *way, play, twayn,* as pronounced by Mr. Ellis, and have reverted nearly to their original sound in our *way, play,* and *twain.* With respect to *way* (written *way, wey*), which undoubtedly rimes, or seems to rime, with *day,* I would suggest that it may have had *two* pronunciations; as was certainly the case with *deye,* to die, which is also spelt *dye,* and made to rime with *remedye,* a remedy. With regard also to such a word as our modern *receive,* we can easily understand that it was once pronounced so as to rime with the modern word *rave,* but the riming of its vowel very nearly with the modern *rive* is much less clear. On this point, therefore, I should plead that some doubt may be allowed to remain.

I may add here that the long sound of *i* is generally denoted by *y* in the Ellesmere MS. Cf. *whylom,* p. 1, l. 134, with *riche* in

---

[1] Not in the Ellesmere MS. only, but in nearly all. *Tweye* occurs 7 times at the end of a line. In 5 places it is spelt with *ey* or *ei* in *all* the 6 MSS.; in 1 place, in 5 of them; and in the last instance, in 4 of them.

the line following. Our modern *j* is commonly written as capital I, as in *Iugement*, B. 688; but the small *i* is sometimes used, as in *ioye*, B. 409. When *u* is written between two vowels, it stands for *v*; as in *euery* (*every*), B. 152; *deuyse* (*devyse*), B. 154; *lyuen* (*lyven*), B. 175. In a few words, *v* is written for *u*, at the beginning; as in *vp, vse, vnto*, for *up, use, unto*.

I now proceed to some general remarks upon the Tales in the present selection.

The Man of Law's Tale. The Introduction to the Man of Law's Prologue (also called, for brevity, the Man-of-Law Headlink) and the Prologue itself, are printed in *The Prioresses Tale,* &c. (Clarendon Press), pp. 1–5. See also the Introduction to that volume, p. xx. The Head-link and Prologue together contain 133 lines, so that the Tale itself begins, in the present volume, with l. 134. I have already stated my belief that The Man of Law's Tale is a piece of Chaucer's earlier workmanship, and that it was revised for insertion among the Tales, with the addition of a Prologue, about 1386. Tyrwhitt has drawn attention to the fact that a story, closely agreeing with The Man of Law's Tale, is found in Gower's Confessio Amantis, Book II. He was misled by the expression "som men wolde sayn" in l. 1009 into supposing that Chaucer took the story from Gower; see note to that line, p. 137. Chronology at once settles the question; for Chaucer's tale, written *before* 1385, could not have been derived from Gower's, written about 1393. The simple explanation of the matter is, that both our poets drew from a common source. That common source has, fortunately, been discovered, in the Life of Constance, as narrated in the Anglo-Norman Chronicle of Nicholas Trivet, written about A.D. 1334. Mr. Thomas Wright, in his edition of the Canterbury Tales, pointed out Trivet's Chronicle as containing the original of the story as told by Gower. That it also contains the original of the story as told by Chaucer, is evident from the publications of the Chaucer Society. Trivet's version of the story was edited for that Society by Mr. Brock in 1872, with an English translation, and a careful line-by-line analysis of it, shewing clearly the exact extent to which Chaucer followed his original. The name of the publication is 'Originals and Analogues of some of Chaucer's Canterbury Tales,' published for the Chaucer Society; Part I, 1872; Part II, 1875. To this I am indebted for much of the information here given[1]. It appears that Nicholas Trivet was an English Dominican friar, who died some time after 1334. A short account of him in Latin, with a list of works ascribed to him, is to be found in Quetif and Echard's *Scriptores Ordinis Praedicatorum*[2], tom. i. pp. 561-565; also a notice in English of his life and some of his works, in the Preface to T. Hog's edition of Trivet's *Annales*. Mr. Brock notices eighteen of his works, amongst which it will suffice to mention here (a) his Annales ab origine mundi ad Christum (Royal MS. 13 B. xvi, &c.); (b) his Annales sex Regum Angliae, qui a comitibus Andegavensibus [counts of Anjou] originem traxerunt (Arundel MSS. 46 and 220, Harl. MSS. 29 and 4322, &c.); and (c) his Anglo-Norman Chronicle, quite a distinct work from the Latin *Annales* (MS. Arundel 56, &c.). Of the last there are numerous copies, MS. Arundel 56 being one of the best, and therefore selected to be printed from for the Chaucer Society. The heading runs thus:—'Ci comence les Cronicles qe Frere Nichol Trivet escript a dame Marie, la fille moun seignour le Roi Edward, le fitz Henri;' shewing that it was written for the princess Mary, daughter of Edward I, born in 1278, who became a nun at Amesbury in 1285. The story of Constance begins on leaf 45, back. Gower follows Trivet rather closely, with but few omissions, and only one addition of any importance, about 30 lines long. 'Chaucer tells the same story as Trivet, but tells it in his own language, and in much shorter compass. He omits little or nothing of importance, and alters only the details. . . . Chaucer's additions are many; of the 1029 lines of which the Tale consists, about 350 are Chaucer's additions. The passages are these:—ll. 190-203; 270-287; 295-315;

---

[1] I sometimes copy Mr. Brock's very words.
[2] The Dominican friars were also called *Friars Preachers*.

330–343; 351–357; 358–371; 400–410; 421–427; 449–462: 470–504; 631–658; 701–714; 771–784; 811–819; 825–868: 925–945; 1037–1043; 1052–1078; 1132–1141' (Brock).

Tyrwhitt pointed out that much the same story is to be found in the Lay of Emarè (MS. Cotton, Calig. A. ii, fol. 69), printed by Ritson in the second volume of his Metrical Romances. He observes:—'the chief differences are, that Emarè is originally exposed in a boat for refusing to comply with the desires of the Emperour her father; that she is driven on the coast of *Galys*, or Wales, and married to the King of that country. The contrivances of the step-mother, and the consequences of them, are the same in both stories.'

Mr. Thomas Wright further observes:—'The treachery of King Ælla's mother enters into the French Romance of the Chevalier au Cigne, and into the still more ancient Anglo-Saxon romance of King Offa, preserved in a Latin form by Matthew Paris. It is also found in the Italian collection, said to have been composed in 1378, under the title of Il Pecorone di ser Giovanni Fiorentino (an imitation of the Decameron), gior. x. no. 1. The treason of the Knight who murders Hermengilde is an incident in the French Roman de la Violette, and in the English metrical romance of Le Bone Florence of Rome (printed in Ritson's collection); and is found in the English Gesta Romanorum, c. 69 (ed. Madden)[1], joined, in the latter place, with Constance's adventure with the steward. It is also found in Vincent of Beauvais[2], and other writers.' The tale in the Gesta Romanorum is called 'Merelaus the Emperor' (MS. Harl. 7333, leaf 201), and is printed in the Originals and Analogues (Chaucer's Society), Part I, pp. 57–70. Mr. Furnivall adds—'This tale was versified by Occleve, who called Merelaus "Gerelaus;" and Warton quotes Occleve's lines describing how the "feendly man" stabs the Earl's child, and then puts the bloody knife into the sleeping Empress's hand—

---

[1] Reprinted for the Early Eng. Text Soc., ed. S. J. Herrtage, 1879; see pp. 311, 493 of this edition.

[2] Warton gives the reference, viz. to his Speculum Historiale, lib. vii. c. 90, fol. 86 a.

'For men shoulde have noon othir deemiug
But she had gilty ben of this murdring.'
See Warton, Hist. Eng. Poetry, ed. 1871, i. 296.'

In the Originals and Analogues, Part i. pp. 71–84, is also printed an extract from Matthew Paris, *Vita Offae Primi*, ed. Wats, 1684, pp. 965–968, containing the story of 'King Offa's intercepted Letters and banished Queen.'

Some account of Ser Giovanni is given in Dunlop's History of Fiction, 3rd ed. 1845, p. 247. He was a Florentine notary, who began his Tales in 1378, at a village in the neighbourhood of Forli. His work is called Il Pecorone, i. e. the Dunce, 'a title which the author assumed, as some Italian academicians styled themselves Insensati, Stolidi, &c., appellations in which there was not always so much irony as they imagined.' The 1st tale of the 10th Day is thus analysed by Dunlop. 'Story of the Princess Denise of France, who, to avoid a disagreeable marriage with an old German prince, escapes in disguise to England, and is there received in a convent. The king, passing that way, falls in love with and espouses her. Afterwards, while he was engaged in a war in Scotland, his wife brings forth twins; but the queen-mother sends to acquaint her son that his spouse had given birth to two monsters. In place of his majesty's answer, ordering them to be nevertheless brought up with the utmost care, she substitutes a mandate for their destruction, and also for that of the queen. The person to whom the execution of this command is entrusted, allows the queen to depart with her twins to Genoa. At the end of some years she discovers her husband at Rome, on his way to a crusade; she there presents him with his children, and is brought back with them in triumph to England.' Dunlop points out the likeness of this story to those told by Chaucer and Gower, mentions the Lay of Emarè, and adds:—'it is the subject, too, of a very old French romance, published in 4to, without date, entitled Le Roman de la Belle Helene de Constantinople. There, as in Emarè, the heroine escapes to England to avoid a marriage, &c. At length she is ordered to be burnt, but is saved by the Duke of Gloster's niece kindly offering to personate her on that occasion.' The story appears again in a collection of tales by Straparola, in the 4th tale of the first night; but Straparola merely borrowed it from Ser Giovanni. See Dunlop, Hist. Fiction, 3rd ed. p. 268.

It occurs to me that Shakespeare, in delineating Imogen, did not forget Chaucer's portrait of Constance.

The Pardoner's Prologue. In this Prologue, the Pardoner is made to expatiate upon the value of his relics. It is very likely that Chaucer here remembered one of the tales in Boccaccio's Decamerone (Day vi. Tale 10), concerning a certain Friar Cipolla, of the Order of St. Anthony, of which Dunlop gives some account in his History of Fiction, 3rd ed. pp. 227, 228. 'He gave a long account (says Dunlop) of his travels as far as India, and told how on his return he had visited the Patriarch of Jerusalem, who had shewn him innumerable relics: among others, a lock of the hair of the seraph that appeared to St. Francis, a paring of the cherub's nail, a few of the rays of the blessed star that guided the Magi in the east, the jawbone of Lazarus,' &c. He adds—'This tale of Boccaccio drew down the censure of the Council of Trent, and is the one which gave the greatest umbrage to the church. The author has been defended by his commentators, on the ground that he did not intend to censure the respectable orders of friars, but to expose those wandering mendicants who supported themselves by imposing on the credulity of the people; that he did not mean to ridicule the sacred relics of the church, but those which were believed so in consequence of the fraud and artifice of monks.' But it must have been hard to draw this line. In the note to l. 349, p. 145, I have drawn attention to Heywood's close plagiarism from Chaucer, in the passage from The Four P.'s, printed in the note to l. 701 of Dr. Morris's edition of Chaucer's Prologue; also to Sir David Lyndesay's Satyre of the Three Estates, ll. 2037-2121.

The Pardoner's Tale. A considerable part of this Tale is occupied with digressions; the Tale itself is told simply, briefly, and well, occupying ll. 463-484, 661-894. Mr. Thomas Wright remarks—'This beautiful moral story appears to have been

taken from a Fabliau, now lost, but of which the mere outline
is preserved [as first noted by Tyrwhitt] in the Cento Novelle
Antiche, Nov. lxxxii, as well as the story itself by Chaucer.'
Dunlop, in his History of Fiction, p. 203, says—'It is evident from
the title of the Cento Novelle *Antiche*, that it was not a new and
original production, but a compilation of stories already current
in the world. The collection was made towards the end of the
13th century, and was formed from episodes in Romances of
chivalry; the Fabliaux of the French Trouveurs; the ancient
chronicles of Italy; recent incidents; or jests and repartees
current by oral tradition. That the stories derived from these
sources were compiled by different authors, is evident from the
great variety of style; but who those authors were, is still a
problem in the literary annals of Italy.' The story is not exactly
the same in all the editions of the Cento Novelle; and two different forms of it have been printed by Mr. Furnivall, in his
Originals and Analogues (Chaucer Soc.), Pt. ii. pp. 131–133. Of
these, the former is from the edition of 1525, with the title Le
Ciento Novelle Antike, where it appears as Nov. lxxxiii. It is very
brief, and to this effect. As Christ was walking with his disciples
through a wild country, some of His disciples espied some golden
piastres, and said, 'Let us take some of these for our use.' But
Christ reproved them, warning them that they would soon see
the fatal effects of avarice. Soon after, two men found the gold;
and one of them went to fetch a mule to carry it off, whilst the
other remained to guard it. On his return with the mule, the
former offered to his companion two loaves which he had bought
for him. The latter refused at the moment, and shortly afterwards took an opportunity of stabbing the other as he chanced
to be stooping down. He then took the two loaves, gave one to
the mule, and ate the other himself. The loaves were poisoned;
and man and mule fell dead. Then our Lord, passing by once
more, pointed out to His disciples the three dead bodies.

The other version is from the edition of 1572, entitled Libro
di Novelle, et di bel Parlar Gentile; where it is Nov. lxxxii.
This is much more like Chaucer's story, and is occasionally

quoted in the Notes as the 'Italian text.' Mr. Furnivall's analysis of the story is as follows.

'A hermit lying down in a cave, sees there much gold. At once he runs away, and meets three robbers. They see no one chasing the hermit, and ask him what he is running away from. "Death, which is chasing me." "Where is he? shew him us." "Come with me, and I will." The hermit takes them to the cave, and shews them Death—the gold. They laugh at him, and make great joy, and say, "The hermit is a fool." Then the three robbers consult as to what they shall do. The second proposes that one shall go to the town, buy bread and wine and all things needful; but the crafty Devil puts into the heart of the robber who goes to the town, that he shall feed himself, poison his mates, and then have all the treasure, and be the richest man in that country. Meantime, the other robbers plot to murder their mate as soon as he comes back with the bread and wine, and then share the treasure. Their mate returns from the city, and they murder him at once. Then they eat the food he has brought, and both fall dead. Thus doth our Lord God requite traitors. The robbers found death. The wise man fled, and left the gold free.'

As the original is not long, I here reprint it, for the reader's convenience.

'Qui conta d' uno Romito che andando per un luogo foresto trouo molto grande Tesoro.

'Andando vn giorno vn Romito per vn luogo foresto: si trouò vna grandissima grotta, laquale era molo celata, et ritirandosi verso là per riposarsi, pero che era assai affaticato; come e' giunse alla grotta si la vide in certo luogo molto tralucere, impercio che vi hauea molto oro: e si tosto come il conobbe, incontanente si partio, et comincio a correre per lo deserto, quanto e' ne potea andare. Correndo cosi questo Romito s' intoppo in tre grandi scherani, liquali stauano in quella foresta per rubare chi unque vi passaua. Ne gia mai si erano accorti, che questo oro vi fosse. Hor vedendo costoro, che nascosti si stauano, fuggir cosi questo huomo, non hauendo

persona dietro che 'l cacciasse, **alquanto** hebbero temenza, ma
pur se li pararono dinanzi per **sapere** perche fuggiua, che di cio
molto si marauigliauano. Ed **elli** rispose et disse. "Fratelli
miei, io fuggo la morte, che mi vien dietro cacciando **mi**." Que'
non vedendo **ne** huomo, ne bestia, che il cacciasse, dissero:
"Mostraci chi ti caccia: et menaci cola oue ella **è**." Allhora il
Romito disse **loro**, "venite meco, et mostrerollaui," pregandoli
tutta via che **non** andassero ad essa, impercio che elli per se la
fuggia. Ed eglino volendola trouare, **per uedere come** fosse
fatta, nol domandouano di altro. Il Romito vedendo che non
potea piu, et hauendo paura di **loro**, gli condusse **alla** grotta,
onde egli s'era partito, e disse loro, "Qui è la morte, che mi
cacciaua," et mostra loro l'oro che u'era, ed eglino il conobbero
incontanente, et molto si cominciarono a rallegrare, **et a** fare
insieme grande sollazzo. Allhora accommiatarono questo buono
huomo; et egli sen'ando per i fatti suoi: et quelli cominciarono
a dire tra loro, come elli era semplice persona. Rimasero questi
scherani tutti e tre insieme, a guardare questo hauere, e incomin-
ciarono a ragionare quello che voleano fare. L'uno rispuose et
disse. "A me pare, da che Dio ci ha dato cosi alta ventura, che
noi non ci partiamo di qui, **insino** a tanto che noi non ne porti-
amo tutto questo hauere." Et l'altro disse: "non facciamo
cosi; l'vno di **noi ne** tolga **alquanto**, et **vada** alla cittade et ven-
dalo, et **rechi del** pane **et del** vino, et di quello che ci bisogna, e
di cio s'ingegni il meglio che puote: faccia egli, pur com' elli ci
fornisca." A **questo** s'accordarono tutti **e** tre insieme. Il Demonio ch'è ingegnoso, e reo d'ordinare di fare quanto male e
puote, mise in cuori a **costui che** andaua alla citta per lo forni-
mento, "da ch'io sarò nella cittade" (dicea fra se medesimo)
"**io voglio** mangiare et bere quanto mi bisogna, et poi fornirmi
di certe cose delle quali io ho **mestiere** hora al presente: et poi
auuelenero quello che io porto a **miei** compagni: si che, da ch'elli
saranno morti **amendue, si saro io** poi Signore di tutto quello
hauere, et secondo **che mi pare** egli è tanto, che io saro poi il
piu ricco huomo di tutto questo paese da parte d'hauere:" et
come li venne in pensiero, cosi fece. Prese viuanda per se

quanto gli bisogno, et poi tutta l' altra auuelenoe, e cosi la porto
a que suoi compagni.   Intanto ch' ando alla cittade secondo che
detto hauemo : se elli pensoe et ordinoe male per uccidere li
suoi compagni, accio che ogni cosa li rimanesse : quelli pensaro
di lui non meglio ch' elli di loro, et dissero tra loro : " Si tosto
come questo nostro compagno tornera col pane et col vino, et
con l' altre cose che ci bisognano, si l' uccideremo, et poi mange-
remo quanto uorremo, e sara poi tra noi due tutto questo grande
hauere.   Et come meno parti ne saremo, tanto n' haueremo mag-
gior parte ciascuno di noi."   Hor viene quelli, che era ito alla
cittade a comperare le cose che bisognaua loro.   Tornato a suoi
compagni incontanente che l' videro, gli furono addosso con le
lancie et con le coltella, et l' uccisero.   Da che l' hebbero morto,
mangiarono di quello che egli hauea recato : et si tosto come
furono satolli, amendue caddero morti : et cosi morirono tutti e
tre : che l' vno vccise l' altro si come vdito hauete, et non hebbe
l' hauere : et cosi paga Domenedio li traditori, che egli andarono
cercando la morte, et in questo modo la trouarono, et si come
ellino n' erano degni.   Et il saggio sauiamente la fuggio, e l' oro
rimase libero come di prima.'

Mr. Furnivall has also reprinted Novella xlii from the Novellae
of Morlinus, ed. Naples, 1520 (reprinted at Paris in 1799); corrected by the Paris edition of Morlinus' Works, 1855.   The
story is very brief, being as follows.

'De illis qui, in Tiberi reperto thesauro, ad inuicem conspirantes, ueneno et ferro periere.

'Magus magico susurro in Tiberi delitere thesaurum quadam
in cauea spirituum reuelatione cognouit : quo reperto, cum mag-
num siclorum cumulum aspiceret, communi uoto pars sociorum
proximum oppidum seu castellum, epulas aliasque res compara-
turi, accedunt : ceteri uero copiosum interea ignem instruunt,
thesaurumque custodiunt.   Dumque in castellum conuenissent,
radice malorum cupiditate affecti, ut consocios thesauri parte
priuarent, diro ueneno illos interimere statuerunt : cum dicto,
in caupona epulantes, ebrii ac uino sepulti, aliquatenus moram
fecere.   In Tiberi expectantes atque esurientes, consocios de

mora incusabant: Iouemque adiurauerunt, repedantes **ex op-
pido** atque castello **et uita** et **thesauri parte** priuare. Sicque ad
inuicem conspirantes, non **multo post** adueniunt **ex pago** illi,
uinarios, utres, **pullos,** pisces, aliaque tucetosi saporis pulmentaria
atque prelectum hircum ferentes. Quibus obuiam dederunt
ieiuni, illosque **omnes** morti imparatos incautosque insecauere
atque **crudeli strage** perdiderunt. Pone sumptis cibariis diro
ueneno tabefactis, insigni iocunditate gnauiter cuncta ministrare
incipiunt; **alter** uerrit, alter sternit, pars coquit, atque tuceta
concinnat. Pone omnibus scitule appositis, ac mensa largiter in-
structa edere ceperunt, omniaque ingurgitauerunt. Commodum
ex **eis mensa** erectis erant (*sic*) **quod,** morte preuenti, cum sociis
uitam fato reddentes, sub elemento mortui et sepulti remansere.

'Nouella **indicat:** nec esse **de malo** cogitandum: nam **quod**
quis seminat, **metit.**'

The Second Nun's Tale. There is a peculiar interest about
this Tale, because, as compared with the rest, it so clearly shews
us Chaucer's mode of compilation ; his advance from close translation to **a more** free handling of materials ; and his change of
rhythm, **from** stanzas to rimed couplets. The closeness of the
translation **and the** rhythm alike point to early workmanship ;
and, most fortunately, **we are not** left **to** conjecture in **this**
matter, since **our** author himself refers to this piece, by the Title
of the *Lyf of Seint Cecile,* in his Prologue to the Legend of Good
Women, l. **426.** It was probably written a considerable time
before **the Legend.** **Mr.** Furnivall assigns to it the conjectural
date of 1373, which cannot be very far wrong. The expression
in l. **78,** 'Yet preye I yow that *reden* that I wryte' clearly shews
that it was neither originally written **as a** tale of the series, nor
properly revised; and the expression in l. 62, 'And though that
I, vnworthy *sone* of Eue,' cannot fail to strike the reader as a
singular one to be put into the mouth of a *nun.* We possess, in
fact, **the Tale in** its original shape, without either revision or
introduction. What is called the ' Prologue' is, in fact, nothing
of the sort; it is merely such an introduction as was suitable for
the Legend at the time of translation. We have no description

of the Second Nun, no introduction of her as a narrator, nor
anything to connect the Tale with those that precede it. There
is no authority, indeed, for attributing it to the Second Nun at
all beyond the mere rubrics printed at pp. 61, 63, and 81.

It is not even made quite clear to us who the Second Nun
was. We may, however, conclude that, as the Prioresse was
herself a Nun, i. e. the *first* nun (see **Prol.** l. 118), the person
intended is the 'Another Nonne' mentioned in the Prologue, l.
163, but mentioned nowhere else. The first line of the Canon's
Yeoman's Prologue (p. 82) merely mentions 'the lyf of Seint
Cecile' without any hint as to the supposed narrator of it. The
Prioress herself, on the other hand, is properly introduced to us,
and her Tale is carefully inserted in its right place.

An analysis of the so-called Prologue to this Tale is given in
the Notes, at p. **165**; cf. note to l. 84, p. 169. Tyrwhitt pointed
out that the Tale itself is translated from the Life of St. Cecilia
as given in the Legenda Aurea (or Golden Legend) of Jacobus
Januensis, or Jacobus a Voragine, who was archbishop of Genoa
at the close of the 13th century. Tyrwhitt calls it 'literally'
translated, but this is not quite the case; for our author has made
several judicious alterations, suppressions, and additions, some of
which are pointed out in the notes; see, e. g. notes to ll. 346,
380, 395, 442, 489, 505, and 535. However, most of the alterations occur towards the end of the story, and Chaucer follows
the original author closely as far as l. 343; see note to l. 346.
The best text of this Life of St. Cecilia is that given in the
second edition of the Aurea Legenda by Dr. Th. Grässe, published at Leipsic in 1850. Mr. Furnivall has printed it at length,
from Grässe's first edition, 1846, in his Originals and Analogues,
Pt. ii. pp. 192–205; side by side with the French version of La
Legende Dorée, as translated by Jehan de Vignay, printed at Paris
in 1513. The suggestion was made in 'Bell's' edition of Chaucer
(really edited by Mr. Jephson), that Chaucer's original was not
the Latin, but the French text. A very slight comparison shews
at once that this idea is wrong (as Mr. Furnivall points out),
and that Chaucer unquestionably followed the *Latin* original; see

note to l. 319, p. 174. It is, however, probable that **Chaucer
may** have seen the French version also, as he seems **to have**
taken from it the **idea** of his first **four** stanzas, ll. 1-28. **But he
has** taken thence merely the general idea, and **no more**; **see**
notes to l. 1, **p. 165,** and to l. 7, **p. 166.** The Invocation to the
Virgin bears some resemblance to the Prioresses Prologue; see
note to l. 50, p. **168.** It contains, moreover, **a passage which is**
a free translation of one in Dante's Paradiso; see note to l. 36,
p. 167. I may add here that Mr. Furnivall has also reprinted
two more lives of St. Cecilia, one from Caxton's Golden Legende,
in English prose, ed. 1483, fol. ccclxxvij, back; the other in
English verse, in a metre similar to that used by Robert **of**
Gloucester, from MS. Ashmole **43,** leaf 185, back, in the **Bod-**
leian library, Oxford. These do not throw much further light
upon the matter; and, in fact, the only text really worth consulting is the Latin one of Jacobus a Voragine, which is frequently quoted in the notes. Of this Dunlop says, in his History
of Fiction, 3rd ed. p. 286—'The grand repertory of pious fiction
seems to have been the Legenda Aurea of Jacobus de Voragine,
a Genoese Dominican, a work entitled Golden from its popu-
larity, on the same principle that this epithet was bestowed on
the 'Ass' of Apuleius. A similar composition in Greek, **by**
Simon Metaphrastes, written about the end of the 10th century,
was the prototype of this work of the 13th century, which com-
prehends the lives of individual saints, whose history had already
been written, or was current from tradition. The Golden
Legend, however, does not consist solely of the lives of saints,
but is said in the colophon to be interspersed with many other
beautiful and strange relations, which were probably extracted
from the Gesta Longobardorum, and other sources too obscure
and voluminous to be easily traced; indeed, one of the original
titles of the Legenda Aurea was Historia Lombardica. The
work of [Jacobus a] Voragine was translated into French by
Jean de Vignai, **and was** one of the three books from which
Caxton's Golden Legend was compiled.'

In The Military and Religious Life in the Middle Ages, by

Paul Lacroix, at p. 426, is the following brief account of Saint Cecilia. 'Under the reign of Alexander Severus, many illustrious martyrs were put to death: St. Cecilia, her husband, and her brother-in-law among the number. St. Cecilia was descended from a very ancient family which dated back to the time of Tarquin the Proud; she belonged to the same house as Metella, many of whose children were raised to the honours of triumph and of the consulate in the heyday of the Roman republic. Her parents gave her in marriage to a young Roman patrician, named Valerian. But Cecilia had dedicated her virginity to God, and her husband, converted to the faith by her arguments and entreaties, respected her vow, and himself converted his brother Tiburcius. They all three relieved their persecuted brethren, and this Christian charity betrayed them. In spite of their distinguished birth, their wealth and their connections, they were arrested, and their refusal to sacrifice to the false gods led to their being condemned to death. We find a multitude of analogous occurrences in Gaul, and also in the most distant provinces of the East.' On the preceding page of the same book is figured a copy of a piece of mosaic work of the third or fourth century, which was taken from the cemetery of St. Sixtus, and is preserved in the church of St. Cecilia, at Rome. It represents St. Cecilia and St. Valerian, with roses and lilies in bloom at their feet, and having on each side of them a palm-tree laden with fruit, a symbol of their victories and of their meritorious martyrdom. Upon one of the palm-trees is a phoenix with a 'gloria' round its head, the ancient symbol of resurrection.

The following interesting account of the church and statue of St. Cecilia is extracted from Mrs. Jameson's beautiful work upon Sacred and Legendary Art.

'According to her wish, the house of Cecilia was consecrated as a church, the chamber in which she suffered martyrdom being regarded as a spot of peculiar sanctity. There is mention of a council held in the church of St. Cecilia by Pope Symmachus, in the year 500. Afterwards, in the troubles and invasions of the barbarians, this ancient church fell into ruin, and was rebuilt by

Pope Paschal I. in the ninth century. It is related that, while engaged in this work, Paschal had a dream, in which St. Cecilia appeared to him, and revealed the spot in which she lay buried; accordingly search was made, and her body was found in the cemetery of Calixtus, wrapt in a shroud of gold tissue, and round her feet a linen cloth dipt in her blood: near her were the remains of Valerian, Tibertius, and Maximus, which, together with hers, were deposited in the same church, now St. Cecilia-in-Trastevere. The little room, containing her bath, in which she was murdered or martyred, is now a chapel. The rich frescoes with which it was decorated are in a state of utter ruin from age and damp; but the machinery for heating the bath, the pipes, the stoves, yet remain. This church, having again fallen into ruin, was again repaired, and sumptuously embellished in the taste of the sixteenth century, by Cardinal Sfondrati. On this occasion the sarcophagus containing the body of St. Cecilia was opened with great solemnity in the presence of several cardinals and dignitaries of the Church, among others Cardinal Baronius, who has given us an exact description of the appearance of the body, which had been buried by Pope Paschal in 820, when exhumed in 1599. "She was lying," says Baronius, "within a coffin of cypress wood, enclosed in a marble sarcophagus; not in the manner of one dead and buried, that is, on her back, but on her right side, as one asleep; and in a very modest attitude; covered with a simple stuff of taffety, having her head bound with cloth, and at her feet the remains of the cloth of gold and silk which Pope Paschal had found in her tomb." Clement VIII ordered that the relics should remain untouched, inviolate; and the cypress coffin was enclosed in a silver shrine, and replaced under the altar. This re-interment took place in presence of the pope and clergy, with great pomp and solemnity, and the people crowded in from the neighbouring towns to assist at the ceremony. Stefano Maderno, who was then in the employment of the Cardinal Sfondrati as sculptor and architect, and acted as his secretary, was not, we may suppose, absent on this occasion; by the order of the Cardinal he executed the beautiful and celebrated statue of " St. Cecilia lying dead," which was intended to commemorate the attitude in which she was found. It is thus described by Sir Charles Bell :—" The body lies on its side, the limbs a little drawn up ; the hands are delicate and fine,—they are not locked, but crossed at the wrists : the arms are stretched out. The drapery is beautifully modelled, and modestly covers the limbs. The head is enveloped in linen, but the general form is seen, and the artist has contrived to convey by its position, though not offensively, that it is separated from the body. A gold circlet is round the neck, to conceal the place of decollation(?). It is the statue of a lady, perfect in form, and affecting from the resemblance to reality in the drapery of white marble, and the unspotted appearance of the statue altogether. It lies as no living body could lie, and yet correctly, as the dead when left to expire,—I mean in the gravitation of the limbs."

' It must be remembered that Cecilia did not suffer decollation ; that her head was *not* separated from the body ; and the gold band is to conceal the wound in the neck : otherwise, this description of the statue agrees exactly with the description which Cardinal Baronius has given of the body of the saint when found in 1599.

' The ornaments round the shrine, of bronze and rare and precious marbles, are in the worst taste, and do not harmonize with the pathetic simplicity of the figure.

' At what period St. Cecilia came to be regarded as the patron saint of music, and accompanied by the musical attributes, I cannot decide. It is certain that in ancient devotional representations she is not so distinguished ; nor in the old Italian series of subjects from her life have I found any in which she is figured as singing, or playing upon instruments [1].'

The Canon's Yeoman's Prologue, and Tale. The Prologue, as well as the Tale itself, belongs to the very latest period of Chaucer's work. This is clear at once, from its originality, as well as from the metre, and the careless ease of the rhythm,

---

[1] See my note to l. 134 of the Tale, p. 171.

which sometimes almost degenerates into slovenliness, as though our author had written some of it in hot haste, with the intention of revising it more carefully afterwards. Besides, the poet has boldly improved upon his plan of the pilgrims' stories as laid down in his Prologue. We have there no hint of the Canon nor of his Yeoman; they are two new pilgrims who join themselves to the rest upon the road. A dispute arising between the master and the man, the former is put out of countenance, and actually rides away for very sorrow and shame (l. 702); but the man remains, to denounce the cupidity of the alchemists and to expose their trickery. Tyrwhitt remarks :—'The introduction of the Chanouns Yeman to tell a tale, at a time when so many of the original characters remain to be called upon, appears a little extraordinary. It should seem, that some sudden resentment had determined Chaucer to interrupt the regular course of his work, in order to insert a satire against the alchemists. That their pretended science was much cultivated about this time, and produced its usual evils, may fairly be inferred from the Act, which was passed soon after, 5 Henry IV, cap. iv. to make it Felonie *to multiplie gold or siluer, or to vse the art of multiplication.*' He adds—'The first considerable coinage of gold in this country was begun by Edward III in the year 1343, and according to Camden (in his Remains, art. *Money*), "the Alchemists did affirm, as an unwritten verity, that the Rose-nobles, which were coined soon after, were made by projection or multiplication Alchemical of Raymund Lully in the Tower of London." Ashmole, in his *Theatrum Chemicum,* p. 443, has repeated this ridiculous story concerning Lully with additional circumstances, as if he really believed it; though Lully, by the best accounts, had been dead above twenty years before Edward III began to coin gold[1].'

---

[1] Tyrwhitt further explains that a poem in Ashmole's volume, called *Hermes Bird,* and by him attributed to Raymund Lully, is really a poem of Lydgate's, printed by Caxton with the title *The Chorle and the Bird.*

The above-mentioned volume by Ashmole, entitled Theatrum Chemicum [1], is a very singular production. And, perhaps, not the least singular circumstance is that Ashmole actually gives 'The Tale of the Chanon's Yeman, written by our ancient and famous poet, Geoffry Chaucer,' Prologue and all, at full length (pp. 227–256), under the impression, apparently, that Chaucer was really a believer in the science! He says—'One reason why I selected out of Chaucer's Canterbury Tales that of the Chanon's Yeoman was, to let the world see what notorious cheating there has beene ever used, under pretence of this true (though injur'd) Science; Another is, to shew that Chaucer himselfe was a Master therein.' It is indeed true that Chaucer had examined into alchemy very closely, but it is perfectly clear that he had made up his mind, with his strong English common sense, that the whole matter was a delusion. Had he lived in the present century, he could hardly have spoken out in more assured terms. In a similar manner he had studied astrology, and was equally a disbeliever in all but the terms of it and a few of its most general and vague assertions. He says expressly, in his Treatise on the Astrolabie (ed. Skeat, pt. ii. sec. 4, l. 34)—'natheless, theise ben obseruauncez of iudicial matiere & rytes of paiens [pagans], in which my spirit ne hath no feith, ne no knowyng of hir *horoscopum.*' But it is evident that the believers in alchemy had to make the best use they could of Chaucer's language, by applying it as being directed only against notorious cheats; and accordingly, we find in The Ordinall of Alchimy, by Thomas Norton of Bristol, printed in Ashmole's collection, various passages imitated from Chaucer, such as, e.g. that at p. 17 :—

> 'The fals man walketh from Towne to Towne,
> For the most parte in a threed-bare Gowne,' &c.

And again, George Ripley, in his Compound of Alchymie,

---

[1] It is a totally different work from the Latin collection of alchemical works, also called Theatrum Chemicum, so often cited in my notes.

dedicated to King Edward IV, printed in the same collection,
says, at p. 153 :—

> ' Their Clóthes be bawdy and woryn threde-bare,
> Men may them smell for Multyplyers where they go,' &c.[1]

Ashmole's work contains several treatises which profess to ex-
plain alchemy, nearly all alike couched in mysterious, and often
in ridiculous language.   Such are Norton's Ordinall of Alchimy,
Ripley's Compound of Alchymie, Liber Patris Sapientiae, Hermes
Bird (really Lydgate's poem of The Churl and the Bird),
Chaucer's Canon's Yeoman's Tale (!), Pearce the Blacke Monke
upon the Elixir, Charnock's Breviary of Naturall Philosophy[2],
Ripley's Mistery of Alchymists, an extract from Gower's Confessio Amantis, Aristotle's Secreta Secretorum, translated by
Lydgate ; and so on.   On the whole, the book is equally curious
and dull.

It would hardly be possible to give much idea of alchemy in
a brief space, and it would certainly be unprofitable.   The
curious will find an excellent article upon it (entitled ' Alchemy ')
in the new edition of the Encyclopaedia Britannica; and a
history of it, by no means uninteresting, in the first volume
of Thomson's History of Chemistry.   In Whewell's History
of the Inductive Sciences, 2nd edition, 1847, vol. i. p. 320, the
following notice of it occurs, which I quote for the reader's
convenience.—' Like other kinds of Mysticism, Alchemy seems
to have grown out of the notions of moral, personal, and
mythological qualities, which men associated with terms, of
which the primary application was to physical properties.   This
is the form in which the subject is presented to us in the
earliest writings which we possess on the subject of chemistry,

---

[1] At p. 470. Ashmole gives a brief account of Chaucer, made up from
Speght, Bale, Pits, and others, of no particular value.   At p. 226, he gives
an engraving of the marble monument erected to Chaucer's memory in
Westminster Abbey, by Nicholas Brigham, A.D. 1556.

[2] This is somewhat amusing.   Charnock describes his numerous mis-
adventures, and it is not clear that he preserved his faith in alchemy
unshaken.

those of Geber of Seville, who is supposed to have lived in the eighth or ninth century. The very titles of Geber's works show the notions on which this pretended science proceeds. They are, "Of the Search of Perfection;" "Of the Sum of Perfection, or of the Perfect Magistery;" "Of the Invention of Verity, or Perfection." The basis of this phraseology is the distinction of metals into more or less *perfect*; gold being the most perfect, as being the most valuable, most beautiful, most pure, most durable; silver the next; and so on. The "Search of Perfection" was, therefore, the attempt to convert other metals into gold; and doctrines were adopted which represented the metals as all compounded of the same elements, so that this was theoretically possible. But the mystical trains of association were pursued much further than this; gold and silver were held to be the most noble of metals; gold was their King, and silver their Queen. Mythological associations were called in aid of these fancies, as had been done in astrology. Gold was Sol, the sun; silver was Luna, the moon; copper, iron, tin, lead, were assigned to Venus, Mars, Jupiter, Saturn. The processes of mixture and heat were spoken of as personal actions and relations, struggles and victories. Some elements were conquerors, some conquered; there existed preparations which possessed the power of changing the whole of a body into a substance of another kind: these were called *magisteries* [1]. When gold and quicksilver are combined, the king and the queen are married, to produce children of their own kind. It will easily be conceived, that when chemical operations were described in phraseology of this sort, the enthusiasm of the fancy would be added to that of the hopes, and observation would not be permitted to correct the delusion, or to suggest sounder and more rational views.

'The exaggeration of the vague notion of perfection and power in the object of the alchemist's search, was carried further still. The same preparation which possessed the faculty of turning

---

[1] Thomson's Hist. Chemistry, i. 25.

baser metals into gold, was imagined to be also a universal medicine, to have the gift of curing or preventing diseases, prolonging life, producing bodily strength and beauty: the *philosophers' stone* was finally invested with every desirable efficacy which the fancy of the "philosophers" could devise.'

See also Dr. Whewell's account of the doctrine of "the four elements" in the same work; vol. iii. **p. 121.**

The history of the rise and growth of the ideas involved in alchemy is ably treated of in the article in the Encyclopaedia Britannica already referred to; it is of some interest to note how some of the more important notions were developed. From ancient Persia came the idea of a correspondence between the heavenly bodies and parts of the human frame, alluded to in Chaucer's Treatise on the Astrolabie, and in Shakespeare's Twelfth Night, i. 3. 148[1]. From ancient India came the idea of a peregrination of sinful souls through the animal, vegetable, and even the mineral world, till they were absorbed into Deity. Hence was further evolved the notion of a transmutation of elements. The Greeks held that different deities had under their protection and guidance different types of men; an idea still preserved in our words *mercurial, jovial,* and *saturnine.* The school of Hippocrates held the doctrine of the four elements, or primary substances of which all others were made, an idea first mentioned (it is said) by Empedocles; to which Aristotle added a fifth element, that of ether (Arist. de Caelo, i. 2). But this idea is probably older; for we find five *bhúta's,* or elements, enumerated in Sanskrit, viz. **earth,** fire, **water,** air, and ether; see Benfey's Skt. Dict. **s. v.** *bhú,* p. 658. Another very ancient notion is that male and female principles existed in all three worlds alike, animal, vegetable, and mineral; from which it followed that the union of two metals

---

[1] '*Sir To.* What shall we do else? Were we not born under Taurus? *Sir And.* Taurus I that's sides and heart. *Sir To.* No, sir; it's legs and thighs.' Both are wrong, of course, as Shakespeare knew. Chaucer says— '*Aries hath thin heued* [head], *and Taurus thy nekke and thy throte;*' Astrolabie, pt. i. sec. 21. l. 50.

could produce a third. It was argued that 'monstrosities are
the productions of diseased metals (really alloys), which, if
properly treated, may be cured, and will turn to gold, or at
least silver. The second stage in this imitation of nature is
to obtain, by tincture or projection, solid or liquid gold, the
cure of all evils;' Encycl. Brit. i. 463, col. 2. This notion
is still preserved in the word *arsenic* (Gk. ἀρσενικόν, male). It
was universally believed that nature produced changes in the
substance of various metals by slow degrees, and the great object
of alchemy was to produce the same changes quickly. The
chief names in connection with the progress of alchemy are
Geber, a Sabaean, who flourished about A.D. 800; Avicenna,
a native of Shiraz, born A.D. 980, died June, 1037; Albertus
Magnus, born about 1193, died Nov. 15, 1280, who uses much
more intelligible language than alchemists usually indulge in;
Raymund Lully, born at Majorca in 1235, a scholar of Roger
Bacon, who was himself deeply imbued with the mystery of
alchemy; Arnoldus de Villa Nova (mentioned by Chaucer), so
named because born at Villeneuve, in Provence, in 1240; and
others. Paracelsus[1], a Swiss physician (born in 1493, died
1541) was something better than a mere alchemist. He did
something towards destroying the notion of the necessity of
consulting astrological influences, and prepared the way for
the discoveries of Van Helmont (born at Brussels in 1577,
died 1644), with whom the history of modern chemistry may
be said to begin. Van Helmont was the inventor of two new
terms, *gas*[2] and *blas*, the former of which remains in common
use, though the latter is wholly forgotten.

The great store-house of treatises upon alchemy is the Latin
collection, in five volumes, called Theatrum Chemicum. I have
made considerable use of the edition of this work published
in 1660, which I have frequently quoted in the Notes. We

---

[1] See Browning's drama entitled 'Paracelsus.'
[2] It is useless to try and discover an etymology for this word. It was
invented wittingly. The most that can be said was that Van Helmont
may have been thinking of the Dutch *geest*, a spirit; E. *gho-t*.

hence gather that most of the authors upon the subject
wished men to believe that the true secrets of the science
were known to *themselves only;* yet they all learnt more or
less of a certain jargon which they continually repeated, attributing their empirical rules to Hermes, or Geber, or other
supposed masters. The same ideas, alleged results, and supposed principles continually recur; and the brief statement of
a few of these will at once shew what the reader of an alchemical treatise may expect to find. Much depended on the
supposed powers of certain numbers. Thus, there were *three*
primary colours, black, white, and red[1], from which all others
were produced by combination; Theat. Chem. iv. 536. According to Gower, there were really *three* kinds of the phi'o-
sopher's stone, viz. animal, vegetable, and mineral. Some said
it was composed of *three* parts; body, spirit, and soul—*corpus,
spiritus,* and *anima;* Ashmole's Th. Ch. p. 382. Again, there
were *four* elements; *four* complexions of nature or temperaments; *four* colours (said some), viz. white, black, citrine, and
red; *four* savours, insipid, acid, sweet, and bitter; *four* odours,
sweet, fetid, intense, and slight (*remissus*), Theat. Chem. iii.
82. In particular, there were *four* spirits, sulphur, sal ammoniac,
quick-silver, and arsenic; see note to line 778, p. 189; also
four states or conditions, hot, cold, wet, and dry; Theat.
Chem. iv. 537. There were *seven* planets; and *because* there
were seven planets, it followed that every planet had a corresponding note in the musical scale of *seven* notes. Every
planet had its proper colour; and, in this view, there were
seven colours, sable, vert, gules, or, argent, sanguine, and umber;
Batman upon Bartholome, lib. 19, c. 37. Every planet had its
proper metal; there were therefore *seven* metals; see the
extract from Gower, p. 193. Now, as all substances are made
of the same four elements, it follows that if a substance can
be decomposed, and reunited in different proportions, its nature
may be so changed that it shall become another substance.

[1] A strange selection; but due to Aristotle, De Sensu, ii.

Many substances, if subjected to heat, are destroyed; but metals are not so, and therefore became the favourite subject for experiments. It was laid down that one metal could be transmuted into another, but only after having been first **reduced** into its primary elements; Theat. Chem. iv. 531. Ere long, it was accepted as an axiom that all baser metals **could be** transmuted either into gold, or *sol*, typified by the sun, **or** into silver, or *luna*, typified by the moon; these being the two extremes between which the other five metals were ranged. It was agreed that the chief agents in producing this transmutation were quicksilver and sulphur, and of these quicksilver was the more important; so much so, **that the** mention of quicksilver meets us everywhere, and no alchemist could work without it [1]. It was also agreed that certain processes must be gone through in a due order, generally ten or twelve in number; and if *any one* of them failed, the whole work had to be begun afresh. They are commonly described as (1) calcination, (2) solution, (3) separation of the elements, (4) conjunction, (5) putrefaction, (6) coagulation, (7) cibation, (8) sublimation, (9) fermentation, (10) exaltation, (11) augmentation or multiplication; and (12) projection; Theat. Chem. ii. 175, and Ripley's Compound of Alchemy. By insisting on the necessity of all these processes, they sufficiently guarded against all chances of an unfavourable result by securing that a result could not very well be arrived at.

The moment that we attempt to analyse their processes more closely, we are met by two difficulties that are simply insuperable; the first, that the same name is clearly used to denote **quite different** substances, and the second, that the same substance is called **by** many different **names.** Hence also arose **endless evasions,** and arrogant claims to pretended secrets; it

---

[1] The Indian god *Siva* was actually worshipped *under the form of quicksilver*. Professor Cowell refers me to Marco Polo, ed. Yule, ii. 300, and to his own edition of Colebrooke's Essays, i. 433; also to the semi-mythic life of *Sankara* A'chárya, the great reformer of the eighth century.

was often said that the quicksilver of the alchemists was a substance only known to adepts, and that those who used only ordinary quicksilver knew nothing of the matter. The master could thus always mystify his pupils, and make it appear that he alone, and no one else, knew what he was talking about.

Yet it was frequently alleged that the experiments *did* succeed. The easiest explanation of this matter is, that the hopes of the alchemists were doubtless buoyed up by the fact that every now and then the experiments *appeared* to succeed; and it is easy to shew how. The close affinity of quicksilver for gold is well known. I copy the following from a book on experiments, which really suffices to explain the whole matter. ' If a sovereign be rubbed with mercury, it will lose its usual appearance, and appear as if silvered over [1]; the attraction of the gold for the mercury being sufficient to cause a coating of it to remain. When it is wished to remove the silvery appearance, dip the sovereign in a dilute solution of nitric acid, which will entirely take it off.' Now the alchemists tell us that quicksilver must always be used in all experiments; and they constantly recommend the introduction into the substances experimented on of a *small* quantity of gold, which they thought would be increased. The experiments constantly failed; and whenever they failed, the pieces of molten metal were carefully saved, to be used over and over again. The frequent introduction of small quantities of gold caused that metal to accumulate; and if, by any favourable process, the quicksilver was separated from the mass, a considerable quantity of gold would now and then actually appear. This account is so much in accordance with all that we read that we may confidently accept the conclusion of Dr. Thomson, the author of the History of Chemistry, that the vaunted philosopher's stone was certainly an *amalgam of gold;* which, ' if projected into melted lead or tin, and afterwards cupellated,

---

[1] This explains why the alchemists, in seeking gold, sometimes supposed that they had obtained silver.

would leave a portion of gold; all the gold, of course, that existed previously in the amalgam.' He adds that 'the alchemists who prepared the amalgam could not be ignorant that it contained gold;' a statement which I am inclined to modify by suggesting that it may very easily have contained *more gold than they supposed it did*. In a word, we may conclude that some deceived themselves, and others were conscious cheats.

The real secret of the long reign of alchemy, and of the tardy appearance of scientific chemistry, lies in this—that men, as a rule, have more faith in their theoretical notions than in the practical evidence of their senses. The history of alchemy is, in fact, full of instruction, and its lessons have not yet all been learnt. Not to apply them to any of the more popular delusions of the day (which would here be out of place), I would apply them to a subject in which students of Chaucer may be supposed to take a special interest, viz. that of *English etymology*. A good deal of what is called 'etymology' is the merest alchemy; and the guesswork which is sometimes dignified by that name is often as baseless and as valueless as the dreams of the so-called adepts. Perhaps there is no book which better illustrates the history of the English language than Richardson's Dictionary; the value of the profusion of quotations, each with its proper reference, is very great. Yet the etymology is remarkably poor, owing to the number of guesses which were too rashly recorded there. Take, e.g. his account of the word *hod*. '*Hod*, perhaps *hoved*, *hov'd*, *hod*; past part. of A. S. *heafan*, to heave. That which is *heaved* or raised,' &c. Yet the whole of this breaks down when we remember that *hebban* [not *heafan*] is a strong verb, and that its past part. became *hoven*, whilst still conjugated as a strong verb; and afterwards *heav'd*, when it was treated as a weak one : the form *hov'd* being simply impossible either way. Students may do better than this, if they will bear in mind two or three leading principles, such as (1) that the investigation of the *history* of a word must precede all attempts to 'derive' it; (2) that it is of small utility to imagine how a word *might* have been

formed, especially when, as is sometimes the case, there is
good evidence as to how it *was* formed : (3) that the laws
of language must be studied, it being absurd to make up words
in opposition to all that we know of Anglo-Saxon grammar;
and (4) that the light afforded by comparative philology is to
be thankfully accepted, and not shut out as if it were non-
existent. In particular, it is to be remembered that the history
of many words is insufficiently recorded, and in such cases we
have no right to assume an origin which we cannot prove, but
should be content to say that we do not know it. The one
besetting sin of students of English etymology is that few are
content to give up the pursuit of that which lies beyond them;
like the alchemists, men are prone to pretend to know that
of which they can, after all, give no intelligible explanation.
Like the alchemists, many invent their facts, or distort and
wrest them, so as to make them agree with preconceived
theories. This is strikingly exemplified in many of our older
provincial glossaries, wherein the definitions of words, instead
of being honestly stated, are often tortured into agreement
with a supposed 'etymology.' Thus Ray, in his excellent Collection of Provincial Words, defines *belive* as 'anon, by and by,
or *towards night*;' merely in order to introduce his 'etymology,'
that *belive* is a corruption of *by the eve*, with a substitution of
the French *le* for the English *the*. Skinner's Lexicon contains
hundreds of such absurdities, many of which were copied into
Johnson's Dictionary, and some of them are certainly still believed in. For a sample of these, see the 'Garland culled from
Skinner' in my Introduction to Ray's Collection of Provincial
Words, pp. xxi–xxvi, published by the English Dialect Society.
And to this day correspondents write to Notes and Queries about
certain hard words, asking for the 'etymology' of them, instead
of asking for the *history* of them, which is the more important
matter. No wonder that they often receive six or seven different answers, all perhaps equally unsatisfactory and useless,
and learn no more about the matter than they knew at first.
Of course the etymology will explain a word, but only *if it*

happens to be right ; the history of the word is, however, a sure guide, because it deals with quotations and facts, not witl theories and fancies. I fear that we English have still much to learn before we are finally delivered from the alchemy of thos who only work by guess, and from the tyranny of ingeniou assertions.

A list of books most useful for explaining Chaucer, and c the Dictionaries used in compiling the Glossarial Index, is give in my former Introduction, at p. lxxvi.

The present volume is, in the main, my own work. M chief obligations have been to Mr. Furnivall's Six-text editio1 and to Tyrwhitt's notes. I wish to record my thanks to Mi: Gunning, of Cambridge, and Miss Wilkinson, of Dorking, wh considerably lightened the labour of preparing the Glossary b copying out, with proper references, and in many cases, wit explanations, the words explained there. I have added th explanations where they were omitted, and revised the whole the etymological remarks being my own throughout. A con siderable part of the Notes is due to my own reading, and ha not appeared before ; this is particularly the case with respect t the Canon's Yeoman's Tale.

In the present (revised) edition, a few new notes have bee added ; and an Index has been subjoined, shewing where to fin at once the more important explanations of words and subject matter.

Cambridge, Oct. 3, 1879.

NOTE ON THE PARDONER'S TALE.

It has been pointed out by Mr. Tawney and by Mr. Francis that this ta occurs in the Vedabbha Játaka, the 48th in Fausböll's edition. The ta was therefore known to the Buddhists.

ADDITIONS IN THE EDITION OF 1897.

In this edition several emendations have been made, and some errors have been corrected which had previously escaped notice.

The following remarks are added, for the fuller information of the student.

Note on p. xii, l. 17. The remark by Dr. Ellis, that the final *e* 'was never pronounced in *hire*=her' is liable to exception in the case where the word *hire* (usually *here*) happens to occur at *the end of a line*. This is particularly noted at p. 171, in the note to G 150.

Note on p. xxi. It is now recognised, in Sweet's First Middle-English Primer, p. 4, that the diphthongs *ei* and *ai* 'were beginning to be confused, probably through the *a* of *ai* being modified nearly to the sound of *a* in *man*; *ei* probably had the broad sound of the diphthong in the Cockney pronunciation of *name*.'

I do not hesitate to say that, in Chaucer, the diphthongs *ai*, *ay*, *ei*, *ey*, all rime together; and that the common sound was that of *ei* as above described, very nearly that of *ay*, *ey* in the modern English words *pray* and *prey*. The ruling of Dr. Ellis, that their common sound was like that of *ai* in *Isaiah* (p. xi), is quite untenable. Even Dr. Sweet seems to assume that *ai* had this sound originally; but we must not forget that English was spelt by Norman scribes, and there is no evidence that *ai* had the sound of *ai* in *Isaiah* even in late Norman. On the contrary, M. Gaston Paris says, of the Norman *ai* :—'Elle s'est originairement prononcée *ái* [as *ai* in *Isaiah*], mais déjà à l'époque de la dernière rédaction du *Roland* elle se prononce *è* et assone avec *è*.' That is, the symbol *ai* denoted *è* (open *e*), which is much nearer to *ei* than to the original *ai*. I think the reader can hardly go far wrong if he pronounces *ai*, *ay*, *ei*, *ey*, as occurring in Chaucer, with the modern English sound in *praying* or *preying*.

The Man of Lawes Tale.   It has been shewn, in Lounsbury's **Studies** in Chaucer, ii. 333 (a work which deserves to be carefully consulted), that no less than *four* of the stanzas in this Tale were certainly taken from an earlier work by Chaucer, of which the greater part is lost.

In ll. 414–5 of the older Prologue to the Legend of Good Women, Chaucer informs us that he once wrote a piece entitled 'Of the Wreched Engendring of Mankinde, As man may in Pope Innocent yfinde.' That is, he translated a well-known Latin treatise by Pope Innocent III, entitled De Contemptu Mundi sive de Miseria Conditionis Humanae.   This translation, as a whole, is lost ; but parts of it have been preserved by the fact that Chaucer, when revising the present Tale for insertion into the series, took occasion to insert three stanzas of his translation in The Prologue to the Man of Lawes Tale, and four more in the Tale itself, at different places.

The inserted stanzas occur at pp. 11, 23, and 36 of the present volume, and in an omitted passage noticed on p. 29.   The lines are numbered 421–7, 771–7, 925–31, and 1135–41. It is necessary to give the original Latin of these passages, in order to prove the point.

B 421–7 (p. 11).   From De Cont. Mundi, lib. i. c. 23, entitled De Inopinato Dolore. 'Semper enim mundanae laetitiae tristitia repentina succedit.   Et quod incipit a gaudio, desinit in moerore. Mundana quippe felicitas multis amaritudinibus est respersa. Nouerat hoc qui dixerat: Risus dolore miscebitur, et extrema gaudii luctus occupat [Prov. xiv. 13] ... Attende salubre consilium: In die bonorum, non immemor sis malorum' [cf. Eccles. vii. 14 ; xi. 8].   See note to l. 421, at p. 129.

B 771–7 (p. 23).   From De Cont. Mundi, lib. ii. c. 19; De Ebrietate. 'Quid turpius ebrioso? cui fetor in ore, tremor in corpore, qui promittit multa, prodit occulta, cui mens alienatur, facies transformatur?   Nullum enim secretum ubi regnat ebrietas' [Prov. xxxi. 4 ; in the Vulgate].   See note to l. 771, at p. 134.

B 925–31.   From De Cont. Mundi, lib. ii. c. 21. 'O extrema libidinis turpitudo, quae non solum mentem effeminat, **sed etiam corpus** eneruat; **non** solum maculat animam, sed foedat personam.'

B 1135-41 (p. 36). From De Cont. Mundi, lib. i. c. 22; De Breui Laetitia Hominis. 'A mane usque ad uesperam mutabitur tempus [Ecclus. xviii. 26]. ... Quis unquam uel unicam diem totum duxit in sua delectatione iucundum, quem in aliqua parte diei reatus conscientiae, uel impetus irae, uel motus concupiscentiae non turbauerit? Quem liuor inuidiae uel ardor auaritiae uel tumor superbiae non uexauerit? Quem aliqua iactura, uel offensa, uel passio non commouerit?' See note to l. 1135, p. 139.

It is now easy to understand the exact meaning of the Latin sentences quoted in the margins of some MSS., which closely agree with the above quotations. And it will be observed that the four stanzas above referred to are really digressions, having nothing to do with the story itself, though they are introduced suitably enough.

The question as to the relation of Chaucer's Tale to the same story as told by Gower is complicated by the fact that *both* of these poets really produced *two* editions of it. The order of them appears to have been as follows:—

(*a*) Chaucer's first edition.
(*b*) Gower's first edition.
(*c*) Chaucer's second edition.
(*d*) Gower's second edition.

Regarded in this light, it is possible that some of Chaucer's remarks refer to Gower, who copied several of Chaucer's expressions, and may have given some slight offence by doing so. See further, on this subject, in my edition of Chaucer's Complete Works, vol. iii. p. 413.

The Pardoner's Tale. It is necessary to observe that **Chaucer has inserted,** in this Tale also, some passages from Pope Innocent's work just mentioned above. The lines which relate to it are C 483-4, 505-7, 513-6, 521-3, 517-20, 534-6, 537-46, 551-2, 560-1; all from De Cont. Mundi, lib. ii. capp. 17-19.

The Second Nun's Tale. In addition to the Legenda Aurea

(see p. xxxii) Chaucer also consulted the Lives of Valerian and Tiburtius, as given in the Acta Sanctorum (April 14); see my note to l. 369, on p. 176.

Dr. Kölbing has further shewn (in *Englische Studien*, i. 215) that Chaucer only followed the Legenda Aurea down to about l. 348. But *after* this point (and, in a few places, *before* it), he follows another Latin life of St. Cecilia, derived from Simeon Metaphrastes. For this account, see Historiae Aloysii Lipomani de vitis sanctorum, pars II, Lovanii, 1571, p. 32; or the edition entitled De Vitis Sanctorum, ab Aloysio Lipomano, Venetiis, 1581, p. 161. Some of the expressions in Lipomanus which agree with Chaucer are the following :—

l. 189 : [Urbanus] *magno gaudio* est affectus.

ll. 218-9 : Inuenit Caeciliam ... et Angelum Domini *stantem prope eam.*

l. 233 : *assensus es.*

l. 265 : *Quomodo* hoc cognouisti.

l. 315 : Et nos quoque cum eo puniemur, si inuenti fuerimus ad eum ambulantes.

ll. 349-357 : Tunc Valerianus deduxit fratrem suum ad sanctissimum Papam Vrbanum. Cui postquam narrauit omnia ... Deo egit gratias. Acceptum autem cum omni gaudio et exultatione Tibertium, cum ... baptizasset, &c. Quae quidem cum perfecta fuissent eius doctrina, post septem dies Christi militem restituit.

GROUP B.   THE TALE OF THE MAN OF LAWE.

[*The* Introduction to the Man of Law's Prologue, *and the* Prologue *itself, are printed in* The Prioresses Tale, &c. (Clarendon Press Series), pp. 1–5. *A long extract from* The Tale *itself* (ll. 134–693) *is given in* Specimens of Early English, ed. Morris and Skeat, pp. 249–269.]

Here begynneth the man of lawe his tale.

In Surrye whylom dwelte a companye
Of chapmen riche, and therto sadde and trewe,   135
That wyde-wher senten her spicerye,
Clothes of gold, and satins riche of hewe ;
Her chaffar was so thrifty and so newe,
That euery wyght hath deyntee to chaffare
With hem, and eek to sellen hem her ware.   140

Now fel it, that the maistres of that sort
Han shapen hem to Rome for to wende ;
Were it for chapmanhode or for disport,
Noon other message wolde they thider sende,
But comen hem-self to Rome, this is the ende ;   145
And in swich place, as thoughte hem auantage
For her entent, they take her herbergage.

Soiourned han thise marchants in that toun
A certein tyme, as fel to her plesance,
And so bifel, that thexcellent renoun   150
Of themperoures doughter, dame Custance,
Reported was, with euery circumstance,

Vn-to thise Surryen marchants in swich wyse [1],
Fro day to day, as I shal yow deuyse.

This was the commune voys of euery man—   1
'Our Emperour of Rome, god him see,
A doughter hath that, sin the world bigan,
To rekne as wel hir goodnesse as beautee,
Nas neuere swich another as is she;
I prey to god in honour hir susteene,   1
And wolde she were of al Europe the queene.

In hir is hey beautee, with-oute pryde,
Yowthe, with-oute grenehede or folye;
To alle hir werkes vertu is hir gyde,
Humblesse hath slayn in hir al tirannye.   1
She is mirour of alle curteisye;
Hir herte is verray chambre of holynesse,
Hir hand, ministre of fredom for almesse.'

And al this voys was soth, as god is trewe,
But now to purpos lat vs turne agayn;   1
Thise marchants han doon fraught her shippes newe,
And, whan they han this blisful mayden seyn,
Hoom to Surrye ben they went ful fayn,
And doon her nedes as they han doon yore,
And lyuen in wele; I can sey yow no more.   1

Now fel it, that thise marchants stode in grace
Of him, that was the sowdan of Surrye;
For whan they came from any strange place,
He wolde, of his benigne curteisye,
Make hem good chere, and bisily espye   1

---

[1] E. swich a wyse; *but the other MSS. omit* a.

Tydings of sondry regnes, for to lere
The wondres that they myghte seen or here.

Amonges othere thinges, specially
Thise marchants han him told of dame Custance,
So gret noblesse in ernest, ceriously,   185
That this sowdan hath caught so gret plesance
To han hir figure in his remembrance,
That al his lust and al his bisy cure
Was for to loue hir whyl his lyf may dure.

Parauenture in thilke large book   190
Which that men clepe the heuen, ywriten was
With sterres, whan that he his birthe took,
That he for loue shulde han his deth, allas !
For in the sterres, clerer than is glas,
Is writen, god wot, who so coude it rede,   195
The deth of euery man, withouten drede.

In sterres, many a winter ther-biforn,
Was writen the deth of Ector, Achilles,
Of Pompei, Iulius, er they were born ;
The stryf of Thebes ; and of Ercules,   200
Of Sampson, Turnus, and of Socrates
The deth ; but mennes wittes ben so dulle,
That no wyght can wel rede it atte fulle.

This sowdan for his priuee conseil sente,
And, shortly of this mater for to pace,   205
He hath to hem declared his entente,
And seyde hem certein, 'but he myghte haue grace
To han Custance with-inne a litel space,
He nas but deed ;' and charged hem, in hye,
To shapen for his lyf som remedye.   210

Diuerse **men** diuerse thinges seyden ;
They argumenten [1], casten vp and doun ;
Many **a** subtil resoun **forth** they leyden,
They speken of magik and abusioun ;
But finally, as in conclusioun,   215
They can not seen in that non auantage,
Ne in non other wey, saue mariage.

Than seye they ther-in swich difficultee
By way of resoun, for to speke al playn,
By cause that **ther was** swich diuersitee   220
Bitwene her bothe lawes, that **they** sayn,
They trowe ' that no cristen prince wolde fayn
Wedden his child vnder oure lawes swete
That vs were taught by Mahoun **our** prophete.'

And he answerde, ' rather than **I lese**   225
Custance, I wol be cristned doutelees ;
I mot ben hires, I may non other chese.
I prey **yow** holde youre arguments in pees ;
Saueth my lyf, and beth nought recchelees
To getten hir that hath my lyf in cure ;   230
For in this **wo I may** not longe endure.'

What nedeth gretter dilatacioun ?
I seye, by tretys and embassadrye,
And by the popes mediacioun,
And al the chirche, and al the chiualrye,   235
That, in destruccioun of Maumettrye,
And in encrees of cristes lawe dere,
They ben accorded, so as ye shal here ;

----

[1] Harl., Corp. argumentes ; *but see* l. 223.

How that the sowdan and his baronage
And alle his lieges shulde ycristned be,   240
And he shal han Custance in mariage,
And certein gold, I not what quantitee,
And her-to founden suffisant seurtee ;
This same accord was sworn on eyther syde ;
Now, fayre Custance, almyghty god thee gyde !   245

Now wolde som men wayten, as I gesse,
That I shulde tellen al the purveiance
That themperour, of his gretenoblesse,
Hath shapen for his doughter dame Custance.
Wel 'may men knowe that so gret ordinance   250
May no man tellen in a litel clause
As was arrayed for so hey a cause.

Bisshopes ben shapen with hir for to wende,
Lordes, ladyes, knyghtes of renoun,
And other folk ynow, this is the ende ;   255
And notifyed is thurgh-out the toun
That euery wyght, with gret deuocioun,
Shulde preyen crist that he this mariage
Receyue in gree, and spede this viage.

The day is comen of hir departing,   260
I sey, the woful day fatal is come,
That ther may be no lenger tarying,
But forthward they hem dressen, alle and some ;
Custance, that was with sorwe al ouercome,
Ful pale arist, and dresseth hir to wende ;   265
For wel she seeth ther is non other ende.

Allas! what wonder is it though she wepte,
That shal be sent to strange nacioun
Fro frendes, that so tendrely hir kepte,
And to be bounden vnder subieccioun   270
Of oon, she knoweth not his condicioun.
Housbondes ben alle goode, and han ben yore,
That knowen wyues, I dar say yow no more.

'Fader,' she sayde, 'thy wrecched child Custance,
Thy yonge doughter, fostred vp so softe,   275
And ye, my mooder, my soueráyn plesance
Ouer alle thing, out-taken crist on lofte,
Custance, your child, hir recomandeth ofte
Vn-to your grace, for I shal to Surryĕ,
Ne shal I neuer seen yow more with yĕ.   280

Allas! vn-to the Barbre nacioun
I moste gon, sin that it is your wille;
But crist, that starf for our sauacioun,
So yeue me grace, his hestes to fulfille;
I, wrecche womman, no fors though I spille.   285
Wommen are born to thraldom and penance,
And to ben vnder mannes gouernance.'

I trowe, at Troye whan Pirrus brak the wal
Or Ylion[1] brende, at Thebes the citee,
Nat[2] Rome, for the harm thurgh Hanybal   290
That Romayns hath venquisshed tymes thre,
Nas herd swich tendre weping for pitee

---

[1] *All the best MSS. read* ylion, *which should therefore be retained;* at *before* Thebes *is inserted from the* Cambridge MS. Or *is used in the sense of* ere, *and* brende *is intransitive.*

[2] Nat *is the reading of the* Ellesmere, Hengwrt, *and* Cambridge MSS.; *but in this instance it is probably a contraction of* ne at, *instead of being equivalent to* not, *as usual. The* Harl. *MS. reads* Ne at *accordingly.*

As in the chambre was for hir departinge;
Bot forth she moot, wher-so she wepe or singe.

'O firstĕ moeuyng cruel firmament,   295
With thy diurnal sweigh that crowdest ay
And hurlest al from Est til Occident,
That naturelly wolde holde another way,
Thy crowding set the heuen in swich array
At the biginning of this fiers viage,   300
That cruel Mars hath slayn this mariage.

Infortunat ascendent tortuous,
Of which the lord is helplees falle, allas!
Out of his angle in-to the derkest hous.
O Mars, O Atazir, as in this cas!   305
O feble moone, vnhappy ben thy pas!
Thou knittest thee ther thou art not receyued,
Ther thou were wel, from thennes artow weyued.

Imprudent emperour of Rome, allas!
Was ther no philosophre in al thy toun?   310
Is no tyme bet than other in swich cas?
Of viage is ther non eleccioun,
Namely to folk of hey condicioun,
Not whan a rote is of a birthe yknowe?
Allas! we ben to lewed or to slowe.   315

To shippe is brought[1] this woful faire mayde
Solempnely with euery circumstance.
'Now Iesu crist be with yow alle,' she sayde,
Ther nis no more but 'farewel! faire Custance!'
She peyneth hir to make good countenance,   320
And forth I lete hir sayle in this manere,
And turne I wol agayn to my matere.

[1] E. come; brought in the rest.

The mooder of the sowdan, welle of vices,
Espyed hath hir sones pleyn entente,
How he wol lete his olde sacrifices,   325
And ryght anon she for hir conseil sente;
And they ben come, to knowe what she mente.
And when assembled was this folk in-fere,
She sette hir doun, and sayde as ye shal here.

'Lordes,' quod she [1], 'ye knowen euerichon,   330
How that my sone in point is for to lete
The holy lawes of oure Alkaron,
Yeuen by goddes message [2] Makomete.
But oon auow to grete god I hete,
The lyf shal rather out of my body sterte   335
Than Makometes lawe out of myn herte!

What shulde vs tyden of this newe lawe
But thraldom to our bodies and penance?
And afterward in helle to be drawe
For we reneyed Mahoun our creance?   340
But, lordes, wol ye maken assurance,
As I shal seyn, assenting to my lore,
And I shall make vs sauf for euermore?'

They sworen and assenten, euery man,
To lyue with hir and dye, and by hir stonde;   345
And euerich, in the beste wyse he can,
To strengthen hir shal alle his frendes fonde;
And she hath this emprise ytake on honde,
Which ye shal heren that I shal deuyse,
And to hem alle she spak ryght in this wyse.   350

[1] E. she seyde ; quod she *in the rest.*
[2] messager Corp., Petw., *and* Lands. MSS. ; *but see the note.*

'We shul first feyne vs cristendom to take,
Cold water shal not greue vs but a lyte;
And I shal swich a feste and reuel make,
That, as I trowe, I shal the sowdan quyte.
For though his wyf be cristned neuer so whyte,   355
She shal haue nede to wasshe awey the rede,
Though she a font-ful water with hir lede.'

O sowdanesse, rote of iniquitee,
Virago, thou Semyram the secounde,
O serpent vnder femininitee,   360
Lyk to the serpent depe in helle ybounde,
O feyned womman, al that may confounde
Vertu and Innocence, thurgh thy malice,
Is bred in thee, as nest of euery vice!

O Satan, enuious sin thilke day   365
That thou were chased fro our heritage,
Wel knowestow to wommen the olde way!
Thou madest Eua bringe vs in seruage.
Thou wolt fordoon this cristen mariage.
Thy instrument, so, weylawey the whyle!   370
Makestow of wommen, whan thou wolt begyle.

This sowdanesse, whom I thus blame and warye,
Let priuely hir conseil goon her way.
What shulde I in this tale lenger tarye?
She rydeth to the sowdan on a day,   375
And seyde him, that she wold reneye hir lay,
And cristendom of preestes handes fonge,
Repenting hir she hethen was so longe,

Biseching him to doon hir that honour,
That she moste han the cristen men to feste;   380
'To plesen hem I wol do my labour.'
The sowdan seith, 'I wol doon at your heste,'
And kneling thanketh hir of that requeste.
So glad he was, he niste what to seye;
She kiste hir sone, and hom she goth hir weye.   385
    Explicit prima pars.   Sequitur pars secunda.

Arryued ben this cristen folk to londe,
In Surrye, with a greet solempne route,
And hastily this sowdan sent his sonde,
First to his mooder, and al the regne aboute,
And seyde, his wyf was comen, out of doute,   390
And preyde hir for to ryde agayn the queene,
The honour of his regne to susteene.

Gret was the prees, and riche was tharray
Of Surryens and Romayns met yfere;
The mooder of the sowdan, riche and gay,   395
Receyueth hir with al so glad a chere
As any mooder myghte hir doughter dere,
And to the nexte cite ther bisyde
A softe pas solempnely they ryde.

Nought trowe I the triumphe of Iulius,   400
Of which that Lucan maketh swich a bost,
Was roialler, ne¹ more curious
Than was thassemblee of this blissful host.
But this scorpioun, this wikked gost,
The sowdanesse, for all hir flateringe,   405
Caste vnder this ful mortally to stinge.

---

¹ E. or; ne *in the rest.*

The sowdan comth him-self soone after this
So roially, that wonder is to telle,
And welcometh hir with al joye and blis.
And thus in merthe and ioye I lete hem dwelle.   410
The fruyt of this matere is that I telle.
Whan tyme cam, men thoughte it for the beste
That [1] reuel stinte, and men goon to hir reste.

The tyme cam, this olde sowdanesse
Ordeyned hath this feste of which I tolde,   415
And to the feste cristen folk hem dresse
In general, ye ! bothe yonge and olde.
Here may men feste and roialtee biholde,
And deyntees mo than I can yow deuyse,
But al to dere they boughte it er they ryse.   420

O sodeyn wo ! that euer art successour
To worldly blisse, spreynd with bitternesse ;
Thende [2] of the ioye of our worldly labour ;
Wo occupieth the fyn of our gladnesse.
Herke this conseil for thy sikernesse,   425
Vp-on thy glade day haue in thy mynde
The vnwar wo or harm that comth bihynde.

For shortly [3] for to tellen at a word,
The sowdan and the cristen euerichone
Ben al tohewe and stiked at the bord,   430
But it were only dame Custance allone.
This olde sowdanesse, this [4] cursed crone,
Hath with her frendes doon this cursed dede,
For she hir-self wold al the contree lede.

----

[1] E. The; That *in the rest.*
[2] *So in* Camb. ; *the rest have* The ende.   [3] *So in the rest;* E. soothly.
[4] *So in* Petw. *and* Harl. ; *the rest omit* this.

Ne ther[1] was Surryen noon that was conuerted   435
That of the conseil of the sowdan wot,
That he nas al tohewe er he asterted.
And Custance han they take anon, foot-hot,
And in a shippe al sterelees, god wot,
They han hir set, and bidde[2] hir lerne sayle   440
Out of Surrye agaynward to Itayle.

A certein tresor that she thider[3] ladde,
And, soth to sayn, vitaille gret plentee
They han hir yeuen, and clothes eek she hadde,
And forth she sayleth in the salte see.   445
O my Custance, ful of benignytee,
O emperoures yonge doughter dere,
He that is lord of fortune be thy stere I

She blesseth hir, and with ful pitous voys
Vn-to the croys of crist thus seyde she,   450
'O cleere, o welful[4] auter, holy croys,
Reed of the lambes blood full of pitee,
That wesh the world fro the olde iniquitee,
Me fro the feend, and fro his clawes kepe
That day that I shal drenchen in the depe.   455

Victorious tree, proteccioun of trewe,
That only worthy were for to bere
The king of heuen with his woundes newe,
The whyte lomb, that hurt was with the spere,
Flemer of feendes out of hym and here   460

---

[1] *So in the rest;* E. *omits* ther.
[2] Heng. *and* Camb. bidde ; Corp. *and* Petw. bidden ; Lansd. beden; E. biddeth ; Harl. bad.
[3] E. with hire; *but the rest have* thider.
[4] E. woful; *the rest,* welful, wilful, weleful.

On which thy lymes feithfully extenden,
Me keep [1], and yif me myght my lyf tamenden.'
Yeres and dayes fleet [2] this creature
Thurghout the see of Grece vn-to the strayte
Of Marrok, as it was hir auenture;   465
On many a sory meel now may she bayte;
After her deeth ful often may she wayte,
Er that the wilde wawes wole hir dryue
Vn-to the place [3], ther she shal arryue.

Men myghten asken why she was not slayn?   470
Eek at the feste who myghte hir body saue?
And I answere to that demaunde agayn,
Who saued danyel in the horrible caue,
Ther euery wyght saue he, maister and knaue,
Was with the leoun frete er he asterte?   *asterted*   475
No wyght but god, that he bar in his herte.

God list to shewe his wonderful miracle
In hir, for we shulde seen his myghty werkes;
Crist, which that is to euery harm triacle,
By certein menes ofte, as knowen clerkes,   480
Doth thing for certein ende that ful derk is
To mannes wit, that for our ignorance
Ne conne not knowe his prudent purueiance.

Now, sith she was not at the feste yslawe,
Who kepte hir fro the drenching in the see?   485
Who kepte Ionas in the fisshes mawe
Til he was spouted vp at Niniuee?
Wel may men knowe it was no wyght but he

---

[1] Camb., Lands. kep; Heng., Petw., Harl. kepe; Corp. keepe: E. helpe.
[2] E. fleteth; *but the form* fleet *occurs in* Heng., Corp., *and* Petw.
[3] *Probably read* placë; Harl. *alone inserts* as *after* ther.

That kepte peple Ebrayk fro hir drenching,
With drye feet thurgh-out the see passing.   49c

Who bad the foure spirits of tempest,
That power han tanoyen lond and see,
'Bothe north and south, and also west and est,
Anoyeth neither see, ne lond, ne tree?'
Sothly the comaundour of that was he   495
That fro the tempest ay this womman kepte
As wel whan she wook as whan she slepte.

Wher myghte this womman mete and drinke haue?
Thre yeer and more how lasteth her vitaille?
Who fedde the Egypcien Marie in the caue,   500
Or in desert? no wyght but crist, sans faille.
Fyue thousand folk it was as gret meruaille
With loues fyue and fisshes two to fede.
God sente his foyson at hir grete nede.

She dryueth forth in-to our occean   505
Thurgh-out our wilde see, til, atte laste,
Vnder an hold that nempnen I ne can,
Fer in Northumberlond the wawe hir caste,
And in the sond hir ship stiked so faste,
That thennes wolde it noght of al a tyde,   510
The wille of crist was that she shulde abyde.

The constable of the castel doun is fare
To seen this wrak, and al the ship he soughte,
And fond this wery womman ful of care;
He fond also the tresor that she broughte.   515
In hir langage mercy she bisoughte
The lyf out of hir body for to twinne,
Hir to deliuere of wo that she was inne.

A maner latyn corrupt was hir speche,
But algates ther-by was she vnderstonde;   520
The constable, whan him list no lenger seche,
This woful womman brought he to the londe;
She kneleth doun, and thanketh goddes sonde.
But what she was she wolde no man seye,
For foul ne fayr, thogh that she shulde deye.   525

She seyde, she was so mased in the see
That she forgat hir mynde, by hir trewthe;
The constable hath of hir so gret pitee,
And eek his wyf, that they wepen for rewthe,
She was so diligent, with-outen slewthe,   530
To serue and plese[n] euerich in that place
That alle hir louen that looken on[1] hir face.

This constable and dame Hermengild his wyf
Were payens, and that contree euery-where;
But Hermengild louede hir ryght as hir lyf,   535
And Custance hath so longe soiourned[2] there,
In orisons, with many a bitter tere,
Til Iesu hath conuerted thurgh his grace
Dame Hermengild, constablesse of that place.

In al that lond no cristen durste route,   540
Alle cristen folk ben fled fro that contree
Thurgh payens, that conquereden al aboute
The plages of the North, by land and see;
To Walys fled the cristianitee
Of olde Britons, dwellinge in this Ile;   545
Ther was hir refut for the mene whyle.

---

[1] E. *and* Camb. in; *the rest* on.   [2] Harl. *only has* herberwed.

But yet nere cristen Britons so exiled
That ther nere somme that in hir priuitee
Honoured crist, and hethen folk bigiled;
And neigh the castel swiche ther dwelten three.   550
That oon of hem was blynd, and myghte not see
But it were with thilke yĕn'of his mynde,
With whiche men seen, whan that they ben blynde.

Bryght was the sonne as in that someres day,
For which the constable and his wyf also   555
And Custance han ytake the ryghte way
Toward the see, a furlong wey or two,
To playen and to romen to and fro;
And in hir walk this blynde man they mette
Croked and old, with yĕn faste y-schette.   560

'In name of Crist,' cryede this blynde [1] Britoun,
· 'Dame Hermengild, yif me my syghte agayn.'
This lady wex affrayed of the soun,
Lest that hir housbond, shortly for to sayn,
Wolde hir for Iesu cristes loue han slayn,   565
Til Custance made hir bold, and bad hir werche
The wil of Crist, as doughter of his chirche.

The constable wex abasshed of that sight,
And seyde, 'what amounteth al this fare?'
Custance answerde, 'sire, it is Cristes might   570
That helpeth folk out of the feendes snare.'
And so ferforth she gan our lay declare,
That she the constable, or that it were eue,
Conuerted [2], and on Crist made [3] him bileue.

[1] E. olde; Harl. old; *but the rest* blynde *or* blynd.
[2] Harl. Conuerted; Camb. Conuertid; *the rest* Conuerteth.
[3] E. maketh; Lansd. maad; *the rest* made.

This constable was no-thing lord of this place   575
Of which I speke, ther he Custance fond,
But kepte it strongly, many wintres space,
Vnder Alla, king of al Northumberlond,
That was ful wys, and worthy of his hond
Agayn the Scottes, as men may wel here,   580
But turne I wol agayn to my matere.

Sathan, that euer vs waiteth to bigyle,
Sey of Custance al hir perfeccioun,
And caste anon how he myghte quyte hir whyle,
And made a yong knyght, that dwelte in that toun,   585
Loue hir so hote of foul affeccioun,
That verraily him thoughte he shulde spille
But he of hir myghte ones haue his wille.

He woweth hir, but it auailleth nought,
She wolde do no sinne, by no weye ;   590
And, for despit, he compassed in his thought
To maken hir on shamful deth to deye.
He wayteth whan the constable was aweye,
And priuely, vp-on a nyght, he crepte
In Hermengildes chambre whyl she slepte.   595

Wery, for-waked in her orisouns,
Slepeth Custance, and Hermengild also.
This knyght, thurgh Sathanas [1] temptaciouns,
Al softely is to the bed ygo,
And kitte the throte of Hermengild atwo,   600
And leyde the blody knyf by dame Custance,
And wente his weye, ther god yeue him meschance !

---

[1] E. *and* Heng. Sathans ; Harl. Satanas ; *but* Sathanas *in* Corp., Petw., *and* Lansd.

Sone after comth this constable hoom agayn,
And eek Alla, that king was of that lond,
And sey his wyf despitously yslayn,   605
For which ful ofte he weep[1] and wrong his hond,
And in the bed the blody knyf he fond
By dame Custance; allas! what myghte she seye?
For verray wo hir wit was al aweye.

To king Alla was told al this meschance,   610
And eek the tyme, and wher, and in what wyse
That in a ship was founden dame Custance,
As her-biforn that ye han herd deuyse.
The kinges herte of pitee gan agryse,
Whan he sey so benigne a creature   615
Falle in disese and in misauenture.

For as the lomb toward his deth is brought,
So stant this Innocent bifore the king ;
This false knyght that hath this tresoun wrought
Berth[2] hir on hond that she hath doon this thing.   620
But natheles, ther was gret moorning[3]
Among the peple, and seyn, ' they can not gesse
That she hath doon so gret a wikkednesse.

For they han seyn hir euer so vertuous,
And louing Hermengild ryght as her lyf.'   625
Of this bar witnesse euerich in that hous
Saue he that Hermengild slow with his knyf.
This gentil king hath caught a gret motyf
Of this witnesse, and thoughte he wolde enquere
Depper in this, a trewthe for to lere.   630

---

[1] E. Hn. weep *or* weepe ; Camb. Corp. Petw. wepte.
[2] *So in* E; *the rest* Bereth.   [3] Tyr. murmuryng; *see note to l.* 248.

'Allas! Custance! thou hast no champioun
Ne fyghte canstow nought, so weyawley!
But he, that starf for our redempcioun
And bond Sathan (and yit lyth ther he lay)
So be thy stronge champioun this day!   635
For, but-if crist open miracle kythe,
Withouten gilt thou shalt be slayn as swythe.

She sette¹ her doun on knees, and thus she sayde,
'Immortal god, that sauedest Susanne
Fro false blame, and thow, merciful mayde,   640
Mary I mene, doughter to Seint Anne,
Bifore whos child aungeles singe Osanne,
If I be giltlees of this felonye,
My socour be, for ² elles I shal dye I'

Haue ye not seyn som tyme a pale face,   645
Among a prees, of him that hath be lad
Toward his deth, wher as him gat no grace,
And swich a colour in his face hath had,
Men myghte knowe his face, that was bistad,
Amonges alle the faces in that route: 650
So stant Custance, and looketh her aboute.

O queenes, lyuinge in prosperitee,
Duchesses, and ladyes euerichone,
Haueth som rewthe on hir aduersitee;
An emperoures doughter stant allone;   655
She hath no wight to whom to make hir mone.
O blood roial! that stondest in this drede,
Fer ben thy frendes at thy grete nede!

¹ E. sit; Heng. Camb. Petw. sette.
² E. or; *the rest* for.

C 2

This Alla king hath swich compassioun,
As gentil herte is fulfild of pitee,   650
That from his yën ran the water doun.
' Now hastily do fecche a book,' quod he,
' And if this knyght wol sweren how that she
This womman slow, yet wole we vs auyse
Whom that we wole that shal ben our Iustyse.'   665

A Briton book, writen with Euangyles,
Was fet, and on this book he swor anoon
She gilty was, and in the mene whyles
A hand him smot vpon the nekke-boon,
That doun he fel atones as a stoon,   670
And both his yën braste out of his face
In sight of euery body in that place.

A voys was herd in general audience,
And seyde, ' thou hast disclaundered giltelees
The doughter of holy chirche in hey presence ;   675
Thus hastou doon, and yet holde I my pees.' ?
Of this meruaille agast was al the prees ;
As mased folk they stoden euerichone,
For drede of wreche, saue Custance allone.

Gret was the drede and eek the repentance   680
Of hem that hadden wrong suspeccioun
Vpon this sely innocent Custance ;
And, for this miracle, in conclusioun,
And by Custances mediacioun,
The king, and many another in that place,   685
Conuerted was, thanked be cristes grace !

This false knyght was slayn for his vntrewthe
By Iugement of Alla hastily;
And yet Custance hadde of his dethe gret rewthe.
And after this Iesus, of his mercy,   690
Made Alla wedden ful solempnely
This holy mayden, that is so bright and sheene,
And thus hath Crist ymaad Custance a queene.

But who was woful, if I shal nat lye,
Of this wedding but Donegild, and na mo,   695
The kinges moder, ful of tirannye?
Hir thoughte hir cursed herte brast atwo;
She wolde nought hir sone had do so;
Hir thoughte a despit, that he sholde take
So strange a creature vn-to his make.   700

Me list nat of the chaf nor [1] of the stree
Maken so long a tale, as of the corn.
What sholde I tellen of the roialtee
At mariage [2], or which cours goth biforn,
Who bloweth in a [3] trompe or in an horn?   705
The fruyt of euery tale is for to seye;
They ete, and drinke, and daunce, and singe, and pleye.

.   .   .   .

[*King Alla is called away to Scotland, to fight against enemies;
he leaves Constance in the care of his Constable.*]

[1] Cm. nor; E. or; *the rest* ne.
[2] E. Hn. mariages; Hl. (Of) mariage; Ln. þe mariage; *the rest* mariage.
[3] E. the; Hn. Pt. *omit*; *the rest* a.

The tyme is come, a knaue child she ber;
Mauricius at the fontstoon they him calle;
This Constable doth forth come a messager,
And wroot vn-to his king, that cleped was Alle,   725
How that this blisful tyding is bifalle,
And othere tydings speedful for to seye;
He taketh the lettre, and forth he goth his weye.

This messager, to don his auantage,
Vn-to the kinges moder rydeth swythe,   730
And salueth hir ful fayre in his langage,
'Madame,' quod he, 'ye may be glad and blythe,
And thanke [1] god an hundred thousand sythe;
My lady queen hath child, with-outen doute,
To Ioye and blisse of [2] al this regne aboute.   735

Lo, heer the lettres seled of this thing,
That I mot bere with al the haste I may;
If ye wol ought vn-to your sone the king,
I am your seruant, bothe nyght and day.'
Donegild answerde, 'as now at this tym, nay;   740
But heer al nyght I wol thou take thy reste,
Tomorwe wol I sey thee what me leste.'

This messager drank sadly ale and wyn,
And stolen were his lettres priuyly
Out of his box, whyl he sleep as a swyn;   745
And countrefeted was ful subtilly
Another lettre, wrought ful sinfully,
Vn-to the king direct of this matere
Fro his Constable, as ye shul after here.

---

[1] Cp. Hl. thanke; E. Hn. thanketh; Cm. thankede; Pt. Ln. thonketh.
[2] E. Cm. to; *the rest* of.

The lettre spak, ' the queen deliuered was   750
Of so horrible a feendly creature,
That in the castel noon so hardy was
That any whyle dorste ther endure.
The moder was an elf, by auenture
Ycome, by charmes or by sorcerye,   755
And euery wyght[1] hateth hir companye.'

Wo was this king whan he this lettre had seyn,
But to no wyghte he tolde his sorwes sore,   ·
But of his owen honde he wroot agayn,
' Welcome the sonde of crist for euermore   760
To me, that am now lerned in his lore ;
Lord, welcom be thy lust and thy plesaunce,
My lust I putte al in thyn ordinaunce !

Kepeth this child, al be it foul or fayr,
And eek my wyf, vn-to myn hoom-cominge ;   765
Crist, whan him list, may sende me an heyr
More agreable than this to my lykinge.'
This lettre he seleth, priuely wepinge,
Which to the messager was take sone,
And forth he goth ; ther is no more to done.   770

O messager, fulfild of dronkenesse,
Strong is thy breeth, thy lymes faltren ay,
And thou biwreyest alle secrenesse.
Thy mynd is lorn, thou Ianglest as a Iay,
Thy face is turned in a newe array !   775
Ther dronkenesse regneth in any route,
Ther is no conseil hid, with-outen doute.

---

[1] E. Hn. *omit* wyght.

O Donegild, I ne haue noon english digne
Vn-to thy malice and thy tirannye !
And therfor to the fende I thee resigne,   780
Let him endyten of thy traitorye !
Fy, mannish, fy ! o nay, [parfay], I lye,
Fy, *feendly* spirit, for I dar wel telle,
Though thou heer walke, thy spirit is in helle !

This messager comth fro the king agayn,   785
And at the kinges modres court he lyghte,
And she was of this messager ful fayn,
And plesed him in al that euer she myghte.
He drank, and wel his girdel vnderpyghte.
He slepeth, and he snoreth in his gyse   790
Al nyght, vn-til[1] the sonne gan aryse.

Eft were his lettres stolen euerichon
And countrefeted lettres in this wyse ;
' The king comandeth his Constable anon,
Vp peyne of hanging and of[1] hey Iuÿse,   795
That he ne scholde suffren in no wyse
Custance in-with his regne for tabyde
Thre dayes and a quarter of a tyde ;

But in the same ship as he hir fond
Hir and hir yonge son, and al hir gere,   800
He sholde putte, and croude hir fro the lond,
And charge hir that she neuer eft com there.'
O my Custance, wel may thy gost haue fere
And sleping in thy dreem been in penance,
When Donegild caste al this ordinance !   805

---

[1] Hl. vn-to ; *the rest* til ; *but* vn-til (*as in* Tyrwhitt) *seems better.*
[2] Hl. of ; E. Hn. on ; *the rest corrupt.*

This messager on morwe, whan he wook,
Vn-to the castel halt the nexte wey,
And to the Constable he the **lettre** took;
And whan that he this pitous lettre sey,
Ful ofte he **seyde** ' allas !' and 'weylawey!'   810
/ 'Lord crist,' quod he, 'how may this world endure ? `
So ful of sinne is many a creature !

O **myghty god,** if that it **be thy** wille,
Sith thou art ryghtful Iuge, **how** may it be
That thou wolt suffren Innocents to spille,   815
And wikked folk regne in prosperite?
O **good** Custance, allas ! so **wo** is me
That I mot be thy tormentour, or deye
` **On shames**[1] **deeth;** ther **is noon** other **weye !'**

Wepen both yonge and olde in al that place,   820
Whan that the king this cursed lettre sente,
And Custance, with a deedly pale face,
The ferthe day toward hir[2] ship she wente.
But natheles she taketh in good entente
/ **The** wille of Crist, and, kneling on the stronde,`   825
She seyde, ' lord ! ay wel-com be thy sonde !

He that me kepte fro the false blame
Whyl I was on the londe amonges yow,
He can me kepe from harme and **eek** fro shame
In **salte see,** al-though I **se nat** how.   830
As strong as euer he was, he is yet now.
In him triste I, **and** in his moder dere,
That is to me **my seyl and** eek my stere.'

---

[1] *So all but* Ill., *which has* schamful.   [2] E. Ln. the; *the rest* hir.

Hir litel child lay weping in hir arm,
And kneling, pitously to him she seyde,   835
'Pees, litel sone, I wol do thee noon harm.'
With that hir kerchef[1] of[2] hir heed she breyde,
And ouer his litel yën she it leyde ;
And in hir arm she lulleth it ful faste,
And in-to heuen hir yën vp she caste.   840

'Moder,' quod she, 'and mayde bright, Marye,
Soth is that thurgh womannes eggement
Mankynd was lorn and damned ay to dye,
For which thy child was on a croys yrent;
Thy blisful yën seye al his torment;   845
Than is ther no comparisoun bitwene
Thy wo and any wo man may sustene.

Thou sey thy child yslayn bifor thyn yën,
And yet now lyueth my litel[3] child, parfay !
Now, lady bryght, to whom alle woful cryën,   850
Thou glorie of wommanhede, thou fayre may,
Thou hauen of refut, bryghte sterre of day,
Rewe on my child, that of thy gentillesse
Rewest on euery rewful in distresse !

O litel child, allas ! what is thy gilt,   855
That neuer wroughtest sinne as yet, parde,
Why wil thyn harde fader han thee spilt ?
O mercy, dere Constable !' quod she ;
'As lat my litel child dwelle heer with thee ;
And if thou darst not sauen him, for blame,   860
So[4] kis him ones in his fadres name !'

---

[1] Ln. Hl. kerchef; Pt. keerchef; E. Hn. couerchief; Cm. couerchif;
Cp. couerchef.
[2] E. Hn. Cm. ouer (*wrongly*); *the rest* of.
[3] E. Ln. *om.* litel; *the rest have it.*   [4] E. Yet; *the rest* So.

Ther-with she loketh [1] bakward to the londe,
And seyde, 'far-wel, housbond rewthelees !'
And vp she rist, and walketh doun the stronde
Toward the ship; hir folweth al the prees,   865
And euer she preyeth hir child to holde his pees;
And taketh hir leue, and with an holy entente
She blisseth hir; and in-to ship she wente.

Vitailled was the ship, it is no drede,
Habundantly for hir ful longe space,   870
And other necessaries that sholde nede
She hadde ynough, heried be goddes grace !
For wynd and weder almyghty god purchace
And bringe hir hoom ! I can no bettre seye;
But in the see she dryueth forth hir weye.   875

   Explicit secunda pars.   Sequitur pars tercia.

Alla the king comth hoom, sone after this,
Vnto his castel of the which I tolde,
And axeth wher his wyf and his child is.
The Constable gan aboute his herte colde,
And pleynly al the maner he him tolde   880
As ye han herd, I can telle it no bettre,
And sheweth the king his seel and [eek] [2] his lettre,

And seyde, 'lord, as ye comaunded me
Vp peyne of deeth, so haue I doon certeyn.'
This messager tormented was til he   885
Moste biknowe and tellen, plat and pleyn,
Fro nyght to nyght, in what place he had leyn.
And thus, by wit and subtil enqueringe,
Ymagined was by whom this harm gan springe.

---

[1] E. Ln. Hl. looked, loked; *the rest* looketh, loketh.
[2] *The word eek seems wanted; but is not in the MSS.*

The hond was knowe that the lettre wroot,   890
And al the venim of this cursed dede,
But in what wyse certeynly I noot.
Theffect is this, that Alla, out of drede,
His moder slow, that men may pleynly rede,
For that she traytour was to hir ligeaunce.   895
Thus endeth olde Donegild with meschaunce.

The sorwe that this Alla nyght and day
Maketh for his wyf and for his child also,
Ther is no tonge that it telle may.
But now wol I vn-to Custance go,   900
That fleteth in the see, in peyne and wo,
Fyue yeer and more, as lyked cristes sonde,
Er that hir ship approched vn-to [1] londe.

Vnder an hethen Castel, atte laste,
Of which the name in my text nought I fynde,   905
Custance and eek hir child the see vp-caste.
Almighty god, that saueth [2] al mankynde
Haue on Custance and on hir child som mynde,
That fallen is in hethen land eft-sone,
In point to spille, as I shal telle yow sone.   910

Doun from the Castel comth ther many a wyght
To gauren on this ship and on Custance.
But shortly, from the Castel on a nyght
The lordes styward—god yeue him meschaunce !—
A theef, that had reneyed our creaunce,   915
Com in-to [3] ship allone, and seyde he sholde
Hir lemman be, wher-so she wolde or nolde.

---

[1] So Hn. Cp. Pt. Hl.; E. Ln. vn-to the; Cm. to the.
[2] E. saued; the rest saueth.   [3] E. Cm. in-to the; the rest omit the.

[The story relates that, by God's grace, the thief fell
overboard and was drowned.]

. . . .

How may this wayke womman han this strengthe
Hir to defende agayn this renegat?
O Golias, vnmesurable of lengthe,
How myghte Dauid make thee so mat,   935
So yong and of armure so desolat?
How dorste he loke vp-on thy dredful face?
Wel may men seen it nas[1] but goddes grace!

Who yaf Iudith corage or hardinesse
To sleen him, Olofernus[2], in his tente,   940
And to deliueren out of wrecchednesse
The peple of god? I seye for this entente,
That ryght as god spirit of vigour sente
To hem, and saued hem out of meschance,
So sente he myght and vigour to Custance.   945

Forth goth hir ship thurgh-out the narwe mouth
Of Iubaltar and Septe, dryuing alway[3],
Som-tyme West, and som-tym North and South,
And som-tyme Est, ful many a wery day,
Til cristes moder (blessed be she ay!)   950
Hath shapen, thurgh hir endeles goodnesse,
To make an ende of al hir heuinesse.

---

[1] *So* E. Hl.; Ln. is; *the rest* was.
[2] E. Oloferne; Hl. Olefernes; *the rest* Olofernus, Olefernus, *or* Oles-
phernus; *see note.*
[3] E. *has* alway; *the rest* ay. *The latter would be better, but is hardly
admissible on account of its terminating* l. 950.

Now lat vs stinte of Custance but a throwe,   *free*
And speke we of the Romayn Emperour,
That out of Surrye hath by lettres knowe   955
The slaughtre of cristen folk, and dishonour
Don to his daughter by a fals traytour,
I mene the cursed wikked sowdanesse,
That at the feste leet sleen both more and lesse.

For which this emperour hath sent anoon   960
His senatour, with roial ordinance,
And othere lordes, got wot, many oon,
On Surryens to taken hey vengeance.
They brennen, sleen, and bringe hem to meschance
Ful many a day; but shortly, this is thende,   965
Homward to Rome thei shapen hem to wende.

This senatour repaireth with victorie
To Romeward, sayling ful roially,
And mette the ship dryuing, as seith the storie,
In which Custance sit ful pitously.   970
No-thing ne[1] knew he what she was, ne why
She was in swich array; ne she nil seye
Of hir estaat, although[2] she sholde deye.

He bringeth hir to Rome, and to his wyf
He yaf hir, and hir yonge sone also;   975
And with the senatour she ladde her lyf.
Thus can our lady bringen out of wo
Woful Custance, and many another mo.
And longe tyme dwelled she in that place,
In holy werkes euer, as was hir grace.   980

---

[1] E. Cm. *om.* ne ; *the rest have it.*
[2] Hl. although ; Pt. though that ; *the rest* though.

The senatoures wyf hir aunte was,
But for al that she knew hir neuer the more;
I wol no lenger tarien in this cas,
But to king Alla, which I spak of yore,
That for his wyf wepeth[1] and syketh sore,   985
I wol retourne, and lete I wol Custance
Vnder the senatoures gouernance.

King Alla, which that hadde his moder slayn,
Vpon a day fil in swich repentance,
That, if I shortly tellen **shal and** playn,   990
To Rome he comth, **to** receyuen his penance
And putte him in the **popes** ordinance
In hey and low, and **Iesu** Crist bisoughte
Foryeue his wikked werkes that he wroughte.

The fame anon through Rome toun[2] **is** born,   995
How Alla king shal come in pilgrimage,
By herbergeours that wenten him biforn;
For which the senatour, **as** was vsage,
Rood him agayn, and many of his linage,
As wel to shewen his hey magnificence   1000
As to don any king a reuerence.

Greet chere doth this noble senatour
To king Alla, and he to him also;
Euerich of hem doth other greet honour;
And so bifel that, in a day or two,   1005
This senatour is to king Alla go
To feste, and shortly, if I shal nat lye,
Custances **sone wente** in his companye.

---

[1] So all **but** E., *which puts* weepeth *after* That.
[2] E. through out the toun; *the rest* through Rome toun.

Som men wolde seyn, at requeste of Custance,
This senatour hath lad this child to feste;   1010
I may nat tellen euery circumstance,
Be as be may, ther was he at the leste.
But soth is this, that, at his modres heste,
Biforn Alla, during the metes space,
The child stood, loking in the kinges face.   1015

This Alla king hath of this child greet wonder,
And to the senatour he seyde anon,
'Whos is that fayre child that stondeth yonder?'
'I noot,' quod he, '[parfay], and by seint John!
A moder he hath, but fader hath he non   1020
That I of wot'—but shortly, in a stounde,
He told Alla how that this child was founde.

.   .   .   .

Now was this child as lyk vn-to Custance   1030
As possible is a creature to be.
This Alla hath the face in remembrance
Of dame Custance, and ther-on mused he
If that the childes moder were aught she
That was his wyf, and priuely he syghte,   1035
And spedde him fro the table that he myghte.

'Parfay,' thoughte he, 'fantome is in my heed!
I oughte deme, of skilful Iugement,
That in the salte see my wyf is deed.'
And afterward he made his argument—   1040
'What wot I, if that Crist haue [1] hider ysent [2]
My wyf by see, as wel as he hir sente
To my contree fro thennes that she wente?'

---

[1] E. haue ; *the rest* hath.   [2] E. ysent; Cm. I-sent; *the rest* sent.

And, after noon, hoom with the senatour
Goth Alla, for to seen this wonder chaunce.   1045
This senatour doth Alla greet honour,
And hastily [1] he sente after Custaunce.
But trusteth wel, hir liste nat to daunce
Whan that **she** wiste wherefor was that sonde.
Vnnethe vp-on hir feet she myghte stonde.   1050

Whan Alla sey his wyf, fayre he hir grette,
And weep, that it was rewthe for to see.
For at the firste look he on hir sette
He knew wel verraily that **it** was she.
And she for sorwe as domb stant as a tre ;   1055
So was hir herte shet in hir distresse
Whan she remembred his vnkyndenesse.

T'wyes she swowned in **his** owen syghte ;
He weep, and him excuseth pitously :—
'Now god,' quod he, 'and alle [2] his halwes bryghte 1060
'Sò wisly **on my** soule as̄ haue mercy,
That **of your** harm as giltelees am I
As **is Maurice** my sone so lyk your face ;
Elles the feend me fecche out of this place ! '

Long was the sobbing and the bitter **peyne**   1065
Er that her woful hertes myghte cesse ;
Greet was the pite for to here hem pleyne
Thurgh whiche pleyntes **gan** her **wo** encresse.
I prey yow al my labour to relesse ;
I may **nat telle** her wo vn-til tomorwe,   1070
I am so **wery for to speke of** sorwe.

---

[1] E. Pt. hastifly ; *the rest* hastily, hastely.
[2] Hl. alle ; *which the rest omit.*

But fynally, when that the soth is wist
That Alla giltelees was of hir wo,
I trowe an hundred tymes been [1] they kist,
And swich a blisse is ther bitwix hem two   1075
That, saue the Ioye that lasteth euermo,
Ther is noon lyk that any creature
Hath seyn or shal, whyl that the world may dure.

Tho preyde she hir housbond mekely,
In relief of hir longe pitous pyne,   1080
That he wold preye hir fader specially
That, of his magestee, he wolde enclyne
To vouche sauf som day with him to dyne;
She preyde him eek, he sholde [2] by no weye
Vn-to hir fader no word of hir seye.   1085

Som men wold seyn, how that the child Maurice
Doth this message vn-to this emperour;
But, as I gesse, Alla was nat so nyce
To him, that was of so souereyn honour
As he that is of cristen folk the flour,   1090
Sente any child, but it is bet to deme
He wente him-self, and so it may wel seme.

This emperour hath graunted gentilly
To come to dyner, as he him bisoughte ;
And wel rede I, he loked bisily   1095
Vp-on this child, and on his daughter thoughte.
Alla goth to his in, and, as him oughte,
Arrayed for this feste in euery wyse
As ferforth as his conning may suffyse.

---

[1] *So in all the seven MSS.*   [2] E. wolde ; *the rest* sholde.

The morwe cam, and Alla gan him dresse, 1100
And eek his wyf, this emperour to mete;
And forth they ryde in Ioye and in gladnesse.
And whan she sey hir fader in the strete,
She lyghte doun, and falleth him to fete.
'Fader,' quod she, 'your yonge child Custance 1105
Is now ful clene out of your remembrance.

I am your doughter Custance¹,' quod she,
'That whylom ye han sent vn-to Surrye.
It am I, fader, that in the salte see
Was put allone and dampned for to dye. 1110
Now, good fader, mercy I yow crye,
Send me namore vn-to noon hethenesse,
But thonketh my lord heer of his kyndenesse.'

Who can the pitous Ioye tellen al
Bitwix hem thre, sin they ben thus ymette? 1115
But of my tale make an ende I shal;
The day goth faste, I wol no lenger lette.
This glade folk to dyner they hem sette;
In Ioye and blisse at mete I lete hem dwelle
A thousand fold wel more than I can telle. 1120

This child Maurice was sithen emperour
Maad by the pope, and lyued cristenly.
To Cristes chirche he dide gret honour;
But I lete al his storie passen by,
Of Custance is my tale specially. 1125
In olde Romayn gestes may men fynde
Maurices lyf; I bere it nought in mynde.

¹ *So in all the MSS.; to be read as* Cústancë *(three syllables). See the note.*

This king Alla, whan he his tyme sey,
With his Custance, his holy wyf so swete,   25
To Engelond ben they come the ryghte wey,   1130
Wher-as they lyue in Ioye and in quiete.
But litel whyl it lasteth, I yow hete,
Ioye of this world, for tyme wol nat abyde ;
Fro day to nyght it changeth as the tyde.

Who lyued euer in swich delyt o day   1135
That him ne moeued other conscience,
Or Ire, or talent, or som kin[1] affray,   *effroi*
Envie, or pryde, or passion, or offence ?
I ne sey but for this ende this sentence,
That litel whyl in Ioye or in plesance   1140
Lasteth the blisse of Alla with Custance.

For deth, that taketh of hey and low his rente,
Whan passed was a yeer, euen as I gesse,
Out of this world this king Alla he hente,
For whom Custance hath ful gret heuynesse.   1145
Now lat vs preyen[2] god his soule blesse !
And dame Custance, fynally to seye,
Towards the toun of Rome goth hir weye.

To Rome is come this holy creature,
And fyndeth ther[3] hir frendes hole and sounde :   1150
Now is she scaped al hir auenture ;
And whan that she hir fader hath yfounde,
Doun on hir kneës falleth she to grounde ;
Weping for tendrenesse in herte blythe,
She herieth god an hundred thousand sythe.   1155

---

[1] E. som kynnes ; Cm. sumkenys ; Hl. som maner ; Hn. Cp. Pt. som kyn ;
Ln. sumkin.
[2] E. praye to ; Hl. pray that ; *the rest* preyen, prayen, preien, *or* preyne.
[3] *Supplied from* Hl.   *The rest omit* ther, *but the omission spoils the line.*

In vertu and in holy almes-dede
They lyuen alle, and neuer a-sonder wende;
Til deth departed hem, this lyf they lede.
And fareth now wel, my tale is at an ende.
Now Iesu Crist, that of his myght may sende   1160
Ioye after wo, gouerne vs in his grace,
And kepe vs alle that ben in this place ! Amen.

Heere endeth the tale of the man of Lawe.

[*Here follows* **The** Shipman's Prologue (*miscalled in most MSS.*
The Squire's Prologue), ll. 1163-1190; *printed in* ' The Prioresses
Tale, &c., **ed. Skeat,** p. 6. *See that volume for an account of the
rest of* Group B.]

GROUP C. THE PARDONER'S TALE.

[Group **C** *begins with* The Phisiciens (*or* Doctor's) Tale,
ll. 1–286. *After which there follows*—]

The wordes of the Hoost to the Phisicien and the Pardoner.

Our hoste gan to swere as he were wood,
'Harrow!' quod he, 'by nayles and by blood,
This was a fals cherl and a fals Iustise !
As shamful deeth as herte may deuyse   290
Come to thise Iuges [1] and her aduocats !
Algate this sely mayde is slayn, allas ! [2]
Allas ! to dere boughte she beautee !
Wherfor I seye al day, as men may see,
That yiftes of fortune or [3] of nature   295
Been cause of deeth to [4] many a creature.
Hir beautee was hir deeth, I dar wel sayn ;
Allas ! so pitously as she was slayn ! [5]
Of bothe yiftes that I speke of now
Men han ful ofte more harm [6] than prow.   300

---

[1] E. false Iuges; *but no other MS. inserts* false.
[2] *Lines* 291, 292, *stand thus in* E. Hn. Cm. Pt.; *but* Cp. *has*—So falle
vpon his body and his bones The deuyl I bekenne him al at ones; *so also*
Ln. Hl.
[3] E. Hn. and; *the rest* or.
[4] *So* E. Hn.; *the rest* of.
[5] *So* Cp. Ln. Hl. ; E. Hn. Cm. Pt. *omit ll.* 297, 298.
[6] E. Hn. for harm; *the rest omit* for.   Hl. *omits ll.* 299, 300.

But trewely, myn owen mayster dere,
This is a pitous tale for to here.
But natheles, passe ouer, is[1] no fors ;
I prey to god, so saue thy gentil cors,

. . . . 305

Thyn Ypocras, and eek thy Galianes,
And euery boist ful of thy letuarie ;
God blesse hem, and our lady seinte Marie !
So mot I theen, thou art a propre man,
And lyk a prelat, by seint Ronyan ! 310
Seyde I nat wel? I can nat speke in terme ;
But wel I wot, thou dost my herte to erme,
That I almost haue caught a cardiacle.
By corpus bones! byt I haue triacle,
Or elles a draught of moyste and corny ale, 315
Or but I here anon a mery tale,
Myn herte is lost for pitee of this mayde.
Thou bel amy, thou pardoner,' he seyde,
'Tel vs som mirthe or Iapes ryght anon.'
'It shall be doon,' quod he, ' by seint Ronyon ! 320
But first,' quod he, 'heer at this ale-stake
I wol both drinke, and eten of a cake.'
But[2] ryght anon thise gentils gonne to crye,
'Nay! lat him telle vs of no ribaudye[3] ;
Tel vs som moral thing, that we may lere 325
Som wit, and thanne wol we gladly here.'
'I graunte, ywis,' quod he, ' but I mot thinke[4]
Vp-on som honest thing, whyl that I drinke.

---

[1] Hl. this is ; *the rest omit* this.
[2] E. Hn. And ; *the rest* But.
[3] E. Hn. Cp. Hl. ribaudye ; Ln. rebaudie ; Cm. rebaudrye ; Pt. rybaudrye.
[4] *For ll.* 326, 327, Hl. *has*—Gladly, quod he, and sayde as ye schal heere.
But in the cuppe wil I me bethinke.

Heere folweth the Prologe of the Pardoners Tale.

Radix malorum est Cupiditas : Ad Thimotheum, sexto.   VI 10.

Lordings,' quod he, ' in chirches whan I preche,
I peyne me to han an hauteyn speche,   330
And ringe it out as round as goth a belle,
For I can al by rote that I telle.
My theme is alwey oon, and euer was—
" *Radix malorum est Cupiditas.*"

First I pronounce whennes that I come,
And than my bulles shewe I, alle and somme.   335
Our lige lordes seel on my patente
That shewe I first, my body to warente,
That no man be so bold, ne preest ne clerk,
Me to destourbe of Cristes holy werk ;   340
And after that than telle I forth my tales,
Bulles of popes and of cardinales,
Of patriarkes, and bishoppes I shewe ;
And in Latyn I speke a wordes fewe,
To saffron with my predicacioun,   345
And for to stire men[1] to deuocioun.
Than shewe I forth my longe cristal stones,
Ycrammed ful of cloutes and of bones ;
Reliks been they, as wenen they echoon.
Than haue I[2] in latoun a shoulder-boon   350
Which that was of an holy Iewes shepe
' Good men,' seye I,[3] ' tak of my wordes kepe ;
If that this boon be wasshe in any welle,
If cow, or calf, or sheep, or oxe swelle
That any worm hath ete, or worm ystonge,   355
Tak water of that welle, and wash his tonge,

---

[1] E. Hn. Hl. hem ; *the rest* men.   [2] E. omits I *by accident.*
[3] E. Hn. I seye ; *the rest* say I, saie I.

And it is hool anon; and forthermore,
Of pokkes and of scabbe, and euery sore
Shal euery sheep be hool, that of this welle
Drinketh a draughte; tak kepe eek what I telle.　360
If that the good-man, that the bestes oweth,
Wol every wike, er that the cok him croweth,
Fastinge, drinken of this welle a draughte,
As thilke holy Iewe our eldres taughte,
His bestes and his stoor shal multiplye.　365
And, sirs [1], also it heleth Ialousye;
For, though a man be falle in Ialous rage,
Let maken with this water his potage,
And neuer shal he more his wyfe mistriste,
Though he the soth of hir defaute wiste.　370
Al had she taken preestes two or three

　Heer is a miteyn eek, that ye may see.
He that his hond wol putte in this miteyn,
He shal haue multiplying of his greyn,
Whan he hath sowen, be it whete or otes,　375
So that he offre pens, or elles grotes.
　Good [2] men and wommen, o thing warne I yow,
If any wight be in this chirche now,
That hath doon sinné horrible, that he
Dar nat, for shame, of it yshriuen be,　380
Or any woman, be she yong or old,
That hath y-maad hir housbond cokewold,
Swich folk shul haue no power ne no grace
To offren to my reliks in this place.
And who so fyndeth him out of swich blame [3],　385
He [4] wol com vp and offre in [5] goddes name,

[1] E. Hn. sire; *the rest* sires, sirs.　[2] E. Hn. Goode; *the rest* And.
[3] E. fame; *the rest* blame.　[4] Hn. He; *the rest* They.
[5] E. on; Hn. a; *the rest* in.

And I assoille him [1] by the auctoritee
Which that by bulle ygraunted was to me.'
    By this gaude haue I wonne, yeer by yere,
An hundred mark sith I was Pardonere.   390
I stonde lyk a clerk in my pulpet,
And whan the lewed peple is doun yset,
I preche, so as ye haue herd bifore,
And telle an hundred false Iapes more.
Than peyne I me to strecche forth the nekke,   395
And est and west vpon the peple I bekke,
As doth a dowue sitting on a berne.
Myn hondes and my tonge goon so yerne,
That it is Ioye to se my bisynesse.
Of auarice and of swich cursednesse   400
Is al my preching, for to make hem fre
To yeue her pens, and namely vn-to me.
For my entent is nat but for to winne,
And no-thing for correccioun of sinne.
I rekke neuer, whan that [2] they ben beryed,   405
Though that her soules goon a blakeberyed!
For certes, many a predicacioun
Comth ofte tyme of yuel entencioun ;
Som for plesaunce of folk and flaterye,
To been auaunced by ypocrisye,   410
And som for veyne glorie, and som for hate.
For, whan I dar noon other weyes debate,
Than wol I stinge him with my tonge smerte
In preching, so that he shal nat asterte
To been defamed falsly, if that he   415
Hath trespased to my brethren or to me.
For, though I telle nought his propre name,
Men shal wel knowe that it is the same

---

[1] E. Hl. hem; *the rest* him *or* hym.   [2] E. Hl. *omit* that; *the rest have it.*

By signes and by othere circumstances.
Thus quyte I folk that doon vs displesances;   420
Thus spitte I out my venim vnder hewe
Of holynesse, to seme holy and trewe.

    But shortly myn entente I wol deuyse;
I preche of no-thing but for coueityse.
Therfor my theme is yet, and euer was—   425
"*Radix malorum est cupiditas.*"
Thus can I preche agayn that same vice
Which that I vse, and that is auarice.
But, though my-self be gilty in that sinne,
Yet can I maken other folk to twinne   430
From auarice, and sore to repente.
'But that is nat my principal entente.
I preche no-thing but for coueityse;
Of this matere it oughte ynough suffyse.

    Than telle I hem ensamples many oon   435
Of olde stories, longe tyme agoon :
For lewed peple louen tales olde ;
Swich thinges can they wel reporte and holde.
What? trowe ye that, whyles[1] I may preche,
And winne gold and siluer for I teche,   440
That I wol lyue in pouert wilfully?
Nay, nay, I thoughte it neuer trewely !
For I wol preche and begge in sondry londes;
I wol not do no labour with my hondes,
Ne make baskettes, and lyue therby,   445
Because I wol nat beggen ydelly.
I wol noon of the apostles counterfete ;
I wol haue money, wolle, chese, and whete,

---

[1] *So* Hn.; E. Pt. the whiles ; Cm. that whilis that ; Cp. Ln. whiles that ;
Hl. whiles.

Al were it yeuen of the pourest [1] page,   *h. p.*
Or of the pourest widwe in a village,   450
Al sholde hir children sterue for famyne.
Nay! I wol drinke licour of the vyne!
And have a joly wenche in every toun!
But herkneth, lordings, in conclusioun ;
Your lyking is that I shal telle a tale.   455
, Now haue I dronke a draughte of corny ale,
⌊[Parfay], I hope I shal yow telle a thing
That shal, by resoun, been at your lyking.
For, though myself be a ful vicious man,
A moral tale yet I yow telle can,   460
Which I am wont to preche, for to winne.
Now holde your pees, my tale I wol beginne.

Heere bigynneth the Pardoners tale.

    In Flaundres whylom was a companye
Of yonge folk, that haunteden folye,
As ryot, hasard, stewes, and tauernes,   465   *guitar*
Wher as, with harpes, lutes, and giternes,
They daunce and pleye at dees bothe day and nyght,
And ete also and drinken ouer her myght,   *scan*
Thurgh which they doon the deuel sacrifyse
With-in that deueles temple, in cursed wyse,   470
By superfluitee abhominable ;
Her othes been so gret and so dampnable,
That it is grisly for to here hem swere ;
Our blissed lordes body they to-tere ;
Hem thoughte Iewes [2] rente him nought ynough ;   475
And ech of hem at otheres sinne lough.
                            laughede

Hl. prestes.
So Cp. Ln. Hl. ; **E.** Hn. Cm. that Iewes ; Pt. þe Iwes.

female tumblers or dancers

And ryght anon than comen tombesteres
Fetys and smale, and yonge fruytesteres,
Singers with harpes [eek, and] wafereres,
Whiche been the verray deueles officeres   480
To kindle and blowe the fyr of [luxurye],
That is annexed vn-to glotonye;
The holy writ take I to my witnesse,
That luxurie is in wyn and dronkenesse.

          .   .   .   .   .   .

   Herodes (who so wel the stories soughte)[1],   *im. par. sete*
Whan he of wyn was replet at his feste,
Ryght at his owen table he yaf his heste   490 *prin. pai*
To sleen the Baptist Iohn ful giltelees.
   Senek seith eek[2] a good word doutelees;
He seith he can no difference fynde
Bitwix a man that is out of his mynde
And a man which that is dronkelewe,   495 *Seon*
But that woodnesse, yfallen in a shrewe,   *prin. parts.*
Perseuereth lenger than doth dronkenesse.
O glotonye, ful of cursednesse,   *gluttony not*
O cause first of our confusioun,   *than disobede*
O original of our dampnacioun,   *inserted on*
          500
Til Crist had bought vs with his blood agayn!
Lo, how dere, shortly for to sayn,
Abought was thilke cursed vilanye;
Corrupt was al this world for glotonye!
   Adam our fader, and his wyf also,   505
Fro Paradys to labour and to wo
Were driuen for that vice, it is no drede;
For whyl that Adam fasted, as I rede,

---

[1] E. Hn. Cm. Pt. Hl *agree here*; Cp. Ln. *have two additional lines, but
they are probably spurious.*
[2] Cp. Ln. eek; *the rest omit it.*

He was in Paradys; and whan that he
Eet of the fruyt defended on the tree,   510
Anon he was out cast to wo and peyne.
O glotonye, on thee wel oughte vs pleyne!
O, wiste a man how many maladyes
Folwen of excesse and of glotonyes,
He wolde been the more mesurable   515
Of his diete, sittinge at his table.
Allas! the shorte throte, the **tendre** mouth,
Maketh that Est and West, and North and South,
In erthe, in eir, in water men [1] to-swinke
To gete a glotoun deyntee mete and drinke!   520
Of this matere, o Paul, wel canstow trete,
'Mete vn-to wombe, and wombe eek vn-to mete,
Shal god destroyen bothe,' as Paulus seith.
Allas! a foul thing is it, by my feith,
To seye this word, and fouler is the dede,   525
Whan man so drinketh of the whyte and rede,
That of his throte he maketh his pryuee,
Thurgh thilke cursed superfluitee.
    The apostel weping seith ful pitously,
'**Ther** walken many of whiche yow told haue I,   530
I seye it now weping with pitous voys,
That thai [2] been enemys of Cristes croys,
Of whiche the ende is deth, wombe is her god.'

    .   .   .   .

How gret labour and cost is thee to fynde!   537
Thise cokes, how they stampe, and streyne, and grynde,
And turnen substaunce in-to accident,
To fulfille al thy likerous talent!   540

---

[1] E. Hl. man; *the rest* men.
[2] That thai *is* Tyrwhitt's *reading*; Hl. Thay; *but the rest have* Ther,
probably repeated by mistake from l. 530.

Out of the harde bones knokke they
The mary, for they caste nought a-wey
That may go thurgh the golet softe and swote;
Of spicerye, of leef, and bark, and rote
Shal been his sauce ymaked by delyt, 545
To make him yet a newer appetyt.
But certes, he that haunteth swich delices
Is deed, whyl that he lyueth in tho vices.
A [cursed] thing is wyn, and dronkenesse
Is ful of stryuing and of wrecchednesse. 550
O dronke man, disfigured is thy face,
Sour is thy breeth, foul artow to embrace,
And thurgh thy dronke nose semeth the soun
As though thou seydest ay 'Sampsoun, Sampsoun';
And yet, god wot, Sampsoun drank neuer no wyn. 555
Thou fallest, as it were a stiked swyn,
Thy tonge is lost, and al thyn honest cure;
For dronkenesse is verray sepulture
Of mannes wit and his discrecioun.
In whom that drinke hath dominacioun, 560
He can no conseil kepe, it is no drede.
Now kepe yow fro the whyte and fro the rede,
And namely fro the whyte wyn of Lepe,
That is to selle in Fishstrete or in Chepe.
This wyn of Spayne crepeth subtilly 565
In othere wynes, growing faste by,
Of which ther ryseth swich fumositee,
That whan a man hath dronken draughtes thre,
And weneth that he be at hoom in Chepe,
He is in Spayne, ryght at the toune of Lepe, 570
Nat at the Rochel, ne at Burdeux toun;
And thanne wol he seye, 'Sampsoun, Sampsoun.'

[handwritten top margin: t the judgment of any of the afflicted ... we can, a]

But herkneth, lordings[1], o word, I yow preye,
That alle the souereyn actes, dar I seye,
Of victories in the olde testament,   575
Thurgh verray god, that is omnipotent,
Were doon in abstinence and in preyere;
Loketh the Bible, and ther ye may it lere.

Loke, Attila, the grete conquerour,
Deyde in his sleep, with shame and dishonour,   580
Bledinge ay at his nose in dronkenesse;
A capitayn shoulde lyue in sobrenesse.
And ouer al this, auyseth yow ryght wel
What was comaunded vn-to Lamuel—
Nat Samuel, but Lamuel, seye I—   585
Redeth the Bible, and fynde it expresly
Of wyn-yeuing to hem that han Iustise;
Namore of this, for it may wel suffise.

And now that[2] I haue spoke of glotonye,
Now wol I yow defenden hasardrye.   590
Hasard is verray moder of lesinges,
And of deceit, and cursed forsweringes,
Blaspheme[3] of Crist, manslaughtre, and wast also
Of catel and of tyme; and forthermo,
It is repreue and contrarie of honour   595
For to ben holde a commune hasardour.
And euer the heyer he is of estaat,
The more is he holden desolaat.
If that a prince vseth hasardrye,
In alle gouernaunce and policye   600
He is, as by commune opinoun,
Yholde the lasse in reputacioun.

[1] E. lordes; *the rest* lordinges, lordynges, lordyngs.
[2] E. Hl. *om.* that; *the rest have it.*
[3] E. Blasphemyng; *the rest* Blaspheme.

Stilbon, that was a wys embassadour,
Was sent to Corinthe, in ful greet honour,
Fro Lacidomie, to make her alliaunce.   605
And whan he cam, him happede, par chaunce,
That alle the grettest, that were of that lond,
Pléyinge átte hásard hé hem foñd.
For which, as sone as it myghte be,
He stal him hoom agayn to his contree,   610
And seyde, 'ther wol I nat lese my name ;
Ne I[1] wol nat take on me so great defame,
Yow for to allye vn-to none hasardours.
Sendeth som[2] othere wyse embassadours ;
For, by my trouthe, me were leuer dye,   615
Than I yow sholde to hasardours allye.
For ye that been so glorious in honours
Shul nat allyen yow with hasardours
As by my wil, ne as by my tretee.'
This wyse philosophre thus seyde he.   620
    Loke eek that to[3] the king Demetrius
The king of Parthes, as the book seith vs,
Sente him a paire of dees of gold in scorn,
For he hadde vsed hasard ther-biforn ;
For which he heeld his glorie or his renoun   625
At no value or reputacioun.
Lordes may fynden other maner pley
Honeste ynough to dryue the day awey.
    Now wol I speke of othes false and grete
A word or two, as olde bokes trete.   630
Gret swering is a thing abhominable,
And fals swering is yet[4] more repreuable.

---

[1] Hn. Ny; Cm. Nay (*both put for* Ne I) *which shews the scansion.*
[2] Tyrwhitt *inserts* som ; *it is not in our MSS.*
[3] Hn. Cm. Cp. Pt. to; *which* E. Ln. Hl. *omit.*
[4] Cp. Ln. Hl. *om.* yet.

The heye god forbad swering at al,
Witnesse on Mathew; but in special
Of swering seith the holy Ieremye,   635
'Thou shalt seye sooth thyn othes, and nat lye,
And swere in dome, and eek in ryghtwisnesse;'
But ydel swering is a cursednesse.
Bihold and se, that in the firste table
Of heye goddes hestes honurable,   640
How that the seconde heste of him is this—
'Tak nat my name in ydel or amis.'
Lo, rather he forbedeth swich swering
Than homicyde or many a[1] cursed thing;
I sey that, as by ordre, thus it stondeth;   645
This knowen, that his hestes vnderstondeth,
How that the second heste of god is that.
And forther ouer, I wol thee telle al plat,
That vengeance shal nat parten from his hous,
That of his othes is to outrageous.   650
'By goddes precious herte, and by his nayles,
And by the blode of Crist, that it is in Hayles,
Seuen is my chaunce, and thyn is cink and treye;
By goddes armes, if thou falsly pleye,
This dagger shal thurgh-out thyn herte go'—   655
This fruyt cometh of the bicched[2] bones two,
Forswering, ire, falsnesse, homicyde.
Now, for the loue of Crist that for vs dyde,
Leueth[3] your othes, bothe grete and smale;
But, sirs, now wol I telle forth my tale.   660
    Thise ryotoures three, of whiche I telle,
Longe erst er pryme rong of any belle,

---

[1] Hn. Cm. Hl. many a; E. any; Cp. Pt. Ln. eny other.
[2] *So* E. Cp.; Hl. bicchid; Ln. becched; Hn. Cm. bicche; Pt. thilk.
[3] E. Hn. Lete; *the rest* Leueth.

Were set hem in a tauerne for [1] to drinke;
And as they satte, they herde a belle clinke
Biforn a cors, was caried to his graue;   665
That oon of hem gan callen to his knaue,
'Go bet,' quod he, 'and axe redily,
What cors is this that passeth heer forby;
And look that thou reporte his name wel.'
    'Sir,' quod this boy, 'it nedeth neueradel.   670
It was me told er ye cam heer two houres;
He was, parde, an old felawe of youres;
And sodeynly he was yslayn to-nyght,
For-dronke, as he sat on his bench vpryght;
Ther cam a priuee theef, men clepeth deeth,   675
That in this contree al the peple sleeth,
And with his spere he smoot his herte atwo,
And wente his wey with-outen wordes mo.
He hath a thousand slayn this pestilence:
And, maister, er ye come in his presence,   680
Me thinketh that it were necessarie
For to be war of swich an aduersarie:
Beth redy for to mete him euermore.
Thus taughte me my dame, I sey namore.'
    'By seinte Marie,' seyde this tauerner,   685
'The child seith sooth, for he hath slayn this yeer,
Henne ouer a myle, with-in a greet village,
Both man and wŏmman, child and hyne, and page.
I trowe his habitacioun be there;
To been auysed greet wisdom it were,   690
Er that he dide a man a dishonour.'
'Ye, goddes armes,' quod this ryotour,

[1] Cp. Pt. Hl. for; *which the rest omit.*

E 2

'Is it swich peril with him for to mete?
I shal him seke by weye and eek by strete,
I make auow to goddes digne bones!   695
Herkneth, felawes, we thre been al ones;
Lat ech of vs holde vp his hond til other,
And ech of vs bicomen otheres brother,
And we wol sleen this false traytour deeth;
He shal be slayn, which that so many sleeth,   700
By goddes dignitee, er it be nyght.'
    Togidres han thise thre her trouthes plyght,
To lyue and dyen ech of hem for other,
As though he were his owen yboren [1] brother.
And vp they sterte al [2] dronken, in this rage,   705
And forth they goon towardes that village,
Of which the tauerner had spoke biforn,
And many a grisly ooth than han they sworn,
And Cristes blessed body they to-rente—
'Deeth shal be deed, if that they may him hente.'   710
    Whan they han goon nat fully half a myle,
Ryght as they wolde han troden ouer a style,
An old man and a poure with hem mette.
This olde man ful mekely hem grette,
And seyde thus, 'now, lordes, god yow see!'   715
    The proudest of thise ryotoures three
Answerde agayn, 'what? carl, with sory grace!
Why artow al forwrapped saue thy face?
Why lyuestow so longe in so greet age?'
    This olde man gan loke in his visage,   720
And seyde thus, 'for I ne can nat fynde
A man, though that I walked in-to Ynde,
Neither in citee nor in no village,

[1] E. yborn; Hn. ybore; Cm. bore; Pt. born; Cp. Ln. Hl. sworne.
[2] Hn. Cp. Ln. Hl. al; E. Cm. Pt. and.

That wolde chaunge his youthe for myn age;
And therfore mot I han myn age stille,   725
As longe time as it is goddes wille.

   Ne deeth, allas! ne wol nat han my lyf;
Thus walke I, lyk a restelees caityf,
And on the ground, which is my mōdres gate,
I knokke with my staf, bothe erly and late,   730
And seye, "leue moder, leet me in!
Lo, how I vanish, flesh, and blood, and skin!
Allas! whan shul my bones been at reste?
Mōder, with yow wolde I chaungen my cheste,
That in my chambre longe tyme hath be,   735
Ye! for an heyre clowt to wrappe me!"
But yet to me she wol nat do that grace,
For which ful pale and welked is my face.

   But, sirs, to yow it is no curteisye
To speken to an old man vilanye,   740
But he trespasse in wōrd, or elles in dede.
In holy writ ye may your-self wel rede,
"Agayns an old man, hoor vpon his heed,
Ye sholde aryse," wherfor I yeue yow reed,
Ne doth vn·to an old man noon harm now,   745
No more than [1] ye wolde men dide to yow
In age, if that ye so longe abyde;
And god be with yow, wher ye go or ryde.
I mot go thider as I haue to go.'
'Nay, olde cherl, by god, thou shalt nat so,'   750
Seyde this other hasardour anon,
'Thou partest nat so lyghtly, by seint Iohn!
Thou spak ryght now of thilke traitour deeth,
That in this contree alle our frendes sleeth.

---

[1] E. Hn. than that; *the rest omit* that.

truly as

Haue heer my trouthe, as thou art his aspye,　　755
Tel wher he is, or thou shalt it abye,
By god, and by the holy sacrament!
For soothly thou art oon of his assent,　　*conspire*
To sleen vs yonge folk, thou false theef!'
'Now, sirs,' quod he, 'if that yow[1] be so leef　　760
To fynde deeth, turne vp this croked wey,
For in that groue I lafte him, by my fey,
Vnder a tree, and ther he wol abyde;
Nat for your bost he wol him no-thing hyde.
Se ye that ook? ryght ther ye shul him fynde.　　765
God saue yow, that boughte agayn mankynde,
And yow amende!'—thus seyde this olde man.
And euerich of thise ryotoures ran,
Til he cam to that tree, and ther they founde
Of florins fyne of golde ycoyned rounde　　770
Wel ny an eighte busshels, as hem thoughte.
No lenger thanne after deeth they soughte,
But ech of hem so glad was of that syghte,
For that the florins been so fayre and bryghte,
That doun they sette hem by this precious hord.　　775
The worste of hem he spak the firste word.
　　'Brethren,' quod he, 'tak kepe what I seye;
My wit is greet, though that I bourde and pleye.
This tresor hath fortune vn-to vs yeuen,
In mirthe and Iolitee our lyf to lyuen,　　780
And lyghtly as it comth, so wol we spende.
Ey! goddes precious dignitee! who wende
To-day, that we sholde han so fayr a grace?
But myght this gold be caried fro this place
Hoom to myn hous, or elles vn-to youres—　　785

---

[1] E. Cm. ye; Hn. Hl. yow; Cp. Pt. Ln. to you.

For wel ye wot that al this gold is oures—
Than were we in hey felicitee.
But trewely, by daye it may nat be;
Men wolde seyn that we were theues stronge,
And for our owen tresor doon vs honge.   790
This tresor moste ycaried be by nyghte
As wysly and as slyly as it myghte.
Wherfore I rede that cut among vs alle
Be drawe, and lat se wher the cut wol falle;
And he that hath the cut with herte blythe   •   795
Shal renne to the[1] toune, and that ful swythe,
And bringe vs breed and wyn ful priuely.
And two of vs shul kepen subtilly
This tresor wel; and, if he wol nat tarie,
Whan it is nyght, we wol this tresor carie   800
By oon assent, wher as vs thinketh best.'
That oon of hem the cut broughte in his fest,
And bad him drawe, and loke wher it wolde[2] falle;
And it fil on the youngest of hem alle;
And forth toward the toun he wente anon.   805
And al so sone as that he was gon,
That oon of hem[3] spak thus vn-to that other,
'Thou knowest wel thou art my sworen[4] brother,
Thy profit wol I telle thee anon.
Thou wost wel that our felawe is agon;   810
And heer is gold, and that ful greet plentee,
That shal departed been among vs thre.
But natheles, if I can shape it so
That it departed were among vs two,

---

[1] Hl. Ln. the; *which the rest omit.*
[2] E. Hn. Cp. wol; Hl. wil; Cm. Pt. Ln. wolde.
[3] E. *omits* of hem ; *the rest have it.*
[4] *This seems best;* E. Hn. Pt. sworn ; Cm. swore ; Cp. Ln. Hl. sworne.

Hadde I nat doun a frendes tŏrn to thee?'   815
   That other answerde, 'I not how that may be;
He wot how that the gold is with vs tweye,
What shal we doon, what shal we to him seye?'

: *rede*

   'Shal it be cŏnseil?' seyde the firste shrewe,
'And I shal tellen thee [1], in [2] wōrdes fewe,   820
What we shal doon, and bringe it wel aboute.'   J *she*
   'I graunte,' quod that other, 'out of doute,
That, by my trouthe, I shal thee nat biwreye.'
   'Now,' quod the firste, 'thou wost wel we be tweye,
And two of vs shul strenger be than oon.   825
Lok whan that he is set, and ryght [3] anoon
Arys, as though thou woldest with him pleye;
And I shal ryue him thurgh the sydes tweye
Whyl that thou strŏgelest with him as in game,
And with thy dagger lok thou do the same;   830
And than shal al this gold departed be,
My dere frend, bitwixen me and thee;
Than may we bothe our lustes al fulfille,
And pleye at dees ryght at our owen wille.'
And thus acorded been thise shrewes tweye   835
To sleen the thridde, as ye han herd me seye.

   This yŏngest, which that wente vn-to the toun,
Ful ofte in herte he rolleth vp and doun
The beautee of thise florins newe and bryghte.
'O lord!' quod he, 'if so were that I myghte   840
Haue al this tresor to my self allone,
Ther is no man that lyueth vnder the trone
Of god, that sholde lyue so mery as I!'
And atte laste the feend, our enemy,

[1] Hl. the; *which the rest omit.*
[2] E. Hn. Cm. in a; *the rest omit* a.
[3] E. Hn. Cm. that right; Hl. and þat; Cp. and thanne; Pt. Ln. and
that. *I take* and *from* Cp. Pt. Ln., *and* ryght *from* E. Hn. Cm.

Putte in his thought that he shold poyson beye,   845
With which he myghte sleen his felawes tweye;
For why the feend fond him in swich lyuinge,
That he had leuehim [1] to sorwe bringe,
For this was outrely his ful entente
To sleen hem bothe, and neuer to repente.   850
And forth he goth, no lenger wolde he tarie,
Into the toun, vn-to a pothecarie,
And preyede him that he him wolde selle
Som poyson, that he myghte his rattes quelle;
And eek ther was a polcat in his hawe,   855
That, as he seyde, his capouns hadde yslawe,
And fayn he wolde wreke him, if he myghte,
On vermin, that destroyede him by nyghte.
   The pothecarie answerde, 'and thou shalt haue
A thing that, al so god my soule saue,   860
In al this world ther nis [2] no creature,
That ete or dronke hath of this confiture
Nought but the mountance of a corn of whete,
That he ne shal his lyf anon forlete;
Ye, sterue he shal, and that in lasse whyle   865
Than thou wolt gon a paas nat but a myle;
This poyson is so strong and violent.'
   This cursed man hath in his hond yhent
This poyson in a box, and sith he ran
In-to the nexte strete, vn-to a man,   870
And borwed of [3] him large botels thre;
And in the two his poyson poured he;
The thridde he kepte clene for his [4] drinke.
For al the nyght he shoop him for to swinke

[1] E. Cm. hem; *the rest* hym *or* him.
[2] E. Hn. Cm. is; *the rest* nys *or* nis.   [3] Tyr. of; *which the MSS. omit.*
[4] E. his owene; *but the rest omit* owene.

In caryinge of the gold **out of** that place. 875
And whan this ryotour, with sory grace,(¹)
Had filled with wyn his grete botels thre,
To his felawes agayn repaireth he.
What nedeth it to sermone of it more?
For ryght as ¹ they had cast his deeth bifore, 880
Right so they han him slayn, and that anon.
And whan **that** this was doon, thus spak that oon,
'Now lat vs sitte and drinke, and make vs merie,
And afterward we wol his body berie.'
And with that word it happede him, par cas, 885
To take the botel ther the poyson was,
And drank, and yaf his felawe drinke also,
For which anon they storuen bothe two.
But, certes, I suppose that Auicen
Wroot neuer in no canon, ne in no fen, 890
Mo wonder signes ² of empoisoning
Than hadde thise wrecches two, er her ending.
Thus ended been thise homicydes two,
And eek the false empoysoner also.

O cursed sinne, ful of³ cursednesse! 895
O traytours homicyde, o wikkednesse!
O glotonye, luxúrie, and hasardrye!
Thou blasphemour of Crist with vilanye
And othes grete, of vsage and of pryde!
Allas! mankynde, how may it **bityde,** 900
That to thy creatour which **that thee** wroughte,
And with his precious herte-blood thee boughte,
Thou **art so fals** and so vnkynde, allas!
Now, good men, god foryeue yow your trespas,

¹ E. so as; *the rest omit* so.
² E. Hn. Cm. signes; Cp. Ln. Hl. sorwes; Pt. sorowes.
³ E. Hn. Cm. of alle; Cp. Ln. Hl. ful of; Pt. full of al.

And ware yow fro the sinne of auarice.   905
Myn holy pardoun may yow alle warice,
So that ye offre nobles or sterlinges,
Or elles siluer broches, spones, ringes.
Boweth your heed vnder this holy bulle!
Cometh[1] vp, ye wyues, offreth of your wolle!   910
Your name[2] I entre heer in my rolle anon;
In-to the blisse of heuen shul ye gon;
I yow assoile, by myn hey power,
Yow that wol offre, as clene and eek as cleer
As ye were born, and, lo, sirs, thus I preche.   915
And Iesu Crist, that is our soules leche,
So graunte yow his pardon to receyue;
For that is best; I wol yow nat deceyue.

  But sirs, o word forgat I in my tale,
I haue reliks and pardon in my male,   920
As fayre as any man in Engelond,
Whiche were me yeuen by the popes hond.
If any of yow wol, of deuocioun,
Offren, and han myn absolucioun,
Cometh[3] forth anon, and kneleth heer adoun,   925
And mekely receyueth my pardoun:
Or elles, taketh pardon as ye wende,
Al newe and fresh, at euery myles ende,
So that ye offren alwey newe and newe
Nobles and[4] pens, which that be gode and trewe.   930
It is an honour to euerich that is heer,
That ye mowe haue a suffisant pardoneer
Tassoille yow, in contree as ye ryde,
For auentures which that may bityde.

[1] E. Com; *the rest* Cometh, Comyth.
[2] E. Hl. names; *the rest* name.
[3] E. Hn. Com; *the rest* Cometh, Comyth.
[4] E. Hn. or; *the rest* and.

Perauenture ther may fallen oon or two   935
Doun of his hors, and breke his nekke atwo.
Lok which a seurtee is it to yow alle
That I am in your felawship yfalle,
That may assoille yow, both more and lasse,
Whan that the soule shal fro the body passe.   940
I rede that our host heer shal biginne,
For he is most envoluped in sinne.
Com forth, sir host, and offre first anon,
And thou shalt kisse the¹ reliks euerychon,
Ye, for a grote! vnbokel anon thy purs.'   945
      'Nay, nay,' quod he, 'than haue I Cristes curs!
Lat be,' quod he, 'it shal nat be, so theech!²
Thou woldest make me kisse thyn olde breech,
And swere it were a relik of a seint!'

        .   .   .   .

      This pardoner answerde nat a word;   956
So wroth he was, no word ne wolde he seye.
      'Now,' quod our host, 'I wol no lenger pleye
With thee, ne with noon other angry man.'
But ryght anon the worthy knyght bigan,   960
Whan that he sey that al the peple lough,
'Namore of this, for it is ryght ynough;
Sir pardoner, be glad and mery of chere;
And ye, sir host, that ben to me so dere,
I prey yow that ye kisse the pardoner.   965
And pardoner, I prey thee, draw thee neer,
And, as we diden, lat vs laughe and pleye.'
Anon they kiste, and riden forth her weye.

Heere is ended the Pardoners tale.

¹ E. my; Cm. myne; *the rest* the.   ² *So all but* Hn.; Hn. thee ich.

GROUP G. THE SECOND NUN'S TALE.

The **prologe** of the Seconde Nonnes tale.

THE ministre and the norice vn-to vices,
    Which that men clepe in English ydelnesse,
That porter of the gate is of delices,
To eschúe, and bý hir cóntrarie) hir opprésse,   *offrin*
That is to seyn, by leueful bisinesse,   5 *law*
Wel oughten we to doon al our entente,
Lest that the feend thurgh ydelnesse vs hente[1].

For he, that with his thousand cordes slye
Continuelly vs waiteth to biclappe,   *watel*
Whan he may man in ydelnesse espye,   10
He can so lyghtly cacche him in his trappe,
Til that a man be hent ryght by the lappe,
He nis nat war the feend hath him in honde ;   *is attending* [1]
Wel oughte vs werche, and ydelnes withstonde.

And though men dradden neuer for to dye,   15
Yet seen men wel by resoun doutelees,
That ydelnesse is roten [2] slogardye,
Of which ther neuer comth no good encrees[3] ;
And seen, that slouthe hir [4] holdeth in a lees
Only to slepe, and for to ete and drinke,   20
And to deuouren al that othere swinke.   *get by toil*

---

[1] Hn. Cm. Cp. Hl. hente ; E. shente, Pt. shent. Ln. schent, *wrongly.*
[2] *So* E. Hn. Pt. Ln. ; Cm. rote ; Cp. hoten ; Hl. *also has* roten.
[3] E. Hn. no good nencrees ; Cp. Pt. Ln. noon encrese ; Hl. good encres ;
Cm. encrees.
[4] Cm. hire ; Pt. hure ; Hn. Cp. Ln. hir ; Hl. her.

And for to putte vs fro swich ydelnesse,
That cause is of so greet confusioun,
I haue heer doon my feithful bisinesse,
After the legende, in translacioun   25
Right of thy glorious lyf and passioun,
Thou with thy gerland wrought of [1] rose and lilie;
Thee mene I, mayde and martir seynt [2] Cecilie!

Inuocacio ad Mariam.

And thou that flour of virgines art alle,
    Of whom that Bernard list so wel to wryte,   30
To thee at my biginning first I calle;
Thou comfort of vs wrecches, do me endyte [3]
Thy maydens deeth, that wan thurgh hir meryte
The eternal lyf, and of the feend victorie,
As man may after reden in hir storie.   35

Thou mayde and moder, doughter of thy sone,
Thou welle of mercy, sinful soules cure,
In whom that god, for bountee, chees to wone,
Thou humble, and hey ouer euery creature,
Thou nobledest so ferforth our nature,   40
That no desdeyn the maker hadde of kynde,
His sone in blode and flesshe to clothe and wynde.

Withinne the cloistre blisful of thy sydes
Took mannes shap the eternal loue and pees,
That of the tryne compas lord and gyde is,   45
Whom erthe and see and heuen, out of relees,
Ay herien; and thou, virgin wemmeless,

---

[1] Hn. Cp. Pt. of; E. Cm. Ln. Hl. with.
[2] Cp. Hn. Cm. Pt. Ln. martir seint; Hl. martir; E. mooder.
[3] Hn. mendite (*shewing the scansion*).

Bar of thy body, and dweltest mayden pure,
The creatour of euery creature.

Assembled is in thee magnificence   50
With mercy, goodnesse, and with swich pitee
That thou, that art the sonne of excellence,
Nat only helpest hem that prayen thee,
But ofte tyme, of thy benignitee,
Ful frely, er that men thyn help biseche,   55
Thou goost biforn, and art her lyues leche.

Now help, thou meke and blisful fayre mayde,
Me, flemed wrecche, in this desert of galle;
Think on the womman Cananee, that sayde
That whelpes eten somme of the crommes alle   60
That from her lordes table been yfalle;
And though that I, vnworthy sone of Eue,
Be sinful, yet accepte my bileue.

And, for that feith is deed with-outen werkes,
So for to worchen yif me wit and space,   65
That I be quit fro thennes that most derk is!
O thou, that art so fayr and ful of grace,
Be myn aduocat in that heye place
Ther as withouten ende is songe 'Osanne,'
Thou Cristes moder, doughter dere of Anne!   70

And of thy lyght my soule in prison lyghte,
That troubled is by the contagioun
Of my body, and also by the wyghte
Of erthly lust and fals affeccioun;
O hauen of refut, o saluacioun   75
Of hem that been in sorwe and in distresse,
Now help, for to my werk I wol me dresse.

Yet preye I yow that reden that I wryte,
Foryeue me, that I do no diligence`
This ilke storie subtilly to endyte[1] ;   80
For both haue I the wordes and sentence
Of him [2] that at the seintes reuerence
The storie wroot, and folwe [3] hir legende,
And prey [4] yow, that ye wol my werk amende.

[THE PROEM.]

Interpretacio nominis Cecilie, quam ponit frater Iacobus
Ianuensis in legenda.

First wolde I yow[5] the name of seint Cecilie   85
Expoune, as men may in hir storie see,
It is to seye in english 'heuenes lilie,'
For pure chastnesse of virginitee ;
Or, for she whytnesse hadde of honestee,
And grene of conscience, and of good fame   90
The sote savour [6], 'lilie' was hir name.

Or Cecile is to seye 'the wey to blynde,'
For she ensample was by good techinge ;
Or elles Cecile, as I writen fynde,
Is ioyned, by a manere conioyninge   95
Of 'heuene' and 'lia' ; and heer, in figuringe,
The 'heuen' is set for thought of holinesse,
And 'lia' for hir lasting bisinesse.

---

[1] Hn. tendite (*shewing the scansion*).
[2] *So* E. Hn. Cm. Hl. ; *but* Cp. Pt. Ln. hem.
[3] Cm. folwe ; E. Hn. Hl. folwen ; Cp. Pt. Ln. folowen.
[4] E. I pray ; Cp. And pray I ; *the rest* And pray (*or* prei, *or* preye).
[5] E. *omits* yow ; *the rest retain it.*
[6] E. favour ; *the rest* savour ; *see* l. 229.

Cecile may eek be seyd in this manere,
'Wanting of blyndnesse,' for hir grete lyghte   100
Of sapience, and for hir thewes clere ;
Or elles, lo ! this maydens name bryghte
Of 'heuene' and 'leos' comth, for which by ryghte
Men myghte hir wel 'the heuen of peple' calle,
Ensample of gode and wyse werkes alle.   105

For 'leos' 'peple' in english is to seye,
And ryght as men may in the heuene see
The sonne and mone and sterres euery weye,
Ryght so men gostly, in this mayden free,
Seyen of feith the magnanimitee,   110
And eek the cleernesse hool of sapience,
And sondry werkes, bryghte of excellence.

And ryght so as thise philosophres wryte
That heuen is swift and round and eek brenninge,
Ryght so was fayre Cecilie the whyte   115
Ful swift and bisy euer in good werkinge,
And round and hool in good perseueringe,
And brenning euer in charite ful bryghte ;
Now haue I yow declared what she hyghte.

Explicit.

**Here bigynneth the Seconde Nonnes tale, of the lyf
of Seinte Cecile.**

This mayden bryght Cecile, as hir lyf seith,   120
Was comen of Romayns, and of noble kynde,
And from hir cradel vp fostred in the feith

Of Crist, and bar his gospel in hir mynde;
She neuer cessede, as I writen fynde,
Of hir preyere, and god to loue and drede,
Biseking him to kepe hir maydenhede.

And whan this mayden sholde vnto a man
Ywedded be, that was ful yong of age,
Which that ycleped was Valerian,
And day was comen of hir mariage,
She, ful devout and humble in hir corage,
Vnder hir robe of gold, that sat ful fayre,
Had next hir flesshe yclad hir in an heyre.

And whyl the organs [1] maden melodye,
To god alone in herte thus sang she;
'O lord, my soule and eek my body gye
Vnwemmed, lest that I [2] confounded be:'
And, for his loue that deyde vpon a tree,
Euery seconde or [3] thridde day she faste,
Ay biddinge in hir orisons ful faste.

[The tyme is comen, whan she moste] gon
With hir housbonde, as ofte is the manere,
And priuely to him she seyde anon,
'O swete and wel biloued spouse dere,
Ther is a conseil, and ye wolde it here,
Which that ryght fayn I wolde vnto yow seye,
So that ye swere ye shul me [4] nat biwreye.'

Valerian gan faste vnto hir swere,
That for no cas, ne thing that myghte be,
He sholde neuer mo biwreyen here;

[1] Hl. Hn. organs; Ln. orgens; E. Orgues; Cp. Orgles; Pt. Orgels.
[2] E. it; *the rest* I.   [3] E. Hn. and; *the rest* or.
[4] E. me; *the rest* it; **see** *l.* 150.

And thanne at erst to him thus seyde she,
'I haue an angel which that loueth me,
That with greet loue, wher so I wake or slepe,
Is redy ay my body for to kepe.'

.   .   .   .

Valerian, corrected as god wolde,
Answerde agayn, 'if I shal trusten thee,
Lat me that angel se, and him biholde;
And if that it a verray angel be,   165
Than wol I doon as thou hast preyed me;
And if thou loue another man, for sothe
Ryght with this swerd than wol I sle yow bothe.'

Cecile answerde anon ryght in this wyse,
'If that yow list, the angel shul ye see,   170
So that ye trowe in Crist and yow baptyse.
Goth forth to Via Apia,' quod she,
'That fro this toun ne stant but myles three,
And, to the poure folkes that ther dwelle,
Sey hem ryght thus, as that I shal yow telle.   175

Telle hem that I, Cecile, yow to hem sente,
To shewen yow the gode Vrban the olde,
For secre nedes [1] and for good entente.
And whan that ye seint Vrban han biholde,
Telle him the wordes whiche I [2] to yow tolde;   180
And whan that he hath purged yow fro sinne,
Thanne shul ye se that angel, er ye twinne.'

---

[1] E. thynges; *the rest* nedes, nedis, needes.
[2] E. Cp. Ln. Hl. whiche þat I ; *but* Hn. Cm. Pt. *omit* that.

Valerian is to the place ygon,
And ryght as him was taught by his lerninge,
He fond this holy olde Vrban anon   185
Among the seintes buriels lotinge.
And he anon, with-outen taryinge,
Dide his message ; and whan that he it tolde,
Vrban for ioye his hondes gan vp holde.

The teres from his yën leet he falle—   190
'Almyghty lord, o Iesu Crist,' quod he,
'Sower of chast conseil, herde of vs alle,
The fruyt of thilke seed of chastitee
That thou hast sowe in Cecile tak to thee!
Lo, lyk a bisy bee, with-outen gyle,   195
Thee serueth ay thyn owen thral Cecile!

For thilke spouse, that she took but[1] now
Ful lyk a fiers leoun, she sendeth here,
As meke as euer was any lamb, to yow!'
And with that worde, anon ther gan appere   200
An old man, clad in whyte clothes clere,
That hadde a book with lettre of golde in honde,
And gan biforn[2] Valerian to stonde.

Valerian as deed fil doun for drede
Whan he him sey, and he vp hente him tho,   205
And on his book ryght thus he gan to rede—
'Oo Lord, oo feith, oo god with-outen mo,
Oo[3] Cristendom, and fader of alle also,
Abouen alle and[4] ouer al euerywhere '—
Thise wordes al with golde ywriten were.   21c

---

[1] E. Hl. right ; *the rest* but.
[2] E. bifore ; Hl. to-forn ; *the rest* biforn, biforne, beforne.
[3] E. Hn. Cm. O ; Hl. On ; Cp. Pt. Ln. Of.
[4] E. *omits* and ; *the rest have it.*

Whan this was rad, than seyde this olde **man,**
' Leuestow this thing or **no?** sey ye or nay.'
' I leue al this thing,' quod Valerian,
' For sother[1] thing than this, I dar wel say,
Vnder the **heuen** no wyght thinke may.'   215
Tho vanisshed the [2] olde man, he niste where,
And Pope Vrban him cristened ryght there.

Valerian gooth hoom, and fynt Cecilie
With-inne his chambre with an angel stonde ;
This angel hadde of roses and of lilie   220
Corones two, the which he bar in honde ;
And first to Cecile, as I vnderstonde,
He yaf that oon, and after gan he take
That other to Valerian, hir make.

' With body clene and with vnwemmed thought   225
Kepeth ay wel thise corones,' quod he [3];
' Fro Paradys to yow haue I hem brought,
Ne neuer mo ne shal they roten be,
Ne lese her sote sauour, trusteth me ;
Ne neuer wyght shal seen hem with his yĕ,   230
But he be chaast and hate vilanyĕ.

And thou, Valerian, for thou so sone
Assentedest to good conseil also,
Sey what thee list, and thou shalt han thy bone.'
' I haue a brother,' quod Valerian tho,   235
' **That** in this world I loue no man so.
I pray yow that my brother may han grace
To knowe the trouthe, as I do in this place.'

[1] E. oother ; *the rest* sother.
[2] E. Hn. Cm. this ; Pt. that ; Cp. Ln. the ; *see note.*
[3] E. three ; Hl. thre ; *the rest* quod he.

The angel seyde, 'god lyketh thy requeste,
And bothe, with the palm of martirdom,   240
Ye shullen come vnto his blisful feste.'
And with that word Tiburce his brother com.
And whan that he the sauour vndernom
Which that the roses and the lilies caste,
With-inne his herte he gan to wondre faste,   245

And seyde, ' I wondre this tyme of the yeer
Whennes that sote sauour cometh so
Of rose and lilies that I smelle heer.
For though I hadde hem in myn hondes two,
The sauour myghte in me no depper go.   250
The sote [1] smel that in myn herte I fynde
Hath chaunged me al in another kynde.'   *nature*

Valerian seyde, ' two corones han we,
Snow-whyte and rose-reed, that shynen clere,
Whiche that thyn yĕn han no myght to see ;   255
And as thou smellest hem thurgh my preyere,
So shaltow seen hem, leue brother dere,
If it so be thou wolt, withouten slouthe,
Bileue aryght and knowen verray trouthe.'

Tiburce answerde, ' seistow this to me   260
In sothnesse, or in dreem I herkne this ?'
' In dremes,' quod Valerian, ' han we be
Vnto this tyme, brother myn, ywis.
But now at erst in trouthe our dwelling is.'
' How wostow this,' quod Tiburce, 'in what wyse ? 265
Quod Valerian, 'that shal I thee deuyse.

---

[1] *The MSS. have* swete *here; but in* l. 247 *we find only* sote, soote,
swote, suote, *except* swete *in* Pt.; *in* l. 229 *we find* E. soote; Hn. swote;
Cm. sote; Hl. soote; Cp. Pt. Ln. swete.

The angel of god hath me the [1] trouthe ytaught
Which thou shalt seen, if that thou wolt reneye
The ydoles and be clene, and elles naught.'—
And óf the mirácle óf thise corónes tweye   270
Seint Ambrose in his preface list to seye ;
Solempnely this noble doctour dere
Commendeth it [2], and seith in this manere :

The palm of martirdom for to receyue,
Seint Cecilie, fulfild of goddes yifte,   275
The world and eek hir chambre gan she weyue ;
Witnes Tyburces and Valerians [3] shrifte,
To whiche god of his bountee wolde shifte
Corones two of floures wel smellinge,
And made his angel hem the corones bringe :   280

The mayde hath broght thise [4] men to blisse aboue ;
The world hath wist what it is worth, certeyn,
Deuocioun of chastitee to loue.—
Tho shewede him Cecile al [5] open and pleyn
That alle ydoles nis but a thing in veyn ;   285
For they been dombe, and therto they been deue,
And charged him his ydoles for to leue.

'Who so that troweth nat this, a beste he is,'
Quod tho Tiburce, 'if that I shal nat lye.'
And she gan kisse his brest, that herde this,   290
And was ful glad he coude trouthe espye.
'This day I take thee for myn allye,'
Seyde this blisful fayre mayde dere ;
And after that she seyde as ye may here :

---

[1] E. Ln. Hl. *omit* the; *the rest have it.*   [2] E. hym; *the rest* it.
[3] *The MSS. have* Cecilies, *wrongly; see note.*
[4] E. Hn. *omit* thise ; *but the rest retain it, except* Cm., *which has* brought
hem to blysse.   [5] Cp. Pt. Ln. *omit* al; *but the rest retain it.*

'Lo, ryght so as the loue of Crist,' quod she,   295
'Made me thy brotheres wyf, ryght in that wyse
Anon for myn allye heer take I thee,
Sin that thou wolt thyn ydoles despyse.
Go with thy brother now, and thee baptyse,
And make thee clene; so that thou mowe biholde   300
The angels face of which thy brother tolde.'

Tiburce answerde and seyde, ' brother dere,
First tel me whider I ¹ shal, and to what man?'
'To whom?' quod he, ' com forth with ryght good
    chere,
I wol thee lede vnto the pope Vrban.'   305
'Til Vrban? brother myn, Valerian,'
Quod tho Tiburce, ' woltow me thider lede?
Me thinketh that it were a wonder dede.

Ne menestow nat Vrban,' quod he tho,
'That is so ofte dampned to be deed,   310
And woneth in halkes alwey to and fro,
And dar nat ones putte forth his heed?
Men sholde him brennen in a fyr so reed
If he were founde, or that men myghte him spye;
And we also, to bere him companye—   315

And whyl we seken thilke diuinitee
That is yhid in heuene priuely,
Algate ybrend in this world shul we be !'
To whom Cecile answerde boldely,
'Men myghten dreden wel and skilfully   320
This lyf to lese, myn owen dere brother,
If this were lyuinge only and non other.

_____

¹ E. Hn. Cm. that I; *the rest omit* that.

But ther is better lyf in other place,
That neuer shal be lost, ne dred thee nought,
Which goddes sone vs tolde thurgh his grace ;   325
That fadres sone hath alle thinges wrought[1] ;
And al that wrought is with a skilful thought,
The gost, that fro the fader gan procede,
Hath sowled hem, withouten any drede.   *given*

By word and by miracle goddes sone,   330
Whan he was in this world, declared here
That ther was other lyf ther men may wone.'
To whom answerde Tiburce, 'o suster dere,
Ne seydestow ryght now in this manere,
Ther nis but o god, lord in sothfastnesse ;   335
And now of three how maystow bere witnesse ?'

'That shal I telle,' quod she, 'er I go.
Ryght as a man hath sapiences three,   *im*
Memorie, engyn, and intellect also,
So, in o[2] being of diuinitee,   340
Thre persones may ther ryght wel be.'
Tho gan she him ful bisily to preche
Of Cristes come, and of his peynes teche,

And many pointes of his passioun ;
How goddes sone in this world was withholde,   345
To doon mankynde pleyn remissioun,
That was ybounde in sinne and cares colde :
Al this thing she vnto Tiburce tolde.
And after this Tiburce, in good entente,
With Valerian to pope Vrban he wente,   350

---

[1] E. thyng ywroght ; Hn. Cm. thynges wroght.
[2] E. *omits* o ; *the rest have it.*

That thanked god; and with glad herte and lyght
He cristned him, and made him in that place
Parfit in his lerninge, goddes knyght.
And after this Tiburce gat swich grace,
That euery day he sey, in tyme and space,   355
The angel of god; and euery maner bone
That he god axed, it was sped ful sone.

It were ful hard by ordre for to seyn
How many wondres Iesus for hem wroughte;
But atte laste, to tellen short and pleyn,   360
The sergeants of the toun of Rome hem soughte,
And hem biforn Almache the prefect broughte,
Which hem opposed [1], and knew al her entente,
And to the image of Iupiter hem sente,

And seyde, 'who so wol nat sacrifyse,   365
Swap of his heed, this is [2] my sentence here.'
Anon thise martirs that I yow deuyse
Oon Maximus, that was an officere
Of the Prefectes and his corniculere,
Hem hente; and whan he forth the seintes ladde,   370
Him-self he weep, for pitee that he hadde.

Whan Maximus had herd the seintes lore,
He gat him of the tormentoures leue,
And ladde hem to his hous withoute more;
And with her preching, er that it were eue,   375
They gonnen fro the tormentours to reue,
And fro Maxime, and fro his folk echone
The false feith, to trowe in god allone.

---

[1] Hl. apposed; *the rest* opposed.
[2] E. Cm. Hl. *omit* is; *the rest have it.*

Cecilie cam, whan it was woxen nyght,
With prestes that hem cristnede alle yfere,   380
And afterward, whan day was woxen lyght,
Cecile hem seyde with a ful sobre [1] chere,
' Now, Cristes owen knyghtes leue and dere,
Caste alle awey the werkes of derknesse,
And **armeth** yow in armure of bryghtnesse.   385

Ye **han for** sothe ydoon a greet bataille,
Your cours is doon, your feith han ye conserued,
Goth to the corone of lyf that may nat faille ;
The ryghtful Iuge, which that ye han serued,
Shall yeue it yow, as ye han it deserued.'   390
And whan this thing **was seyd** as I deuyse,
Men ladde hem forth to **doon** the sacrifyse.

But whan **they** weren to the place brought,
To tellen shortly the conclusioun,
They nolde encense **ne** sacrifice ryght nought,   395
But on hir knees they **setten** hem adoun
With humble herte and **sad** deuocioun,
And losten bothe, hir hedes in the place.
Hir soules wenten to the king of grace.

This **Maximus,** that sey this thing **bityde,**   400
With pitous teres tolde it anon ryght,
That he her soules sey to heuen glyde
With angels ful of cleerness and **of** lyght,
And with his [2] word conuerted many a wyght ;
For **which** Almachius dide him so to-bete [3]   405
With whippe **of** leed, **til** he his [4] lyf gan lete.

---

[1] E. Hn. Hl. ful stedefast ; **Cm.** ful sobere ; Cp. Pt. Ln. sobre.
[2] E. this ; *the rest* his.
[3] E. Hn. Cm. Hl. so bete ; Cp. Pt. Ln. so to-bete ; *see the note.*
[4] E. **the ;** *the rest* his.

Cecile him took and buryed him **anoon**
By Tiburce and Valerian softely,
Withinne hir burying-place, vnder the stoon.
And after this Almachius hastily   410
Bad his ministres fecchen openly
Cecile, so that she myghte in his presence
Doon sacrifice, and Iupiter encense.

But they, conuerted at hir wyse lore,
Wepten ful sore, and yauen ful credence   415
Vnto hir word, and cryden more and more,
'Crist, goddes sone withouten difference,
Is verray god, this is al[1] our sentence,
That hath so good a seruant him to serue ;
This with o voys we trowen, though we sterue !'   420

Almachius, that **herde of** this doinge,
Bad fecchen Cecile, **that he myghte** hir see,
And alderfirst, lo ! **this** was his axinge,
'What maner womman **artow** ?' tho[2] quod he.
'**I am a** gentil womman born,' quod she.   425
'**I axe thee**,' quod he, 'though it thee greue,
Of thy **religioun and of** thy bileue.' ·

fool   '**Ye** han bigonne your questioun folily,'
Quod she, 'that wolden **two** answeres conclude
In **oo** demande ; ye axed lewedly.'   430
wicked use   Almache answerde vnto that similitude,
rare in E)   'Of whennes comth thyn answering so rude ?'
'Of whennes ?' quod she, whan that she was freyned,
'Of conscience and of good feith vnfeyned.'

---

[1] E. *omits* al; *the rest have it.*
[2] Cp. Pt. **Ln.** tho ; *which the rest omit.*

Almachius seyde, 'ne takestow noon hede   435
Of my power?' and she answerde him this[1]—
'Your myght,' quod she, 'ful litel is to drede;
For euery mortal mannes power nis
But lyk a bladdre, ful of wynd, ywis.
For with a nedles poynt, whan it is blowe,   440
May al the bost of it be leyd ful lowe.'

'Ful wrongfully bigonne thou,' quod he,
'And yet in wrong is thy perseueraunce;
Wostow nat how our myghty princes free
Han thus comanded and maad ordinaunce,   445
That euery cristen wyght shal han penaunce
But if that he his cristendom withseye,
And goon al quit, if he wol it reneye?'

'Your princes erren, as your nobley doth,'
Quod tho Cecile, 'and with a wood sentence   450
Ye make vs gilty, and it[2] is nat soth;
For ye, that knowen wel our innocence,
For as muche as we doon a reuerence
To Crist, and for we bere a cristen name,
Ye putte on vs a cryme, and eek a blame.   455

But we that knowen thilke name so
For vertuous, we may it nat withseye.'
Almache answerde, 'chees oon of thise two,
Do sacrifice, or cristendom reneye,
That thou mow now escapen by that weye.'   460
At which the holy blisful fayre mayde
Gan for to laughe, and to the Iuge seyde,

---

[1] Hn. Hl. this; Cm. Cp. Pt. Ln. thus; E. *omits*.
[2] E. Hn. Cm. *omit* it; *the rest have it*.

'O Iuge, confus in thy nycetee,
Woltow that I reneye innocence,
To make me a wikked wyght?' quod she;   465
of all   'Lo! he dissimuleth here in audience,
He stareth and¹ woodeth in his aduertence!'
To whom Almachius, 'vnsely wrecche,
Ne wostow nat how far my myght may strecche?

Han nought our myghty princes to me yeuen,   470
Ye, bothe power and auctoritee
To maken folk to deyen or to lyuen?
Why spekestow so proudly than to me?'
'I speke nought but stedfastly,' quod she,
'Nat proudly, for I seye², as for my syde,   475
We haten deedly thilke vice of pryde.

And if thou drede nat a soth to here,
Than wol I shewe al openly, by ryght,
That thou hast maad a ful gret lesing here.
Thou seyst, thy princes han thee yeuen myght   480
Bothe for to sleen and for to quike a wyght;
Thou, that ne mayst but only lyf bireue,
Thou hast noon other power ne no leue!

But thou mayst seyn, thy princes han thee maked
Ministre of deth; for if thou speke of mo,   485
Thou lyest, for thy power is ful naked.'
'Do wey thy boldnes,' seyde Almachius tho,
'And sacrifice to our goddes, er thou go;
I recche nat what wrong that thou me profre,   *chan...*
For I can suffre it as a philosophre;   490

¹ E. and he; *the rest omit* he.
² E. speke; *the rest* seye.

But thilke wronges may I nat endure
That thou spekest of our goddes here,' quod he.
Cecile answerde, ' o nyce creature,
Thou seydest no word sin thou spak to me,
That I ne knew therwith thy nycetee ;   495
And that thou were, in euery maner wyse,
A lewed officer and a veyn Iustise.

Ther lakketh no thing to thyn utter yën
That thou nart blynd, for thing that we seen alle
That it is stoon, that men may wel espyen,   500
That ilke stoon a god thou wolt it calle.
I rede thee, lat thyn hand vpon it falle,
And taste it wel, and stoon thou shalt it fynde,
Sin that thou seest nat with thyn yën blynde.

It is a shame that the peple shal   505
So scorne thee, and laughe at thy folye ;
For communly men wot it wel oueral,
That myghty god is in his heuenes hye,
And thise images, wel thou mayst espye,
To thee ne to hem-self [1] mowe nought profyte,   510
For in effect they been nat worth a myte.'

Thise wordes and swiche othere seyde she,
And he weex wroth, and bad men sholde hir lede
Hom til hir hous, ' and in hir hous,' quod he,
' Brenne hir ryght in a bath of flambes rede.'   515
And as he bad, ryght so was doon in dede ;
For in a bath they gonne hir faste shetten,
And nyght and day greet fyr they vnder betten.

---

[1] E. Ln. *insert* ne *before* mowe ; *the rest omit it.*

The longe nyght and eek a day also,
For al the fyr and eek the bathes hete,
She sat al cold, and feelede no wo,
It made hir nat a droppe for to swete.
But in that bath hir lyf she moste lete;
For he, Almachius, with ful[1] wikke entente
To sleen hir in the bath his sonde sente.

Thre strokes in the nekke he smoot hir tho,
The tormentour, but for no maner chaunce
He myghte nought smyte al hir nekke atwo;
And for ther was that tyme an ordinaunce,
That no man sholde doon man[2] swich penaunce
The ferthe strook to smyten, softe or sore,
This tormentour ne dorste do namore.

But half-deed, with hir nekke ycoruen there,
He lefte hir lye, and on his wey is[3] went.
The cristen folk, which that aboute hir were,
With shetes han the blood ful faire yhent.
Thre dayes lyued she in this torment,
And neuer cessed hem the feith to teche;
That she hadde fostred, hem she gan to preche;

And hem she yaf hir moebles and hir thing,
And to the pope Vrban bitook hem tho,
And seyde, ' I axed this at[4] heuene king,
To han respyt thre dayes and namo,
To recomende to yow, er that I go,
Thise soules, lo! and that I myghte do werche
Here of myn hous perpetuelly a cherche.'

---

[1] E. Hn. a ful; Cm. a; *the rest* ful.
[2] E. men; *the rest* man.
[3] Cm. is went; *the rest* he wente (*or* he went) *wrongly; see the note.*
[4] E. at; *the rest* of; *see* G 621.

Seint Vrban, with his deknes, priuely
The[1] body fette, and buried it by nyghte
Among his othere seintes honestly.
Hir hous the chirche of seint Cecilie hyghte ;　　550
Seint Vrban halwed it, as he wel myghte ;
In which, into this day, in noble wyse,
Men doon to Crist and to his seint seruyse.

Heere is ended the Seconde Nonnes tale.

[1] E. This ; *the rest* The.

GROUP G. THE CANON'S YEOMAN'S TALE.

The prologe of the Chanons yemannes tale.

Whan ended was[1] the lyf of seint Cecile,
Er we had riden fully fyue myle, 555
At Boughton vnder Blee vs gan atake
A man, that clothed was in clothes blake,
And vndernethe he wered a surplys[2].
His hakeney, that[3] was al pomely grys,
So swatte, that it wonder was to see ; 560
It semed he[4] had priked myles three.
The hors[5] eek that his yeman rood vpon
So swatte, that vnnethe myghte it gon.
Aboute the peytrel stood the foom ful hye,
He was of fome al flekked as a pye[6]. 565
A male tweyfold on[7] his croper lay,
It semed that he caried lyt array.
Al lyght for somer rood this wörthy man,
And in myn herte wondren[8] I bigan
What that he was, til that I vnderstood 570
How that his cloke was sowed to his hood ;
For which, when I had longe auysed me,
I demede him som chanon for to be.

---

[1] E. toold was al; Cm. told **was**; *the rest* ended was.
[2] *So* E. ; *the rest have* And vnder that he hadde a whit surplis.
[3] E. which þat; *the rest omit* which.
[4] E. as he ; Cm. that he; *the rest* he.   [5] E. hakeney ; *the rest* hors.
[6] E. omits ll. 564, 565; *the rest retain them.*
[7] E. vpon ; *the rest* on.   [8] E. to wondren ; *the rest omit* to.

His hat heng at his bak doun by a laas,
For he had riden more than trot or paas ;   575
He had ay priked lyk as he were wood.
A clote-leef he hadde vnder his hood
For swote, and for to kepe his heed from hete.
But it was ioye for to seen him swete !
His forhed dropped as a stillatorie,   580
Were ful of plantayn and of paritorie.
And whan that he was come, he gan to crye,
'God saue,' quod he, 'this ioly companye !
Faste haue I priked,' quod he, 'for your sake,
By cause that I wolde yow atake,   585
To ryden in this[1] mery companye.'
His yeman eek was ful of curteisye,
And seyde, 'sirs, now in the morwe tyde
Out of your hostelrye I sey you ryde,
And warned heer my lord and my souerayn,   590
Which that[2] to ryden with yow is ful fayn,
For his desport ; he loueth daliaunce.'
    'Frend, for thy warning god yeue thee good[3] chaunce,'
Than seyde our host, 'for certes[4], it wolde seme
Thy lord were wys, and so I may wel deme ;   595
He is ful iocund also, dar I leye.
Can he aught telle a mery tale or tweye,
With which he glade may this companye ?'
    'Who, sir ? my lord ? ye, ye, withouten lye,
He can of murthe, and eek of Iolite   600
Nat but ynongh ; also sir, trusteth me,
And ye him knewe as wel as do I,
Ye wolde wondre how wel and craftily[5]

---

[1] E. som ; *the rest* this.   [2] E. *omits* that.
[3] E. *omits* good.   [4] E. certein ; *the rest* certes.
[5] *So* E. Cm.; *the rest* thriftily.

G 2

He coude werke, and that in sondry wyse.
He hath take on him many a greet empryse,   605
Which were ful hard for any that is here
To bringe aboute, but they of him it lere.
As homly as he rit amonges yow,
If ye him knewe, it wolde be for your prow ;
Ye wolde nat forgon his aqueyntaunce   610
For mochel good, I dar leye in balaunce
Al that I haue in my possessioun.
He is a man of hey discrecioun,
I warne you wel, he is a passing man.'
    'Wel,' quod our host, 'I pray thee, tel me than,   615
Is he a clerk, or noon? tel what he is.'
    'Nay, he is gretter than a clerk, ywis,'
Seyde this yeman, 'and in wordes fewe,
Host, of his craft som-what I wol yow shewe.
    I seye, my lord can swich subtilitee—   620
(But al his craft ye may nat wite at[1] me ;
And som-what helpe I yet to his werkinge)—
That al this ground on which we been rydinge,
Til that we come to Caunterbury toun,
He coude al clene turne it vp so doun,   625
And paue it al of siluer and of gold.'
    And whan this yeman hadde thus[2] ytold
Vnto our host, he seyde, 'benedicite!
This thing is wonder merueillous to me,
Sin that thy lord is of so hey prudence,   630
By cause of which men sholde him reuerence,
That of his worship rekketh he so lyte ;
His oversloppe nis nat worth a myte,

---

[1] E. for ; Hl. of ; *the rest* at.
[2] E. this tale ; Cm. this ; *the rest* thus.

As in effect, to him, so mot I go !
It is al baudy and to-tore also.   635
Why is thy lord so sluttish, I thee preye,
And is of power better cloth to beye,
If that his dede accorde with thy speche ?
Telle me that, and that I thee biseche.'
    ' Why ? ' quod this yeman, ' wherto axe ye me ?   640
God help me so, for he shal neuer thee !
(But I wol nat auowe that I seye,
And therfor kepe it secre, I yow preye).
He is to wys, in feith, as I bileue ;
That that is ouerdoon, it wol nat preue   645
Aryght, as clerkes seyn, it is a vice.
Wherfor in that I holde him lewed and nyce.
For whan a man hath ouer-greet a wit,
Ful oft him happeth to misusen it ;
So doth my lord, and that me greueth sore.   650
God it amende, I can sey yow namore.'
    ' Ther-of no fors, good yeman,' quod our host ;
' Sin of the conning of thy lord thou wost,
Tel how he doth, I pray thee hertely,
Sin that he is so crafty and so sly.   655
Wher dwellen ye, if it to telle be ?'
    ' In the suburbes of a toun,' quod he,
' Lurkinge in hernes and in lanes blynde,
Wher as thise robbours and thise theues by kynde
Holden her pryue fereful residence,   660
As they that dar nat shewen her presence ;
So faren we, if I shal seye the sothe.'
    ' Now,' quod our host, ' yit[1] lat me talke [2] to thee ;

    [1] Cm. Hl. yit, *which the rest omit.*
    [2] E. telle ; Cm. speke ; *the rest* talke.

Why artow so discoloured of thy face ?'
   'Peter !' quod he, 'god yeue it harde grace,   665
I am so vsed in the fyr to blowe,
That it hath chaunged my colour, I trowe.
I am nat wont in no mirour to prye,
But swinke sore and lerne multiplye.
We blundren euer and pouren in the fyr,   670
And for al that we fayle of our desyr,
For euer we lakken our[1] conclusioun.
To mochel folk we doon illusioun,
And borwe gold, be it a pound or two,
Or ten, or twelue, or many sommes mo,   675
And make hem wenen, at the leste weye,
That of a pound we coude make tweye !
Yet is it fals, but ay we han good hope   hope
It for to doon, and after it we grope.
But that science is so fer vs biforn,   680
We mowen nat, al though we hadde it[2] sworn,
It ouertake, it slit awey so faste ;
It wol vs maken beggers atte laste.'
   Whyl this yeman was thus in his talking,
This chanoun drough him neer, and herde al thing 685
Which this yeman spak, for suspecioun
Of mennes speche euer hadde this chanoun.
For Catoun seith, that he that gilty is   de se putat conscius ipse
Demeth al thing be spoke of him, ywis.
That was the cause he gan so ny him drawe   690
To his yeman, to herknen al his sawe.
And thus he seyde vn-to his yeman tho,
'Hold thou thy pees, and spek no wordes mo,
For if thou do, thou shalt it dere abye ;
Thou sclaundrest me heer in this companye,   695

---

[1] E. of oure; *the rest omit* of.   [2] E. *omits* it.

And eek discouerest that thou sholdest hyde.'
    'Ye,' quod our host, 'telle on, what so bityde ;
Of al his[1] threting rekke[2] nat a myte !'
    'In feith,' quod he, 'namore I do but lyte.'
    And whan this chanon sey it wolde nat be,   700
But his yeman wolde telle his priuyte,
He fledde awey for verray sorwe and shame.
    'A !' quod the yeman, 'heer shall aryse game,
Al that I can anon now wol I telle.
Sin he is gon, the foule fend him quelle !   705
For neuer her-after[3] wol I with him mete
For peny ne for pound, I yow bihete !
He that me broughte first vnto that game,
Er that he deye, sorwe haue he and shame !
For it is ernest to me, by my feith ;   710
That fele I wel, what so[4] any man seith.
And yet, for al my smert and al my grief,
For al my sorwe, labour, and meschief,
I coude neuer leue it in no wyse.
Now wolde god my wit myghte suffyse   715
To tellen al that longeth to that art !
But[5] natheles yow wol I tellen part ;
Sin that my lord is gon, I wol nat spare ;
Swich thing as that I knowe, I wol declare.—   719

**Heere endeth the prologe of the Chanouns
yemannes tale.**

---

[1] *So* E. ; *the rest* this.
[2] *So* E. Cm. ; Cp. recche I ; Hl. Pt. Ln. recche thee.
[3] *So* Hl. Cp. Pt. Ln. ; E. *omits* after, *having* heer *only.*
[4] E. that ; *the rest* so.   [5] E. And ; *the rest* But.

Heer biginneth the Chanouns yeman his tale.

[*Prima pars.*]

With this chanoun I dwelt haue seuen yeer,   720
And of his science am I neuer the neer.
Al that I hadde, I haue ylost ther-by;
And god wot, so hath many mo than I.
Ther I was wont to be ryght fresh and gay
Of clothing and of other good array,   725
Now may I were an hose vpon myn heed;
And wher my colour was bothe fresh and reed,
Now is it wan and of a¹ leden hewe;
Who so it vseth, sore shal he rewe.
And of my swink yet blered is myn yĕ,   730
Lo! which auantage is to multiplye!
That slyding science hath me maad so bare,
That I haue no good, wher that euer I fare;
And yet I am endetted so ther-by
Of gold that I haue borwed, trewely,   735
That whyl I lyue, I shal it quyte neuer.
Lat euery man be war by me for euer!
What maner man that casteth him ther-to,
If he continue, I holde his thrift ydo.
So² helpe me god, ther-by shal he nat winne,   740
But empte his purs, and make his wittes thinne.
And whan he, thurgh his madnes and folye,
Hath lost his owen good thurgh Iupartye,
Thanne he excyteth other folk ther-to,
To lese her good as he him-self hath do.   745
For vnto shrewes ioye it is and ese
To haue her felawes in peyne and disese;

---

¹ E. *omits* a.   ² E. Pt. Ln. For so; *but* Cp. *omits* For.

Thus was I ones lerned of a clerk.

Solamen miseri
habuisse dolori
in marlowe's F.
ii, i, 42.

Of that no charge, I wol speke of our werk.

   Whan we been ther as we shul exercyse   750

Our eluish craft, we semen wonder wyse,

Our termes been so clergial and so queynte.   *original was elaborate*

I blowe the fyr til that myn herte feynte.

   What sholde I tellen ech proporcioun

Of thinges whiche that we werche vpon,   755

As on fyue or sixe ounces, may wel be,

Of siluer or som other quantite,

And bisie me to telle yow the names

Of orpiment, brent bones, yren squames,

That into poudre grounden been ful smal?   760

And in an erthen potte how[1] put is al,

And salt yput in, and also pepeer[2],

Biforn thise poudres that I speke of heer,

And wel ycouered with a lampe[3] of glas,   *lame of plate of dampness*

And mochel other thing which that ther was?   765

And of the pot and glasses enluting,

That of the eyre myghte passe out no thing?

And of the esy fyr and smart also,

Which that was maad, and of the care and wo

That we hadde in our matires sublyming,   770

And in amalgaming and calcening

Of quik siluer, yclept Mercurie crude?

For alle our sleightes we can nat conclude.

Our orpiment and sublymed Mercurie,

Our grounden litarge eek on[4] the porphurie,   775

---

[1] E. *omits* how ; *the rest have it.*
[2] *The MSS. have* papeer, paupere. Tyrwhitt *reads* pepere.
[3] *The MSS. have* lampe, *or* laumpe. *See the note.*
[4] E. in ; Cm. & ; *the rest on.*

Of[1] ech of thise of ounces a certeyn——
Nought helpeth vs, our labour is in veyn.
Ne eek our spirites ascencioun,
Ne our materes that lyen al fixe adoun,
Mowe in our werking no thing vs auayle.
For lost is al our labour and trauayle,
And al the cost, a[2] twenty deuel weye,
Is lost also, which we vpon it leye.
   Ther is also ful many another thing
That is vnto our craft apertening ;
Though I by ordre hem nat reherse can,
By cause that I am a lewed man,
Yet wol I telle hem as they come to mynde,
Though I ne can nat sette hem in her kynde ;
As bole armoniak, verdegrees, boras,
And sondry vessels maad of erthe and glas,
Our [many botels] and our descensories,
Violes, croslets, and sublymatories,
Cucurbites, and alembykes eek,
And othere swiche, dere ynough a leek.
Nat nedeth it for to reherse hem alle,
Watres rubifying and boles galle,
Arsenik, sal armoniak, and brimstoon ;
And herbes coude I telle eek many oon,
As egremoin, valerian, and lunarie,
And othere swiche, if that me liste tarie.
Our lampes brenning bothe nyght and day,
To bringe aboute our craft, if that[3] we may.
Our fourneys eek of calcinacioun,
And of watres albificacioun,

---

[1] E. And; *the rest* Of.
[2] E. Cm. a; Ln. in; *the rest* on.
[3] E. purpos if; *the rest* craft if that.

Vnslekked lym, chalk, and gleyre of an[1] ey,
Poudres diuerse, asshes, [and muk], and cley,   *longe, passe*
Cered pokets[2], sal peter, vitriole ;
And diuers fyres maad of wode and cole ;
Sal tartre, alkaly, and sal preparat,   810
And combust materes and coagulat,
Cley maad with hors or[3] mannes heer, and oile
Of tartre, alum[4], glas, berm, wort, and argoile,   *yeast, unfer beer, moth vinegar*
found & ctue Resalgar, and our materes enbibing;   *absorption*
And eek of our materes encorporing,   815
And of our siluer citrinacioun,   *turning to the colour.*
Our[5] cementing and fermentacioun,
Our ingottes, testes, and many mo.   *test tubes*
    I wol yow telle, as was me taught also,
The foure[6] spirites and the bodies seuene,   820
By ordre, as ofte I herde my lord hem neuene.
The firste spirit quik-siluer called is,
sulphide senic The second orpiment, the thridde, ywis,
onium chloride Sal armoniak, and the ferthe brimstoon.
The bodies seuene eek, lo! hem heer anoon :   825
Sol gold is, and Luna siluer we threpe,   *call*
Mars yren, Mercurie quik siluer wel clepe,
Saturnus leed, and Iupiter is tin,
And Venus coper, by my fader kin !
    This cursed craft who so wol exercyse,   830
He shal no good han that him may suffyse ;
For al the good he spendeth ther-aboute,
He lese shal, ther-of haue I no doute.
Who so[7] that listeth outen his folye,
Lat him come forth, and lerne multiplye ;   835

---

[1] *The MSS. all retain* an.   [2] *Miswritten* pottes *in* E.
[3] E. and; *the rest* or.   [4] *Accent* alum *on the* u.
[5] E. And of oure; *the rest omit* And of.   [6] E. seuene; *the rest* foure.
[7] E. omits so; *the rest have it.*

And euery man that ought hath in his cofre,

Of quarter Lat him appere, and wexe a philosofre.

Ascaunce that craft is so lyght to lere ?

Nay, nay, god wot, al be he monk or frere,

Preest or chanoun, or any other wyght,   840

Though he sitte at his book bothe day and nyght,

In lernyng of this eluish nyce lore,

Al is in veyn, and parde, mochel more !

To lerne a lewed man this subtilte,

Fy ! spek nat ther-of, for it wol nat be ;   845

Al[1] conne he letterure, or conne he noon,

As in effect, he shal fynde it al oon.

For bothe two, by my sauacioun,

Concluden, in multiplicacioun,

Ylyke wel, whan they han al ydo ;   850

This is to seyn, they faylen bothe two.

   Yet forgat I to make rehersaille

Of watres corosif and of lymaille,   *metal filings*

And of bodies mollificacioun,

And also of her induracioun,   855

Oyles, ablucions, and metal fusible,

To tellen al wolde passen any bible

That owher is ; wherfor, as for the beste,

Of alle thise names now wol I me reste.

For, as I trowe, I haue yow told ynow   860

To reyse a feend, al loke he neuer so row.

   A ! nay ! lat be ; the philosophres stoon,

Elixir clept, we sechen faste echoon ;

For, hadde we him, than were we[2] siker ynow.

But, vnto god of heuen I make avow,   865

For al our craft, whan we han al ydo,

And[3] al our sleighte, he wol nat come vs to.

---

[1] E. Cm. And; *the rest* Al.   [2] E. it ; *the rest* we.

He hath ymaad vs[1] spenden mochel good,
For sorwe of which almost we wexen wood,
But that good hope crepeth in our herte,   870
Supposinge euer[2], though we sore smerte,
To be releued by him afterward;
Swich supposing and hope is sharp and hard;
I warne **yow wel**, it is to seken euer;
That futur temps hath maad men to[3] disseuer   875
In trust therof, from al that euer they hadde.
Yet of that art they can nat wexen sadde,
For vnto hem it is a bitter swete;
So semeth it; for nadde they but a shete
Which that they myghte wrappe hem inne a nyght, 880
And a bak[5] to walken inne by day-lyght,
They wolde hem selle and spenden on this[6] craft;
They can nat stinte til **no** thing be laft.
And euermore, wher that euer they goon,
Men may hem knowe by smel of brimstoon;   885
For al the world, they stinken as a goot;
Her **sauour is** so rammish and so hoot,
That, though **a** man from hem a myle[7] be,
The sauour wol infecte him, trusteth[8] me;
Lo[9], thus by smelling[10] and threedbare array   890
If that men list, this folk they knowe may.
And if a man wol aske hem pryuely,
Why they been clothed so vnthriftily,
They ryght anon wol rownen in his ere,
And seyn, that if that they espyed were,   895

---

[1] Cm. I-mad vs; Hl. i-made vs; E. maad vs; *the rest* vs made.
[2] E. *omits* euer; *the rest have it.*   [3] Cm. to, *which the rest omit.*
[4] E. Inne at; *the rest* in a.   [5] E. brat; *the rest* bak; *see note.*
[6] E. the; *the rest* this.
[7] E. a Mile from hem; *the rest* from hem a myle.
[8] E. truste; *the rest* trusteth.   [9] E. And; *the rest* Lo.
[10] E. smel; *the rest* smellyng.

Men wolde hem slee, by cause of her science;
Lo, thus this folk bitrayen innocence !
   Passe ouer this ; I go my tale vn-to.
Er than[1] the pot be on the fyr ydo,
Of metals with a certeyn quantite,   900
My lord hem tempreth, and no man but he—
Now he is goon, I dar seyn boldely—
For, as men seyn, he can doon craftily;
Algate I wot wel he hath swich a name,
And yet ful ofte he renneth in a blame ;   905
And wite ye how? ful ofte it happeth so,
The pot tobreketh, and farewel ! al is go !
Thise metals been of so greet violence,
Our walles mowe nat make hem resistence,
But if they weren wrought of lym and stoon ;   910
They percen so, and thurgh the wal they goon,
And somme of hem sinken in-to the ground—
Thus han we lost by tymes many a pound—
And somme are scatered al the floor aboute,
Somme lepe[2] in-to the roof; with-outen doute;   915
Though that the feend nought in our syghte him shewe,
I trowe he with vs be, that ilke shrewe !
In helle wher that he is lord[3] and sire,
Nis ther more wo, ne more rancour ne ire.//
Whan that our pot is broke, as I haue sayd,   920
Euery man chit, and halt him yuel apayd.
   Som seyde, it was long[4] on the fyr-making,
Som seyde, nay ! it was on the blowing;
(Than was I fered, for that was myn office);
'Straw!' quod the thridde, 'ye been lewed and nyce,

---

[1] E. Ln. that ; *the rest* than.   [2] E. lepte ; *the rest* lepe, lepen.
[3] E. lord is ; *the rest* is lord.   [4] E. Cm. along ; *the rest* long.

It was nat tempred as it oughte be.' 926
'Nay!' quod the ferthe, 'stint, and herkne me;
By cause our fyr ne was nat maad of beech,
That is the cause, and other noon, so theech!'
I can nat telle wher-on it was long[1], 930
But wel I wot greet stryf is vs[2] among.
    'What!' quod my lord, 'ther is namore to done,
Of thise perils I wol be war eft-sone;
I am ryght siker that the pot was crased.
Be as be may, be ye no thing amased; 935
As vsage is, lat swepe the floor as swythe,
Plukke vp your hertes, and beth gladde and blythe.'
    The mullok on an hepe ysweped[3] was,
And on the floor ycast a canevas,
And al this mullok in a syve ythrowe, 940
And sifted, and ypiked many a throwe.
    'Parde,' quod oon, 'somwhat of our metal
Yet is ther heer, though that we han nat al.
Al-though this thing mishapped haue as now,
Another tyme it may be wel ynow, 945
Vs moste putte our good in auenture;
A marchant, parde! may nat ay endure,
Trusteth me wel, in his prosperite;
Somtym his good is drenched in the see,
And somtym comth it sauf vn-to the londe.' 950
    'Pees!' quod my lord, 'the next tyme I wol[4] fonde
To bringe our craft al in another plyte;
And but I do, sirs[5], lat me han the wyte;
Ther was defaute in som what, wel I wot.'
    Another seyde, the fyr was ouer hot:— 955

[1] Cm. Hl. long; *the rest* along; *see* l. 922.   [2] E. vs is; *the rest* is vs.
[3] Cm. I-swepid; Ln. yswepped; E. sweped; Cp. Pt. Hl. yswoped.
[4] E. shal; *the rest* wol, wil, wele.   [5] E. *omits* sirs; *the rest have* it.

But [1], be it hot or cold, I dar seye this,
That we concluden euermore amis.
We fayle of that which that we wolden haue,
And in our madnesse euermore we raue.
And whan we been togidres euerichoon,   96
Euery man semeth a Salomon.
But al [2] thing which that shyneth [3] as the gold
Nis nat gold, as that I haue herd it [4] told;
Ne euery appel that is fair at [5] yë
Ne is [6] nat good, what so men clappe or crye.   96
Ryght so, lo! [7] fareth it amonges vs;
He that semeth the wysest, by Iesus!
Is most fool, whan it cometh to the preef;
And he that semeth trewest is a theef;
That shul ye knowe, er that I fro yow wende,   97
By that I of my tale haue maad an ende.

Explicit prima pars.   Et sequitur pars secunda.

     Ther is [8] a chanoun of religioun
Amonges vs, wolde infecte al a toun,
Though it as greet were as was Niniue,
Rome, Alisaundre, Troye, and othere three.   97
His sleightes [9] and his infinit falsnesse
Ther coude no man wryten, as I gesse,
Though that he myghte lyue [10] a thousand yeer.
In al this world of falshede nis [11] his peer;
For in his termes so he wolde him wynde,   98
And speke his wordes in so sly a kynde,

---

[1] E. And; *the rest* But.   [2] E. euery; *the rest* al, alle.
[3] Cm. schynyth; Ln. schyneth; Hl. schineth; E. seineth; Cp. semeth.
[4] Cp. Pt. Ln. it; E. Cm. Hl. *omit* it.   [5] E. to; *the rest* at.
[6] E. Nis; *the rest* Ne is.   [7] E. *omits* lo; *the rest have* it.
[8] E. was; *the rest* is. Cf. l. 987.   [9] E. Hl. sleighte; *the rest* sleightes.
[10] E. lyue myghte; *the rest* myghte lyue.
[11] E. nas; Ln. ne is; *the rest* nis, nys.

Whan he commune shal with any wyght,
That he wol make him doten anon ryght,
But it a feend be, as him-seluen is.
Ful many a man hath he bigyled er this,   985
And wol, if that he lyue may a whyle;
And yet men ryde and goon ful many a myle
Him for to seke and haue his aqueyntaunce,
Nought knowinge of his false gouernaunce.
And if yow list to yeue me audience,   990
I wol it tellen heer in your presence.

    But worshipful chanouns religious,
Ne demeth nat that I sclaundre¹ your hous,
Al-though² my tale of a chanoun be.
Of euery ordre som shrewe is, parde,   995
And god forbede that al a companye
Sholde rewe a singuler mannes folye.
To sclaundre yow is no thing myn entente,
But to correcten that is mis I mente.
This tale was nat only told for yow,   1000
But eek for othere mo ; ye wot wel how
That, among Cristes apostelles twelue,
Ther nas no traytour but Iudas him-selue.
Than why sholde al the remenant haue blame³
That giltlees were? by yow I seye the same.   1005
Saue only this, if ye wol herkne me,
If any Iudas in your couent be,
Remeueth him bitymes, I yow rede,
If shame or los may causen any drede.
And beth no thing displesed, I yow preye,   1010
But in this cas herkneth what I shal seye.

---

¹ E. desclaundre ; *the rest* sclaundre ; *see* l. 998.
² E. Al-though that ; *the rest omit* that.
³ E. Hl. a blame ; *the rest omit* a.

In London was a preest, an[1] annueleer,
That therin dwelled hadde[2] many a yeer,
Which was so plesaunt and so seruisable
Vnto the wyf, wher as he was at table,
That she wolde suffre him no thing for to paye
For bord ne clothing, wente he neuer so gaye;
And spending siluer hadde he ryght ynow.
Therof no fors; I wol procede as now,
And telle forth my tale of the chanoun,
That broughte this preest to confusioun.

   This false chanoun cam vp-on a day
Vnto this preestes chambre, wher he lay,
Biseching him to lene him a certeyn
Of gold, and he wolde quyte it him ageyn.
'Lene me a mark,' quod he, 'but dayes three,
And at my day I wol it quyten thee.
And if so be that thou me fynde fals,
Another day do hange me by the hals!'

   This preest him took a mark, and that as swythe,
And this chanoun him thanked ofte sithe,
And took his leue, and wente forth his weye,
And at the thridde day broughte his moneye,
And to the preest he took his gold agayn,
Wherof this preest was wonder glad and fayn.

   'Certes,' quod he, 'no thing anoyeth me
To lene a man a noble, or two or thre,
Or what thing were in my possessioun,
Whan he so trewe is of condicioun,
That in no wyse he breke wol his day;
To swich a man I can neuer seye nay.'

---

[1] E. *omits* an; *the rest have it.*
[2] E. had dwelled; *the rest* dwelled hadde (*or* had).

'What l' quod this chanoun, 'sholde I be vntrewe?
Nay, that were thing[1] yfallen al of-newe.
Trouthe is a thing that I wol euer kepe
Vn-to[2] that day in which that I shal crepe   1045
In-to my graue, and[3] elles god forbede;
Bileueth this as siker as your[4] crede.
God thanke I, and in good tyme be it sayd,
That ther was neuer man yet yuel apayd
For gold ne siluer that he to me lente,   1050
Ne neuer falshede in myn herte I mente.
And sir,' quod he, 'now of my priuetee,
Sin ye so goodlich han been vn-to me,
And kythed to me so greet gentillesse,
Somwhat to quyte with your kyndenesse,   1055
I wol yow shewe, and, if[5] yow list to lere,
I wol yow teche pleynly the manere,
How I can werken in philosophye.
Taketh good heed, ye shul wel seen at yë,
That I wol doon a maistrie er I go.'   1060
     'Ye,' quod the preest, 'ye, sir[6], and wol ye so?
Marie ! ther-of I pray yow hertely !'
     'At your comandement, sir, trewely,'
Quod the chanoun, 'and elles god forbede !'
     Lo, how this theef coude his seruyse bede !   1065
Ful soth it is, that swich profred seruyse
Stinketh, as witnessen thise olde wyse;
And that ful sone I wol it verifye
In this chanoun, rote of al trecherye,
That euer-more delyt hath and gladnesse—   1070
Swich feendly thoughtes in his herte impresse—

---

[1] E. Cm. a thyng; *the rest omit* a.   [2] E. Ln. In-to; *the rest* Vn-to.
[3] E. or; *the rest* and.   [4] E. the; Hl. your; *the rest* is your.
[5] E. if that; *the rest* and if (or yif).
[6] *After* sir, E. *wrongly inserts* quod he.

H 2

How Cristes peple he may to **meschief** bringe ;
God kepe **vs** from his fals dissimulinge !
    Nought **wiste** this preest with whom that he delte,
Ne of his harm cominge he no thing felte.   1075
O sely preest ! o sely Innocent !
With coueityse anon thou shalt be blent !
O gracelees, ful blynd is thy conceit,
No thing ne artow war of the deceit
Which that this fox yshapen hath to[1] thee !   1080
His wyly wrenches thou ne mayst nat flee.
Wherfor, to go to the conclusioun
That refereth to thy confusioun,
Vnhappy man ! anon I wol me hye
To tellen thyn vnwit and thy[2] folye,   1085
And eek the falsnesse of that other wrecche,
As ferforth as that[3] my conning may strecche.
    This chanoun was my lord, ye wolden wene ?
Sir host, in feith, and by the heuenes quene,
It **was** another chanoun, and nat he,   1090
That can an hundred fold more subtilte !
He hath bitrayed folkes many tyme ;
Of his falshede it **dulleth** me to ryme.
Euer whan that I speke of his falshede,
For shame of him my chekes wexen rede ;   1095
Algates, they biginnen for to glowe,
For reednesse haue I noon, ryght wel I knowe,
In my visage ; for fumes dyuerse
Of metals, which ye han herd me reherse,
Consúmed ánd wastéd han mý reednésse.   1100
Now tak heed of this chanouns cursednesse !

---

[1] E. for; _the rest_ to.   [2] E. his; Cm. heigh; _the rest_ thy.
         [3] Cm. that, _which seems required; yet the rest omit it._

'Sir,' quod he to the preest, 'lat your man gon
For quik-siluer, that we it hadde [1] anon;
And lat him bringen ounces two or three;
And whan he comth, as faste shul ye see   1105
A wonder thing which ye sey neuer er this.'
    Sir,' quod the preest, 'it shall be doon, ywis.'
He bad his seruaunt fecchen him this thing,
And he al redy was at his bidding,
And wente him forth, and cam anon agayn   1110
With this quik-siluer, sothly for to sayn,
And took thise ounces thre to the chanoun;
And he hem [2] leyde fayre and wel adoun,
And bad the seruaunt coles for to bringe,
That he anon myghte go to his werkinge.   1115
    The coles ryght anon weren yfet,
And this chanoun took out a crosselet
Of his bosom, and shewed it the [3] preest.
'This instrument,' quod he, 'which that thou seest,
Tak in thyn hand, and put thy-self ther-inne   1120
Of this quik-siluer an ounce, and heer biginne,
In the name of Crist, to wexe a philosofre.
Ther been ful fewe, whiche that [4] I wolde profre
To shewen hem thus muche of my science.
For ye shul seen heer, by experience,   1125
That this quik-siluer wol I mortifye
Ryght in your syghte anon, withouten [5] lye,
And make it [6] as good siluer and as fyn
As ther is any in your purs or myn,

---

[1] E. Cm. hadde it; *the rest* it hadde.   [2] E. Cm. hem; *the rest* it.
[3] E. to the; *the rest omit* to.
[4] E. to whiche; Cm. to whiche that; *the rest* whiche that.
[5] E. I wol nat; Hl. with-outen; Cm. with·outyn; *the rest* withoute (*or* without.)   [6] E. *omits* it; *the rest have it.*

Or elleswher, and make it malliable;   1130
And elles, holdeth me fals and vnable
Amonges folk for euer to appere !
I haue a poudre heer, that coste me dere,
Shal make al good, for it is cause of al
My conning, which that I yow [1] shewen shal.   1135
Voydeth your man, and lat him be ther-oute,
And shet the dore, whyls we been aboute
Our priuetee, that no man vs espye
Whyls that we werke in this philosophye.'
Al as he bad, fulfilled was in dede,   1140
This ilke seruant anon-ryght out yede,
And his maister shette the dore anon,
And to her labour speedily they gon.

   This preest, at this cursed chanouns bidding,
Vp-on the fyr anon sette this thing.   1145
And blew the fyr, and bisied him ful faste;
And this chanoun in-to the croslet caste
A poudre, noot I wher-of that it was
Ymaad, other of chalk, other [2] of glas,
Or som what elles, was nat worth a flye,   1150
To blynde with the preest; and bad him hye
The coles for to couchen al aboue
The croslet, ' for, in tokening I thee loue,'
Quod this chanoun, ' thyn owene hondes two
Shul werchen [3] al thing which shal heer be do.'   1155

   ' Graunt mercy,' quod the preest, and was ful glad,
And couched coles [4] as the [5] chanoun bad.
And whyle he bisy was, this feendly wrecche,
This fals chanoun, the foule feend him fecche !

---

[1] E. to yow; *the rest omit* to.   [2] E. or; Pt. or ellis; *the rest* other.
[3] *The MSS. have* werche, worche, wirche; *spoiling the metre; see* l. 1058.
[4] E. Cm. cole; *the rest* coles.   [5] E. that; Cm. that the; *the rest* the.

Out of his bosom took [1] a bechen cole,   1160
In which ful subtilly was maad an hole,
And ther-in put was of siluer lymaille
An ounce, and stopped was, with-outen fayle,
The hole with wex, to kepe the lymail in.
And vnderstondeth, that this false gin   1165
Was nat maad ther, but it was maad bifore;
And othere thinges I shal telle more
Herafterward, which that he with him broughte;
Er he cam ther, him to bigyle he thoughte,
And so he dide, er that they wente atwinne;   1170
Til he had terved him, he coude not blinne.
It dulleth me whan that I of him speke,
On his falshede fayn wolde I me wreke,
If I wiste how; but he is heer and ther;
He is so variaunt, he [2] abit no wher.   1175
    But taketh heed now, sirs, for goddes loue !
He took his [3] cole of which I spak aboue,
And in his hond he baar it priuely.
And whyles the [4] preest couched busily
The coles, as I tolde yow er this,   1180
This chanoun seyde, 'frend, ye doon amis;
That is nat couched as it oughte be;
But sone I shal amenden it,' quod he.
'Now lat me medle therwith but a whyle,
For of yow haue I pite, by seint Gyle !   1185
Ye been ryght hoot, I se wel how ye swete,
Haue heer a cloth, and wype awey the wete.'
And whyles that the preest wyped his face,
This chanoun took his cole with harde grace [5],

---

[1] E. he took; *the rest omit* he.   [2] E. Cp. that he; *the rest omit* that.
[2] E. this; *the rest* his; *see* l. 1189.   [4] *Read* this? *See* ll. 1181, 1030.
[5] *So* E.; Cm. with sory grace (*see* l. 665). *Most MSS. have* I shrewe his
face, *and make* l. 1188 *end with* him wyped has.

And leyde it vp aboue, on [1] the midward   1190
Of the croslet, and blew wel afterward,
Till that the coles gonne faste brenne.

inf.   ' Now yeue vs drinke,' quod the chanoun thenne,
' As swythe al shal be wel, I vndertake ;
Sitte we doun, and lat vs mery make.'   1195
And whan that this chanounes bechen cole
Was brent, all the lymaille, out of the hole,
Into the croslet fil anon adoun ;
And so it moste nedes, by resoun,
Sin it so euen aboue [2] couched was ;   1200
But ther-of wiste the preest no thing, alas !
He demed alle the coles yliche good,
For of that sleighte he no thing vnderstood.
And whan this alkamistre sey his tyme,
' Ris vp,' quod he, ' sir preest, and stondeth [3] by me ;
And for I wot wel ingot haue I noon,   1206
Goth, walketh forth, and brynge vs a chalk-stoon ;
For I wol make oon of the same shap
That is an ingot, if I may han hap.   *good luck*
And bringeth eek with yow a bolle or a panne,   1210
Ful of water, and ye shul se wel thanne
How that our bisinesse shal thryue and preue.
der that   And yet, (for ye shul han no misbileue
ny have   Ne wrong conceit of me in your absence,)
I ne wol nat been out of your presence,   1215
But go with yow, and come with yow ageyn.'
The chambre dore, shortly for to seyn,
They opened and shette, and wente her wey.
And forth with hem they carieden the key,

---

[1] *I propose this reading ;* E. *has* aboue vp on ; Cm. *the same, but omitting* it ;
Hl. abouen on ; *the rest* vpon abouen.   [2] E. abouen it ; *the rest* aboue.
[3] Lichf. Cp. Pt. stondeth ; Ln. Hl. stonde ; Cm. stand ; E. sit.

And come agayn with-outen any delay.   1220
What sholde I tarien al the longe day ?
He took the chalk, and shoop it in the wyse
Of an ingot, as I shal yow deuyse.

    I seye, he took out of his owen sleue,
A teyne of siluer (yuel moot he cheue !)   1225
Which that ne [1] was nat but an ounce of weighte ;
And taketh heed now of his cursed sleighte !

    He shoop his ingot, in lengthe and eek [2] in brede,
Of this [3] teýne, with-oúten ány dréde,
So slyly, that the preest it nat espyde ;   1230
And in his sleue agayn he gan it hyde ;
And fro the fyr he took vp his matere,
And in thingot putte it with mery chere,
And in the water-vessel he it caste
Whan that him luste, and bad the preest as_faste,   1235
‘ Look what ther is [4], put in thyn hand and grope,
Thow fynde shalt ther siluer, as I hope ;
What, [by myn honour,] sholde it elles be ?
Shauing of siluer siluer is, parde ! ’ [5]
He putte his hond in, and took vp a teyne   1240
Of siluer fyn, and glad in euery veyne
Was this preest, whan he sey that [6] it was so.
‘ Goddes blessing, and his modres also,
And alle halwes haue ye, sir chanoun,’
Seyde this preest, ‘ and I her malisoun,   1245
But, and ye vouche-sauf to techen me
This noble craft and this subtilite;

---

[1] Cm. ne ; *which the rest omit.*   [2] E. eek; *which the rest omit.*
[3] Tyrwhitt *reads* Of thilke; *I propose*—As of this teyne.
[4] E. What that heer is ; *the rest* Look what ther is.
[5] E. *omits* ll. 1238, 1239.
[6] E. Hl. *omit* that ; *it is found in* Cm. Cp. Pt. Ln.

I wol be your in al that euer I may !'
    Quod the chanoun [1], ' yet wol I make assay
The second tyme, that ye may taken hede   1250
And been expert of this, and in your nede
Another day assaye in myn absence
This disciplyne and this crafty science.
Lat take another ounce,' quod he tho,
' Of quik-siluer, with-outen wordes mo,   1255
And do ther-with as ye han doon er this
With that other, which that now siluer is.'
    This preest him bisieth in al that he can
To doon as this chanoun, this cursed man,
Comanded him, and faste he blew the fyr,   1260
For to come to theffect of his desyr.
And this chanoun, ryght in the mene whyle,
Al redy was, the preest eft to bigyle,
And, for a countenaunce, in his honde he bar
An holwe stikke, (tak keep and be war !)   * 1265
In thende of which an ounce, and namore,
Of siluer lymail put was, as bifore
Was [2] in his cole, and stopped with wex wel
For to kepe in his lymail euery del.
And whyl this preest was in his bisinesse,   1270
This chanoun with his stikke gan him dresse
To him anon, and his pouder caste in
As he did er; (the deuel out of his skin
Him terve [3], I pray to god, for his falshede;
For he was euer fals in thought and dede);   1275
And with this stikke aboue the croslet,
That was ordeyned with that false get [4],

---

[1] E. preest; *the rest* chanoun.   [2] E. *omits* Was; *the rest have it.*
[3] E. terve; Cm. Pt. turne; *the rest* torne.
[4] E. Cm. Iet (=jet); Hl. get; Ln. gett; Cp. Pt. gette.

He stired the coles til relente gan
The wex agayn the fyr, as euery man,
But it a fool be, wot wel it mot nede,   adv.   1280
And al that in the stikke was out yede,
And in the croslet hastily it fel.

   Now gode sirs, what wol ye bet than wel?[1]
Whan that this preest thus was bigyled ageyn[2],
Supposing nought but trewthe, soth to seyn,   1285
He was so glad, that I can[3] nat expresse
In no manere his mirthe and his gladnesse,
And to the chanoun he profred eftsone
Body and good; 'ye,' quod the chanoun sone,
'Though poure I be, crafty thou shalt me fynde;   1290
I warne thee, yet is ther more bihynde.
Is ther any coper her-inne?' seyde he.
'Ye,' quod the preest, 'sir, I trowe wel ther be.'
'Elles go by vs som, and that as swythe,
Now, gode sir, go forth thy wey and hy the.'   1295

   He wente his wey, and with the coper cam,
And this chanoun it in his hondes nam,
And of that coper weyed out but an ounce.
Al to simple is my tonge to pronounce,
As ministre of my wit, the doublenesse   1300
Of this chanoun, rote of al cursednesse.
He semed frendly to hem that knewe him nought,
But he was feendly bothe in herte and thought.
It werieth me to telle of his falsnesse,
And nathelees yet wol I it expresse,   1305
To thentent that men may be war therby,
And for noon other cause, trewely.

[1] Cp. Pt. Ln. The preest supposede nothing but wel.
[2] Cp. Pt. Ln. But busyed him faste, and was wonder fayn.
[3] E. ne kan; *the rest omit* ne.

He putte his [1] ounce of coper in the croslet,
And on the fyr as swythe he hath it set,
And caste in poudre, and made the preest to blowe,
And in his werking for to stoupe lowe,   1311
As he dide er, and al nas but a Iape ;
Ryght as him liste, the preest he made his ape ;
And afterward in thingot he it caste,
And in the panne putte it at the laste   1315
Of water, and [2] in he putte his owen hond.
And in his sleue, (as ye biforn-hond
Herde me telle,) he [3] hadde a siluer teyne.
He slyly took it out, this cursed heyne—
Vnwiting this preest of his false craft—   1320
And in the pannes botme he hath it laft ;
And in the water rombled to and fro,
And wonder priuely took vp also
The coper teyne, nought knowing this preest,
And hidde it, and him hente by the breest,   1325
And to him spak, and thus seyde in his game,
'Stoupeth adoun, [parde], ye be to blame,
Helpeth me now, as I [4] dide yow whyl-er,
Putte in your hond, and loketh what is ther.'

This preest took vp this siluer teyne anon,   1330
And thanne seyde the chanoun, 'lat vs gon
With thise thre teynes, which that we han wrought,
To som goldsmith, and wite if they been ought.
For, by my feith, I nolde, for myn hood,
But if that they were siluer, fyn and good,   1335
And that as swythe preued shal it [5] be.'
Vn-to the goldsmith with thise teynes three

---

[1] Cm. his ; E. the ; *the rest* this.   [2] E. the water ; *the rest* water and.
[3] E. *omits* he ; *the rest have* it.   [4] E. a ; *the rest* I.
[5] E. it shal ; Ln. schal he ; *the rest* shal it.

They wente, and putte thise teynes in assay
To fyr and hamer ; myghte no man sey nay,
But that they weren as hem oughte be.   1340
    This sotted preest, who was gladder than he ?
Was neuer brid gladder agayn the day,
Ne nyghtingale, in the sesoun of May,
Nas neuer **noon**[1] that luste bet to singe;
Ne lady lustier in carolinge   1345
Or for to speke of love and wommanhede,
Ne knyght in armes to doon an hardy **dede**,
To stonde in grace of his lady dere,
Than had this preest this sory craft to lere ;
And to the chanoun thus **he** spak and seyde,   1350
'For loue of god, that for vs alle deyde,
And as I may deserue it vn-to yow,
What shall this receit coste ? telleth now !'
    ' By our lady,' quod this chanoun, ' it is dere,
I warne yow wel; for, saue I and a frere,   1355
In Engelond ther can no man it make.'
    ' No fors,' quod he, ' now, sir, for goddes sake,
What shal I paye ? telleth me, I preye.'
    ' Ywis,' quod he, ' it is ful dere, I seye;
Sir, at o word, if that thee list it haue,   1360
Ye shul paye fourty pound, so god me saue !
And, nere the frendship that ye dide er **this**
To me, ye sholde paye more, y-wis.'
    This preest the somme of fourty pound anon
Of nobles fette, and took hem euerichon   1365
To **this** chanoun, for this ilke receit;
Al his werking nas but fraude and deceit.
    ' Sir preest,' he seyde, ' I kepe han no loos
Of my craft, for I wolde it kept were cloos;

[1] E. man; *the rest* noon (non).

And as ye loue me, kepeth it secre;   1370
For, and men knewen al my sotilte,
[Parde], they wolden han so greet enuye
To me, by cause of my philosophye,
I sholde be deed, ther were noon other weye.'
  ' God it forbede!' quod the preest, ' what sey ye?
Yet hadde I leuer spenden al the good   1376
Which that I haue (and¹ elles wexe I wood!)
Than that ye sholden falle in swich mescheef.'
  ' For your good wil, sir, haue ye ryght good preef,'
Quod the chanoun, ' and farwel, grant mercy!'   1380
He wente his wey and neuer the preest him sy
After that day; and whan that this preest sholde
Maken assay, at swich tyme as he wolde,
Of this receit, farwel! it wolde nat be!
Lo, thus byiaped and bigyled was he!   1385
Thus maketh he his introduccioun
To bringe folk to her² destruccion.—

  Considereth, sirs, how that, in ech estaat,
Bitwixe men and gold ther is debaat
So ferforth, that vnnethes is ther noon.   1390
This multiplying blent so many oon,
That in good feith I trowe that it be
The cause grettest of swich scarsete.
Philosophres speken so mistily
In this craft, that men can nat come therby,   1395
For any wit that men han now a dayes.
They mowe wel chiteren, as doon thise³ Iayes,
And in her termes sette her lust and peyne,
But to her purpos shul they neuer atteyne.

  ¹ E. or; *the rest* and.   ² E. Cm. *omit* her.
  ³ E. as that doon; Cm. as don; *the rest* as doon thise.

A man may lyghtly lerne, if he haue ought,
To multiplye, and bringe his good to nought!
   Lo! swich a lucre is in this lusty game,
A mannes mirthe it wol torne vn-to grame,
And empten also grete and heuy purses,
And maken folk for to purchasen curses
Of hem, that han her good therto ylent.
O!¹ fy! for shame! they that han been brent,
Allas! can thei nat flee the fyres hete?
Ye that it vse, I rede ye it lete,
Lest ye lese al; for bet than neuer is late.
Neuer to thryue were to long a date.
Though ye prolle ay, ye shul it neuer fynde;
Ye been as bolde as is Bayard the blynde,
That blundreth forth, and peril casteth noon;
He is as bold to renne agayn a stoon
As for to gon besydes in the weye.
So fare ye that multiplye, I seye.
If that your yёn can nat seen aryght,
Loke that your mynde lakke nought his syght.
For, though ye loke neuer so brode, and stare,
Ye shul nat winne a myte² in that chaffare,
But wasten al that ye may rape and renne.
Withdrawe the fyr, lest it to faste brenne;
Medleth namore with that art, I mene,
For, if ye doon, yowr thrift is goon ful clene.
And ryght as swythe I wol yow tellen here,
What³ philosophres seyn in this matere.
   Lo, thus seith Arnold of the newe toun,
As his Rosarie maketh mencioun;

¹ E. *omits* O; *the rest have it.*
² E. Cm. no thyng wynne; *the rest* nat wynne a myte.
³ Tyr. What; Cm. What that ʒe; *the rest* What that the (*badly*).

He seith **ryght thus,** with-outen any lye,   1430
'Ther may no man Mercurie mortifye,
But it be with his brother knowleching;
Lo, how[1] that he, which that first seyde this thing,
Of philosophres fader was[2], Hermes;
He seith, how that the dragoun, doutelees,   1435
Ne deyeth nat, but if that he be slayn
With his brother; and that is for to sayn,
By the dragoun, Mercurie and noon other
He vnderstood; and brimstoon by his brother,
That out of *sol* and *luna* were ydrawe.   1440
And therfor,' seyde he, 'tak heed to my sawe,
Let no man bisy him this art for to seche,
But if that he thentencioun and speche
Of philosophres vnderstonde can;
And if he do, he is a lewed man.   1445
For this science and this conning,' quod he,
'Is of the secre of secrees[3], parde.'

  Also ther was a disciple of Plato,
That on a tyme seyde his maister to,
As his book Senior wol bere witnesse,   1450
And this was his demande in sothfastnesse:
'Tel me the name of the priuy stoon?'
  And Plato answerde vnto him anoon,
'Tak the stoon that Titanos men name.'
  'Which is that?' quod he.   'Magnesia is the same,'
Seyde Plato.   'Ye, sir, and is it thus?   1456
This is *ignotum per ignotius.*
What is Magnesia, good sir, I yow preye?'
  'It is a water that is maad, I seye,

---

[1] Tyr. Lo how; MSS. How; *see* l. 1428.
[2] E. first was; *the rest omit* first.
[3] E. Cm. of the secretes; Pt. of secrees; Hl. of secretz; Ln. of secretees.

Of elementes foure,' quod Plato.   1460
   ' Tel me the rote [1], good sir,' quod he tho,
' Of that water, if that [2] it be your wil?'
   ' Nay, nay,' quod Plato, 'certein, that I nil.
The philosophres sworn were euerichoon,
That they sholden discouere it vn-to noon,   1465
Ne in no book it wryte in no manere;
For vn-to god [3] it is so leef and dere
That he wol nat that it discouered be,
But wher it lyketh to his deite
Man for tenspyre, and eek for to defende   1470
Whom that him lyketh; lo, this is the ende.'
   Than thus conclude I [4]; sith that god of heuene
Ne wol nat that the philosophres neuene
How that a man shal come vn-to this stoon,
I rede as [5] for the beste, let it goon.   1475
For who so maketh god his aduersarie,
As for to werche any thing in contrarie
Of his wil, certes neuer shal he thryue,
Though that he multiplye terme of his [6] lyue.   *ace of*
And ther a poynt; for ended is my tale;   1480
God sende euery trewe man bote of his bale!—

Heere is ended the Chanouns Yemannes tale.

[1] E. roote; *the rest* roche, rooche, roches.
[2] Cm. that; *which the rest omit.*
[3] *So the* Lichfield MS.; *the rest have* Crist; *see* l. 1476.
[4] *So* Tyr.; MSS. conclude I thus.   [5] E. vs; *the rest* as.
[6] E. Cm. **omit** his; *the rest have* it.

GROUP H. THE MANCIPLE'S PROLOGUE.

Heere folweth the Prologe of the Maunciples
Tale.

Wite[1] ye nat wher ther stant a litel toun
Which that ycleped is Bob-vp-and-doun,
Vnder the Blee, in Caunterbury weye?
Ther gan our hoste for to Iape and pleye,
And seyde, 'sirs, what! Dun is in the myre!   5
Is ther no man, for preyer ne for hyre,
That wol awake our felawe heer[2] bihynde?
A theef myghte him ful lyghtly robbe and bynde.
Se how he nappeth! se[3], for cokkes bones,
As he wol falle from his hors at ones.   10
Is that a cook of Londoun, with meschaunce?
Do him come forth, he knoweth his penaunce,
For he shal telle a tale, by my fey!
Al-though it be nat worth a botel hey.
Awake, thou cook,' quod he, 'god yeue the sorwe,   15
What eyleth the to slepe by the morwe?
Hastow had fleen al nyght, or artow dronke,

  .   .   .   .

So that thou mayst nat holden vp thyn heed?'
   This cook, that was ful pale and no-thing reed,   20

---

[1] E. Hn. Woot; Cp. Hl. Wot; Cm. Wote; Pt. Ln. Wete; *but* Wite *is
better, as in* l. 82.
[2] Cm. here; E. Hn. Hl. al; *the rest insert neither.*
[3] *So* Cp. Hl.; E. see how; Hn. Cm. se how.

Seyd to our host, 'so god my soule blesse,
As ther is falle on me swich heuinesse,
Not I nat why, that me were leuer slepe
Thán the béste gáloun wýn [1] in Chépe.'

   'Wel,' quod the maunciple, 'if it may doon ese   25
To thee, sir cook, and to no wyght displese
Which that heer rydeth in this companye,
And that our host wol of his curteisye,
I wol as [2] now excuse thee of thy tale;
For, in good feith, thy visage is ful pale,   30
Thyn yën daswen [3] eek, as that me thinketh,
And wel I wot, thy breeth ful soure stinketh,
That sheweth wel thou art not wel disposed;
Of me, certein, thou shalt nat been yglosed.
Se how he ganeth, lo, this dronken wyght,   35
As though he wolde vs swolwe [4] anon ryght.

. . . .

Thy cursed breeth infecte wol vs alle;
Fy, stinking swyn, fy! foule mot thee [5] falle!   40
A! taketh heed, sirs, of this lusty man.
Now, swete sir, wol ye Iusten atte fan?
Ther-to me thinketh ye been wel yshape!
I trowe that ye dronken han wyn ape,
And that is whan men pleyen with a straw.'   45
And with this speche the cook wex wroth and wraw,
And on the maunciple he gan nodde faste
For lakke of speche, and doun the hors him caste,
Wher as he lay, til that men him vp [6] took;
This was a fayr chiuache of a cook!   50

---

[1] Tyr. wyn that is; MSS. *omit* that is; *see note.*
[2] E. *omits* as; *the rest have it.*
[3] *So* E. Hn. Hl.; Cm. daswe; Cp. dasewen; Pt. dasen; Ln. dasoweþe
[4] *So* Cp. Ln.; *the rest* swolwe vs.   [5] E. thou; *the rest* thee *or* the.
[6] E. Hn. vp hym; *the rest* him vp.

Allas ! he nadde holde him by his ladel !
And, er that he agayn were in his sadel,
Ther was greet showuing bothe to and fro,
To lifte him vp, and mochel care and wo,
So vnweldy was this sory palled gost   55
And to the maunciple than spak our host,
' By-cause drink hath dominacioun
Vpon this man, by my sauacioun,
I trowe he lewedly[1] wold telle his tale.
For, were it wyn, or old or moysty ale,   60
That he hath dronke, he speketh in his nose,
And fneseth[2] faste, and eek he hath the pose.
He hath also to do more than ynough
To kepe him and his capel out of slough ;
And, if he falle from his capel eft-sone,   65
Than shul we alle haue ynough to done,
In liftinge vp his heuy dronken cors.
Tel on thy tale, of him make I no fors.
    But yet, maunciple, in feith thou art to nyce,
Thus openly repreue him of his vyce.   70
Another day he wol, perauenture,
Reclayme thee, and bringe thee to lure ;
I mene, he speke wol of smale thinges,
As for to pinchen at thy rekeninges,
That wer not honeste, if it cam to preef.'   75
' No,' quod the maunciple, ' that were a[3] greet mescheefl
So myghte he lyghtly bringe me in the snare.
Yet hadde I leuer payen for the mare
Which[4] he rit on, than he shold with me stryue ;
I wol nat wrathe him, al-so mot I thryue !   80

---

[1] E. Cm. Ln. put lewedly before he.
[2] So E. Hn. Cp. Ln. Hl.; Cm. sneseth; Pt. galpeth.
[3] All the 7 MSS. retain a; see the note. Hl omits No.
[4] E. Which that ; the rest omit that.

That that I spak, I seyde it in my bourde,
And wite ye what? I haue heer, in a gourde,
A draught of wyn, ye, of a rype grape,
And ryght anon ye shul seen a good Iape.
This cook shal drinke ther-of, if[1] I may;   85
Vp peyne of deeth, he wol nat sey me nay!'
    And certeinly, to tellen as it was,
Of this vessel the cook drank faste, allas!
What neded him[2]? he drank ynough biforn.
And whan he hadde pouped in this horn,   90
To the maunciple he took the gourde agayn;
And of that drink the cook was wonder fayn,
And thanked him in swich wyse as he coude.
    Than gan our host to laughen wonder loude,
And seyde, 'I se wel, it is necessarie,   95
Wher that we goon, good[3] drink we with vs carie,
For that wol turne rancour and disese
Tacord[4] and loue, and many a wrong apese.
    O thou[5] Bachus, yblessed be thy name,
That so canst turnen ernest in-to game!   100
Worship and thank be to thy deitee!
Of that matere ye gete namore of me.
Tel on thy tale, maunciple, I thee preye.'
    'Wel, sir,' quod he, 'now herkneth what I seye.'

[*Here follows* The Manciple's Tale, ll. 105–362, *with which*
Group H *ends*.]

---

[1] E. Pt. if that; *the rest omit* that.
[2] *So* E.; Cm. nedith hym; Hn. Hl. neded it; *the rest* needeth it.
[3] E. that; *the rest* good.
[4] *So* E. Hn.; Cm. Cp. Ln. Hl. To acord; Pt. To pees.
[5] Hl. thou; *which the rest omit.*

GROUP I. THE PARSON'S PROLOGUE.

Heere folweth the Prologe of the Persones Tale.

By that the maunciple hadde his tale al ended,
The sonne fro the south lyne was[1] descended
So lowe, that he nas nat, to my syghte,
Degreës nyne and twenty as in hyghte.
Foure[2] of the clokke it was tho, as I gesse;
For eleuen foot, or litel more or lesse,
My shadwe was at thilke tyme, as there,
Of swich feet as my lengthe parted were
In six feet equal of proporcioun.
Ther-with the mones[3] exaltacioun,
I mene[4] Libra, alwey gan ascende,
As we were entringe at a thropes ende;
For which our host, as he was wont to gye,
As in this cas, our Ioly companye,
Seyde in this wyse, 'lordings euerichoon,
Now lakketh vs no tales mo than oon.
Fulfild is my sentence and my decree;
I trowe that we han herd of ech degree.
Almost fulfild is al myn ordinaunce,
I prey to god, so yeue him ryght good chaunce,
That telleth this tale to vs lustily.
Sir preest,' quod he, 'artow a vicary?

[1] E. Cm. was; *the rest is.*   [2] *The MSS. have* Ten; *but see the note.*
[3] *Perhaps for* the mones *we should read* Saturnes; *see the note.*
[4] *So all but* Hl., *which has* In mena.

Or art a person? sey soth, by my fey!
Be what thou be, ne brek thou nat our pley;
For euery man, saue thou, hath told his tale,   25
Vnbokel, and shew vs what is in thy male;
For trewely, me thinketh, by thy chere,
Thou sholdest knitte vp wel a greet matere.
Tel vs a tale anon, for cokkes bones!'
    This persone him¹ answerde, al at ones,   30
'Thou getest fable noon ytold for me;
For Paul, that wryteth vnto Timothee,
Repreueth hem that weyuen sothfastnesse
And tellen fables and swich wrecchednesse.
Why sholde I sowen draf out of my feste,   35
Whan I may sowen whete, if that me leste?
For which I seye, if that yow list to here
Moralitee and vertuous matere,
And than that ye wol yeue me audience,
I wol ful² fayn, at Cristes reuerence,   40
Do yow plesaunce leueful, as I can.
But trusteth wel, I am a Southren man,
I can nat geste—rom, ram, ruf—by lettre,
Ne, god wot, rym holde I but litel bettre;
And therfor, if yow list, I wol not glose.   45
I wol yow telle a mery tale in prose
To knitte vp al this feste, and make an ende.
And Iesu, for his grace, wit me sende
To shewe yow the wey, in this viage,
Of thilke perfit glorious pilgrimage   50
That hyghte Ierusalem celestial.
And, if ye vouche sauf, anon I shal
Biginne vpon my tale, for which I preye
Telle your auys, I can no bettre seye.

¹ Tyr. him; *which the MSS. omit.*   ² E. omits ful; *the rest have it.*

But natheles, this meditacioun   55
I putte it ay vnder correccioun
Of clerkes, for I am nat textuel;
I take but the [1] sentens, trusteth wel.
Therfor I make protestacioun
That I wol stonde to correccioun.'   60
  Vp-on this word we han assented sone,
For, as vs [2] semed, it was for to done,
To enden in som vertuous sentence,
And for to yeue him space and audience;
And bede our host he sholde to him seye,   65
That alle we to telle his tale him preye.
  Our host hadde the wordes for vs alle :—
'Sir preest,' quod he, ' now fayre yow bifalle !
Sey what yow list, and we wol gladly here'—
And with that word he seyde in this manere—   70
'Telleth,' quod he, ' your meditacioun.
But hasteth yow, the sonne wol adoun ;
Beth fructuous, and that in litel space,
And to do wel god sende yow his grace !'   ·

Explicit prohemium.

[*Here follows* The Parson's Tale, *with which* Group I *ends.*]

---

[1] E. *omits* the; *the rest have it.*   [2] So E.; *the rest* it, *which is inferior.*

NOTES.

THE TALE OF THE MAN OF LAWE (GROUP **B**).

A story, agreeing closely with **The** Man of Lawes Tale, **is** found in Book II. of Gower's Confessio Amantis, from which Tyrwhitt supposed that Chaucer borrowed it. But I have shewn, **in the Preface,** that Gower's **version** is later than Chaucer's, and that Chaucer and **Gower** were **both alike** indebted to the version of the story in French **prose** (by **Nicholas** Trivet) in MS. Arundel 56, printed for **the** Chaucer Society in 1872. In some places Chaucer agrees with this **French** version rather closely, but he makes variations and additions at pleasure.

The first ninety-eight lines of **the** preceding Prologue are written in **couplets, in** order to link the Tale **to the others of the** series; but there is nothing to show which of the other tales it was intended to follow. Next follows a more special Prologue of thirty-five lines, in five stanzas of seven lines each; so that the first line in the Tale is l. 134 of Group B, the second of the fragments into which the Canterbury Tales are broken up, owing to the incomplete state in which Chaucer left them.

Wherever a final *e* occurs, it **is,** in general, to be pronounced as a distinct syllable, unless elided before a vowel or *h* following. In like manner *-es* and *-ed* generally form distinct syllables. There are, **in** general, **sufficient** reasons for the full pronunciation of **these final** syllables, but these cannot here be stated. The reader is **referred to** Morris's edition of Chaucer's Prologue and Knightes Tale (Clarendon Press Series), p. xliv. and to the Preface to my edition of The Prioresses Tale, pp. xlviii.-lxxii. for general rules; and to Ellis's Early English Pronunciation for **a** full discussion of the subject. **In the** first stanza, for example, the word *trewe* is dissyllabic, being plural: *hewe* is so, **because** it is a dative case governed by the prep. *of*, which formerly governed **a** dative, though now associated with the idea of a possessive case; *newe* **is** so, because modified from the A. S. dissyllabic *niwe*. *Chaffare* (l. **139**) is a gerund, and gerunds are commonly marked by the termination *-e* or *-en* (A. S. *-anne*). *Ware* is dissyllabic, being the A.S. *ware*. Sometimes **an** *e* is sounded in the middle of a word, as in *wydewher* (three syllables). Observe also *elothès* (A.S. *clǒðas*). In some French words, such **as** *companye,* the pronunciation of the *e* final is less **certain,** and seems to partake of poetic license; yet there is nothing very remarkable in the assumption, since the same word contains four syllables to this day, and is accented on the penultimate, both in Spanish and Italian ; cf. Span. *compañia* and Ital. *compagnia*. Again, such words as *grace, space,* from the Latin *gratiam, spatium,* may fairly be allowed two syllables ; especially when we find *cause* (Lat. *causam*) with two syllables ; Cant. Tales, 4142, 5705. If, however, the final *e* be followed by a vowel, or (in some cases) by the letter *h,* it is elided, or, to speak more strictly, slurred over by rapid pronunciation. This is the case in the words *dwelte* (134), *riche, sadde* (135), and *riche* again (137). Chaucer's lines, if read with attention, are beautifully melodious.

Line 134. *Surrye,* Syria ; called *Sarazine* (Saracen-land) by N. Trivet.
l. 143. *Were it,* whether it were.
l. 144. *Message,* messenger, *not* message ; see l. 333, and the note.
l. 145. The final *e* in *Rome* is pronounced, as in l. 142 ; but the words *the ende* are to be run together, forming but *one* syllable, *thende,* according to Chaucer's usual practice ; cf. note to l. 255. Indeed, in l. 423, it is actually so spelt ; just as, in l. 150, we have *thexcellent,* and in l. 151, *themperoures.*
l. 151. *Themperoures,* the emperor's. Gower calls him Tiberius Constantine, who was Emperor (not of Rome, but) of the East, A.D. 578, and was succeeded, as in the story, by Maurice, A.D. 582. His capital was Constantinople, whither merchants from Syria could easily repair ; but the greater fame of Rome caused the substitution of the Western for the Eastern capital.
l. 156. *God him see,* God protect him. See note to C. 715.
l. 161. *Al Europe.* In the margin of MSS. E. Hn. Cp. Pt. Ln. is written the note 'Europa est tercia pars mundi.'
l. 166. *Mirour,* mirror. Such French words are frequently accented on the *last* syllable. Cf. *ministr'* in l. 168.
l. 171. *Han doon fraught,* have caused to be freighted. All the MSS. have *fraught,* not *fraughte.* In the Glossary to Specimens of English, I marked *fraught* as being the infinitive mood, as Dr. Stratmann supposes, though he notes the lack of the final *e.* I have now no doubt that *fraught* is nothing but the past participle, as in William of Palerne, l. 2732—
'And feithliche *fraught* ful of fine wines.'
which is said of a ship. The use of this past participle after a *perfect* tense is a most remarkable idiom, but there is no doubt about its occurrence in the Clerkes Tale, Group E. 1098, where we find 'Hath doon yow *kept,*' where Tyrwhitt has altered *kept* to *kepe.* On the other hand, Tyrwhitt actually notes the occurrence of 'Hath doon *wrought*' in Kn. Tale, 1055, which he calls an irregularity. A better name for it is idiom. I find similar instances of it in another author of the same

'Thai strak his hed of, and syne,it
Thai *haf gert saltit* in-til a kyt.'

Barbour's Bruce, ed. Skeat. xviii. 167.

I. e. they have caused it (to be) salted. And again in the same, bk. viii.
l. 13, we have the expression *He gert held*, as if 'he caused to be
held;' but it may mean 'he caused to incline.' Compare also the
following :—

'And thai sall *let thame trwmpit* ill;' id. xix. 712.

I.e. and they shall consider themselves as evilly deceived.

The infinitive appears to have been *fraughten*, though the earliest certain
examples of this form seem to be those in Shakespeare, Cymb. i. 1. 126,
Temp. i. 2. 13. The proper form of the pp. was *fraughted* (as in Marlowe,
2 Tamb. i. 2. 33), but the loss of final -*ed* in past participles of verbs of
which the stem ends in *t* is common ; cf. *set, put*, &c. Hence this form
fraught as a pp. in the present instance. It is a Scandinavian word, from
Swed. *frakta*, Dan. *fragte*. At a later period we find *freight*, the mod. E.
form. The vowel-change is due to the fact that there was an intermediate
form *fret*, borrowed from the French form *fret* of the Scandinavian word.
This form *fret* disturbed the vowel-sound, without wholly destroying
the recollection of the original guttural *gh*, due to the Swed. *k*. For an
example of *fret*, we have only to consult the old black-letter editions of
Chaucer printed in 1532 and 1561, which give us the present line in the
form—' These marchantes han don *fret* her ships new.'

l. 185. *Ceriously*, with great minuteness of detail. Used by Fabyan,
who says that 'to reherce *ceryously*' all the conquests of Henry V
would fill a volume; Chron., ed. Ellis, p. 589. It is the Low Latin
seriose, used in two senses; (1) seriously, gravely; (2) minutely, fully.
In the latter case it is perhaps to be referred to the Lat. *series*, not *serius*.
A similar word, *cereatly* (Lat. *seriatim*), is found three times in the
Romance of Partenay, ed. Skeat, with the sense of *in due order*.

l. 190. This refers to the old belief in astrology and the casting of
nativities. Cf. Prol. 414-418.

l. 197. Tyrwhitt shews that this stanza is imitated closely from some
Latin lines, some of which are quoted in the margin of many MSS. of
Chaucer. He quotes them at length from the Megacosmos of Bernardus
Silvestris, a poet of the twelfth century (extant in MS. Bodley 1265).
The lines are as follows, it being premised that those printed in italics
are cited in the margin of MSS. E. Hn. Cp. Pt. and Ln. :—

'Præiacet in stellis series, quam longior ætas
  Explicet et spatiis temporis ordo suis,
Sceptra Phoronei, fratrum discordia Thebis,
Flamma Phaethontis, Deucalionis aquæ.
In stellis Codri paupertas, copia Croesi,
  Incestus Paridis, Hippolytique pudor.

In stellis Priami *species, audacia* Turni,
Sensus Ulixeus, Herculeusque **uigor**.
In stellis pugil **est** Pollux et **nauita** Typhis,
Et Cicero rhetor et geometra Thales.
In stellis lepidum dictat Maro, **Milo** figurat,
Fulgurat in Latia nobilitate Nero.
Astra notat Persis, Ægyptus parturit artes,
Græcia docta legit, prælia Roma gerit.'

The names *Ector* (Hector), &c. are too well known to require comment. The death of Turnus is told at the end of Virgil's Æneid.

ll. 207, 208. Here *haue* seems to be used as the form of the auxiliary verb, whilst *han* (for *hauen*) signifies possession. See *han* again in l. 241.

l. 211. Compare Squieres Tale, F. **202, 203**, and the note thereon.

l. 224. *Mahoun*, Mahomet. The French version does not mention Mahomet. This is an anachronism on **Chaucer's part**; the Emperor Tiberius II died A.D. 582, when Mahomet was but twelve years old.

l. 228. *I prey yow holde,* I pray you to hold. Here *holde* is the infinitive mood. The imperative plural would be *holdeth*; see *saueth*, next line.

l. 236. *Maumettrye*, idolatry; from the Mid. E. *maumet*, an idol, corrupted from Mahomet. The confusion introduced by using the word *Mahomet* for an idol may partly account for the anachronism in l. 224. The Mahometans were falsely supposed by our forefathers to be idolaters.

l. 242. *Not*, put for *ne wot*, know not.

l. 248. An imperfect line. There are a few such lines in Chaucer, in which the cæsural pause seems to count for a syllable. Scan it thus:—

That thém | peróur ‖ — óf | his grét | noblésse ‖

Again, l. 621 below may be read in a similar manner:—

But ná | thelés ‖ — thér | was grét | moorníng ‖

l. 253. 'So, when Ethelbert married Bertha, daughter of the Christian King Charibert, she brought with her, to the court of her husband, a Gallican bishop named Leudhard, who was permitted to celebrate mass in the ancient British Church of **St. Martin**, at Canterbury.' Note in Bell's Chaucer.

l. 255. *Ynow*, being plural, may take a final *e*; we should then read *th'ende*, as explained in note to l. 145. The pl. *inoȝhe* occurs in the **Ormulum**.

l. 263. *Alle and some*, collectively and individually; one and all. See Cler. Tale, E. 941.

l. 277. The word *alle*, being plural, is dissyllabic. *Thing* is often a plural form, being an A.S. neuter noun. The words *ouer, euer, neuer* are, in Chaucer, generally monosyllables, or nearly so; just as *o'er, e'er, ne'er* are treated as monosyllables by our poets in general. Hence the scansion is—'O'er al | le thing | ,' &c.

l. 289. The word *at* is inserted from the Cambridge MS.; all the

other six MSS. omit it, which makes the passage one of extreme
difficulty. Tyrwhitt reads 'Or Ylion brent, or Thebes the citee.' Of
course he means *brende*, past tense, not *brent*, the past participle; and
his conjecture amounts to inserting *or* before Thebes. It is better to
insert *at*, as proposed by Mr. Gilman. The sense is—'When Pyrrhus
broke the wall, before Ilium burnt, (nor) at the city of Thebes, nor
at Rome,' &c. Tyrwhitt well observes that 'Thebes the citee' is a
French phrase. He quotes 'dedans Renes *la cite*,' Froissart, v. i.
c. 225. Chaucer regarded Ilium as the *citadel* of Troy.

1. 295. In the margin of the Ellesmere MS. is written—'Vnde Ptholo-
meus, libro i. cap. 8. Primi motus celi duo sunt, quorum vnus est qui
mouet totum semper ab Oriente in Occidentem vno modo super orbes,
&c. Item aliter vero motus est qui mouet orbem stellarum currencium
contra motum primum, videlicet, ab Occidente in Orientem super alios
duos polos.' The old astronomy imagined nine spheres revolving round
the central stationary earth ; of the seven innermost, each carried with it
one of the seven planets, viz the Moon, Venus. Mercury, Sun, Mars,
Jupiter, and Saturn ; the eighth sphere, that of the fixed stars, had a
slow motion from west to east, to account for the precession of the
equinoxes, whilst the ninth or outermost sphere, called the *primum
mobile,* or the sphere of first motion, had a diurnal revolution from east
to west, carrying everything with it. This exactly corresponds with
Chaucer's language. He addresses the outermost sphere or *primum
mobile* (which is the *ninth* if reckoning from within, but the *first* from
without), and accuses it of carrying with it everything in its irresistible
westward motion ; a motion contrary to that of the 'natural' motion,
viz. that in which the sun advances along the signs of the zodiac. The
result was that the evil influence of the planet Mars prevented the
marriage. It is clear that Chaucer was thinking of certain passages
in Boethius, as will appear from consulting his own translation of
Boethius, ed. Morris, pp. 21, 22, 106, and 110. I quote a few lines
to shew this :—

'O þou maker of þe whele þat bereþ þe sterres, whiche þat art fastned
to þi perdurable chayere, and turnest þe heuene wiþ a rauyssyng *sweighe*,
and constreinest þe sterres to suffren þi lawe ;' pp. 21, 22.

' þe regioun of þe fire þat eschaufiþ by þe swifte *moeuyng of þe firmament* ;' p. 110.

The original is—

> 'O stelliferi conditor orbis
> Qui perpetuo nixus solio
> *Rapidum cœlum turbine uersas,*
> Legemque pati sidera cogis;'
>
> Boeth. Cons. Phil. lib. i. met. 5.
> 'Quique *agili motu* calet *ætheris* ;' id. lib. iv. met. 1.

Compare also the following passage :—

> 'The earth, in roundness of a perfect ball,
> Which as a point but of this mighty all
> Wise Nature fixed, that permanent doth stay,
> Wheras the spheres by a *diurnal* sway
> Of the first Mover carried are about.'

Drayton : The Man in the Moon.

l. 299. *Crowding*, pushing. This is still a familiar word in East Anglia. Forby, in his Glossary of the East Anglian Dialect, says— '*Crowd*, v. to push, shove, or press close. To the word, in its *common* acceptation, *number* seems necessary. With us, *one* individual can *crowd* another.' To *crowd* a wheelbarrow means to push it. The expression '*crod* in a barwe,' i.e. wheeled or pushed along in a wheelbarrow, occurs in the Paston Letters, A.D. 1477, ed. Gairdner, iii. 215.

l. 302. A planet is said to ascend directly, when in a direct sign ; but tortuously, when in a tortuous sign. The tortuous signs are those which ascend most obliquely to the horizon, viz. the signs from Capricornus to Gemini inclusive. Chaucer tells us this *himself* ; see his Treatise on the Astrolabe, ed. Skeat, part ii. sect. 28. The most 'tortuous' of these are the two middle ones, Pisces and Aries. Of these two, Aries is called the mansion of Mars, and we may perhaps suppose the ascending sign to be Aries, the lord of which (Mars) is said to have fallen 'from his angle into the darkest house.' The words 'angle' and 'house' are used technically. The whole sphere was divided into twelve equal parts, or 'houses.' Of these, four were termed 'angles,' four others 'succedents,' and the rest 'cadents.' It appears that Mars was not then situate in an 'angle' or lucky 'house,' but in the unluckiest or 'darkest' house ; this was generally considered to be the eighth, or, in the present case, Scorpio. And Mars in Scorpio portended great disaster.

l. 305. The meaning of *Atazir* has long remained undiscovered. But by the kind help of Mr. Bensly, one of the sub-librarians of the Cambridge University Library, I am enabled to explain it. *Atazir* or *atacir* is the Spanish spelling of the Arabic *al-tasir*, influence, given at p. 351 of Richardson's Pers. Dict., ed. 1829. It is a noun derived from *asara*, a verb of the second conjugation, meaning to leave a mark on, from the substantive *asar*, a mark ; the latter substantive is given at p. 20 of the same work. Its use in astrology is commented upon by Dozy, who gives it in the form *atacir*, in his Glossaire des Mots Espagnols dérivés de l'Arabique, p. 207. It signifies the *influence* of a star or planet upon other stars, or upon the fortunes of men. In the present case it is clearly used in a bad sense ; we may therefore translate it by 'evil influence.' On this common deterioration in the meaning of words, see Trench, Study of Words, p. 52. The word *craft*, for example, is a very similar instance ; it originally meant *skill*, and hence, a trade, and we find *star-craft* used in particular to signify the science of astronomy.

l. 307. 'Thou art in conjunction in an unfavourable position; from the position in which thou wast favourably placed thou art moved away.'

l. 312. 'Is there no choice as to when to fix the voyage?' The favourable moment for commencing a voyage was one of the points on which it was considered desirable to have an astrologer's opinion. Travelling, at that time, was a serious matter. Yet this was only one of the many undertakings which required, as was thought, to be begun at a favourable moment. Whole books were written on 'elections,' i.e. favourable times for commencing operations of all kinds. Chaucer was thinking, in particular, of the following passage, which is written in the margins of the Ellesmere and Hengwrt MSS. 'Omnes concordati sunt quod elecciones sint debiles nisi in diuitibus: habent enim isti, licet debilitentur eorum elecciones, radicem, i. [*id est*] natiuitates eorum, que confortat omnem planetam debilem in itinere.' The sense of which is—'For all are agreed, that "elections" are weak, except in the case of the rich; for these, although their elections be weakened, have a "root" of their own, that is to say, their nativities (*or* horoscopes); which root strengthens every planet that is of weak influence with respect to a journey.' This is extracted, says Tyrwhitt, from a Liber Electionum by a certain Zael; see MS. Harl. 80; MS. Bodley 1648. This is a very fair example of the jargon to be found in old books on astrology. The old astrologers used to alter their predictions almost at pleasure, by stating that their results depended on several causes, which partly counteracted one another; an arrangement of which the convenience is obvious. Thus, if the aspect of the planets at the time inquired about appeared to be adverse to a journey, it might still be the case (they said) that such evil aspect might be overcome by the fortunate aspect of the inquirer's horoscope; or, conversely, an ill aspect in the horoscope could be counteracted by a fit election of a time for action. A rich man would probably be fitted with a fortunate horoscope, or else why should he buy one? Such horoscope depended on the aspect of the heavens at the time of birth or 'nativity,' and, in particular, upon the 'ascendant' at that time; i.e. upon the planets lying nearest to the point of the zodiac which happened, at that moment, to be *ascending*, i.e. just appearing above the horizon. So Chaucer, in his Treatise on the Astrolabe, ed. Skeat, bk. ii. § 4, explains the matter, saying—'The assendent sothly, as wel in alle natiuitez as in questiouns and *elecciouns of tymes*, is a thing which þat thise Astrologiens gretly obseruen;' &c. The curious reader may find much more to the same effect in the same Treatise, with directions to 'make roots' in pt. ii. § 44.

The curious may further consult the Epitome Astrologiæ of Johannes Hispalensis. The whole of Book iv. of that work is 'De Electionibus,' and the title of **cap. xv. is** 'Pro Itinere.'   **See Chaucer's** Astrolabe, ed. Skeat, pref. p. liv.

Lydgate, in his Siege of Thebes, just at the beginning, describes the astronomers as casting the horoscope of the infant Œdipus. They were expected

> 'to yeue a judgement,
> The roote i-take at the ascendent,
> Truly sought out, by minute and degre,
> The selfe houre of his natiuite,
> Not foryet the heauenly mansions
> Clerely searched by smale fraccions,' &c.

To take a different example, Ashmole, in his Theatrum Chemicum, 1652, says in a note on p. 450—' Generally in all Elections the Efficacy of the Starrs are (*sic*) used, as it were by a certaine application made thereof to those unformed Natures that are to be wrought upon; whereby to further the working thereof, and make them more available to our purpose. . . . . . And by such Elections as good use may be made of the Celestiall influences, as a Physitian doth of the variety of herbes. . . . . . . But Nativities are the Radices of Elections, and therefore we ought chiefly to looke backe upon them as the principal Root and Foundation of all Operations; and next to them the quality of theThing we intend to fit must be respected, so that, by an apt position of Heaven, and fortifying the Planets and Houses in the Nativity of the Operator, and making them agree with the thing signified, the impression made by that influence will abundantly augment the Operation,' &c. ; with much more to the same effect. Several passages in Norton's Ordinall, printed in the same volume (see pp. 60, 100), shew clearly what is meant by Chaucer in his Prologue, ll. 415–7. The Doctor could ' fortune a person's ascendent,' i.e. render his horoscope lucky, by the election of a time, *suitable to that horoscope*, when the prescribed remedies were to be applied.

l. 314. *Roote* is the astrological term for the epoch from which to reckon. The exact moment of a nativity being known, the astrologers were supposed to be able to calculate everything else. See the last note.

l. 332. *Alkaron*, the Koran ; *al* is the Arabic article.

l. 333. Here *Makomete* is used instead of *Mahoun* (l. 224). See Irving's Life of Mahomet.

Message, messenger. This is a correct form, according to the usages of Middle English ; cf. l. 144. In like manner, we find *prison* used to mean a *prisoner*, which is often puzzling at first sight.

l. 340. 'Because we denied Mahomet, our (object of) belief.'

l. 360. 'O serpent under the form of woman, like that Serpent that is bound in hell.' The allusion here is not a little curious. It clearly refers to the old belief that the serpent who tempted Eve appeared to her *with a woman's head*, and it is sometimes so represented. I observed it, for instance, in the chapter-house of Salisbury Cathedral; and see the woodcut at p. 73 of Wright's History of Caricature and Grotesque in Art. In Peter Comestor's Historia Libri Genesis, we read of Satan—'Elegit etiam quoddam genus serpentis (vt ait Beda) *virgineum vultum* habens.' In the alliterative Troy Book, ed. Panton and Donaldson, p. 144, the Tempter is called Lyuyaton (i. e. Leviathan), and it is said of him that he

'Hade a face vne fourmet *as a fre maydon*;' l. 4451.

And, again, in Piers the Plowman, B. xviii. 355, Satan is compared to a 'lusarde [lizard] *with a lady visage*.' In the Ancren Riwle, p. 207, we are gravely informed that a scorpion is a kind of serpent that has a face somewhat like that of a woman, and puts on a pleasant countenance. To remember this gives peculiar force to ll. 370, 371.

l. 367. *Knowestow* is probably a trisyllable; and *the olde* to be read *tholdè*. But in l. 371, the word *Makestow*, being differently placed in the line, is to be read with the *e* slurred over, almost a dissyllable.

l. 380. *Moste*, might. It is not always used like the modern *must*.

l. 421. See Lucan's Pharsalia.

l. 404. There are undoubtedly a few lines in Chaucer, in which the first foot consists of one syllable only; this is one of them, the word *But* standing by itself as a foot. So also in B. 497, G. 341, &c. See Ellis's Early English Pronunciation, pp. 333, 649. This peculiarity was pointed out by me in 1866, in the Aldine edition of Chaucer, i. 174. For the sense of *scorpion*, see the extract from the Ancren Riwle, in note to l. 360. So also *wikked gost* means the Evil Spirit, the Tempter.

l. 421. Pronounce *euer* rapidly, and accent *successour* on the first syllable. In the margin of MSS. E., Hn., Pt., and Cp. is the following note: 'Nota, de inopinato dolore. Semper mundane leticie tristicia repentina succedit. Mundana igitur felicitas multis amaritudinibus est respersa. Extrema gaudii luctus occupat. Audi ergo salubre consilium; in die bonorum ne immemor sis malorum.' These maxims seem to be scraps taken from different authors. I have found one of them in Boethius, De Consolatione Philosophiæ, lib. ii. pr. 4—'Quam multis amaritudinibus humanæ felicitatis dulcedo respersa est;' which Chaucer translated by—'þe swetnesse of mannes wellfulnesse is y-spranid wiþ manye *bitternesses*;' ed. Morris, p. 42: and the same expression is repeated here, in l. 422. Gower quotes the same passage from Boethius in the prologue to his Confessio Amantis. The next sentence is from Prov. xiv. 13—'Risus dolore miscebitur, et *extrema gaudii luctus occupat*.' With the last clause, in ll. 426. 427, compare Eccl. xi. 8.

l. 438. Compare Trivet's French prose version:—'Dount ele fist estoriez vne neef de vitaile, de payn quest apele bisquit, & de peis, & de feues, de sucre, & de meel, & de vyn, pur sustenaunce de la vie de la pucele pur

treis aunz ; e en cele neef fit mettre la richesse & le tresour que lempirə
Tiberie auoit maunde oue la pucele Constaunce, sa fille ; e en cele neef
fist la soudane mettre la pucele saunz sigle, & sauntz neuiroun, & sauntz
chescune maner de eide de homme.' I.e. 'Then she caused a ship to be
stored with victuals, with bread that is called biscuit, with peas, beans,
sugar, honey, and wine, to sustain the maiden's life for three years. And
in this ship she caused to be placed the riches and treasure which the
Emperor Tiberius had sent with the maid Constance his daughter ; and
in this ship the Sultaness caused the maiden to be put, without sail or
oar, or any kind of human aid.'

Foot-hot, hastily. It occurs in Gower, in The Romaunt of the Rose,
l. 3827, and in Barbour's Bruce. iii. 418, xiii. 454. Compare the term *hot-
trod*, explained by Sir W. Scott to mean the pursuit of marauders with
bloodhounds ; see note 3 H to the Lay of the Last Minstrel. We also find
hot fot, i.e. immediately, in the Debate of the Body and the Soul, l. 481.

ll. 451–462. Compare these lines with verses 3 and 5 of the hymn
'Lustra sex qui iam peregit' in the office of Lauds from Passion
Sunday to Wednesday in Holy Week inclusive, in the Roman breviary.

'Crux fidelis, inter omnes
Arbor una nobilis :
Silua talem nulla profert
Fronde, flore, germine :
Dulce ferrum, dulce lignum,
Dulce pondus sustinent. . . . . .

Sola digna tu fuisti
Ferre mundi uictimam ;
Atque portum præparare,
Arca mundo naufrago,
Quam sacer cruor perunxit,
Fusus Agni corpore.'

See the translation in Hymns Ancient and Modern, No. 97, part 3
(new edition), beginning—' Now the thirty years accomplished.'

l. 460. *Hym and here*, him and her, i.e. man and woman ; as in Piers
the Plowman, A. Pass. i. l. 100. The allusion is to the supposed power
of the cross over evil spirits. See The Legends of the Holy Rood, ed.
Morris ; especially the story of the Invention of the Cross by St. Helen,
p. 160—'And anone, as he had made the [sign of the] crosse, þe grete
multitude of deuylles vanyshed awaye ;' or, in the Latin original,
'statimque ut edidit signum crucis, omnis illa daemonum multitudo
euanuit ;' Aurea Legenda, ed. Grässe, 2nd ed. p. 311. Cf. Piers Plowman, B. xviii. 429-431.

l. 461. The reading of this line is certain, and must not be altered. But
it is impossible to *parse* the line without at once noticing that there is
a great difficulty in the construction. The best solution is obtained by

taking *which* in the sense of *whom*. A familiar example of this use of *which* for *who* occurs in the Lord's Prayer. See also Abbot's Shakespearian Grammar, Sect. 265. The construction is as follows—'O victorious tree, protection of true people, that alone wast worthy to bear the King of Heaven with His new wounds—the White Lamb that was hurt with the spear—O expeller of fiends out of both man and woman, on whom (i.e. the men and women on whom) thine arms faithfully spread out,' &c. *Lymes* means the arms of the cross, spread before a person to protect him.

l. 464. *See of Greece*, here put for the Mediterranean Sea.

l. 465. *Marrok*, Morocco; alluding to the Strait of Gibraltar; cf. l. 947.

l. 474. *Ther*, where; as usual.

l. 475. 'Was eaten by the lion ere he could escape.' Cf. l. 437.

l. 491. See Revelation vii. 1-3.

l. 497. Here *As* seems to form a foot by itself. See note to l. 404.

l. 500. Alluding to St. Mary the Egyptian (*Maria Egiptiaca*), who, according to the legend, after a youth spent in debauchery, lived entirely alone for the last forty-seven years of her life in the wilderness beyond the Jordan. She lived in the fifth century. Her day is April 9. See Mrs. Jameson's Sacred and Legendary Art; Rutebuef, ed. Jubinal, ii. 106-150; Maundeville's Travels, ed. Halliwell, p. 96; Aurea Legenda, ed. Grässe, cap. lvi. She was often confused with St. Mary Magdalen.

l. 508. *Northumberlond*, the district, not the county. Yorkshire is, in fact, meant, as the French version expressly mentions the Humber.

l. 510. *Of al a tyde*, for the whole of an hour.

l. 512. *The constable*: named *Elda* by Trivet and Gower.

l. 519. Trivet says that she answered Elda in his own language, 'en sessoneys,' in Saxon, for she had learnt many languages in her youth.

l. 525. The word *deye* seems to have had two pronunciations; in l. 644 it is *dye*, with a different rime. In fact, Mr. Cromie's 'Ryme-Index' to Chaucer proves the point. On the one hand *deye* rimes to *aweye*, *disobeye, dreye, preye, seye, tweye, weye;* and on the other *dye* rimes to *avoutrye, bigamye, compaignye, Emelye, genterye, lye, maladye,* &c.

l. 527. *Forgat hir mynde*, lost her memory.

l. 531. The final *e* in *plese* is preserved from elision by the cæsural pause. Or, we may read *plesen;* yet the MSS. have *plese.*

l. 578. *Alla*, i.e. Ælla, king of Northumberland, A.D. 560-567; the same whose name Gregory (afterwards Pope) turned, by a pun, into Alleluia, according to the version of the celebrated story about Gregory and the English slaves, as given in Beda, Eccl. Hist. b. ii. c. 1.

l. 584. *Quyte her whyle*, repay her time; i.e. her pains, trouble; as when we say 'it is worth *while*.' *Wile* is *not* intended.

l. 585. 'The plot of the knight against Constance, and also her subsequent adventure with the steward, are both to be found, with some variations, in a story in the Gesta Romanorum, ch. 101; MS. Harl.

2270. Occleve has versified the whole story;' Tyrwhitt. See the Preface for further information. Compare the conduct of Iachimo, in Cymbeline.

l. 620. *Berth hir on hond,* affirms falsely; lit. bears her in hand. Chaucer uses the phrase 'to bere in hond' with the sense of false affirmation, sometimes with the idea of accusing falsely, as here and in the Wyf of Bathes Prologue. C. T. 5975; and sometimes with that of persuading falsely, C. T. 5814, 5962. In Shakespeare the sense is rather—'to keep in expectation, to amuse with false pretences;' Nares's Glossary. Barbour uses it in the more general sense of 'to affirm,' or 'to make a statement,' whether falsely or truly.

l. 634. 'And bound Satan; and he still lies where he (then) lay.' In the Apocryphal Gospel of Nicodemus, Christ descends into hell, and (according to some versions) binds him with chains; see Piers Plowman, B. xviii. 401.

l. 639. *Susanne;* see the story of Susannah, in the Apocrypha.

l. 641. The Virgin's mother is called Anna in the Apocryphal Gospel of James. Her day is July 26. See Aurea Legenda, ed. Grässe, cap. cxxxi; Cowper's Apocryphal Gospels, p. 4.

l. 645. Here *pale* is pronounced as a dissyllable.

l. 647. 'Where that he gat (could get) for himself no favour.'

l. 660. 'For pite renneth sone in gentil herte;' Knightes Tale, l. 903. And see note to Sq. Tale, F. 479.

l. 664. *Vs auyse,* deliberate with ourselves, consider the matter again. Compare the law-phrase *Le roi s'avisera,* by which the king refuses assent to a measure proposed. 'We will consider whom to appoint as judge.'

l. 666. I.e. a copy of the Gospels in Welsh or British, called in the French prose version 'liure des Ewangeiles.' Agreements were sometimes written on the fly-leaves of copies of the Gospels, as may be seen in two copies of the A.S. version of them.

l. 669. A very similar miracle is recorded in the old alliterative romance of Joseph of Arimathea, l. 362. The French version has :—'a peine auoit fini la parole, qe vne mayn close, com poyn de homme. apparut deuant Elda et quant questoient en presence, et ferri tiel coup en le haterel le feloun, que ambedeus lez eus lui enuolerent de la teste, & les dentz hors de la bouche; & le feloun chai abatu a la terre; et a ceo dist vne voiz en le oyance de touz: Aduersus filiam matris ecclesie ponebas scandalum; hec fecisti, et tacui.' I.e. 'Scarcely had he ended the word, when a closed hand, like a man's fist, appeared before Elda and all who were in the presence, and smote such a blow on the nape of the felon's neck that both his eyes flew out of his head, and the teeth out of his mouth; and the felon fell smitten down to the earth; and thereupon a voice said in the hearing of all, "Against the daughter of Mother Church thou wast laying a scandal; this hast thou done, and I held my peace."' The reading *tacui* suggests that, in l. 676, the word *holde* should rather be *held ;* but the MSS. do not recognise this reading.

l. 697. *Hir thoughte*, it seemed to her ; *thoughte* is here impersonal ; so in l. 699. The French text adds that Domulde (Donegild) was, moreover, jealous of hearing the praises of Constance's beauty.

l. 701. *Me list nat*, it pleases me not, I do not wish to. He does not wish to give every detail. In this matter Chaucer is often very judicious ; Gower and others often give the more unimportant matters as fully as the rest. Cf. l. 706 ; and see Squyeres Tale, F. 401.

l. 703. *What*, why. Cf. Squyeres Tale, F. 283, 298.

l. 707. Trivet says—' Puis a vn demy aan passe, vint nouele al Roy que les gentz de Albanie, qe sountz les Escotz, furent passes lour boundes et guerrirent les terres le Roy. Dount par comun counseil, le Roi assembla son ost de rebouter ses enemis. Et auant son departir vers Escoce, baila la Reine Constaunce sa femme en la garde Elda, le Conestable du chastel, et a Lucius, leuesqe de Bangor ; si lour chargea qe quant ele fut deliueres denfaunt, qui lui feisoient hastiuement sauoir la nouele ;' i.e. 'Then, after half-a-year, news came to the king that the people of Albania, who are the Scots, had passed their bounds, and warred on the king's lands. Then by common counsel the king gathered his host to rebut his foes. And before his departure towards Scotland, he committed Queen Constance his wife to the keeping of Elda, the constable of the castle, and of Lucius, bishop of Bangor, and charged them that when she was delivered, they should hastily let him know the news.'

l. 722. *Knaue child*, male child ; as in Clerkes Tale, E. 444.

l. 723. *At the fontstoon*, i.e. at his baptism ; French text—' al baptisme su nome Moris.'

l. 729. *To don his auantage*, to suit his convenience. He hoped, by going only a little out of his way, to tell Donegild the news also, and to receive a reward for doing so. Trivet says that the old Queen was then at Knaresborough, situated ' between England and Scotland, as in an intermediate place.' Its exact site is less than seventeen miles west of York. Donegild pretends to be very pleased at the news, and gives the man a rich present.

l. 736. *Lettres ;* so in all 7 MSS. ; Tyrwhitt reads *lettre*. But it is right as it is. *Lettres* is sometimes used, like Lat. *literæ*, in a singular sense, and the French text has 'les lettres.' Examples occur in Piers Plowman, B. ix. 38 ; Bruce, ii. 80. See l. 744, and note to l. 747.

l. 738. *If ye wol ought*, if you wish (to say) anything.

l. 740. *Donegild* is dissyllabic here, as in l. 695, but in l. 805 it appears to have three syllables. I have before remarked that Chaucer alters proper names so as to suit his metre ; see Pref. to Prioresses Tale, p. lxiii. l. 13, or p. lxiv. l. 12 (2nd ed.).

l. 743. *Sadly*, steadily, with the idea of long continuance.

l. 747. *Le'tre*; here the singular form is used, but it is a matter of indifference. Exactly the same variation occurs in Barbour's Bruce, ii. 80:—

> 'And, among othir, *lettres* ar gayn
> To the byschop off Androwis towne,
> That tauld how slayn wes that baroun.
> The *lettir* tauld hym all the deid,' &c.

This circumstance, of exchanging the messenger's letters for forged ones, is found in Matthew Paris's account of the Life of Offa the first; ed. Wats, pp. 965–968. See the Preface.

l. 748. *Direct*, directed, addressed ; French text 'maundez.'

l. 751. Pronounce *horrible* as in French.

l. 752. The last word in this line should certainly be *nas* (= was not), as has kindly been pointed out to me ; though the seven MSS. all have *was*. By this alteration we secure a true rime.

l. 754. *Elf*; French text—' ele fu malueise espirit en fourme de femme,' she was an evil spirit in form of woman. *Elf* is the A.S. *ælf*, Icel. *álfr*, G. *alp* and *elfe*; Shakespeare writes *ouphes* for *elves*. 'The Edda distinguishes between Ljósálfar, the elves of light, and Dökkálfar, elves of darkness; the latter are not elsewhere mentioned either in modern fairy tales or in old writers. ... In the Alvismál, elves and dwarfs are clearly distinguished as different. The abode of the elves in the Edda is 'Alfheimar, fairy land, and their king the god Frey, the god of light. In the fairy tales the Elves haunt the hills ; hence their name Huldufólk, hidden people ; respecting their origin, life, and customs, see Íslenzkar þjóðsögur, i. 1. In old writers the Elves are rarely mentioned ; but that the same tales were told as at present is clear ;' note on the word *álfr*, in Cleasby and Vigfusson's Icelandic Dictionary. See also Keight ley's Fairy Mythology, and Brand's Popular Antiquities. The word is here used in a bad sense, and is nearly equivalent to witch. In the Prompt. Parv. we find—' Elfe, spryte. *Lamia*;' and Mr. Way notes that these elves were often supposed to bewitch children, and to use them cruelly.

l. 767. Pronounce *agreable* as in French, and with an accent on the first syllable.

l. 769. *Take*, handed over, delivered. *Take* often means to give or hand over in Middle English : very seldom to convey or bring.

l. 771. In the margin of MSS. E., Hn., Cp., and Pt. is written—' Quid turpius ebrioso, cui fetor in ore, tremor in corpore, qui promit stulta, prodit occulta, cuius mens alienatur, facies transformatur ? nullum enim latet secretum ubi regnat ebrietas.' This is no doubt the original of the stanza, ll. 771–777; cf note to C. 561. There is nothing answering to it in Trivet.

l. 778. 'O Donegild, I have no language fit to tell,' &c.

l. 782. *Mannish*, man-like, i.e. harsh and cruel, not mild and gentle like a woman. But Chaucer is not satisfied with the epithet, and says he ought rather to call her ' fiend-like.'

l. 789. 'He stowed away plenty (of wine) under his girdle,' i.e. drank his fill.

l. 794. Pronounce *coustábl'* much as if it were French, with an accent on *a*. In l. 808 the accent is on *o*. Lastly, in l. 858 all three syllables are fully sounded.

l. 798. 'Three days and a quarter of an hour;' i.e. she was to be allowed only three days, and after that to start off as soon as possible. *Tide* (like *tið* in Icelandic) sometimes means an hour. The French text says—'deynz quatre iours,' within four days.

l. 801. *Croude*, push; see ll. 296, 299 above.

ll. 813-826. Lines 813-819 are not in the French, and ll. 820-826 are not at all close to the original.

ll. 827-833. The French text only has—'en esperaunce qe dure comencement amenera dieu a bon fyn, et qil me purra en la mere sauuer, qi en mere et en terre est de toute puissaunce.'

l. 835. The beautiful stanzas in ll. 834-868 are all Chaucer's own; and of the next stanza, ll. 869-875, the French text gives but the merest hint.

l. 842. *Eggement*, incitement. The same word is used in other descriptions of the Fall. Thus, in Piers Plowman, B. i. 65, it is said of Satan that 'Adam and Eue he *egged* to ille;' and in Allit. Poems, ed. Morris, B. 241, it is said of Adam that 'thurgh the *eggyng* of Eue he ete of an apple.'

l. 859. *As lat*, pray, let. See note to Clerkes Prologue, E. 7.

l. 873. *Purchace*, provide, make provision. So in Troilus, bk. ii. 1125, the line 'And of some goodly answer yon purchace' means—and provide yourself with some kind answer, i.e. be ready with a kind reply.

ll. 875-884. Much abridged from the French text.

l. 885. *Tormented*, tortured. However, the French text says the messenger acknowledged his drunkenness freely. Examination by torture was so common, that Chaucer seems to have regarded the mention of it as being the most simple way of telling the story.

l. 893. *Out of drede*, without doubt, certainly; cf. l. 869. The other equally common expression *out of doute* comes to much the same thing, because *doute* in Middle-English has in general the meaning of *fear* or *dread*, not of hesitation. See Group E. 634, 1155; and Prol. 487.

l. 894. *Pleynly rede*, fully read, read at length. In fact, Chaucer judiciously omits the details of the French text, where we read that King Ælla rushed into his mother's room with a drawn sword as she lay asleep, roused her by crying 'traitress!' in a loud voice, and, after hearing the full confession which she made in the extremity of her terror, slew her and cut her to pieces as she lay in bed.

l. 901. *Fleteth*, floats. French text—'le quinte an de cest exil, come ele fu *flotaunt* sur le mere,' &c.

l. 905. The name of the castle is certainly not given in the French text, which merely says it was ' vn chastel dun Admiral de paens,' i.e. a castle of an admiral of the Pagans.

l. 912. *Gauren*, gaze, stare. See note to Squ. Tale, F. 190.

l. 913. *Shortly*, briefly ; because the poet considerably abridges this part of the narrative. The steward's name was Thelous.

ll. 932–945. These two stanzas are wholly Chaucer's, plainly written as a parallel passage to that in ll. 470-504 above.

l. 934. *Golias*, Goliath. See 1 Samuel xvii. 25.

l. 940. See the story of Holofernes in the Monkes Tale, B. 3741 ; and the note. I select the spelling *Olofernus* here, because it is that of the majority of the MSS., and agrees with the title *De Oloferno* in the Monkes Tale.

l. 947. In l. 465 Chaucer mentions the 'Strait of Marrok,' i.e. Morocco, though there is no mention of it in the French text ; so here he alludes to it again, but by a different name, viz. ' the mouth of Jubalter and Septe.' *Jubaltar* (Gibraltar) is from the Arabic *jabâlu't târik*, i.e. the mountain of Tarik ; who was the leader of a band of Saracens that made a descent upon Spain in the eighth century. *Septe* is Ceuta, on the opposite coast of Africa.

l. 965. *Shortly*, briefly ; because Chaucer here again abridges the original, which relates how the Romans burnt the Sultaness, and slew more than 11,000 of the Saracens, without a single death or even wound on their own side.

l. 967. *Senatour.* His name was Arsemius of Cappadocia ; his wife's name was Helen. Accent *victorie* on the o.

l. 969. *As seith the storie*, as the history says. The French text relates this circumstance fully.

l. 971. The French text says that, though Arsemius did not recognise Constance, she, on her part, recognised him at once, though she did not reveal it.

l. 981. *Aunte.* Helen, the wife of Arsemius, was daughter of Sallustius, brother of the Emperor Tiberius, and Constance's uncle. Thus Helen was really Constance's first cousin. Chaucer may have altered it purposely ; but it looks as if he had glanced at the sentence—' Cest heleyne, la nece Constaunce, taunt tendrement ama sa nece,' &c., and had read it as—' This Helen. . . . loved her *niece* so tenderly.' In reality, the word *nece* means ' cousin ' here, being applied to Helen as well as to Constance.

l. 982. *She*, i.e. Helen ; for Constance knew Helen.

l. 991. *To receyuen*, i.e. to submit himself to any penance which the Pope might see fit to impose upon him. Journeys to Rome were actually made by English kings ; Ælfred was sent to Rome as a boy, and his father, Æthelwulf, also spent a year there, but (as the Chronicle tells us) he went 'mid micelre weorðnesse,' with much pomp.

l. 994. *Wikked werkes;* especially the murder of his mother, as Trivet says. See note to l. 894.

l. 999. *Rood him agayn,* rode towards him, rode to meet him; cf. l. 391. See Cler. Tale, E. 911, and the note.

l. 1009. *Som men wolde sayn,* some relate the story by saying. The expression occurs again in l. 1086. On the strength of it, Tyrwhitt concluded that Chaucer here refers to Gower, who tells the story of Constance in Book ii. of his Confessio Amantis. He observes that Gower's version of the story includes both the circumstances which are introduced by this expression. But this is not conclusive. It appears, rather, that Gower's version of the story is the later one of the two, and there is no reason why the expression *som men* may not refer to Nicholas Trivet, who also makes mention of these circumstances. See this further discussed in the Preface. In the present instance the French text has—'A ceo temps de la venuz le Roi a Rome, comensca Moris son diseotisme aan. Cist estoit *apris priuement de sa mere Constance, qe, quant il irreit a la feste ou son seignur le senatour,'* &c.; i.e. At this time of the king's coming to Rome, Maurice began his eighteenth year. *He was secretly instructed by his mother Constance, that, when he should go to the feast with his lord the senator,* &c. See also the note to l. 1086 below.

l. 1014. *Metes space,* time of eating. This circumstance strikingly resembles the story of young Roland, who, whilst still a child, was instructed by his mother Bertha to appear before his uncle Charlemagne, by way of introducing himself. The story is well told in Uhland's ballad entitled 'Klein Roland,' a translation of which is given at pp. 335-340 of my 'Ballads and Songs of Uhland.'

> 'They had but waited a little while,
>   When Roland returns more bold;
> With hasty step to the king he comes,
>   And seizes his cup of gold.
> "What ho, there! stop! you saucy imp!"
>   Are the words that loudly ring.
> But Roland clutches the beaker still
>   With eyes fast fixed on the king.
> The king at the first looked fierce and dark,
>   But soon perforce he smiled—
> "Thou comest,' he said, "into golden halls
>   As though they were woodlands wild,"' &c.

The result is also similar; Bertha is reconciled to Charlemagne, much as Custance is to Ælla.

l. 1034. *Aught,* in any way, at all ; lit. 'a whit.'

l. 1035. *Syghte,* sighed. So also *pyghte,* 'pitched;' *plyghte,* 'plucked;' and *shryghte,* 'shrieked.' It occurs again in the Romaunt of the Rose, l. 1746 :—

'Than **took** I with myn hondes tweye
The arwe, **and** ful faste it out *flyghte*,
And in the pulling sore I *syghte*.'

l. 1036. *That he myghte*, as fast as he could.

l. 1038. 'I ought to suppose, in accordance with reasonable opinion.'
Chaucer tells the story quite in his own way. There is no trace of
ll. 1038-1042 in the French, and scarcely any of ll. 1048-1071, which is
all in his own excellent strain.

l. 1056. *Shet*, shut, closed. Compare the description of Griselda in
the Clerkes Tale, E. 1058-1061.

l. 1058. Both *twyes* and *owen* are dissyllabic.

l. 1060. *Alle his halwes*, all His saints. Hence the term All-hallow-
mas, i.e. All Saints' day.

l. 1061. *Wisly*, certainly. **As haue**, I pray that he may have; see
note to l. 859 above. 'I pray He may so surely have mercy on my
soul, as that I am as innocent of your suffering as Maurice my son is
like you in the face.'

l. 1078. After this line, **the** French text tells us that King Ælla
presented himself before Pope Pelagius, who absolved him for the death
of his mother.

l. 1086. Here again Tyrwhitt supposes Chaucer to follow Gower.
But, in fact, Chaucer and Gower both consulted Trivet, who says
here—'Constaunce charga son fitz Morice del messager [or message]
.... Et puis, quant Morice estoit deuaunt lempereur venuz, oue la
compaignie honurable, et auoit son message fest de part le Roi son
pere,' &c.; i.e. 'Constance charged her son Maurice with the message
.... and then, when Maurice was come before the emperor, with the
honourable company, and had done his message on behalf of the king
his father,' &c.

l. 1090. *As he;* used much as we should now use 'as one.' It refers
to the Emperor, of course.

l. 1091. *Sente*, elliptical for 'as that he would send.' Tyrwhitt reads
send; but it is best to leave an expression like this as it stands in the
MSS. It was probably a colloquial idiom ; and, in the next line, we have
wente. Observe that *sente* is in the subjunctive mood, and is equivalent
to 'he would send.'

l. 1107. Chaucer so frequently varies the length and accent of a proper
name that there is no objection to the supposition that we are here to
read *Cústancë* in three syllables, with an accent on the first syllable. In
exactly the **same** way, we find *Grisildis* in three syllables (E. 948),
though in most **other** passages it is *Grisild*. We have had *Cústance*,
accented on the first syllable, several times; see ll. 438, 556, 566,
576, &c.; also *Custáncë*, three syllables, ll. 184, 274, 319, 612, &c.

Perhaps it improves the line, but it is better to leave the text untouched.

l. 1109. *It am I;* it is I. It is the usual idiom. So in the A. S. version of St. John vi. 20, we find 'ic hyt eom,' i.e. I it am, and in a Dutch New Testament, A.D. 1700, I find 'Ick ben 't,' i.e. I am it. The Mœso-Gothic version omits *it,* having simply 'Ik im;' so does Wyclif's, which has 'I am.' Tyndale, A.D. 1526, has 'it ys I.'

l. 1113. *Thonketh,* pronounced *thonk'th;* so also *eyl'th,* B. 1171, *Abyd'th,* B. 1175: Prioresses Tale, &c. p. 6. So also *tak'th,* l. 1142 below. *Of,* for.

l. 1123. The French text tells us that he was named **Maurice** of Cappadocia, and was also known, in Latin, as *Mauritius Christianissimus Imperator.* Trivet tells us no more about him, except that he accounts for the title 'of Cappadocia' by saying that Arsemius (the senator who found Constance and Maurice and took care of them) was a Cappadocian. Gibbon says—'The Emperor Maurice derived his origin from ancient Rome; but his immediate parents were settled at Arabissus in Cappadocia, and their singular felicity preserved them alive to behold and partake the fortune of their august son. . . . . Maurice ascended the throne at the mature age of 43 years; and he reigned above 20 years over the east and over himself.' Decline and Fall of the Roman Empire, cap. xlv. He was murdered, with all his seven children, by his successor, Phocas the Usurper; Nov. 27, A.D. 602. His accession was in A.D. 582.

l. 1127. The statement 'I bere it not in mynde,' i.e. I do not remember it, may be taken to mean that Chaucer could find nothing about Maurice in his French text beyond the epithet *Christianissimus,* which he has skilfully expanded into l. 1123. He vaguely refers us to 'olde Romayn gestes,' that is, to lives of the Roman emperors, for he can hardly mean the *Gesta Romanorum* in this instance. In the Marchauntes Tale, where he really refers to the *Gesta,* he uses the definite article, and calls them '*the* Romain gestes;' C. T. 10158. Gibbon refers us to Evagrius, lib. v. and lib. vi.; Theophylact, Simocatta; Theophanes, Zonaras, and Cedrenus.

l. 1132. In the margin of MSS. E., Hn., Cp., Pt. is written—'A mane usque ad vesperam mutabitur tempus. Tenent tympanum et gaudent ad sonum organi, &c.'

l. 1135. In the margin of MSS. E., Hn., Cp., Pt. is written—'Quis vnquam vnicam diem totam duxit in sua dilectione [*vel* delectatione] iocundam? quem in aliqua parte diei reatus consciencie, vel impetus Ire, vel motus concupiscencie non turbauerit? quem liuor Inuidie, vel Ardor Auaricie, vel tumor **superbie non** vexauerit? quem aliqua inactura vel offensa, vel passio non commouerit, &c.' Cp. Pt. insert *inde* before *non turbauerit.* This corresponds to nothing in the French text, but is what Chaucer in l. 1139 calls 'a sentence,' i.e. a choice saying.

Innocent III

l. **1143.** *I gesse*, I suppose. Chaucer somewhat alters the story. Trivet says that Ælla died at the end of nine months after this. Half-a-year after, **Constance** repairs to Rome. Thirteen days after her arrival, her father Tiberius **dies.** A year later, Constance herself dies, on St. Clement's day (**Nov. 23**), A.D. 584, and is buried at Rome, near her father, in St. Peter's church. The date 584, here given by Trivet, should rather be 583; the death of Tiberius took place on Aug. 14, **582 ; see** Gibbon.

NOTES TO THE PARDONERES TALE (GROUP C).

The Words of the Host.

l. **287.** *Wood,* mad, frantic, furious; especially applied to the transient madness of anger. See Kn. Ta. 443, 471, 720; also Mids. Nt. Dream, ii. 1. 192. Cf. G. *wuthend,* raging.

l. **288.** *Harrow,* also spelt *haro,* a cry of astonishment; see Non. Prest. Tale, **225.** '*Haro,* the ancient Norman hue and cry; the exclamation of a person to procure assistance when his person or property was in danger. To cry out *haro* on any one, to denounce his evil doings;' Halliwell's Dictionary. Spenser has it, F. Q. ii. 6. 43; see *Harrow* in Kitchin's Gloss. to Spenser, bk. ii.

On the oaths used by the Host, see note to l. 651 below.

l. **289.** The Host is denouncing the decemvir Appius Claudius, whose false judgment had previously been described by the Doctor, in telling the story of Virginia.

l. **293.** 'She (Virginia) bought her **beauty** too dear;' she paid too high a price; it cost her her life.

l. **299.** *Bothe yiftes,* both (kinds of) gifts; i.e. gifts of fortune, such as wealth, and of nature, such as beauty. Compare Dr. Johnson's poem on The **Vanity** of Human Wishes, imitated from the tenth satire of Juvenal.

l. **302.** *Pitous,* piteous, pitiful. Such is the reading of all the seven best MSS. Tyrwhitt found the reading *erneful* in some MSS., which he correctly supposes to be bad spelling for *ermful,* miserable, from A.S. *earm,* wretched; see note to l. 312. The meaning, in fact, is the same.

l. **303.** *Is no fors,* it is no matter. Here *it* must be supplied, the full phrase being *it is no fors.* In some cases Chaucer not only omits *it,* but *is* also; writing simply *no fors,* as in Group E. 1092, 2430. We also find *I do no force,* i.e. I care not, C. T. 6816; and *They yeve no force,* they care not, Romaunt of the Rose, 4826. Palsgrave has—'I gyue no force, I care nat for a thyng. *Il ne men chault.*'

l. 306. *Ypocras* is the usual spelling, in English MSS., of *Hippocrates;* see Prologue, l. 431. So also in the Book of the Duchess, 571, 572:—

> 'Ne hele me may no physicien,
> Nought Ipocras, ne Galien.'

In the present passage it does not signify the physician himself, but a beverage named after him. 'It was composed of wine, with spices and sugar, strained through a cloth. It is said to have taken its name from *Hippocrates' sleeve,* the term apothecaries gave to a strainer;' Halliwell's Dict. s.v. *Hippocras.* In the same work, s.v. *Ipocras,* are several receipts for making it, the simplest being one copied from Arnold's Chronicle:—'Take a quart of red wyne, an ounce of synamon, and half an unce of gynger; a quarter of an ounce of greynes, and long peper, and halfe a pounde of sugar; and brose all this, and than put them in a bage of wullen clothe, made therefore, with the wyne; and lete it hange over a vessel, tyll the wyne be rune thorowe.' Halliwell adds that—'Ipocras seems to have been a great favourite with our ancestors, being served up at every entertainment, public or private. It generally made a part of the last course, and was taken immediately after dinner, with wafers or some other light biscuits;' &c. See Pegge's Form of Cury, p. 161; Babees Book, ed. Furnivall, pp. 125-128, 267; and Nares's Glossary, s.v. *Hippocras.*

Galianes. In like manner this word (hitherto unexplained as far as I am aware) must signify drinks named after Galen, whose name is spelt *Galien* (in Latin, *Galienus*) not only in Chaucer, but in other authors, as pointed out by Tyrwhitt. See the sixth line on this page.

l. 310. *Lyk a prelat,* like a dignitary of the church, like a bishop or abbot. Mr. Jephson, in Bell's edition, suggests that the Doctor was in holy orders, and that this is why we are told in the Prologue, l. 438, that 'his studie was but litel on the bible.' I see no reason for this guess, which is quite unsupported. Chaucer does not say he *is* a prelate, but that he is *like* one; because he had been highly educated, as a member of a 'learned profession' should be.

Ronyan is here of three syllables and rimes with *man;* in l. 320 it is of two syllables, and rimes with *anon.* It looks as if the Host and Pardoner were not very clear about the saint's name, only knowing him to swear by. In Pilkington's Works (Parker Society), we find a mention of 'St. Tronian's fast,' p. 80; and again, of 'St. Rinian's fast,' p. 551, in a passage which is a repetition of the former. The forms *Ronyan* and *Rinian* are evidently corruptions of *Ronan,* a saint whose name is well known to readers of 'St. Ronan's Well.' Of St. Ronan scarcely anything is known. The fullest account that can easily be found is the following:—

'Ronan, B. and C. Feb. 7.—Beyond the mere mention of his com memoration as S. Ronan, bishop at Kilmaronen, in Levenax, in the body of the Breviary of Aberdeen, there is nothing said about this saint. . . Camerarius (p. 86) makes this Ronanus the same as he who is mentioned by Beda (Hist. Ecc. lib. iii. c. 25). This Ronan died in A.D. 778. The Ulster annals give at [A.D.] 737 (736)—"Mors Ronain Abbatis Cinngaraid." Ængus places this saint at the 9th of February,' &c.; Kalendars of Scottish Saints, by Bp. A. P. Forbes, 1872, p. 441. Kilmaronen is Kilmaronock, in the county and parish of Dumbarton. There are traces of St. Ronan in about seven place-names in Scotland, according to the same authority. Under the date of Feb. 7 (February, vol. ii. 3 B), the Acta Sanctorum has a few lines about St. Ronan, who, according to some, flourished under King Malduin, A.D. 664-684; or according to others, about 603. The notice concludes with the remark —'Maiorem lucem desideramus.' Beda says that 'Ronan, a Scot by nation, but instructed in ecclesiastical truth either in France or Italy,' was mixed up in the controversy which arose about the keeping of Easter, and was 'a most zealous defender of the true Easter.' This controversy took place about A.D. 652, which does not agree with the date above.

l. 311. Tyrwhitt thinks that Shakespeare remembered this expression of Chaucer, when he describes the Host of the Garter as frequently repeating the phrase 'said I well:' Merry Wives of Windsor, i. 3. 11; ii. 1. 226; ii. 3. 93, 99.

In terme, in learned terms; cf. Prol 323.

l. 312. *Erme*, to grieve. For the explanation of unusual *words*, the Glossary should, in general, be consulted; the Notes are intended, for the most part, to explain only phrases and allusions, and to give illustrations of the use of words. Such illustrations are, moreover, often omitted when they can easily be found by consulting such a work as Stratmann's Old English Dictionary. In the present case, for example, Stratmann gives ten instances of the use of *earm* or *arm* as an adjective, meaning wretched; four examples of *ermlic*, miserable: four of *earming*, a miserable creature; and five of *earmthe*, misery. These twenty-three additional examples shew that the word was formerly well understood. It may be added, that a particular interest attaches to this word, in con- nection with Shakespeare. We may first note that a later instance of *ermen* or *erme*, to grieve, occurs in Caxton's translation of Reynard the Fox, A.D. 1481; see Arber's reprint p. 48, l. 5. 'Thenne departed he fro the kynge so heuyly that many of them *ermed*,' i. e. then departed he from the king so sorrowfully that many of them mourned, or were greatly grieved. Now it is my firm belief that this verb to *erme*, slightly corrupted to *erne*, is the source of the verb to *earn* in Shake- speare, which has been further obscured by being changed into *yearn* in

modern editions. Examples are (using the modern corrupt spelling) :
'It *yearns* me not when men my garments wear,' i. e. it grieves me not ;
Hen. V. iv. 3. 26. 'My manly heart doth *yearn*,' i.e. grieve ; Hen. V. ii.
3. 3. 'Falstaff he is dead, and we must *yearn* therefore ;' Hen. V. ii. 3. 6.
'That every like is not the same, O Cæsar, The heart of Brutus *yearns*
to think upon ;' Jul. Cæsar, ii. 2. 129. It is remarkable that Shakespeare *never* uses the verb to *yearn* in the modern sense ; he expresses
that idea solely by the verb to *long*, which he uses more than *sixty*
times. The prefixed *y*, found sometimes in old editions also, means no
more than the *y* in the prov. E. *yale* for *ale*. And cf. note to l. 302.

l. 314. The Host's form of oath is amusingly ignorant ; he is con-
fusing the two oaths ' by corpus Domini ' and ' by Christes bones,' and
evidently regards *corpus* as a genitive case. Tyrwhitt alters the phrase
to ' By corpus domini,' which wholly spoils the humour of it.

Triacle, a restorative remedy ; see Man of Lawes Tale, Group B,
l 479.

l. 315. *Moyste*, new. The word retains the sense of the Lat. *musteus*
and *mustus*. In Group II. 60 (see p. 116), we find *moysty ale* spoken of as
differing from *old ale*. But the most peculiar use of the word is in the
Prologue, l. 457, where the Wyf of Bath's shoes are described as being
moyste and newe.

l. 318. *Bel amy*, good friend ; a common form of address in old
French. We also find *biaus douz amis*, sweet good friend ; as in—

' Charlot, Charlot, *biaus doux amis* ;'

Rutebuef ; La Disputoison de Charlot et du Barbier, l. 57.
Belamy occurs in an Early Eng. Life of St. Cecilia, MS. Ashmole 43,
l. 161. Similar forms are *beau filtz*, dear son (Piers Plowman, B. vii.
162) ; *beau pere*, good father ; *beau sire*, good sir. Cf. *beldame*.

l. 321. *Ale-stake*, inn-sign. Speght interprets this by ' may-pole.' He
was probably thinking of the *ale-pole*, such as was sometimes set up
before an inn as a sign ; see the picture of one in Larwood and Hotten's
History of Signboards, Plate II. But the *ale-stakes* of the fourteenth
century were differently placed ; instead of being perpendicular, they
projected horizontally from the inn, just like the bar which supports
a painted sign at the present day. At the end of the ale-stake a large
garland was commonly suspended, as mentioned by Chaucer himself
(Prol. 667), or sometimes a bunch of ivy, box, or evergreen, called
a ' bush ;' whence the proverb ' good wine needs no *bush*,' i.e. nothing
to indicate where it is sold ; see Hist. Signboards, pp. 3, 4, 6, 233. The
clearest information about ale-stakes is obtained from a notice of them
in the Liber Albus, ed. Riley, where an ordinance of the time of Richard
II is printed, the translation of which runs as follows : 'Also, it was
ordained that whereas the *ale-stakes*, projecting in front of the taverns in
Chepe and elsewhere in the said city, extend too far over the king's

highways, to the impeding of riders and others. and, by reason of their excessive weight, to the great deterioration of the houses to which they are fixed, ... it was ordained, ... that no one in future should have a stake *bearing either his sign or leaves* [i.e. a bush] extending or lying over the King's highway. *of greater length than 7 feet at most,'* &c. And, at p. 292 of the same work, note 2, Mr. Riley rightly defines an *ale-stake* to be 'the pole projecting from the house, and supporting a bunch of leaves.'

The word *ale-stake* occurs in Chatterton's poem of Ælla. stanza 30, where it is used in a manner which shews that the supposed 'Rowley' did not know what it was like. See my note on this; Essay on the Rowley Poems, p. xix.

l. 322. *Of a cake*; we should now say, a bit of bread; the modern sense of 'cake' is a little misleading. The old cakes were mostly made of dough, whence the proverb 'my cake is dough,' i e. is not properly baked; Taming of the Shrew, v. 1. 145. Shakespeare also speaks of 'cakes and ale,' Tw. Nt. ii. 3. 124. The picture of the 'Simnel Cakes' in Chambers' Book of Days, i. 336, illustrates Chaucer's use of the word in the Prologue, l. 668.

l. 324. The Pardoner was so ready to tell some 'mirth or japes' that the more decent folks in the company try to repress him. It is a curious comment on the popular estimate of his character. He has, moreover, to refresh himself, and to think awhile before he can recollect 'some honest (i.e. decent) thing.'

ll. 327, 328. The Harleian MS. has—

> 'But in the cuppe wil I me bethinke
> Upon som honest tale, whil I drinke.'

The Pardoneres Prologue.

TITLE. The Latin text is copied from l. 334 below; it appears in the Ellesmere and Hengwrt MSS. The A. V. has—'the love of money is the root of all evil;' 1 Tim. vi. 10. It is well worth notice that the novel by Morlinus, quoted in the Preface as a source of the Pardoner's Tale, contains the expression—'radice malorum cupiditate affecti.' See the Preface.

l. 336. *Bulles*, bulls from the pope, whom he here calls his 'liege lord;' see Prol. 687, and Piers the Plowman, B. Prol. 69.

Alle and somme, one and all. Cp. Clerkes Tale. E 941, and the note.

l. 337. *Patente*; defined by Webster as 'an official document, conferring a right or privilege on some person or party;' etc. It was so called because 'patent' or open to public inspection. 'When indulgences came to be sold. the pope made them a part of his ordinary revenue; and, according to the usual way in those, and even in much later times, of farming the revenue, he let them out usually to the Dominican friars ;' Massingberd, Hist. Eng. Reformation, p. 126.

l. 345. 'To colour my devotion with.' For *saffron*, MS. Harl. reads *savore*. Tyrwhitt rightly prefers the reading *saffron*, as 'more expressive, and less likely to have been a gloss.' And he adds—'Saffron was used to give colour as well as flavour.' For example, in the Babees Book, ed. Furnivall, p. 275, we read of 'capons that ben coloured with saffron.' And in Winter's Tale, iv. 3. 48, the Clown says—' I must have saffron to colour the warden pies.' Cf. Sir Thopas, Group B, l. 1920. As to the position of *with*, cp. Sq. Ta. 471, 641.

l. 346. According to Tyrwhitt, this line is, in some MSS., replaced by three, viz.—

> 'In euery village and in euery toun,
> This is my terme, and shal, and euer was,
> *Radix malorum est cupiditas.*'

l. 347. *Cristal stones*, evidently hollow pieces of crystal in which relics were kept; so in the Prologue, l. 700, we have—

> 'And in a *glas* he hadde pigges bones.'

l. 348. *Cloutes*, rags, bits of cloth. 'The origin of the veneration for relics may be traced to Acts xix. 12. Hence *clouts*, or *cloths*, are among the Pardoner's stock ;' note in Bell's edition.

l. 349. *Reliks*. In the Prologue, we read that he had the Virgin Mary's veil and a piece of the sail of St. Peter's ship. Below, we have mention of the shoulder-bone of a holy Jew's sheep, and of a miraculous mitten. See Heywood's impudent plagiarism from this passage in his description of a Pardoner, as printed in the note to l. 701 of Dr. Morris's edition of Chaucer's Prologue. See also a curious list of relics in Chambers' Book of Days, i. 587; and compare the humorous descriptions of the pardoner and his wares in Sir David Lyndesay's Satyre of the Three Estates, ll. 2037-2121.

l. 350. *Latoun*. The word *latten* is still in use in Devon and the North of England for plate tin, but as Halliwell remarks, that is not the sense of *latoun* in our older writers. It was a kind of mixed metal, much resembling brass both in its nature and colour. It was used for helmets (Rime of Sir Thopas, B. 2067), lavers (P. Pl. Crede, 196), spoons (Nares), sepulchral memorials (Way in Prompt. Parv.), and other articles. Todd, in his Illustrations of Chaucer, p. 350, remarks that the escutcheons on the tomb of the Black Prince are of *laton* over-gilt, in accordance with the Prince's instructions; see Nichols's Royal Wills, p. 67. He adds—'In our old Church Inventories a *cross of laton* frequently occurs.' See Prol. 699.

l. 351. The expression 'holy Jew' is remarkable, as the usual feeling in the middle ages was to regard all Jews with abhorrence. It is suggested, in a note to Bell's edition, that it 'must be understood of some Jew before the Incarnation.' Perhaps the Pardoner wished it to be understood that the sheep was once the property of Jacob; this would help to give force to l. 365. Cp. Gen. xxx.

The best comment on the virtues of a sheep's shoulder-bone is afforded by a passage in the Persones Tale (De Ira), where we find— 'Swering sodenly without avisement is also a gret sinne. But let us go now to that horrible swering of adiuration and coniuration, as don thise false enchauntours and nigromancers in basins ful of water, or in a bright swerd, in a cercle, or in a fire, or in a *sholder-bone of a shepe;*' &c. Sir David Lyndesay inserts a cow's horn and a cow's tail in his list of pardoner's relics; cp. note to l. 349 above.

In Part I of the Records of the Folk-lore Society is an article by Mr. Thoms on the subject of divination by means of the shoulder-bone of a sheep. He shews that it was still practised in the Scottish Highlands down to the beginning of the present century, and that it is known in Greece. He further cites some passages concerning it from some scarce books; and ends by saying—'let me refer any reader desirous of knowing more of this wide-spread form of divination to Sir H. Ellis's edition of Brand's Popular Antiquities, iii. 179, ed. 1842, and to much curious information respecting *Spatulamancia*, as it is called by Hartlieb, and an analogous species of divination *ex anserino sterno*, to Grimm's Deutsche Mythologie, 2nd ed. p. 1067.'

l. 355. **The sense is**—'which any snake has bitten or stung.' The reference is to the poisonous effects of the bite of an adder or venomous snake. The word *worm* is used by Shakespeare to describe the asp whose bite was fatal to Cleopatra; and it is sometimes used to describe a dragon of the largest size. In Icelandic, the term 'miðgarðsormr,' lit. worm of the middle-earth, signifies a great sea-serpent encompassing the entire world.

l. 363. *Fastinge.* This word is spelt with a final *e* in all seven MSS.; and as it is emphatic and followed by a slight pause, perhaps the final *e* should be pronounced. Cp. A.S. *fæstende*, the oldest form of the present participle.

It is not, perhaps, absolutely essential to the metre, for the word may be pronounced *fásting*, with an accent on the first syllable, thus making the first foot consist of but one syllable. See other examples of this in my Preface to the Prioresses Tale, p. lxiii (or p. lxiv, 2nd ed.).

l. 366. For *heleth*, MS. Hl. has *kelith*, i.e. cooleth.

l. 379. The final *e* in *sinne* must not be elided; it is preserved by the cæsura. Besides, *e* is only elided before *h* in the case of certain words; see Pref. to Prioresses Tale, p. liv (or p. lv, 2nd ed.).

l. 387. *Assoille*, absolve. In Michelet's Life of Luther, tr. by W. Hazlitt. chap. ii, there is a very similar passage concerning Tetzel, the Dominican friar, whose shameless sale of indulgences roused Luther to his famous denunciations of the practice. Tetzel 'went about from town to town, with great display, pomp, and expense, hawking the commodity [i.e. the indulgences] in the churches, in the public streets, in taverns and ale-houses. He paid over to his employers as little as possible, pocketing the balance, as was subsequently proved against him. The faith of the buyers diminishing, it became necessary to exaggerate to the fullest extent the merit of the specific. . . . The intrepid Tetzel stretched his rhetoric to the very uttermost bounds of amplification. Daringly piling one lie upon another, he set forth, in reckless display, the long list of evils which this panacea could cure. He did not content himself with enumerating known sins; he set his foul imagination to work, and invented crimes, infamous atrocities, strange, unheard of, unthought of; and when he saw his auditors stand aghast at each horrible suggestion, he would calmly repeat the burden of his song:—Well, all this is expiated the moment your money chinks in the pope's chest.' This was in the year 1517.

l. 390. *An hundred mark.* A mark was worth about 13s. 4d., and 100 marks about £66 13s. 4d. In order to make allowance for the difference in the value of money in that age, we must at least multiply by ten; or we may say in round numbers, that the Pardoner made at least £700 a year. We may contrast this with Chaucer's own pension of twenty marks, granted him in 1367, and afterwards increased till, in the very last year of his life, he received in all, according to Sir Harris Nicolas, as much as £61 13s. 4d. Even then his income did not quite attain to the hundred marks which the Pardoner gained so easily.

l. 397. *Dowue*, a pigeon; lit. a dove. Chaucer, in the Milleres Tale, has a line very like this, viz.—

        'As any swallow sitting on a berne.'

l. 402. *Namely*, especially, in particular; cf. Kn. Ta. 410.

l. 405. *Blakeberyed.* The line means—'Though their souls go a blackberrying;' i.e. wander wherever they like. This is a well-known *crux*, which all the editors have given up as unintelligible. I have been so fortunate as to obtain the complete solution of it, which was printed in Notes and Queries, 4 S. x. 222, xii. 45, and again in my preface to the C-text of Piers the Plowman, p. lxxxvii. The simple explanation is that, by a grammatical construction which was probably really due (as will be shewn) to an error, the verb go could be combined with what was *apparently* a past participle, in such a manner as to give the participle the force of a verbal substantive. In other words, instead of saying 'he goes a-hunting,' our forefathers sometimes said 'he goes a-hunted.' The examples of this use are at least six. The clearest is in Piers Plowman, C. ix. 138, where we read of 'folk that gon a-begged,' i.e. folk that go a-begging. In Chaucer, we not only have an instance

in the present passage, but another in the Wyf of Bath's Tale, Group D,
l 354, where we have 'to gon a-caterwawed,' with the sense of 'to go
a-caterwauling;' and it is a fortunate circumstance that in both these
cases the unusual forms occur at the end of a line, so that the rime has
preserved them from being tampered with.   Gower (Conf. Amant.
bk. i. ed. Chalmers, pp. 32, 33, or ed. Pauli, i. 110) speaks of a king of
Hungary riding out 'in the month of May,' adding—

'This king with noble purueiance
Hath for him-selfe his chare [*car*] arayed,
Wherein he wolde ryde *amayed*,' &c.

that is, wherein he wished to ride a-*Maying*.   Again (in bk. v, ed.
Chalmers, p. 124, col. 2, or ed. Pauli, ii. 132) we read of a drunken priest
losing his way :—

'This prest was dronke, and *goth a-strayed*;'

i.e. he goes a-straying, or goes astray.

The explanation of this construction I take to be this; the *-ed* was
not really a sign of the past participle, but a corruption of the ending
-eth (A.S. *-að*) which is sometimes found at the end of a verbal substantive. Hence it is that, in the passage from Piers Plowman above
quoted, one of the best and earliest MSS. actually reads 'folk that gon
a-beggeth.' And again, in another passage (P. Pl. C. ix. 246) is the
phrase 'gon abrybeth,' or, in some MSS., 'gon abrybed,' i e. go
a-bribing or go a-thieving, since Mid. Eng *briben* often means to rob.
This form is clearly an imitation of the form *a-hunteth* in the old
phrase *gon a-hunteth* or *riden an honteth*, used by Robert of Gloucester
(Specimens of English, ed. Morris and Skeat, p. 14, l. 387)—

'As he *rod an honteth*, and par-auntre [h]is hors spurnde.'

Now this *honteth* is the dat. case of a substantive, viz. of the A. S.
huntað or *huntoð*. This substantive would easily be mistaken for a part
of a verb, and, particularly, for the past participle of a verb; just as
many people at this day are quite unable to distinguish between the
true verbal substantive and the present participle in *-ing*. This mistake
once established, the ending *-ed* would be freely used after the verbs go
or *ride*.

The result is that the present phrase, hitherto so puzzling, is a mere
variation for 'gon a blake-berying,' i.e. 'go a-gathering blackberries,' a
humorous expression for 'wander wherever they please.' A not very
dissimilar expression occurs in the proverbial saying—'his wits are gone
a-wool-gathering.'

The Pardoner says, in effect, 'I promise them full absolution;
however, when they die and are buried, it matters little to me in what
direction their souls go.'

l. 407. Tyrwhitt aptly adduces a parallel passage from the Romaunt
of the Rose, l. 5766—

'For oft good predicatioun
Cometh of euil intentioun.'

'Some indeed preach Christ even of envy and strife;' Phil. **i. 15**.

l. **413**.   In Piers Plowman (B-text), **v. 87**, it is said of Envy that—

'Eche a worde that he warpe • **was** of an addres tonge.'

Cf. Rom. iii. **13** ; Ps. **cxl. 3**.

l. **440**. *For I teche*, because I teach, by my teaching.

l. **441**. *Wilful pouerte* signifies voluntary poverty.   This is well illustrated by the following lines concerning Christ in Piers Plowman, B. xx. 48, 49 :—

'Syth he that wroughte al the worlde • was *wilfullich* nedy,

Ne neuer **non so** nedy • ne pouerer deyde.'

Several examples occur in Richardson's Dictionary in which *wilfully* has the sense of *willingly* or *voluntarily*.   Thus—'If they *wylfully* would renounce the sayd place and put them in his grace, he wolde vtterlye pardon theyr trespace ;' Fabyan's Chronicle, c. 114.   It even means *gladly*; thus in Wyclif's Bible, Acts xxi. **17**, we find, 'britherin res-seyuyden vs *wilfulli*.'   Speaking of palmers, Speght says—'The *pilgrim* travelled at his own charge, the *palmer* professed wilful poverty.'

The word *wilful* still means *willing* in Warwickshire ; see Eng. Dialect Soc. Gloss. **C. 6**.

l. **445**. The context seems to imply that some of the apostles made baskets.   So in Piers Plowman, B. xv. 285, we read of St. Paul—

'**Poule**, after his prechyng • *panyers* he made.'

Yet in Acts xviii. 3 we only read that he wrought as a tent-maker. However, it was St. Paul who set the example of labouring with his hands ; and, in imitation of him, we find an early example of basket-making by St. Arsenius, 'who, before he turned hermit, had been the tutor of the emperors Arcadius and Honorius,' and who is represented in a fresco in the Campo Santo at Pisa, by Pietro Laurati, as 'weaving baskets of palm-leaves ;' whilst beside him another hermit is cutting wooden spoons, and another is fishing.   See Mrs. Jameson's Sacred and Legendary Art, 3rd ed. ii. 757.

l. **448**. The best description of the house-to-house system of begging, as adopted by the mendicant friars, is near the beginning of the Sompnour's Tale.   They went in pairs to the farm-houses, begging a bushel of wheat, or malt, or rye, or a piece of cheese or brawn, or bacon or beef, or even a piece of an old blanket.   Nothing seems to have come amiss to them.

l. **450**. See Prologue, l. 255 ; and cf. the description of the poor widow at the beginning of the Nonne Prestes Tale.

The Pardoneres Tale.

For some account of the source of this Tale, see the Preface. The account which I here quote as the 'Italian' text is that contained in Novella lxxxii of the Libro di Novelle.

l. 463. In laying the scene in Flanders, Chaucer probably followed an original which is now lost. Andrew Borde, in his amusing Introduction of Knowledge, ch. viii, says:—'Flaunders is a plentyfull countre of fyshe & fleshe & wyld fowle. Ther shal a man be clenly serued at his table, & well ordred and vsed for meate & drynke & lodgyng. The countre is playn, & somwhat sandy. The people be gentyl, but the men be great drynkers; and many of the women be vertuous and wel dysposyd.' He describes the Fleming as saying—

> 'I am a Fleming, what for all that,
> Although I wyll be dronken other whyles as a rat?
> "Buttermouth Flemyng" men doth me call,' &c.

l. 464. *Haunteden*, followed after; cf. note to l. 547. The same expression occurs in The Tale of Beryn, a spurious (but not ill-told) addition to the Canterbury Tales:—

> '*Foly, I haunted it ever*, ther myght no man me let;' l. 2319.

l. 473. *Grisly*, terrible, enough to make one shudder. It is exactly the right word; see the Glossary. The mention of these oaths reminds us of the admission of my Uncle Toby in Sterne's Tristram Shandy, ch. xi, that 'our armies swore terribly *in Flanders*.'

l. 474. *To-tere*, tear in pieces, dismember. Cf. *to-rente* in Gloss. to Prioresses Tale (Clar. Press). Chaucer elsewhere says—'For Cristes sake swere not so sinnefully, in *dismembring* of Crist, by soule, herte, bones, and body; for certes it semeth, that ye thinken that the cursed Iewes dismembred him not ynough, but ye dismembre him more;' Persones Tale. *De Ira.* And see ll. 629-659 below.

'And than Seint Johan seid—"These [who are thus tormented in hell] ben thei that sweren bi Goddes membris, as bi his nayles and other his membris, and thei thus dismembrid God in horrible swerynge bi his limmes;' Vision of Wm. Staunton (A.D. 1409), quoted in Wright's St. Patrick's Purgatory, p. 146. In the Plowman's Tale (Chaucer, ed. 1561, fol. xci) we have—

> 'And Cristes membres al to-tere
> On roode as he were newe yrent.'

Barclay, in his Ship of Fools (ed. Jamieson. i. 97), says—

> 'Some sweryth armes, naylys, herte, and body,
> Terynge our Lord worse than the Jowes hym arayed.'

swearing **by 'his** holy membres,' **by** his 'blode,' by 'his face, his herte, or **by** his croune of thorne,' etc. Todd, in his Illustrations of Chaucer, p. 264, quotes (from an old MS.) **the** old second commandment in the following form :—

> 'II. **Thi** goddes name and b[e'autte
> Thou shalt not **take** for wel nor wo;
> Dismembre hym not that on rode-tre
> **For the** was mad boyth blak **and blo.'**

477. *Tombesteres,* **female** dancers. 'Sir Perdicas, whom that kinge Alysandre made **to** been his **heire** in Grece, was of no kinges blod; his dame [*mother*] was a tombystere;' Testament of Love, Book ii. ed. 1561, fol. ccxcvi b.

Tombestere is the feminine form; the A.S. spelling **would be** *tumb-estre;* the masc. form is the A.S. *tumbere,* which is glossed by *saltator,* **i.e.** a dancer; the verb is *tumbian,* **to** dance, used of Herodias's **daughter** in the A.S. version of Mark vi. 22.

On the feminine termination *-ster* (formerly *-estre,* **or -stre)** see the remarks in Marsh's Lectures on **the** English Language, printed in (the so-called) Smith's Student's Manual **of** the English Language, ed. 1862, **pp. 207,** 208, with an additional **note** at p. 217. Marsh's remarks are, in **this** case, less clear than usual. He shews that the termination was not always used as **a** feminine, and that, in fact, its force was early lost. It is, however, **merely a** question of chronology. That the termination was *originally* feminine in Anglo-Saxon, **is** sufficiently proved by the A.S. version of the Gospels. There we find the word *witega* frequently used in **the** sense of *prophet;* **but,** in one instance, where it is necessary to express the *feminine,* we find this accomplished by the use **of** this very termination. 'And anna wæs *witegystre* (another MS. *witegestre*);' i.e. and Anna was a *prophetess,* **Luke ii. 36.** Similar instances might **easily** be multiplied; see **Dr. Morris's Hist.** Outlines of Eng. Accidence, pp. **89, 90.** Thus, *wasshestren* (pl.) **is used** as **the translation of** *lotrices;* Old Eng. Homilies, ed. Morris, ii. 57. But it is also **true that,** in the fourteenth **century,** the feminine force of this termination **was** becoming very weak, **so that,** whilst in P. Plowman, B. v. 306, **we find 'Beton the** *brewestere'* applied **to a** female brewer, we cannot **thence** certainly conclude that 'brewestere' was always feminine at that period. On the other hand, we may **point to** one word, *spinster,* which has remained feminine to this very day.

Dr. Morris **remarks** that *tombestere* is a hybrid word; in which I believe he has **been misled by the** spelling. It is a pure native word, **from** the A.S. *tumbian,* but **the** scribes have turned it from *tumbestere* **into** *tombestere,* by confusion with the French *tomber.* Yet even the Fr. *tomber* was once spelt *tumber* (Burguy, Roquefort), being, in fact, **a** word of Germanic origin. An acrobat **can** still be called a *tumbler;*

we find 'rope dancers and *tumblers*' in Locke ; Conduct of the Under-standing, § 4. Indeed, the Cambridge MS. has here the true spelling *tumbesteris*, whilst the Corpus, Petworth, and Lansdowne MSS. have the variations *tomblisteres* and *tomblesters*.

As to the *source* of the suffix *-ster*, it is really a compound suffix, due to composition either of the Aryan suffixes *-es-* and *-ter-*, or of *-yans-* and *-ter-*; cf. Lat. *mag-is-ter*, *min-is-ter*, *poet-as-ter*. The feminine use is peculiar to Anglo-Saxon and to some other Teutonic languages.

l. 478. *Fruytesteres*, female sellers of fruit ; see note to last line.

l. 479. *Wafereres*, sellers of confectionery, confectioners. The feminine form *wafrestre* occurs in Piers Plowman, v. 641. From Beaumont and Fletcher we learn that ' wafer-women ' were often employed in amorous embassies, as stated in Nares' Glossary, q. v.

l. 483 *Holy writ*. In the margin of the MSS. E., Hn., Cp., Pt., and Hl. is the note—'Nolite inebriari vino, in quo est luxuria,' quoted from the Vulgate version of Eph. v. 18.

l. 488. ' Herod, (as may be seen by any one) who would consult the "stories" carefully.' The Harleian MS. has the inferior reading *story* ; but the reference is particular, not vague. Peter Comestor (died A.D. 1198) was the author of an Historia Scholastica, on which account he was called ' the maister of stories,' or ' clerk of the stories,' as explained in the note to Piers Plowman, vii. 73 (Clar. Press). The use of the *plural* is due to the fact that the whole Historia Scholastica, which is a sort of epitome of the Bible, with notes and additions, is divided into sections, *each* of which is *also* called ' Historia.' The account of Herod occurs, of course, in the section entitled Historia Evangelica, cap. lxxii ; De decollatione ioannis. Cf. Matt. xiv ; Mark vi.

l. 492. *Senek*, Seneca. The reference appears to be, as pointed out by Tyrwhitt, to Seneca's Letters ; Epist. lxxxiii : ' Extende in plures dies illum ebrii habitum : numquid de furore dubitabis ? nunc quoque non est minor, sed brevior.'

l. 496. ' Except that madness when it has come upon a man of evil nature, lasts longer than does a fit of drunkenness.'

l. 499. ' First cause of our misfortune ;' alluding to the Fall of Adam. See l. 505.

l. 501. *Bought us agayn*, redeemed us ; a translation of the Latin *redemit*. Hence we find Christ called, in Middle English, the *Aȝenbyer*. 'See now how dere he [Christ] boughte man, that he made after his owne ymage, and how dere he *aȝenboght* us, for the grete love that he hadde to us ;' Sir J. Maundeville, Prologue to his Voiage (Specimens of Eng. 1298-1393, p. 165). See l. 766 below.

l. 505. Here, in the margin of MS. E., Hn., Cp., Pt., Hl. is a quotation from ' Hieronymus contra Jovinianum ' (i.e. from St. Jerome): ' Quamdiu iciunauit Adam, in Paradiso fuit ; comedit et eiectus est ;

statim duxit uxorem.' See Hieron. contra Jov. lib. ii. c. 15 ; ed. Migne, ii. 305.

l. 510. *Defended,* forbidden. Even Milton has it ; see P. Lost, xi. 86. See also l. 590 below.

l. 512. '*O gluttony! it would much behove us to complain of thee!'*

l. 522. In the margin of MSS. E. and Hn. is written the quotation— ' Esca ventri, et venter escis. Deus autem et hunc et illam destruet.' For *illam,* the usual reading of the Vulgate is *has* ; see 1 Cor. vi. 13.

l. 526. *Whyte and rede,* white wine and red wine ; see note to Piers Plowman, B. prol. 228 (Clar. Press).

l. 529. In the margin of MSS. E. and Hn. is written—' Ad Philipenses, capitulo tertio.' See Phil. iii. 18.

l. 537. ' How great toil and expense (it is) to provide for thee!' Chaucer is here addressing man's appetite for delicacies. Cf. *fond,* Non. Pr. Tale, 9.

l. 539. Here Chaucer humorously alludes to the famous disputes in scholastic philosophy between the Realists and Nominalists. To attempt any explanation of their language is to become lost in subtleties of distinction. It would seem however that the Realists maintained that everything possesses a *substance,* which is inherent in itself, and distinct from the *accidents* or outward phenomena which the thing presents. According to them, the form, smell, taste, colour, of anything are merely *accidents,* and might be changed without affecting the *substance* itself. See the excellent article on *Substance* in the Engl. Cyclopædia ; also that on *Nominalists.*

According to Chaucer, then, the cooks who toil to satisfy man's appetite change the nature of the things cooked so effectually as to confound *substance* with *accident.* Translated into plain language, it means that those who partook of the meats so prepared, could not, by means of their taste and smell, form any precise idea as to what they were eating. The art is not lost.

l. 547. *Haunteth,* practises, indulges in ; cf. l. 464. In the margin of MSS. E. and Hn. is written—' Qui autem in deliciis est, viuens mortuus est.' This is a quotation from the Vulgate version of 1 Tim. v. 6, but with *Qui* for *quæ,* and *mortuus* for *mortua.*

l. 549. In the margin of MSS. E. and Hn. is written—' Luxuriosa res vinum, et contumeliosa ebrietas.' The Vulgate version of Prov. xx. 1 agrees with this nearly, but has *tumultuosa* for *contumeliosa.* This is of course the text to which Chaucer refers. And see note to B. 771.

l. 554. He means that the drunkard's stertorous breathing seems to repeat the sound of the word *Sampsoún.* The word was probably chosen for the sake of its nasal sounds, to imitate a sort of grunt. Pronounce the *m* and *n* as in French, but with exaggerated emphasis. So also in l. 572.

l. 555. See note to the Monkes Tale, Group B, line 3245. In Judges
xiii. 4, 7, the command to drink no wine is addressed, not to Samson,
but to his mother. Of Samson himself it is said that he was 'a
Nazarite,' which implies the same thing; see Numbers vi. 3, 5.

l. 561. In Chaucer's Tale of Melibeus (Six-text, B. 2383) we find—
'Thou shalt also eschue the conseiling of folk that been dronkelewe; for
they can no conseil hyde; for Salomon seith, Ther is no priuctee ther-as
regneth dronkenesse;' and see B. 776. The allusion is to Prov. xxxi. 4
—'Noli regibus, O Lamuel, noli regibus dare uinum; quia nullum
secretum est ubi regnat ebrietas.' This last clause is quite different
from that in our own version; which furnishes, perhaps, a reason why
the allusion here intended has not been perceived by previous editors.

l. 563. *Namely*, especially. Tyrwhitt's note is as follows: 'According
to the geographers, Lepe was not far from Cadiz. This wine, of whatever sort it may have been, was probably much stronger than the
Gascon wines, usually drunk in England. La Rochelle and Bordeaux
(l. 571), the two chief ports of Gascony, were both, in Chaucer's time,
part of the English dominions.'

'Spanish wines might also be more alluring upon account of their
great rarity. Among the Orders of the Royal Household, in 1604, is
the following (MS. Harl. 293, fol. 162): "And whereas, in tymes past,
Spanish wines, called Sacke, were little or noe whit used in our courte,
and that in later years, though not of ordinary allowance, it was thought
convenient that noblemen ... might have a boule or glas, &c. We
understanding that it is now used as common drinke ... reduce the
allowance to xii. gallons a day for the court."' &c. Several regulations
to be observed by London vintners are mentioned in the Liber Albus,
ed. Riley, pp. 614-618. Amongst them is—'Item, that white wine of
Gascoigne, of la Rochele, of Spain, or other place, shall not be put in
cellars with Rhenish wines.' See also note to l. 565.

l. 564. *To selle*, for sale; the true gerund, of which *to* is, in Anglo-
Saxon, the sign. So also 'this house *to let*' is the correct old idiom,
needing no such alteration as some would make. Cf Morris, Hist.
Outlines of Eng. Accidence, sect. 290, subsect. 4. Fish Street leads out
of Lower Thames Street, close to the North end of London Bridge.
The Harleian MS. alone reads *Fleet Street*, which is certainly wrong.
Considering that Thames Street is especially mentioned as a street
for vintners (Liber Albus, p. 614), and that Chaucer's own father was a
Thames Street vintner, there can be little doubt about this matter. The
poet is here speaking from his own knowledge; a consideration which
gives the present passage a peculiar interest. *Chepe* is Cheapside.

l. 565. This is a fine touch. The poet here tells us that some of this
strong Spanish wine used to find its way mysteriously into other wines;

but because the vines of Spain notoriously grew so close to those of Gascony that it was not possible to keep them apart! *Crepeth subtilly* = finds its way mysteriously. Observe the humour in the word *growing*, which expresses that the mixture of wines must be due to the proximity of the vines producing them in the vineyards, not to any accidental proximity of the casks containing them in the vintners' cellars. In fact, the different kinds of wine were to be kept in different cellars, as the Regulations in the Liber Albus (pp. 615–618) shew. 'Item, that no Taverner shall put Rhenish wine and White wine in a cellar together.' 'Item, that new wines shall not be put in cellars with old wines.' 'Item, that White wine of Gascoigne, of la Rochele, of Spain, or other place, shall not be put in cellars with Rhenish wines.' 'Item. that white wine shall not be sold for Rhenish wine.' 'Item, that no one shall expose for sale wines counterfeit or mixed, made by himself or by another, under pain of being set upon the pillory.' But pillories have vanished, and all such laws are obsolete.

l. 570. 'He is in Spain;' i.e. he is, as it were, transported thither. He imagines he has never left Cheapside, yet is far from knowing where he is, as we should say.

l. 571. 'Not at Rochelle.' where the wines are weak.

l. 579. 'The death of Attila took place in 453. The commonly received account is that given by Jornandes, that he died by the bursting of a blood-vessel on the night of his marriage with a beautiful maiden, whom he added to his many other wives; some, with a natural suspicion, impute it to the hand of his bride. Priscus observes, that no one ever subdued so many countries in so short a time. . . . Jornandes, *De Rebus Geticis*, and Priscus, *Excerpta de Legationibus*, furnish the best existing materials for the history of Attila. For modern compilations, see Buat, *Histoire des Peuples de l'Europe*; De Guignes, *Hist. des Huns*; and Gibbon, capp. xxxiv and xxxv;' English Cyclopædia. And see Amédée Thierry, *Histoire d'Attila*.

Mr. Jephson (in Bell's Chaucer) quotes the account of Attila's death given by Paulus Diaconus, *Gest. Rom.* lib. xv: 'Qui reuersus ad proprias sedes, supra plures quas habebat uxores, valde decoram, indicto nomine, sibi in matrimonium iunxit. Ob cuius nuptias profusa conuiuia exercens, dum tantum uini quantum nunquam antea insimul bibisset, cum supinus quiesceret, eruptione sanguinis, qui ei de naribus solitus erat effluere, suffocatus et extinctus est.'

l. 585. *Lamuel*, i.e. King Lemuel, mentioned in Prov. xxxi. 1. q.v.; not to be confused, says Chaucer, with Samuel. The allusion is to Prov. xxxi. 4, 5; and not (as Mr. Wright suggests) to Prov. xxiii. In fact, in the margin of MSS. E. and Hn. is written—'Noli uinum dare,' words found in Prov. xxxi. 4. See note to l. 561.

l. 591. *Hasard*, gambling. In the margin of MSS. E. and Hn. is written—'Policratici libro primo; Mendaciorum et periuriarum mater est Alea.' This shews that the line is a quotation from lib. i. [cap. 5] of the Polycraticus of John of Salisbury, bishop of Chartres, who died in 1180. See some account of this work in Prof. Morley's Eng. Writers, i. 597. 'In the first book, John treats of temptations and duties and other vanities, such as hunting, *dice*, music, mimes and minstrelsy, magic and soothsaying, prognostication by dreams and astrology.' See also the account of gaming, considered as a branch of Avarice in the Ayenbyte of Inwyt, ed. Morris, pp. 45, 46.

l. 603. *Stilbon.* It should rather be *Chilon.* Tyrwhitt remarks— 'John of Salisbury, from whom our author probably took this story and the following, calls him *Chilon*; Polycrat. lib. i. c. 5. "Chilon Lacedæmonius, iungendæ societatis causa missus Corinthum, duces et seniores populi ludentes inuenit in alea. Infecto itaque negotio reuersus est [dicens se nolle gloriam Spartanorum, quorum uirtus constructo Byzantio clarescebat, hac maculare infamia, ut dicerentur cum aleatoribus contraxisse societatem]." Accordingly, in ver. 12539 [l. 605], MS. C. 1 [i.e. MS. Camb. Univ. Lib. Dd. 4. 24] reads very rightly *Lacedomye* instead of *Calidone*, the common reading [of the old editions]. Our author has used before *Lacedomie* for *Lacedæmon*, v. 11692 [Frank. Tale, F 1380].'

In the Petw. MS., the name *Stilbon* is explained as meaning *Mercurius.* So, in Liddell and Scott's Gk. Lexicon, we have 'στίλβων, -οντος, ὁ, *the planet Mercury*, Arist. Mund. 2. 9; cf. Cic. Nat. D. 2. 20.' The explanation is clearly wrong in the present instance, yet it points to the original sense of the word, viz. 'shining,' from the verb στίλβειν, to glitter.

l. 608. The first foot has but one syllable, viz. *Pley. Atte*, for *at the.* Tyrwhitt oddly remarks here, that '*atte* has frequently been corrupted into *at the*,' viz. in the old editions. Of course *atte* is rather, etymologically, a corruption of *at the*; Tyrwhitt probably means that the editors might as well have let the form *atte* stand. If so, he is quite right; for, though etymologically a corruption, it was a recognised form at that date.

l. 621. This story immediately follows the one quoted from John of Salisbury in the note to l. 603. After 'societatem,' he proceeds :— 'Regi quoque Demetrio, in opprobrium puerilis leuitatis, tali aurei a rege Parthorum dati sunt.' What Demetrius this was, we are not told; perhaps it may have been Demetrius Nicator, king of Syria, who was defeated and taken prisoner by the Parthians in 138 B.C., and detained in captivity by them for ten years. This, however, is but a guess. Compare the story told of our own king, in Shakespeare's Henry V, Act i. sc. 2.

l. 628. *To dryue the day awey*, to pass the time. The same phrase occurs in Piers Plowman, B. prol. 224, where it is said of the labourers who tilled the soil that they 'dryuen forth the longe day with *Dieu vous saue, Dame emme*,' i.e. amuse themselves with singing idle songs.

l. 633. In the margin of MSS. E., Hn., and Pt. is the quotation
'Nolite omnino iurare,' with a reference (in Hn. only) to Matt. v. The
Vulgate version of Matt. v. 34 is—' Ego autem dico uobis, non iurare
omnino, neque per cælum, quia thronus Dei est.'

l. 635. In the margin of MSS. E., Hn., and Pt. is written—' Ieremie
quarto. Iurabis in veritate, in Iudicio et Iusticia;' see Jer. iv. 2.

There are several points of resemblance between the present passage
and one in the Persones Tale (*De Ira*), part of which has been already
quoted in the note to l. 474. 'Also our Lord Iesu Crist sayth, by the
word of seint Mathew: Ne shal ye nat swere in alle manere, neyther by
heven, &c. And if so be that the lawe compelle you to swere, than
reuleth you after the lawe of god in your swering, as sayth Ieremie;
Thou shalt kepe three conditions; thou shalt swere in trouth, in dome,
and in rightwisenesse, &c. And think wel this, that euery gret swerer,
not compelled lawfully to swere, the plage shal not depart fro his hous,
while he useth unleful swering. Thou shalt swere also in dome, when
thou art constreined by the domesman to witnesse a trouth;' &c. So
also Wyclif:—'ȝit no man schulde swere, nouther for life ne dethe, no
but with these thre condiciones, that is, in treuthe, in dome, and in
rightwisenes, as God sais by the prophet Ieremye;' Works, ed. Arnold,
iii. 483.

l. 639. *The firste table*, i. e. the commandments that teach us our duty
towards God; those in the second table teach us our duty to our
neighbour.

l. 641. *Seconde heste*, second commandment. Formerly, the first two
commandments were considered as one; the third commandment was
therefore the second, as here. The tenth commandment was divided
into two parts, to make up the number. See Wyclif's treatise on 'The
ten Comaundements;' Works, ed. Arnold, iii. 82. Thus Wyclif says—
'The secounde maner maundement of God perteyneth to the Sone.
Thow schalt not take the name of thi Lord God in veyn, nepþer in word,
neiþer in lyvynge.' And see note to l. 474.

l. 643. *Rather*, sooner; because this commandment precedes those
which relate to murder, &c.

l. 646. 'They that understand his commandments know this,' &c.

l. 649. Wyclif says—' For it is written in Ecclesiasticus, the thre and
twenti chapitre, there he seith this: A man much sweringe schal be fulfilled with wickidnesse, and veniaunce schal not go away fro his hous;'
Works, iii. 84. Chaucer here quotes the same text; see Ecclus. xxiii. 11.

l. 651. So Wyclif, iii. 483—' hit is not leeful to swere by creaturis, ne
by Goddys bonys, sydus, naylus, ne armus, or by ony membre of Cristis
body, as þe moste dele of men usen.'

Tyrwhitt says—' *his nayles*, i.e. with which he was nailed to the cross.
Sir J. Maundeville, c. vii—" And thereby in the walle is the place where

the 4 Nayles of our Lord weren hidd ; for he had 2 in his hondes, and 2 in his feet: and one of theise the Emperoure of Constantynoble made a brydille to his hors, to bere him in bataylle ; and thorgh vertue thereof he overcame his enemies," &c.   He had said before, c. ii., that "on of the nayles that Crist was naylled with on the cross" was "at Constantynoble ; and on in France, in the kinges chapelle." '

Mr. Wright adds, what is doubtless true, that these nails 'were objects of superstition in the middle ages.'   Notwithstanding these opinions, I am not satisfied that these comments are *quite* correct.   I strongly suspect that swearers did not stop to think, nor were they at all particular as to the sense in which the words might be used. Here, for example, *nails* are mentioned between *heart* and *blood* ; in the quotation from Wyclif in the note to l. 651, we find mention of 'bones, sides, nails, and arms,' followed by 'any member of Christ's body.'   Still more express is the phrase used by William Staunton (see note to l. 474 above) that 'God's members' include 'his nails.'   On the other hand, in Lewis's Life of Pecock, p. 155 [or p. 107, ed. 1820], is a citation from a MS. to the effect that, in the year 1420, many men died in England 'emittendo sanguinem per iuncturas et per secessum, scilicet in illis partibus corporis per quas horribiliter iurare consueuerunt, scilicet, per oculos Christi, per faciem Christi, per latera Christi, per sanguinem Christi, per cor Christi preciosum, per *clauos* Christi in suis manibus et pedibus.'   A long essay might be written upon the oaths found in our old authors, but the subject is, I think, a most repulsive one.

l. 652. Here Tyrwhitt notes—'The Abbey of Hailes, in Glocestershire, was founded by Richard, king of the Romans, brother to Henry III.   This precious relick, which was afterwards called "the blood of Hailes," was brought out of Germany by the son of Richard, Edmund, who bestowed a third part of it upon his father's Abbey of Hailes, and some time after gave the other two parts to an Abbey of his own foundation at Ashrug near Berkhamsted.   Hollinshed, vol. ii. p. 275.'   'A vial was shewn at Hales in Glocestershire, as containing a portion of our blessed Saviour's blood, which suffered itself to be seen by no person in a state of mortal sin, but became visible when the penitent, by his offerings, had obtained forgiveness.   It was now discovered that this was performed by keeping blood, which was renewed every week, in a vial, one side of which was thick and opaque, the other transparent, and turning it by a secret hand as the case required.   A trick of the same kind, more skilfully executed, is still annually performed at Naples.'—Southey, Book of the Church, ch. xii. He refers to Fuller, b. vi. Hist. of Abbeys, p. 323 ; Burnet, i. 323, ed. 1681.   See also the word *Hales* in the Index to the works published by the Parker Society ; and Pilgrimages to Walsingham and Canterbury (by Erasmus), ed. J. G. Nichols, 2nd ed. 1875, p. 88.

l. 653. 'My chance is seven; yours is five and **three.**' This is an allusion to the particular game called *hazard*, not to a mere comparison of throws to see which is highest. A certain throw (here *seven*) is called the caster's *chance.* This can only be understood by an acquaintance with the rules of the game. See the article *Hazard* in Supplement to Eng. Cyclopædia, or in Hoyle's Games. Cf. Man of Lawes Prologue, B 124; Monkes Tale, B 3851. Compare—'Not unlike the use of foule gamesters, who having lost the maine by [i.e. according to] **true** judgement, thinke to face it out with a false oath;' Lyly's Euphues and his England (qu. in Halliwell's edition of Nares, s.v. *Main*).

l. 656. In the Towneley Mysteries, p. 241, when **the soldiers dice for** Christ's garments, one says—

> 'I was falsly begyled withe thise *byched bones,*
> Ther cursyd thay **be.**'

On the following page (p. 242), Pilate addresses a soldier with the words—'Unbychid, unbayn.' *Unbayn* (Icel. *ú-beinn*) means, literally, **crooked**; metaphorically, perverse; and is a term of reproach. This suggests that *unbychid* could be similarly used.

The readings are :—E. Cp. *bicched*; Ln. *becched*; Hl. *bicched*; Hn. Cm. *bicche*; Pt. and old edd. *thilk, thilke* (wrongly). Besides which, Tyrwhitt cites *bichet*, MS. Harl. 7335; *becched*, Camb. Univ. Lib. Dd. 4. 24; and, from other MSS., *bicched, bicchid, bitched, bicche.* The general consensus of the MS. and the **quotation** from the Towneley Mysteries establish the reading given in the **text** beyond all doubt. Yet Tyrwhitt reads *bicchel*, for which **he adduces** no authority beyond the following. '*Bickel*, as explained by Kilian, is *talus*, ovillus et **lusorius** ; and *bickelen*, talis ludere. See also **Had.** Junii Nomencl. n. 213. Our dice indeed are the ancient *tesseræ* (κύβοι) not *tali* (ἀστράγαλοι); but, both being games of hazard, **the** implements of one might be **easily attributed** to the other. It should seem from Junius, loc. cit., that **the Germans** had preserved the custom of playing with the natural **bones, as** they have different names for a game with *tali ovilli*, and another with *tali bubuli*.'

I find in the Tauchnitz Dutch Dictionary—'*Bikkel*, cockal. *Bikkelen*, to play at cockals.' Here *cockal* is **the** old name for a game with four hucklebones (Halliwell), and **is further made** to mean the hucklebone itself. **The same** Dutch Dictionary gives—'*Bikken*, to notch (the **mill-stone).**'

In Wackernagel's Altdeutsches Handwörterbuch, we **find**—'*Bickel, Pickel*, Spitzhacke; Würfel,' i.e. (1) a pick-axe; (2) a die. Also '*Bickelspil*, Würfelspiel;' i.e. a game at dice. Wackernagel refers the etymology to the verb *bicken* or *picken*, to pick or peck, which is clearly the same as the Dutch *bikken*, to notch.

We may safely conclude (1) that the reading *bicched* is correct;

(2) that the English term *bicched bcon* is equivalent to the Dutch *bikkel*, Ger. *bickel*, as far as the general sense is concerned, since they both relate to things employed in games of chance. Nevertheless, despite their apparent similarity of form, there seems to be no etymological connection between them, but they were named for quite different reasons. The Du. *bikkel* may be referred to the verb *bikken*, to notch, also to pick, peck, or mark; so that the original sense of *bikkel* was 'pick-axe'; however, it afterwards acquired the sense of 'huckle-bone,' and finally, that of 'die.' The history of the word shews that the last sense arose from a transference of use, and not from the fact that the die was spotted or marked by making slight holes in its surface. But the Eng. *bicched* appears to have had the meaning of 'accursed' or 'execrable'; see the New English Dictionary, where it is shewn that it was applied to other things besides dice; as, for example, to a basilisk, a body, a burden, and to the human conscience. It is evidently an opprobrious term, and seems to be derived from the sb. *bitch* (M. E. *bicche*) opprobriously used. Hence *the bicched bones two* refer to 'the two accursed pieces of bone' that are used in playing at hazard.

I add a few more references by way of confirming the derivation of the Dutch *bikkel*.

Hexham's Dutch Dictionary (ed. 1658) gives:—'Een Bickel, ofte [*or*] Pickel, a hucklebone, or a die. Bickel, a pounce, or a graver. Bickelen, ofte Pickelen, to play at dice. Bickelen, ofte Bicken, to cutt, pink, or engrave. Een Bickeler, ofte Bicker, a stone-hewer, a stone-carver, or a cutter. Bicken, to cut or carue.' The Icel. *pikka* means both to pick and to prick. The A.S. *ficung* means a stigma, or mark caused by burning. The German *Pickel* is explained by Heinsius as 'ein kleines Fleck, ein kleines Geschwür auf der Haut;' and *pickeln*, he says, is 'sanft picken, mit etwas Spitzigem leise berühren.' In Küttner and Nicholson's German Dictionary I find 'Picken, to peck with the bill, as birds do. Ein Vogel, der sich picket, a bird that picks, pecks, or proins itself.' This last throws a clear light on *apiked* in Chaucer's Prologue, l. 365.

l. 661. The Pardoner now takes up the tale in earnest, beginning abruptly. The 'three rioters' have not been previously mentioned, though the word *riot* occurs in l. 465.

l. 662. *Pryme*, about nine o'clock; see notes to Non. Pr. Tale, 35; and to Group B. 2015 (Sir Thopas). Here it means the canonical hour for prayer so called, to announce which bells were rung.

l. 664. A hand-bell was carried before a corpse at a funeral by the sexton. See Rock, Church of Our Fathers, ii. 471; Grindal's Works, p. 136.

l. 666. *That oon of them,* the one of them; the old phrase for 'one of them.' *Knaue,* boy.

l. 667. *Go bet,* lit. go better, i.e. go quicker; a term of encouragement to dogs in the chase. So in the Legend of Good Women (Dido, l. 288) we have—

'The herde of hartes founden is **anon,**

With "hey! *go bet!* prick thou! let gon, let gon!"'

Halliwell says—'*Go bet,* an old hunting cry, often introduced in a more general sense. See Songs and Carols, xv; Shak. Soc. Pap. i. 58; Chaucer, C. T. 12601 [the present passage]; Dido, 288; Tyrwhitt's notes, p. 278; Ritson's Anc. Pop. Poetry, p. 46. The phrase is mentioned by [Juliana] Berners in the Boke of St. Alban's, and seems nearly equivalent to *go along.*' It is strange that no editor has perceived the *exact* sense of this very simple phrase. Cf. 'Keep *bet* my good,' i.e. take better care of my property; Shipmannes Tale, third line from the end.

l. 679. *This pestilence,* during this plague. Alluding to the Great Plagues that took place in the reign of Edward III. There were four such, viz. in 1348-9, 1361-2, 1369, and 1375-6. As Chaucer probably had the story from an Italian source, the allusion must be to the first and worst of these, the effects of which spread nearly all over Europe, and which was severely felt at Florence, as we learn from the description left by Boccaccio. See note to Piers Plowman, B. v. 13 (Clar. Press).

l. 684. *My dame,* my mother; as in Piers Plowman, B. v. 37.

l. 695. *Auow,* vow; to *make auow* is the old phrase for *to vow.* Tyrwhitt alters it to *a vow,* quite unnecessarily; and the same alteration has been made by editors in other books, owing to want of familiarity with old MSS. It is true that the form *vow* does occur, as, e.g. in P. Plowm. B. prol. 71; but it is no less certain that *avow* occurs also, and was the older form; since we have *oon auow* (B. 334), and the phrase 'I make myn *avou,*' P. Plowman, A. v. 218; where no editorial sophistication can evade giving the right spelling. Equally clear is the spelling in the Prompt. Parv.—'*Avowe,* Votum. *Awowyn,* or *to make awowe,* Voveo.' And Mr. Way says—'*Auowe,* veu; Palsgrave. This word occurs in R. de Brunne, Wiclif, and Chaucer. The phrase "performed his auowe" occurs in the Legenda Aurea, fol. 47.' Those who are familiar with MSS. know that a prefixed *a* is often written apart from the word; thus the word now spelt *accord* is often written 'a corde;' and so on. Hence, even when the word is really *one* word, it is still often written 'a uow,' and is naturally printed *a vow* in two words, where no such result was intended. Tyrwhitt himself prints *min avow* in the Knightes Tale, l. 1379, and again *this avow* in the same, l. 1556; where no error is possible. See more on this word in my note to l. 1 of Chevy Chase, in Spec. of Eng. 1394-1579. I have there said that the form *vow* does not occur in early writers; I should rather have said, it is by no means the *usual* form. For the etymology, see the Glossary.

l. 698. *Brother*, i.e. sworn friend; see Kn. Tale, 273, 289. In l. 704, *yboren brother* means brother by birth.

l. 709. *To-rente*, tare in pieces, dismembered. See note to l. 474 above.

l. 713. This 'old man' answers to the *romito* or hermit of the Italian text. Note *an old* (indefinite), as compared with *the oldē* (definite) in l. 714.

l. 715. Tyrwhitt, in his Glossary, remarks—'*God you see!* 7751. *God him see!* 4576. May God keep you, or him, in his sight! In Troilus, ii. 85, it is fuller :—*God you save and see!*' Gower has—' And than I bidde, *God hir see!*' Conf. Amant. bk. iv (ed. Chalmers. p. 116, col. 2, or ed. Pauli, ii. 96). Cf. ' now loke the owre lorde !' P. Plowman, B. i. 207. See also l. 766 below.

l. 727. This is a great improvement upon the Italian tale, which represents the hermit as *fleeing* from death. 'Fratelli miei, io fuggo la morte, che mi vien dietro cacciando mi.'

l. 731. *Leue moder*, dear mother Earth.

l. 734. *Cheste*. Mr. Jephson (in Bell's edition) is puzzled here. He takes *cheste* to mean a coffin, which is certainly the sense in the Clerk's Prologue, E. 29. The simple solution is that *cheste* refers here, not to a coffin, but to the box for holding clothes which, in olden times, almost invariably stood in every bedroom, at the foot of the bed. 'At the foot of the bed there was usually an iron-bound hutch or locker, which served both as a seat, and as a repository for the apparel and wealth of the owner, who, sleeping with his sword by his side, was prepared to protect it against the midnight thief;' Our English Home. p. 101. It was also called a coffer, a hutch, or an ark. This makes the sense clear. The old man is ready to exchange his chest, containing all his worldly gear, for a single hair-cloth, to be used as his shroud.

l. 743. In the margin of MSS. E., Hn., and Pt. is the quotation 'Coram canuto capite consurge,' from Levit. xix. 32. Hence we must understand *Agayns* in l. 743, to mean *before*, or *in presence of*.

l. 748. *God be with you* is said, with probability, to have been the original of our modern unmeaning *Good bye! Go or ride*, a general phrase for locomotion; *go* here means *walk*. Cp. 'ryde or go,' Kn. Tale, 493. Cf. note to l. 866.

l. 771. The readings are :—E. Hn. Cm. *an .viij.*; Ln. *a .vij.*; Cp. Pt. Hl. *a seuen*. The word *eighte* is dissyllabic; cf. A. S. *eahta*, Lat. *octo*. *Wel ny an eighte busshels* = very nearly the quantity of eight bushels. The mention of *florins* is quite in keeping with the Italian character of the poem. Those coins were so named because originally coined at

Florence, the first coinage being in 1252; note in Cary's Dante, Inferno, c. xxx. The value of an English florin was 6s. 8d.; see note to Piers Plowman, ii. 143 (Clar. Press). There is an excellent note on *florins* in Thynne's Animadversions on Speght's Chaucer, ed. Furnivall, p. 45.

l. 781. In allusion to the old proverb—'Lightly come, lightly go.' Cotgrave, s.v. *Fleute*, gives the corresponding French proverb thus :—'Ce qui est venu par la fleute s'en retourne avec le tabourin ; that the pipe hath gathered, the tabour scattereth ; goods ill gotten are commonly ill spent.' In German—'wie gewonnen, so zerronnen.'

l. 782. *Wende*, would have weened, would have supposed. It is the past tense subjunctive.

l. 790. *Doon vs honge*, lit. cause (men) to hang us ; we should now say, cause us to be hanged. 'The Anglo-Saxons nominally punished theft with death, if above 12d. value; but the criminal could redeem his life by a ransom. In the 9th of Henry I. this power of redemption was taken away, 1108. The punishment of theft was very severe in England, till mitigated by Peel's acts, 9 and 10 Geo. IV. 1829.'—Haydn, s.v. *Theft*.

l. 793. To *draw cuts* is to draw lots ; see Prologue, 835, 838, 845. A number of straws were held by one of the company ; the rest drew one apiece, and whoever drew the shortest was the one on whom the lot fell. The shortest straw was the *cut*, i.e. the one cut short ; cf. Welsh *cwtau*, to shorten ; *cwta*, short ; *cwtws*, a lot. In France the custom was reversed ; the lot fell on him who drew the longest ; so that their phrase was—'tirer la longue paille.'

l. 797. So in the Italian story—'rechi del pane e del vino,' let him fetch bread and wine.

l. 806-894. Here Chaucer follows the general sense of the Italian story rather closely, but with certain amplifications.

l. 807. *That oon*, the one ; *that other*, the other.

l. 819. *Conseil*, a secret; as in P. Plowman, B. v. 168. We still say—'to keep one's own counsel.'

l. 844. So the Italian story—'Il Demonio . . . mise in cuore a costui,' &c.; the devil put it in his heart.

l. 848. *Leue*, leave. 'That he had leave to bring him to sorrow.'

l. 851-878. Of this graphic description there is no trace in the Italian story as we now have it. Cf. Rom. and Juliet, v. 1.

l. 860. *Al so*, as. The sense is—as (I hope) God may save my soul. That our modern *as* is for *als*, which is short for *also*, from the A.S. *eall-swá*, is now well known. This fact was doubted by Mr. Singer, but Sir F. Madden, in his Reply to Mr. Singer's remarks upon Havelok the Dane, accumulated such a mass of evidence upon the subject as to set the question at rest for ever. It follows that *as* and *also* are doublets, or various spellings of the same word.

l. 865. *Sterue*, die; **A. S.** *stearfan*. The **cognate** German *sterben* retains the old general sense. See l. 888 below.

l. 866. *Goon a paas*, walk at an ordinary **foot-pace**; so also, *a litel more than paas*, a little faster than at a foot-pace, **Prol.** 825. Cotgrave has—' Aller le pas, to pace, or **go at** a foot-pace; **to** walk fair and softly, or faire and leisurely.' *Nat but*, no more than **only**; cf. North of **England** *nobbut*. The time meant would be about twenty minutes at most.

l. 888. In the Italian story—' amendue caddero morti,' both of them **fell** dead.

l. 889. *Avycen*, Avicenna; mentioned in the Prologue, l. 432. **Avi-zenna**, or Ibn-Sina, a **celebrated** Arabian philosopher and physician, born near Bokhara A.D. 980, died A.D. **1037**. His chief work was a treatise on medicine known as the Canon (' Kitâb al-Kânûn fi'l-Tibb,' that is, ' Book of the Canon in Medicine'). This book, alluded to in the next line, is divided into books and sections; **and** the Arabic word for ' section ' is in the Latin version denoted by *fen*, from the Arabic *fann*, a part of any science. Chaucer's expression is not quite correct; **he seems** to have taken *canon* in its usual sense of rule, **whereas it** is **really the title of the whole work.** It is much as if one were to speak of **Dante's work in the** terms—' such as Dante never wrote in any Divina Commedia nor in **any canto.'** Lib. iv. Fen 1 of Avicenna's Canon treats ' De Venenis.'

l. 895. Against this line is written, in MS. E. only, the word ' Auctor;' **to** shew that the paragraph contained in ll. 895–903 **is a** reflection by the author.

l. 897. The final *e* in *glutonye* is preserved by the cæsural pause; but the scansion of the line is more easily seen by supposing it suppressed. Hence in order to scan the line, suppress the final *e* in *glutonye*, lay the accent on the second *u* in *luxúrie*, and slur over the final *-ie* in that **word.** Thus—

        O glút | onýʾ | luxú | rie and hás | ardrýë ‖

l. 904. *Good men* is the common phrase of address to hearers in old homilies, answering to the modern ' dear brethren.' The Pardoner, **having told his tale** (after which Chaucer himself **has** thrown in a moral **reflection**), proceeds to improve his opportunity by addressing the audience **in his** usual professional style; see l. 915.

l. 907. *Noble*, a coin worth 6s. 8d., first coined by Edward III. about 1339. See note **to** P. Plowman, B. iii. 45 (Clar. Press).

l. 908. So in P. Plowman, B. prol. **75**, it is said of the Pardoner that he ' raughte with his ragman [bull] *rynges and broches*.'

l. 910. *Cometh* is to be pronounced *Com'th*, as in Prol. 839; so also in l. 925 below.

l. 920. *Male*, bag; see Prol. 694.

l. 935. The first two syllables in *perauénture* are to be very rapidly pronounced; it is not uncommon to find the spelling *jeraunter*, as in P. Plowman, B. xi. 10.

l. 937. *Which a*, what sort of a, how great a, what a.

l. 945. *Ye, for a grote*, yea, even for a groat, i.e. 4*d.*

l. 946. *Haue I*, may I have; an imprecation.

l. 947. *So theech*, a colloquialism for **so thee ich**, so may I thrive. The Host proceeds to abuse the Pardoner in **not very** decent terms.

l. 962. *Ryght enough*, quite enough; *ryght* is an adverb. Cf. l. 960.

NOTES TO THE SECOND NONNES TALE (GROUP G).

For general remarks on this Tale, see the Preface.

PROLOGUE. This consists of **twelve** stanzas, and is at once divisible into three parts.

(1) The first four stanzas, the idea of which is taken **from** Jehan de Vignay's Introduction to his French translation of the Legenda Aurea. This Introduction is reprinted at length, from the Paris edition of 1513, **in** the Originals and Analogues published by the Chaucer Society, pt. ii. p. 190.

(2) The Invocation to the Virgin, in stanzas 5-11; see note **to** ll. 29, 36.

(3) An Envoy to the reader, **in** stanza 12; see note to l. 78.

Line 1. Jehan de Vignay attributes the idea of this line to St. Bernard. He says—' Et pour ce que oysiuete est tant blasmee que sainct Bernard dit qu'elle est *mere de truffes* [mother of trifles], marrastre de vertus: . . et fait estaindre vertu et *nourrir orgueil*,' &c. Chaucer says again, in his Persones Tale (de Accidia)—' And though that ignorance be the mother of alle harmes, certes, *negligence is the norice.*'

l. 2. *Ydelnesse*, idleness; considered as a branch of Sloth, which was one **of the** Seven Deadly Sins. See Chaucer's Persones Tale, *De Accidia.*

l. 3. **Chaucer** took this idea from the Romaunt of the Rose; see ll. 528-594 **of the** English version, where a lover is described as knocking at the wicket of a garden, which was opened by a beautiful maiden named Idleness. He afterwards repeated it in the Knightes Tale, l. 1082; and again in the Persones Tale (de Accidia)—' Than cometh ydelnesse, that **is** the yate [*gate*] of all harmes. . . . Certes heuen is yeuen to hem that will labour, and not **to** ydel folke.'

l. 4. *To eschue*, to eschew; the gerund. The sentence really begins with l. 6, after which take the words *to eschue*; then take ll. 1-3, followed by the rest of l. 4 and by l. 5.

l. 7. Jehan de Vignay's Introduction begins thus: ' Monseigneur sainct hierosme dit ceste auctorite—" Fays tousiours aucune chose de bien, que le dyable ne te trouue oyseux." ' That is, he refers us to St. Jerome for the idea. We are reminded, too, of the familiar lines by Dr. Watts—

'For Satan finds some mischief still
For idle hands to do.'

l. 8. Cf. Persones Tale (de Accidia)—'An idel man is like to a place that hath no walles, theras deuiles may enter on euery side.'

l. 14. Cf. Pers. Tale (de Accidia)—'Ayenst this roten sinne of accidie and slouthe shulde men exercise hemself, and use hemself to do good werkes;' &c. 'Laborare est orare' was the famous motto of St. Bernard.

l. 15. *Though men dradden neuer*, even if men never feared.

l. 17. *Roten*, rotten; Tyrwhitt's text reads *rote of*, i.e. root of. Yet *roten* seems right; observe its occurrence in the note to l. 14 above.

l. 19. 'And (men also) see that Sloth holds her in a leash, (for her) to do nothing but sleep, and eat and drink, and devour all that others obtain by toil.' The reading *hir* refers to Idleness, which, as I have before explained, was a branch of Sloth, and was personified by a female. See notes to ll. 2 and 3 above. Tyrwhitt has *hem*, which is not in any of our seven MSS.

l. 21. Compare Piers Plowman, B. prol. 21, 22—

'In settyng and in sowyng · swonken ful harde,
And wonnen that wastours · with glotonye destruyeth.'

l. 25. *After the legende*, following the Legend; i.e. the Legenda Aurea. A very small portion is wholly Chaucer's own. He has merely added a line here and there, such as ll. 489-497, 505-511, 535, 536. At l. 346 he begins to be less literal; see notes to 380, 395, 443.

l. 27. St. Cecilia and St. Dorothea are both depicted with garlands. Mrs. Jameson tells us how to distinguish them in her Sacred and Legendary Art, 3rd ed. 591. She also says, at p. 35—'The wreath of roses on the brow of St. Cecilia, the roses or fruits borne by St. Dorothea, are explained by the legends.' And again, at p. 36— 'White and red roses expressed love and innocence, or love and wisdom, as in the garland with which the angels crown St. Cecilia.' *Red* was the symbol of love, divine fervour, &c.; *white*, of light, purity, innocence, virginity. See ll. 220, 244, 279. The legend of St. Dorothea forms the subject of Massinger's Virgin Martyr.

l. 29. *Virgines* must be a trisyllable here; such words are often shortened to a dissyllable. The word *thou* is addressed to the Virgin Mary. In the margin of MSS. E. and IIn. is written—'Inuocatio

l. 30. Speaking of St. Bernard, Mrs. Jameson says—'One of his most celebrated works, the *Missus est*, was composed in her honour [i.e. in honour of the Virgin] as Mother of the Redeemer; and in eighty Sermons on texts from the Song of Solomon, he set forth her divine perfection as the Selected and Espoused, the type of the Church on earth;' Legends of the Monastic Orders, 2nd ed. p. 144.

See a further illustration of the great favour shewn by the Virgin to St. Bernard at p. 142 of the same volume; and, at p. 145, the description of a painting by Murillo, quoted from Stirling's Spanish Painters, p. 914. See also Dante, Paradiso, xxxi. 102.

l. 32. *Confort of us wrecches*, comfort of us miserable sinners; see note to l. 58.

Do me endyte, cause me to indite.

l. 34. *Of the feend*, over the Fiend. Tyrwhitt reads *over* for *of*, but it is unnecessary. Accent *victorie* on the o.

l. 36. Lines 36-51 are a free translation of a passage in Dante's Paradiso, Canto xxxiii. ll. 1-21; and are quoted in the notes to Cary's translation.

l. 36.	'Vergine madre, figlia del tuo Figlio,
l. 39.	Umile ed alta più che creatura,
	Termine fisso d'eterno consiglio,
	Tu se' colei che l' umana natura
ll. 40, 41.	Nobilitastì sì, che il suo Fattore
ll. 41, 42.	Non disdegnò di farsi sua fattura.
l. 43.	Nel ventre tuo si raccese l' amore,
l. 44.	Per lo cui caldo nell' eterna pace
	Così è germinato questo fiore.
	Qui sei a noi meridiana face
	Di caritade, e giuso, intra i mortali,
	Sé' di speranza fontana vivace.
	Donna, se' tanto grande, e tanto vali,
	Che qual vuol grazia, e a te non ricorre,
	Sua disianza vuol volar senz' ali.
ll. 53, 54.	La tua benignità non pur soccorre
ll. 53, 54.	A chi dimanda, ma molte fiate
ll. 55, 56.	Liberamente al dimandar precorre.
l. 51.	In te misericordia, in te pietate,
l. 50.	In te magnificenza, in te s'aduna
	Quatunque in creatura è di bontate.'

The numbers at the side denote the corresponding lines. I add a literal prose rendering of the above passage :—

      Virgin mother, daughter of thy Son,

      Lowly and yet exalted more than (any other) creature,

      Fixed limit of the eternal counsel,

Thou art she who didst so ennoble
Human nature, that its Maker
Disdained not to become His own creation.
Within thy womb love was so rekindled,
By the heat whereof, in eternal peace,
This flower has thus budded.
Here art thou to us the meridian torch
Of love, and beneath, among mortals,
Thou art the living fountain of hope.
Lady! thou art so great, and art of such avail,
That whoso desires grace, and does not resort to thee,
His desire endeavours to fly without wings.
Thy benignity not only brings succour
To him who prays for it, but many times
Bountifully foreruns the prayer.
In thee is mercy, in thee is pity,
In thee is munificence, in thee is united
Whatever excellence is in a created being.

l. 40. *Nobledest*, didst ennoble; Dante's 'nobilitasti.'

l. 42. The translation is inexact. **Dante** says—' that its Maker (i.e. **the Maker of human nature**) did not disdain to become His own creature,' i.e. born of that very human nature which He had Himself created. Cf. l. 49.

l. 45. 'That is, Lord and Guide of the threefold space;' i.e. of the three abodes of things created, viz. the earth, the sea, and the heavens.

l. 46. *Out of relees*, without release, i.e. without relaxation, without ceasing. *Out of* means *without*, as is clear from Prol. 487; Kn. Tale, 283; and *relees* means *acquittance* (O. Fr. *relais*); see **Cler.** Tale, E. 153, and *Relesse* in Gloss. Index to Prioresses Tale, &c. There has been some doubt about the meaning of this phrase, but there need be none; especially when it is remembered that *to release* is another form of *to relax*, so that *relees = relaxation*, i.e. slackening. The idea is the same as that so admirably expressed in the Prolog im Himmel to Goethe's Faust.

l. 50. *Assembled is in thee*, there is united in thee; cf. Dante—'in te s'aduna.' This stanza closely resembles the fourth stanza of the Prioresses Prologue, B. 1664-1670; see Prioresses Tale, p. 10.

l. 52. *Sonne*. By all means let the reader remember that *sonne* was probably feminine in English in Chaucer's time, as it is in German, Dutch, and Icelandic to this day. It will be found, however, that **Chaucer** commonly identifies the sun with Phœbus, making it masculine; see Prol. 8, Kn. Tale 635. Still, there is a remarkable example of the old use in the first rubric of Part ii. of Chaucer's Astrolabie

cours a-bowte.' So again, in Piers Plowman, B. xviii. 243—' And lo!
how the sonne gan louke *her* lighte in *herself*.'

1. 56. *Her lyues leche*, the physician of their lives (*or* life).

1. 58. *Flemed wrecche*, banished **exile**. The proper sense of A. S.
wræcca is an exile, a stranger; and thence, a miserable being, an exile.
The phrase 'fleming of wrecches,' i.e. banishment of the miserable, occurs
in Chaucer's Troilus, iii. 935 (ed. Tyrwhitt). And see above, B. 460.

Galle, bitterness. **There** is probably an allusion to the name Mary,
and to the Hebrew *mar*, fem. *mârâh*, bitter. Cf. Exod. xv. 23; Acts
viii. 23; Ruth **i. 20.** Cf. Chaucer's *A B C*, l. 50.

1. 59. *Womman Cananee*, a translation of *mulier Chananæa* in the
Vulgate version **of** Mat. xv. 22. Wyclif calls her 'a womman **of**
Canane.'

1. 60. Compare Wyclif's version—'for whelpis eten of the crummes
that fallen doun fro the bord of her lordis;' Mat. xv. 27.

1. 62. *Sone of Eue*, son of Eve, i.e. the author himself. This, as
Tyrwhitt remarks (Introd. Discourse, note 30), is a clear proof that the
Tale was never properly revised to suit it for the collection. The
expression is unsuitable for the supposed narrator, the Second Nun.

1. 64. See James ii. 17.

1. 67. *Ful of grace;* alluding to the phrase 'Aue gratia plena' in
Luke i. 28.

1. 68. *Aduócat*, accented on the penultimate.

1. 69. *Ther as*, where that. *Osanne*, Hosanna, i.e. 'Save, we pray,'
from Ps. cxviii. 25. See Concise Dict. of the Bible.

1. 70. The Virgin Mary was said to have been the daughter **of**
Joachim and Anna; see the Protevangelion of James, and the Legenda
Aurea, cap. cxxi—' De natiuitate beatne Mariae uirginis.'

1. 75. *Hauen of refut*, haven of refuge. See the same term similarly
applied in **B. 852,** above. Cf. Chaucer's *A B C*, l. 14.

1. 78. *Reden*, read. This is still clearer proof that the story was not
originally meant to be narrated. Cf. note to l. **62.**

1. 82. *Him*, i.e. Jacobus Januensis; see the Preface. *At the*, &c., out
of reverence for the saint.

1. 83. *Hir legende*, her (St. Cecilia's) legend as told in the Aurea
Legenda.

1. 84. The **five** stanzas in ll. 85–119 really belong to the Legend itself,
and are in the **original** Latin. Throughout the notes to the rest of this
Tale I follow the **2nd** edition of the Legenda Aurea, cap. clxix, as
edited by Dr. Th. Grässe; Leipsic, 1850.

1. 87. Several of the **Legends** of the Saints begin **with** ridiculous
etymologies. Thus the Legend of S. Valentine (Aur. Leg. cap. xlii)
begins with the explanation that Valentinus means *ualorem tenens*,
or else *ualens tyro*. So here, as to the etymology of Cæcilia, we are

generously offered *five* solutions, all of them **being** wrong. As it is **hopeless** to understand them without consulting **the original,** I shall quote as much of it as is necessary, arranged in a less confused order. The true etymology is, of course, that Cæcilia is the feminine of Cæcilius, a name borne by members of the Cæcilia gens, which claimed descent from Cæculus, an ancient Italian hero, son of Vulcan, who is said to have founded Præneste. Cæculus, probably a nickname, can hardly be other than a mere diminutive of *cæcus,* blind. The legendary etymologies are right, accordingly, only so far as they relate to *cæcus.* Beyond that, they are strange indeed.

The following are the etymologies, with their reasons.

(1) Cæcilia = coeli lilia (*sic*), i.e. *heuenes lilie.* Reasons:—'Fuit enim coeleste lilium per uirginitatis pudorem; uel dicitur *lilium,* quia habuit candorem munditiae, uirorem conscientiae, odorem bonae famae.' See ll. 87-91. Thus *grene* (= greenness) translates *uirorem.*

(2) Cæcilia = caecis uia, i.e. *the wey to blynde,* a path for the blind. Reason:—'Fuit enim caecis uia per exempli informationem.' See ll. 92, 93.

(3) Cæcilia is from *coelum* and *lya.* 'Fuit enim ... *coelum* per iugem contemplationem, *lya* per assiduam operationem.' Here *lya* is the same as *Lia,* which is the Latin spelling of Leah in the Book of Genesis. It was usual to consider Leah as the type of activity, or the active life, and Rachael **as** the type of the contemplative life.

(4) Cæcilia, '**quasi** caecitate carens.' This is on the celebrated principle of ' lucus a non lucendo.' Reason:—' fuit caecitate carens per sapientiae splendorem.' See ll. 99-101.

(5) '**Uel** dicitur a *coelo* et *leos,* i.e. populus.' Finally, recourse is had to Greek, viz. Gk. λεώς, the Attic form of λαός. Reason:—'fuit et coelum populi, quia in ipsa tamquam in coelo spirituali populus ad imitandum intuetur coelum, solem, lunam, et stellas, i.e. sapientiae perspicacitatem, fidei magnanimitatem et uirtutum uarietatem.' See ll. 102-112.

ll. 113-118. Chaucer has somewhat varied the order; this last stanza belongs in the Latin to derivation (3), though it may serve also for derivation **(5).** It is probably for this reason that he has reserved it. The Latin **is**—'**Uel** dicitur coelum, quia, sicut dicit Ysidorus, coelum philosophi uolubile, rotundum et ardens **esse** dixerunt. Sic et ipsa fuit uolubilis per operationem sollicitam, rotunda per perseuerantiam, ardens per caritatem succensam.' For the *swiftness* and *roundness* of heaven, see note to B 295. The epithet *burning* **is** due to quite **another** matter, **not** explained **in that** note. The nine astronomical spheres there mentioned did not suffice for the wants of theology. Hence a *tenth* sphere was imagined, external to **the** ninth; but **this** was supposed to **be** fixed. This outermost sphere was called the *empyræum* (from Gk. ἔμπυρος, burning, which from ἐν, in, and πῦρ, fire) where the pure element of fire subsisted alone, and it was supposed to be the abode of saints and angels. Milton, in his Paradise Lost, uses the word *empyrean* six times, ii. 771, iii. 57, vi. 833, vii. 73, 633, x. 321; and the word *empyreal* eleven times.

l. 120. For some account of St. Cæcilia, see the Preface.

l. 133. *An heyre*, a hair shirt. The usual expression; see P. Plowman, B. v. 66. Lat. text—'cilicio erat induta.'

l. 134. *The organs;* Lat. 'cantantibus organis.' We should now say 'the organ;' but in old authors the plural form is commonly employed. Sometimes the word *organ* seems to refer to a single pipe only, and the whole instrument was called 'the organs' or 'a pair of organs,' where *pair* means a *set*, as in the phrase 'a peire of bedes;' Ch. Prol. 159. Thus, in a burlesque poem in Reliquiæ Antiquæ, i. 81, a porpoise is described as playing on the organ :—'On tho *orgons* playde tho porpas.' In a note to Sir J. Cullum's Hist. of Hawsted, 2nd ed. p. 33, the expression 'pair of organs' is shewn to occur in three accounts, dated 1521, 1536, and 1618 respectively. See another example in Dr. Morris's note to Nonne Prestes Tale, l. 31, where Chaucer uses *orgoon* as a plural, equivalent to the Lat. *organa*. On the early meaning of *organum*, see Chappell's Hist. of Music, i. 327. The invention of organs dates from the third century B.C.; id. i. 325. See Dante, Purg. ix. 144, and the note to Cary's translation. It is worth adding, that another interpretation of *organs* is equally possible here; it may mean musical instruments *of all kinds*; since St. Augustine says—'organa dicuntur omnia instrumenta musicorum;' Comment. in Psalm 56; Chappell's Hist. Music, i. 375, note *a*. In accordance with this view, the French text translates *organis* by *les instrumens*.

St. Cecilia is commonly considered the patroness of music; see Dryden's Ode for St. Cecilia's day, and Alexander's Feast, ll. 132–141. But the connection of her with music is not very ancient, as Mrs. Jameson explains. The *reason* for this connection seems to me clear enough, viz. the simple fact that the word *organis* occurs in this very passage. The workers at various trades all wanted patron saints, and must in many cases have been driven to select them on very trivial grounds. Thus, because St. Sebastian was shot by arrows, he became the patron saint of archers; and so on. See several examples in Chambers, Book of Days, iii. 388. Besides, St. Cecilia is here represented as singing *herself*—'in corde soli domino *decantabat* dicens;' see l. 135.

l. 145. *Conseil*, a secret; Lat. 'mysterium.' And so in l. 192, and in P. Plowm. B. v. 168; see note to C. 819 above. *And, if*.

l. 150. *Here*, her, is a dissyllable in Chaucer whenever it ends a line, which it does six times; see e. g. B. 460; Kn. Tale 1199. This is quite correct, because the A.S. form *hire* is dissyllabic also.

l. 173. Chaucer has here mistranslated the **Latin**. It is not said that the Via Appia (which led out of Rome through the Porta Capena to Aricia, Tres Tabernæ, Appii Forum, and so on towards Capua and Brundusium) was situated three miles from Rome; but that Valerian is to go along the Appian Way as far as to the third milestone. 'Uade igitur in tertium milliarium ab urbe uia quae Appia nuncupatur.'

l. **177.** *Vrban.* St. Urban's day is May 25. This is Urban I, pope, who succeeded Calixtus, A.D. 222. Besides the notice of him in this Tale, his legend is given separately in the Legenda Aurea, cap. lxxvii. He was beheaded May 25, 230, and succeeded by Pontianus.

l. 178. *Secre nedes,* secret necessary reasons; Lat. 'secreta mandata.'

l. 181. *Purged yow,* viz. by the rite of baptism.

l. 186. *Seintes buriels,* burial-places of the saints; Lat. 'sepulchra martirum.' It is worth observing, perhaps, that the word *buriels* is properly *singular,* not plural; cf. A. S. *byrigels,* a sepulchre, and see the examples in Stratmann. In P. Plowman, B. xix. 142, the Jews are represented as guarding Christ's body because it had been foretold that He should rise from the tomb—

'þat þat blessed body · of *burieles* shulde rise.'

Of course the mistake of supposing *s* to be the mark of a plural was made in course of time, and the singular form *biryel* was evolved. This mistake occurs as early as in Wyclif's Bible, IV Kings xxiii. 17; see Way's note in Prompt. Parv. p. 37, note 1. Consequently, it is most likely that Chaucer has made the same mistake here.

There is here a most interesting allusion to the celebrated catacombs of Rome, which are subterranean passages cut in the rock, and were used by the early Christians for the purpose of sepulture. See Chambers, Book of Days, i. 101, 102.

Lotinge, lying hid. In MS. E., the Latin word *latitantem* is written above, as a gloss. This was taken from the Latin text, which has —'intra sepulchra martirum latitantem.' Stratmann gives six examples of the use of *lotien* or *lutien,* to lie hid. It occurs once in P. Plowman, B. xvii. 102, where outlaws are described as lurking in woods and under banks:—

'For outlawes in þe wode · and vnder banke *lotyeth.*'

l. 201. *An old man;* i.e. an angel in the form of an old man, viz. St. Paul. Cf. note to l. 207.

l. 202. *With lettre of gold;* Lat. 'tenens librum aureis litteris scriptum.' L. 203 is not in the original.

l. 205. 'When he (Valerian) saw him (the old man); and he (the old man) lifted up him (Valerian); and then he (Valerian) began thus to read in his (the old man's) book.' This is very ambiguous in Chaucer, but the Latin is clear. 'Quem uidens Ualerianus prae nimio timore quasi mortuus cecidit, et a sene leuatus sic legit.'

l. **207.** *Oo lord*, one lord. Tyrwhitt prints *on*, 'to guard against the mistake which the editions generally have fallen into, of considering o, in this passage, as the sign of the vocative case.' For the same reason, I have printed *Oo*, as in MS. Pt., in preference to the single o, as in most MSS. Even one of the scribes has fallen into the trap, and has written against this passage—'Et lamentat.' See MS. Cp., in the Six-text edition. The fact is, obviously, that ll. 207–209 are a close translation of Eph. **iv. 5, 6.** Hence the old man must be St. Paul.

l. **208.** *Christendom*, baptism; Lat. 'baptisma.' See l. 217.

l. **216.** We must read *the* before *oldë*, not *this* or *that*, because *e* in *the* must be elided; otherwise the line will not scan.

l. **223, 224.** *That oon*, the one; sometimes written *the ton* or *the toon*. *That other*, the other; sometimes written *the tother*. 'The ton' is obsolete; but 'the tother' may still be heard. *That* is the neuter of the A. S. def. article *se, seó, þæt;* cf. Germ. *der, die, das.*

As to the signification of the red and white flowers, see note to l. 27 above.

Compare Act v. sc. 1 of Massinger's Virgin Martyr, where an angel brings flowers from St. Dorothea, who is in paradise, to Theophilus. See note to l. 248 below.

l. **232.** *For*, because ; Lat. 'quia.'

l. **236.** Afterwards repeated, very nearly, in Kn. Tale, l. 338.

l. **243.** *Sauour vndernom*, perceived the scent ; Lat. 'sensisset odorem.'

l. **248.** *Rose.* We should have expected *roses*. Perhaps this is due to the peculiar form of the Latin text, which has—'roseus hic odor et liliorum.'

Compare the words of Theophilus in the Virgin Martyr, v. 1 :—

> 'What flowers are these?
> In Diocletian's gardens the most beauteous,
> Compared with these, are weeds; is it not February,
> The second day she died? frost, ice, and snow
> Hang on the beard of winter: where's the sun
> That gilds this summer? pretty, sweet boy, say,
> In what country shall a man find this garden?'

l. **270.** Ll. 270–283 are certainly genuine, and the passage is in the Latin text. It is also in the French version, but it does not appear in the Early English version of the story printed by Mr. Furnivall from MS. Ashmole **43**, nor in the English version printed by Caxton in 1483. Tyrwhitt's supposition is no doubt correct, viz. that this passage 'appears evidently to have been at first a marginal observation and to have crept into the [Latin] text by the blunder of some copyist.' He truly observes that these fourteen lines 'interrupt the narrative awkwardly, and to little purpose.'

l. 271. *Ambrose.* 'Huic miraculo de coronis rosarum Ambrosius attestatur in praefatione, sic dicens,' &c. I cannot find anything of the kind in the indices to the works of St. Ambrose.

l. 276. *Eek hir chambre,* even hir marriage-chamber, i.e. even marriage. *Weyue,* waive, abandon. Lat. 'ipsum mundum est cum thalamis exsecrata.' *Weyue* occurs again in some MSS. of Chaucer's *Truth,* l. 20.

l. 277. *Shrifte,* confession. Lat. 'testis est Ualeriani coniugis et Tiburtii prouocata confessio, quos, Domine, angelica manu odoriferis floribus coronasti.' For *Valerians,* all the MSS. have *Cecilies.* Whether the mistake is Chaucer's or his scribes', I cannot say; but it is so obviously a mere slip, that we need not hesitate to correct it. The French text is even clearer than the Latin; it has—'et de cest tesmoing valerien son mary et tiburcien son frere.' Besides, the express mention of 'these men' in l. 281 is enough, in my opinion, to shew that the slip was *not* Chaucer's own; or, at any rate, was a mere oversight.

l. 282. 'The world hath known (by their example) how much, in all truth, it is worth to love such devotion to chastity.' Lat. 'mundus agnouit, quantum ualeat deuotio castitatis;—haec Ambrosius.' This is quoted as St. Ambrose's opinion. The parenthesis ends here.

l. 288. *Beste,* i.e. void of understanding, as a beast of the field is. Lat. 'pecus est.'

l. 315. *And we.* Tyrwhitt remarks that *we* should have been *us.* But a glance at the Latin text shews what was in Chaucer's mind; he is here merely anticipating the *we* in l. 318. Lat. 'et *nos* in illius flammis pariter inuoluemur, et dum quaerimus diuinitatem latentem in coelis, incurremus furorem exurentem in terris.' The sentence is awkward; but *we* was intended. The idiom has overridden the grammar.

l. 319. *Cecile.* This is one of the clearest instances to shew that Chaucer followed the Latin and not the French version. Lat. 'Cui Caecilia;' Fr. 'et valerien dist.' Mr. Furnivall has noted this and other instances, and there is no doubt about the matter.

l. 320. *Skilfully,* reasonably; the usual meaning at this date. See l. 327.

l. 327. 'And all that has been created by a reasonable Intelligence.'

l. 329. *Hath sowled,* hath endued with a soul, hath quickened; Lat. 'animauit.'

l. 335. *O god,* one God. We must suppose this teaching to be included in the mention of Christ in l. 295; otherwise there is no allusion to it in the words of Cecilia. The doctrine had been taught to Valerian however; see ll. 207, 208.

There are continual allusions, in the Lives of the Saints, to the difficulty of this doctrine.

l. 338. Chaucer is not quite exact. The Latin says that three things

reside in a man's wisdom, the said wisdom being but *one.* 'Sicut in
una hominis sapientia tria sunt, ingenium, memoria et intellectus.' The
notion resembles that in a favourite passage from Isidore quoted in
Piers Plowman, B. xv. 39, to the effect that the soul (*anima*) has
different names according to its functions. When engaged in remem-
bering, we call it memory (*memoria*); when in judging, we call it
reason (*ratio*); and so on. Compare the curious illustrations of the
doctrine of the Trinity in Piers Plowman, B. xvi. 220–224, xvii. 137–
249. The illustration in the text is, as Mr. Jephson points out, by
no means a good one.

l. 341. The word *Thre* stands alone in the first foot.

Thré | persón | es máy | ther ryght | wel bé ‖

See note to l. 353.

l. 343. *Come*, coming, i.e. incarnation; Lat. 'aduentu.' Tyrwhitt
read *sonde*, i.e. sending, message; but incorrectly.

l. 345. *Withholde*, detained, constrained to dwell; Lat. 'tentus;'
Fr. 'tenu.'

l. 346. Hitherto Chaucer's translation is, on the whole, very close.
Here he omits a whole sentence, and begins to abbreviate the story
and alter it to suit himself. See his hint in l. 360.

l. 351. *That*, who. In MS. E. the word is glossed by—'qui, scilicet
Vrbanus.' It is remarkable that the relative *who* (as a *simple* relative,
without *so* suffixed) is hardly to be found in English of this date, in
the *nominative* case. The A.S. *hwá* is only used interrogatively.
'*Hwá* (who) appears as a proper relative first in its dative *wam* or *wan*
in Layamon, ii. 632, iii. 50 [about A.D. 1200]; in its genitive *whas* and
dative *wham* in Ormulum, 3425, 10370 [about the same date]. The
nominative *who* is found sometimes with a pronominal antecedent in
Wycliffe, A.D. 1382–3 (Isaiah i. 10), and becomes common as a full
relative in Berners' Froissart, A.D. 1523;' March, Anglo-Saxon Grammar, p. 179.

l. 353. *Goddes knyght*, God's servant, or rather, God's soldier; see
l. 383, and the note. In the A.S. version of the Gospels Christ's
disciples are called 'leorning-cnihtas.' In the Ormulum and in Wyclif
cniht or *kniȝt* sometimes means a servant, but more commonly a soldier.
Priests are called 'goddes knyghtes' in Piers Plowman, B. xi. 304.
In scanning this line, either *lerninge* is of three syllables (which I doubt)
or else the first syllable in *Parfyt* forms a foot by itself; see note to
l. 341 above.

l. 362. *Almache*; Lat. 'Almachius praefectus.' The reigning emperor
was Alexander Severus (A.D. 222–235).

l. 363. *Apposed*, questioned, examined; written *opposed* in most MSS.,
not without good reason. Ed. 1532 also has *aposed*. A similar
confusion occurs in the Freres Tale, D. 1597, where only two MSS.,

viz. **Pt.** and **Ln.**, have the later spelling *appose*, as against five others which rightly read *opposen*. The later spelling occurs in MSS. of Piers the Plowman, where we find *appose*, to question, B. iii. 5; *apposed*, i. 47; *apposeden*, vii. 138. Skelton has it, in his Colin Clout, 267 :—

> 'For that they are not *apposed*
> By iust examinacyon
> In connyng and conuersacyon.'

Mr. Dyce (note on this line) quotes from Horman—'He was *apposed*, or examyned of his byleue, De religione appellatus est;' Vulgaria, sig. Dii. ed. 1530. In Prompt. Parv. it is confused with *oppose*. Wedgwood explains that *appose*, or *pose*, lit. to lay near (Fr. *apposer*), was used in the particular sense of putting specific questions to a candidate for examination; whence the phrase an *apposite* answer, applied to one that was to the point; see his article on *Pose.* But the New E. Dict. gives *oppose* as the original form.

l. 365. *Sacrifyse,* sacrifice to the idol. This was the usual test to which Christians were subjected; see note to l. 395. Compare Dan. iii. 14, 18. So in the Virgin Martyr, iv. 2 :—

> 'Bow but thy knee to Jupiter, and offer
> Any slight sacrifice; or do but swear
> By Cæsar's fortune, and—be free!'

l. 367. *Thise martirs*; note that this is an accusative case.

l. 369. *Corniculere,* a sort of officer. The note in Bell's edition, that the French version has *prevost* here, is wrong. The word *prevost* (Lat. *praefectus*) is applied to Almachius. Maximus was only a subordinate officer, and is called in the Early Eng. version (MS. Ashmole 43) the 'gailer.' The expression 'Maximo Corniculario' occurs only in the Lives of Valerian and Tiburtius, in the Acta Sanctorum (April 14).

Riddle's Lat. Dict. gives—'*Cornicularius,* -i. m. a soldier who was presented with a *corniculum,* and by means of it promoted to a higher rank; hence, *an assistant of an officer,* Suetonius, Domit. 17; then also in the civil service, *an assistant of a magistrate, a clerk, registrar, secretary;* Cod. Just.'

'*Corniculum,* -i. n. (dimin. of *cornu*). 1. *A little horn,* Pliny; also, *a small funnel of horn,* Columella. *An ornament in the shape of a horn worn on the helmet,* with which officers presented meritorious soldiers; Livy, 10. 44.'

Ducange gives several examples, shewing that the word commonly meant a secretary, clerk, or registrar. Tyrwhitt refers us to Pitiscus Lex. Ant. Rom. s.v. *Cornicularius.*

l. 373. 'He got leave for himself from the executioners.' *Tormentoures,* executioners; Lat. 'carnifices.' See l. 527. Cf. *tormentor* in Matt. xviii. 34; see Eastwood and Wright's Bible Word-book.

l. 380. *Prestes,* priests. The original says that pope Urban came himself.

l. 383. *Knyghtes,* soldiers; as in l. 353. Lat. 'Eia milites Christi, abicite opera tenebrarum, et induimini arma lucis.' See Rom. xiii. 12.

l. 386. Tyrwhitt notes a slight defect in the use of *ydoon* in l. 386, followed by *doon* in l. 387. The first six lines in this stanza are not in the original, but are imitated from 2 Tim. iv. 7, 8.

l. 395. 'This was the criterion. The Christians were brought to the image of Jupiter or of the Emperor, and commanded to join in the sacrifice, by eating part of it, or to throw a few grains of incense into the censer, in token of worship; if they refused, they were put to death. —See Pliny's celebrated letter to Trajan. Those who complied were termed *sacrificati* and *thurificati* by the canons, and were excluded from the communion for seven or ten years, or even till their death, according to the circumstances of their lapse.—See Bingham's *Antiquities,* b. xvi. 4. 5.'—Note in Bell's edition of Chaucer. Cf. note to l. 365.

This stanza is represented in the original (in spite of the hint in l. 394) by only a few words. 'Quarto igitur milliario ab urbe sancti ad statuam Iovis ducuntur, et dum sacrificare nollent, pariter decollantur.'

l. 405. *To-bete,* beat severely; *dide him so to-bete,* caused (men) to beat him so severely, caused him to be so severely beaten. I have no hesitation in adopting the reading of ed. 1532 here. *To-bete* is just the right word, and occurs in MSS. Cp., Pt., Ln.; and, though these MSS. are not the best ones, it is clear that *to-bete* is the original reading, or it would not appear. I give two examples of the use of the word. 'Ure men hi *to-betet,*' i.e. they severely beat our men; Layamon's Brut, l. 3308. 'Me *to-beot* his cheoken, and spette him a schorn;' men severely beat His cheeks, and spit upon Him in scorn; Ancren Riwle, p. 106. See *To-race* and *To-rente* in Gloss. to Chaucer's Prioresses Tale, &c.; see also *Dide* in the same. To scan the line, slur over *-ius* in *Almachius,* and accent *dide.*

l. 406. *Whippe of leed,* i.e. a whip furnished with leaden plummets. Lat. 'eum plumbatis tamdiu caedi fecit,' &c.; French text —'il le fist tant batre de plombees,' &c.; Caxton—'he dyd do bete hym with plomettes of leed.'

l. 413. *Encense,* offer incense to; see note to l. 395.

l. 414. *They.* Over this word is written, in MS. E.—'scilicet Ministres.' The Latin original says that Cecilia converted as many as 400 persons upon this occasion. Hence the expression o voys (one voice) in l. 420.

l. 417. *Withouten difference,* i.e. without difference in might, majesty, or glory.

l. 430. *Lewedly,* ignorantly. The 'two answers' relate to her rank and her religion, subjects which had no real connection.

l. 434. Lat. 'de conscientia bona et fide non ficta;' cf. 1 Tim. i. 5.

l. 437. *To dreede*, to be feared; the gerund, and right according to the old idiom. We still say—'he is *to blame*,' 'this house *to let*.' March, in his Anglo-Saxon Grammar, p. 198, says—'The gerund after the copula expresses what *must*, *may*, or *should* be done.

'Ex. *Mannes sunu is tó syllanne*, the Son of Man must be delivered up, Matt. xvii. 22;' &c.

l. 442. *Bigonne*, didst begin; the right form, for which Tyrwhitt has *begonnest*. For the Mid. Eng. *biginnen* we commonly find *onginnan* in Anglo-Saxon, and the form for the past tense is—*ongan*, *ongunne*, *ongan*; pl. *ongunnon*. The form in Middle English is—*bigan*, *bigunne* (or *bigonne*), *bigan*; pl. *bigunnen* (or *bigonne*). The very form here used occurs in the Ayenbite of Inwyt, ed. Morris, p. 71. The suffix -*st* does not appear in *strong* verbs; cf. *Thou sey*, B. 848; *thou bar*, G. 48.

The whole of ll. 443–467 varies considerably from the original, the corresponding passage of which is as follows: 'Cui Almachius: "ab iniuriis caepisti, et in iniuriis perseueras." Caecilia respondit: "iniuria non dicitur quod uerbis fallentibus irrogatur; unde aut iniuriam doce, si falsa locuta sum, aut te ipsum corripe calumniam inferentem, sed nos scientes sanctum Dei nomen omnino negare non possumus; melius est enim feliciter mori quam infeliciter uiuere." Cui Almachius: "ad quid cum tanta superbia loqueris?" Et illa: "non est superbia, sed constantia." Cui Almachius: "infelix, ignoras,"' &c. (l. 468). However, Chaucer has adopted an idea from this in ll. 473, 475.

l. 463. To scan this, remember that *Iuge* has two syllables; and accent *confus* on the first syllable.

l. 485. Lat. 'es igitur minister mortis, non uitae.'

l. 487. *Do wey*, do away with; Lat. 'depone.' The phrase occurs again in the Milleres Tale; C. T. 3287, ed. Tyrwhitt.

ll. 489–497. These lines are wholly Chaucer's own.

l. 490. To scan the line, elide *e* in *suffre*, and read *philosóphre*.

l. 492. *Spekest*; to be read as *spek'st*.

l. 498. *Utter yen*, outer eyes, bodily eyes. In MS. E. it is glossed by 'exterioribus oculis.' The Latin has—'nescio ubi oculos amiseris; nam quos tu Deos dicis, omnes nos saxa esse uidemus; mitte igitur manum et tangendo disce, quod oculis non uales uidere.'

l. 503. *Taste*, test, try; Lat. 'tangendo disce.' The word is now restricted to one of the five senses; it could once have been used also of the sense of feeling, at the least. Bottom even ventures on the strange expression—'I trust to *taste* of truest Thisbe's *sight*;' Mid. Nt. Dream,

l. 533. Lat. 'eam semiuiuam cruentus carnifex dereliquit.'

l. 534. *Is went*, though only in the (excellent) Cambridge MS., is the right reading; the rest have *he wente*, sometimes misspelt *he went*. In the first place, *is went* is a common phrase in Chaucer; cf. German *er ist gegangen*, and Eng. *he is gone*. But secondly, the false rime detects the blunder at once; Chaucer does not rime the weak past tense *wentë* with a past participle like *yhent*. This was obvious to me at the first glance, but the matter was made sure by consulting Mr. Cromie's excellent 'Ryme-Index.' This at once gives the examples *is went*, riming with pp. *to-rent*, E. 1012 (Clerkes Tale); *is went*, riming with *instrument*, F. 567 (Sq. Tale); *is went*, riming with *innocent*, B. 1730, and *ben went*, riming with *pauement*, B. 1869 (Prioresses Tale); all of which may be found in my edition of The Prioresses Tale, &c. Besides this, there are two more examples, viz. *be they went*, riming with *sacrement*, E. 1701; and *that he be went*, riming with *sent*, A. 3665. On the other hand, we find *wente, sente, hente*, and *to-rente*, all (weak) past tenses, and all riming together, in the Monkes Tale, B. 3446. The student should particularly observe an instance like this. The rules of rime in Chaucer are, on the whole, so carefully observed that, when once they are learnt, a false rime jars upon the ear with such discord as to be unpleasantly remarkable, and should be at once detected.

ll. 535, 536. These two lines are not in the original.

l. 539. 'She began to preach to them whom she had fostered,' i.e. converted. To *foster* is here to nurse, to bring up, to educate in the faith; see l. 122 above. The Latin text has—'omnes quos ad fidem conuerterat, Urbano episcopo commendauit.' Tyrwhitt makes nonsense of this line by placing the comma after *hem* instead of after *fostred*, and other editors have followed him. In MSS. E. and Hn. the metrical pause is rightly marked as occurring after *fostred*. The story here closely resembles the end of the Prioresses Tale, B. 1801–1855.

l. 545. *Do werche*, cause to be constructed.

l. 549. Lat. 'inter episcopos sepeliuit.'

l. 550. 'It is now a church in Rome, and gives a title to a cardinal;' note in Bell's edition. In a poem called the Stacyons of Rome, ed. Furnivall, l. 832, we are told that 100 years' pardon may be obtained by going to St. Cecilia's church. Mr. W. M. Rossetti, in a note on this line, says—'The Church of St. Cecilia, at the end of the Trastevere, near the Quay of Ripa Grande, was built on the site of the saint's own house in 230; rebuilt by pope Paschal I. in 821, and dedicated to God and Sts. Mary, Peter, Paul, and Cecilia; and altered to its present form in 1599 and 1725. In the former of these years, 1599, the body of the saint was found on the spot, with a contemporary inscription identifying her: the celebrated statue by Stefano Maderno, now in the church, represents her in the attitude she was discovered lying in. Francino does not name the 100 years indulgence of the text, but plenary indulgence on St. Cecilia's day.'

l. 553. After this line the Latin adds—'Passa est autem circa annos domini CC et XXIII, tempore Alexandri imperatoris. Alibi autem legitur, quod passa sit tempore Marci Aurelii, qui imperauit circa annos domini CCXX.' The confusion of names here is easily explained. Marcus Aurelius died in 180; but Marcus Aurelius Alexander Severus (for such was his title in full) reigned from 222 to 235. The true date is generally considered to be 230, falling within his reign, as it should do.

NOTES TO THE CANON'S YEOMAN'S TALE.

l. 554. *The lyf of seint Cecile*, i.e. the Second Nun's Tale. This notice is important, because it inseparably links the Canon's Yeoman's Tale to the preceding one.

l. 555. *Fyue myle*, five miles. Tyrwhitt says that it is five miles 'from *some place*, which we are now unable to determine with certainty.' He adds that he is in doubt whether the pilgrims are here supposed to be riding *from* or *towards* Canterbury; but afterwards thinks that 'the manner in which the Yeman expresses himself in ver. 16091, 2 [i.e. ll. 623, 624] seems to shew that he was riding *to* Canterbury.'

It is really very easy to explain the matter, and to tell all about it. It is perfectly clear that these two lines express the fact that they were riding *to* Canterbury. It is even probable that *every one* of the extant Tales refers to the outward journey: for Chaucer would naturally write his first set of Tales before beginning a second, and the extant Tales are insufficient to make even the first set complete. Consequently, we have only to reckon backwards from Boughton (see l. 556) for a five-mile distance along the *old* Canterbury road, and we shall find the name of the place intended.

The answer to this is—Ospringe. The matter is settled by the discovery that Ospringe was, as a matter of fact, one of the halting-places for the night of travellers from London to Canterbury. Dean Stanley, in his Historical Memorials of Canterbury, p. 237, quotes from a paper in the Archæologia, xxxv. 461, by Mr. E. A. Bond, to shew that queen Isabella, wife of Edw. II, rested in London on the 6th of June, 1358; at Dartford on the 7th; at Rochester on the 8th; at *Ospringe* on the 9th; and at Canterbury on the 10th and 11th; and returned, on the 12th, to *Ospringe again*. See this, more at length, in Mr. Furnivall's

Mr. Furnivall quotes again from M. Douet-d'Arcq, concerning a journey made by king John of France from London to Dover, by way of Canterbury, in 1360. On June 30, 1360, king John left London and came to Eltham. On July 1, he slept at Dartford ; on July 2, at Rochester ; on July 3, he dined at Sittingbourne (noted as being 39 miles and three-quarters from London), and slept at *Ospringe;* and on July 4 came to Canterbury (noted as being 54 miles and a half from London).

These extracts clearly shew (1) that the whole journey was usually made to occupy three or four days ; (2) that the usual resting-places were (at least) Dartford, Rochester, and Ospringe ; and (3) that Sittingbourne was considered as being about 15 miles from Canterbury.

Now, in passing from Sittingbourne to Canterbury, we find that the distance is divided into three very nearly equal parts by the situations of Ospringe and Boughton, giving five miles for each portion. The chief difficulty is that raised by Tyrwhitt, that the distance from Ospringe to Canterbury, only ten miles, leaves very little to be done on the last day. There is really no objection here worth considering, because we have Chaucer's express words to the contrary. Chaucer says, as plainly as possible, that the pilgrims really *did* rest all night on the road, at a place which can only be Ospringe ; see ll. 588, 589.

Mr. Furnivall also notes (Temp. Pref. p. 29), that Lydgate, in his Storie of Thebes (in Speght's Chaucer, 1602, fol. 353 back, col. 2) makes the pilgrims, on their return-journey, return from Canterbury to Ospringe to dinner :—

> ' And toward morrow, as soon as it was light,
> Euery pilgrime, both bet and wors,
> As bad our host, tooke anone his hors,
> When the Sunne rose in the East ful clere,
> Fully in purpose to come to dinere
> Unto Ospring, and breake there our fast.'

Further illustrations might, perhaps, be found ; but we scarcely require them.

l. 556. *Boughton-under-Blee.* Here *Blee* is the same as *the blee* in Group H. l. 3, which see. It is now called Blean Forest, and the village is called Boughton-under-Blean, in order to distinguish it from other villages of the same name. I find, in a map, for examples, Boughton Aluph between Canterbury and Ashford, Boughton Malherb between Ashford and Maidstone, and Boughton Monchelsea between Maidstone and Staplehurst.

l. 557. *A man,* i.e. the Canon. This is an additional pilgrim, not described in the Prologue, and therefore described here in ll. 566–581, 600–655, &c.

'The name of Canon, as applied to an officer in the Church, is derived from the Gk. κανών (kanôn) signifying a rule or measure, and also the roll or catalogue of the Church, in which the names of the Ecclesiastics were registered; hence the clergy so registered were denominated Canonici or Canons. Before the Reformation, they were divided into two classes, Regular and Secular. The Secular were so called, because they canonized *in sæculo*, abroad in the world. Regular Canons were such as lived under a rule, that is, a code of laws published by the founder of that order. They were a less strict sort of religious than the monks, but lived together under one roof, had a common dormitory and refectory, and were obliged to observe the statutes of their order. The chief rule for these [regular] canons is that of St. Augustine, who was made bishop of Hippo in the year 395. . . . Their habit was a long black cassock with a white rochet over it, and over that a black coat and hood; from whence they were called *Black* Canons Regular of St. Augustine.'—Hook's Church Dictionary.

There were several other orders, such as the Gilbertine canons of Sempringham in Lincolnshire, the Præmonstratenses or *White* Canons, &c. See also the description of them in Cutts's Scenes and Characters of the Middle Ages, p. 19.

I should imagine, from the description of the Canon's house in l. 657, and from the general tenor of the Tale, that Chaucer's Canon was but a secular one. Still, their rule seems to have been less strict than that of the monks.

l. 561. *Priked myles three*, ridden hard for three miles. The Canon and his yeoman may be supposed to have ridden rather fast for the first two miles; and then, finding they could not otherwise overtake the pilgrims, they took to the best pace they could force out of their horses for three miles more.

l. 562. *Yeman*, yeoman, attendant, servant. His face was all discoloured with blowing his master's fire (ll. 664-667), and he seems to have been the more honest man of the two. He is the teller of the Tale, and begins by describing himself; l. 720.

l. 565. 'He was all spotted with foam, so that he looked like a magpie.' The word *He* (like *his* in l. 566) refers to the Canon, whose clothing was *black* (l. 557); and the white spots of foam upon it gave him this appearance. The horse is denoted by *it* (l. 563), the word *hors* being neuter in the Oldest English. Most MSS. read *he* for *it* in l. 563, but there is nothing gained by it.

l. 566. *Male tweyfold*, a double budget or leathern bag; see Prol. l. 694.

l. 571. Chaucer tells us that the Pardoner's hood, on the contrary, was *not* fastened to his cloak; see Prol. l. 680.

l. 575. 'Rather faster than at a trot or a foot-pace.' Said ironically. Cf. Prol. 825.

l. **577.** *Clote-leef,* the leaf of a burdock. Cotgrave has—'*Lampourde,* f. the *Cloot* or great Burre.' Also—'*Glouteron,* m. The *Clote,* Burre Docke, or great Burre.' And again—'*Bardane,* f. the *Clote,* burre-dock, or great Burre.'

In the Prompt. Parv. we find—'*Clote,* herbe; Lappa bardana, lappa rotunda.' In Wyclif's Version of the Bible, Hosea ix. 6, x. 8, we find *clote* or *cloote* where the Vulgate version has *lappa.* In Vergil, Georg. i. 153, we have—'Lappaeque tribulique,' and a note in the Delphin edition, 1813, says—'Lappa, glouteron, bardane, BURDOCK; herba, capitula ferens hamis aspera, quae vestibus praetereuntium adhaerent.' The Glossary to Cockayne's 'Leechdoms' explains A. S. *cláte* as *arctium lappa,* with numerous references.

The word is closely related to G. *klette,* a bur, a burdock, O. H. G. *chletta, chletto,* Mid. Du. *kladde,* a bur (see Hexham); whence O. F. *gleton,* F. *glouteron* (see above). It is clear that *clote* originally meant the bur *itself,* just as the name of *bur-dock* has reference to the same. The *clote* is, accordingly, the *Arctium lappa,* or Common Burdock, obtaining its name from the *clotes* (i.e. burs or knobs) upon it; and one of the large leaves of this plant would be very suitable for the purpose indicated.

After this we may safely dismiss the suggestion in Halliwell's Dictionary, founded on a passage in Gerarde's Herball, p. 674 D, that the *Clote* here means the yellow water-lily. We know from Cockayne's 'Leechdoms' that the name *cláte seó þe swimman wille* (i.e. swimming clote) was sometimes used for that flower (*Nuphar lutea*), either on account of its large round leaves or its globose flowers; but in the present passage we have only to remember the Canon's haste to feel assured that he might much more easily have caught up a burdock-leaf from the road-side than have searched in a ditch for a water-lily.

l. **578.** *For swote,* to prevent sweat, to keep off the heat. See note to Sir Thopas, B. 2052.

l. **581.** *Were ful,* that might be full, that might chance to be full. *Were* is the subjunctive, and the relative is omitted.

l. **588.** *Now, &c.*; lately, in the time of early morning.

l. **589.** This shews that the pilgrims had rested all night on the road; see note to l. 555, and p. xiii. of Pref. to Prioresses Tale, &c.

l. **597.** *Aught,* in any way, at all. Cf. Kn. Ta. 2187; and Prioresses Tale, B. 1792.

l. **599.** *Ye,* yea. There is a difference between *ye, yea,* and *yis,* yes. The former merely assents, or answers a simple question in the affirmative. The latter is much more forcible, is used when the question involves a negative, and is often followed by an oath. See note to Specimens of Eng. 1394–1579, ed. Skeat, sect. xvii. (D), l. 22; and note to 3is in the Glossary to my edition of William of Palerne. See an example of 3us (yes) after a negative in Piers the Plowman, B. v. 125. Similarly, *nay* is the weaker, *no* the stronger form of negation.

l. 602. A note in Bell's edition makes a difficulty of the scansion of this line. It is perfectly easy. The cæsura (carefully *marked* in MS. E. as occurring after *knewe*) preserves the final *e* in *knewe* from elision.

And yé | him knéw | e, ás | wel ás | do I ‖

Tyrwhitt reads *also* for the former *as*; which is legitimate, because *as* and *also* are merely different spellings of the same word.

It is true that the final *e* in *wondre*, and again that in *werke*, are both elided, under similar circumstances, in the two lines next following; but the cases are not quite identical. The *e* in *knewe*, representing not merely the plural, but also the subjunctive mood, is essential to the conditional form of the sentence, and is of much higher value than the others. If this argument be not allowed, Tyrwhitt's suggestion may be adopted. Or we may rèad *knewen*.

l. 608. *Rit*, contracted from *rideth*; see other examples in Pref. to Prioresses Tale, p. l. See also *slit* for *slideth* in l. 682 below.

l. 611. *Leye in balaunce*, place in the balance, weigh against it.

l. 620. *Can*, knows, knows how to exercise.

l. 622. The Yeoman puts in a word for himself—'and moreover, I am of some assistance to him.'

l. 625. *Vp so doun*, i.e. upside doun, according to our modern phrase. Chaucer's phrase is very common; see Pricke of Conscience, ed. Morris, l. 7230; P. Plowman, B. xx. 53; Gower, Conf. Amantis, &c.

l. 628. *Benedicite*, pronounced *bendiste*, in three syllables, as in B. 1170, 1974. See note to B. 1170 (Prioress's Tale, &c.).

l. 632. *Worship*, dignity, honour; here, respectable appearance.

l. 633. *Ouersloppe*, upper garment. So in Icelandic, *yfirsloppr* means an outer gown; as, 'prestar skrýddir yfirsloppum,' i.e. priests clad in over-slops, Historia Ecclesiastica, i. 473. The word *slop* is preserved in the somewhat vulgar '*slop*-shop,' i.e. shop for second-hand clothes.

l. 635. *Baudy*, dirty. *To-tore*, torn in half. So in Piers Plowman, B. v. 197, Avarice is described as wearing a 'tabard' which is 'al to-torn and baudy.'

l. 639. The second person sing. imperative seldom exhibits a final *e*; but it is sometimes found in weak verbs, *tellen* being one of them. The readings are—*Telle*, E. Cp. Pt. Hl.; *Tel*, Ln. Cm.

l. 641. *For*, &c.; because he shall never thrive. The Yeoman blurts out the truth, and is then afraid he has said too much. In l. 644, he gives an evasive and politer reason, declaring that his lord is 'too wise;' see l. 648.

l. 645. *That that*, that which. In the margin of MS. E. is written—'Omne quod est nimium, &c.;' which is probably short for—'Omne

quod est nimium uertitur in uitium.' We also find—'Omne nimium
nocet.' The corresponding English proverb is—'Too much of one thing
is not good' (Heywood); on which Ray remarks—'Assez y a si trop n'y
a; *French.* Ne quid nimis ; *Terentius.* Μηδὲν ἄγαν. This is an apothegm
of one of the seven wise men ; some attribute it to Thales, some to Solon.
Est modus in rebus, sunt certi denique fines ; *Horat.* Sat. i. 1. 106. L'ab-
bondanza delle cose ingenera fastidio ; *Ital.* Cada dia olla, amargo el
caldo ; *Spanish.*' We also find in Hazlitt's English Proverbs—'Too
much cunning undoes.'—'Too much is stark nought.'—'Too much
of a good thing.'—'Too much spoileth, too little is nothing.' See also
the collection of similar proverbs in Ida v. Düringsfeld's Sprichwörter, i.
37, 38.

l. 648. Cf. Butler's description of Hudibras :—
  'We grant, although he had much wit,
  He was very shy of using it.'

l. 652. *Ther-of no fors,* never mind about that.

l. 656. *If it to telle be,* if it may be told. Cf. note to l. 437.

l. 658. A *blind lane* is one that has no opening at the farther end ;
a *cul de sac.*

l. 659. *Theues by kynde,* thieves by natural disposition.

l. 662. *The sothe,* the truth. The reader should carefully note the full
pronunciation of the final *e* in *sothe.* If he should omit to sound it,
he will be put to shame when he comes to the end of the next line,
ending with *tó thee.* A very similar instance is that of *tyme,* riming
with *bý me,* G. 1204 below. The case is the more remarkable because
the A.S. *sóð,* truth, is a monosyllable; but the truth is that the
definite adjective *the sothe* (A.S. þæt sóðe) may very well have supplied
its place, the adjective being more freely used than the substantive
in this instance. Chaucer has *sothe* at the end of a line in one more
place, where it rimes with the dissyllabic *bothe* ; G. 168.

We may remark that *the sothe* is written and pronounced instead
of *the soth* (as shewn by the metre) in the Story of Genesis and Exodus,
ed. Morris, l. 74 :—
  'He [they] witen the sothe, that is sen.'

l. 665. *Peter !* by St. Peter. The full form of the phrase—'bi seynt
Peter of Rome'—occurs in Piers the Plowman, B. vi. 3. The shorter
exclamation—'Peter !' also occurs in the same, B. v. 544; see my note
on that line.

l. 669. *Multiplye.* This was the technical term employed by alchemists to denote their supposed power of transmuting the baser
metals into gold ; they thought to *multiply* gold by turning as much base
metal as a piece of it would buy into gold itself; see l. 677. Some
such pun seems here intended ; yet it is proper to remember that
the term originally referred solely to the supposed fact that the strength

of an elixir could be multiplied by repeated operations. See the article 'De Multiplicatione,' in Theatrum Chemicum, iii. 301, 818; cf. 131. Cf. Ben Jonson's Alchemist, ii. 1 :—

> 'For look, how oft I iterate the work,
> So many times I add unto his virtue.
> As, if at first one ounce convert a hundred,
> After his second loose, he'll turn a thousand ;
> His third solution, ten ; his fourth, a hundred ;
> After his fifth, a thousand thousand ounces
> Of any imperfect metal, into pure
> Silver or gold, in all examinations
> As good as any of the natural mine.'

l. 686. **To scan** the line, accent *yeman* on the latter syllable, as in ll. 684, 701.

l. 687. **To scan** the line, pronounce *euer* nearly as *e'er*, and remember that *hadde* is of two syllables. The MSS. agree here.

l. 688. *Catoun*, Cato. Dionysius Cato is the name commonly assigned to the author of a Latin work in four books, entitled Dionysii Catonis Disticha de Moribus ad Filium. The work may be referred to the fourth century. It was extremely popular, not only in Latin, but in French and English versions. Chaucer here quotes from Lib. i. Distich. 17 :—

> 'Ne cures si quis tacito sermone loquatur ;
> Conscius ipse sibi de se putat omnia dici.'

See another quotation from Cato in the Nonne Prestes Tale, l. 120; and see my note to Piers the Plowman, B. vi. 316.

It is worth noticing that *Catoun* follows the form of the Lat. *Catonem*, the accusative case. Such is the usual rule.

l. 694. *Dere abye*, pay dearly for it. *Abye* (lit. to buy off) was corrupted at a later date to *abide*, as in Shak. Jul. Caesar, iii. 1. 94.

l. 703. *Game*, amusement. In l. 708, it is used ironically. Cf. *ernest*, i.e. a serious matter, in l. 710.

> 'Rather than I'll be bray'd, sir, I'll believe
> That Alchemy is a pretty kind of game,
> Somewhat like tricks o' the cards, to cheat a man
> With charming.'—The Alchemist, ii. 1.

●

NOTES TO THE CANON'S YEOMAN'S TALE.

l. 720. This Tale is divided, in MS. E, into two parts. *Pars prima* is not really a tale at all, but a description of alchemy and its professors. The real tale, founded on the same subject, is contained in *Pars*

Secunda, beginning at l. 972. The rubric means—'Here the Canon's Yeoman begins his tale.' The word *tale* is not to be taken as a nominative case.

l. 721. *Neer,* nearer; this explains *near* in Macbeth, ii. 3. 146.

l. 724. *Ther,* where; observe the use. In l. 727, we have *wher.*

l. 726. *Hose,* an old stocking, instead of a hood.

l. 730. 'And, in return for all my labour, I am cajoled.' To '*blere* one's eye' is to cajole, to deceive, to hoodwink. See Piers the Plowman, B. prol. 74, and the note.

l. 731. *Which,* what sort of a; Lat. *qualis.* On *multiplye,* see note to l. 669.

l. 739. 'I consider his prosperity as done with.'

l. 743. *Iupartie,* jeopardy, hazard. Tyrwhitt remarks that the derivation is not from *jeu perdu,* as some have guessed, but from *jeu parti.* He adds—'A *jeu parti* is properly a game, in which the chances are exactly even; see Froissart, v. i. c. 234—" Ils n'estoient pas à *jeu parti* contre les François;' and v. ii. c. 9—" si nous les voyons à *jeu parti.*" From hence it signifies anything uncertain or hazardous. In the old French poetry, the discussion of a problem, where much might be said on both sides, was called a *Jeu parti.* See *Poesies du Roy de Navarre,* Chanson xlviii., and *Gloss.* in v. See also Ducange, in v. *Jocus Partitus.*' Ducange has—'*Jocus partitus* dicebatur, cum alicui facultas concedebatur, alterum e duobus propositis eligendi.' Hence was formed not only *jeopardy,* but even the verb to *jeopard,* used in the A.V., Judges v. 18; 2 Macc. xi. 7. Also in Shakespeare's Plutarch, ed. Skeat, p. 139, side-note 2.

l. 746. In the margin of MS. E. is written—'Solacium miseriorum, &c.' In Marlowe's Faustus, ii. 1. 42, the proverb is quoted in the form 'Solamen miseris socios habuisse doloris.' Dr. Wagner says: 'The purport of this line may have been originally derived from Seneca, De Consol. ad Polybium, xii. 2: est autem hoc ipsum solatii loco, inter multos dolorem suum dividere; qui quia dispensatur inter plures, exigua debet apud te parte subsidere.' Cf. Milton, P.R. i. 398. The idea is that conveyed in the fable of the Fox who had lost his tail, and wished to persuade the other foxes to cut theirs off likewise.

l. 752. 'The technical terms which we use are so learned and fine. See this well illustrated in Jonson's Alchemist, ii. 1 :—

> 'What else are all your terms,
> Whereon no one of your writers 'grees with other,
> Of your elixir, your lac virginis,
> Your stone, your medicine, and your chrysosperme,
> Your sal, your sulphur, and your mercury,' &c.

l. 764. *Lampe;* so in the MSS. It is clearly put for *lambe,* a corruption of O. Fr. *lame,* Lat. *lamina.* Were there any MS. authority, it would be better to read *lame* at once. Cotgrave has—'*Lame* ; f. a thin plate of any metall ; also, a blade,' &c. Nares has—'*Lamm*, s. a plate, from Lat. *lamina*. "But he strake Phalantus just upon the gorget, so as he batred the *lamms* thereof, and made his head almost touch the back of his horse ; " Pembr. Arcadia, lib. iii, p. 269.' *Lame* in old French also means, the flat slab covering a tomb ; see Roquefort. So here, after the ingredients have all been placed in a pot, they are covered over with a plate of glass laid flat upon the top.

It is strange that no editor has made any attempt to explain this word. It obviously does not mean *lamp !* For the insertion of the *p*, cf. *solempne* for *solemne*, and *nempne* for *nemne* ; see Gloss. to Prior. Tale.

1. 766. *Enluting.* To *enlute* is to close with *lute*. Webster has— '*Lute*, n. (Lat. *lutum*, mud, clay). A composition of clay or other tenacious substance, used for stopping the juncture of vessels so closely as to prevent the escape or entrance of air, or to protect them when exposed to heat.'

The process is minutely described in a MS. by Sir George Erskine, of Innertiel (temp. James I.), printed by Mr. J. Small in the Proceedings of the Society of Antiquaries of Scotland, vol. xi. 1874–75. p. 193, as follows :—' Thairfoir when all the matter which must be in, is gathered together into the pot, tak a good *lute* maid of potters clay, and mix it with bolus and rust of iron tempered with whitts of eggs and chopt hair, and mingle and worke thame weill togither, and lute ȝoure pott ane inch thick thairwith, and mak a stopple of potters earth weill brunt, to shut close in the hole that is in the top of the cover of the pott, and lute the pott and the cover very close togither, so as no ayre may brek furth, and when any craks cum into it, in the drying of the lute, dawbe them up againe ; and when the lute is perfectly drie in the sunne, then take a course linen or canvas, and soke it weill in the whitts of eggs mixt with iron rust, and spred this cloth round about the luting, and then wet it weill again with whitts of eggs and upon the luting ; ' &c.

1. 768. The alchemists were naturally very careful about the heat of the fire. So in The Alchemist, ii. 1 :—

> ' Look well to the register,
>
> And let your heat still lessen by degrees.'

And again, in iii. 2 :—

> ' We must now increase
>
> Our fire to *ignis ardens*, we are passed
>
> *Fimus equinus*, *balnei*, *cineris*,
>
> And all those lenter heats.'

1. 770. *Matires sublyming*, sublimation of materials. To ' sublimate ' is to render vaporous, to cause matter to pass into a state of vapour by the application of heat. ' Philosophi considerantes eorum materiam, quæ est in vase suo, et calorem sentit, evaporatur in speciem fumi, et ascendit

in capite vasis: et vocant *sublimationem;*' Theatrum Chemicum, 1659, vol. ii. p. 125.

> *Subtle.* How do you sublime him [mercury]?
> *Face.* With the calce of egg-shells,
> White marble, talc.' The Alchemist. ii. 1.

l. 771. *Amalgaming.* To 'amalgamate' is to compound or mix intimately, especially used of mixing quicksilver with other metals. The term is still in use; thus 'an *amalgam* of tin' means a mixture of tin and quicksilver.

Calcening. To 'calcine' is to reduce a metal to an oxide, by the action of heat. What is now called an oxide was formerly called 'a metallic calx;' hence the name. The term is here applied to quicksilver or mercury. For example—' When mercury is heated, and at the same time exposed to atmospheric air, it is found that the volume of the air is diminished, and the weight of the mercury increased, and that it becomes, during the operation, a red crystalline body, which is the binoxide of mercury, formed by the metal combining with the oxygen of the air;' English Cyclopædia, Div. Arts and Sciences, s. v. *Oxygen.* 'The alchemists used to keep mercury at a boiling heat for a month or longer in a matrass, or a flask with a tolerably long neck, having free communication with the air. It thus slowly absorbed oxygen, becoming converted into binoxide, and was called by them *mercurius precipitatus per se.* It is now however generally prepared by calcination from mercuric nitrate;' id., s. v. *Mercury.*

l. 772. *Mercurie crude*, crude Mercury. See note to l. 820. See the description of Mercury in Ashmole's Theat. Chem. p. 272. The alchemists pretended that *their* quicksilver, which they called the Green Lion, was something different from quicksilver as ordinarily found. See treatise on 'The Greene Lyon,' in Ashmole's Theat. Chem. p. 280.

l. 774. Note the accents—'súblyméd Mercúrie.'

l. 778. Here the 'ascension of spirits' refers to the rising of gases or vapours from certain substances; and the 'matters that lie all fix adown' are the materials that lie at the bottom in a fixed (i.e. in a solid) state. There were four substances in particular which were technically termed 'spirits;' viz. sulphur, sal ammoniac, quicksilver, and arsenic, or (as some said) orpiment. See Theatrum Chemicum, iii. 81, 129; ii. 430; iii. 276.

l. 782. Here *a* = in; being short for *an*, a variant of *on*, used in the old sense of 'in.' The expression signifies, literally, in the manner of twenty devils, i. e. in all sorts of evil and accursed ways.

l. 790. *Bole armoniak.* The latter word should rather be *Armeniak*, i. e. Armenian, but we have *armoniak* again below, in l. 798; see note to that line.

'*Bole*, a kind of fine, compact, or earthy clay, often highly coloured with iron, and varying in shades of colour from white to yellowish, reddish, blueish, and brownish. Fr. *bol*, Lat. *bolus*, Gk. βῶλος, a clod or lump of earth ; ' Webster's Dict., ed. Goodrich and Porter. Cotgrave has—'*Bol*, m. the astringent and medicinable red earth or minerall called *Bolearmenie* . . . *Bol Oriental*, et *Bol Armenien Oriental*, Oriental Bolearmenie; the best and truest kind of Bolearmenie, ministred with good effect against all poisons, and in pestilent diseases ; and more red than the ordinary one, which should rather be tearmed Sinopian red earth than Bolearmeny.' And again—'*Rubrique Sinopique*, Sinopian red earth, a heavy, massive, liver-coloured, and astringent earth, or minerall, which, put into water, soon moulders, and fals into pieces. This may very well be the ordinarie *Bolearmonie* [sic] that is, at this day, used by many surgeons in the staunching of blood, &c., but is not the true (Orientall) one, redder then it, and not so easily dissolved by water as it.'

Verdegrees looks at first like a corruption of *verd-de-gris*, but that would mean 'green of gray,' which is nonsense. It is really an English version of O. F. *vert de Grece*, 'green of Greece ;' which, possibly, was confused with the Eng. *grease*, from the notion that it is of a greasy nature. The French *verderis* is from the Latin *viride æris*, the green of brass. This term (*viride æris*) is the common one in the old Latin treatises on alchemy. See the chapter in Albertus Magnus—'Quomodo viride æris fit, et quomodo rubificatur, et super omnia valet ad artem istam ; ' Theatrum Chemicum, ii. 436. It is the bibasic acetate of copper.

l. 794. *Cucurbites*, vessels supposed to bear some resemblance to a gourd, whence the name (Lat. *cucurbita*, a gourd). ' Cucurbita est uas quod debet stare in aqua, usque ad juncturam firmatum in caldario, ut non moueatur ; nec cucurbita debet tangere fundum, quia frangeretur ; et cum aqua minuitur, fundas aliam, scilicet calidam et non frigidam, quia uas frangeretur ; ' Theatrum Chemicum, ii. 452.

l. 795. *Dere ynough a leek*, dear enough at the price of a leek. Cf. Clerkes Tale, E. 999.

l. 797. *Watres rubifying*, reddening waters. This is well illustrated by a long passage in The Boke of Quinte Essence, ed. Furnivall, p. 13, where instructions are given for extracting the quintessence out of the four elements. After various processes, we are directed to put the vessel into ' the fier of flawme right strong, and the *reed water* schal ascende ; ' and again—' thanne yn the stillatorie, to the fier of bath, cleer water schall asende ; and in the botum shall remayne the *reed water*, that is, the element of fier.' A long and unintelligible passage about ' rubrificatio ' and ' aqua spiritualis rubea ' occurs in the Theatrum Chemicum, iii. 41. See also ' modus rubrificandi ' and the recipe for

Chemicum, iii. 177; also p. 110, and ii. 238. *Sal armoniacum* was another of them (see l. 824) and is constantly mentioned in the old treatises; see 'præparatio salis Armoniaci secundum Rasim;' Theat. Chem. iii. 179; also pp. 89, 94, 102; ii. 445. In vol. ii. p. 138 of the same work, it is twice called '*sal armeniacum.*' See the account of *sal ammoniac* in Thomson, Hist. of Chemistry, i. 124. *Brimstoon* was also a 'spirit' (see l. 824); it is only another name for sulphur.

l. 800. *Egrimoin*, common agrimony, *Ægrimonia officinalis;* valerian, *Valeriana officinalis; lunarie*, a kind of fern called in English moon-wort, *Botrychium lunaria.* The belief in the virtue of herbs was very strong; hence even Spenser says (F. Q. i. 2. 10) that the magician Archimago was thus enabled to turn himself into the shape of various animals, adding—

'O who can tell

The hidden power of herbs, and might of magic spell.'

The root of valerian yields valerianic acid. The following quotation is from the English Encyclopædia, s.v. *Botrychium:*—

'In former times the ferns had a great reputation in medicine, not so much on account of their obvious as their supposed virtues. The lunate shape of the pinnæ of this fern (*B. lunaria*) gave it its common name, and was the origin of much of the superstitious veneration with which it was regarded. When used it was gathered by the light of the moon. Gerarde says—" it is singular [i. e. sovereign] to heal green and fresh wounds. It hath been used among the *alchymists and witches* to do wonders withall, who say that it will loose locks and make them to fall from the feet of horses that grase where it doth grow, and hath been called of them *Martagon*, whereas in truth they are all but drowsy dreams and illusions; but it is singular for wounds as aforesaid."'

In Ashmole's Theatrum Chemicum, p. 348, is a full description of 'lunayrie,' with an engraving of it. It is there also called *asterion*, and we are told that its root is black, its stalk red, and its leaves round; and moreover, that the leaves *wax and wane with the moon*, and on each of them is a mark of the breadth of a penny. See also pp. 315, 318 of the same work.

l. 805. *Albificacioun*, i.e. the rendering the water of a white colour, as distinguishing from the reddening of it, mentioned in l. 797. In a long chapter printed in the Theatrum Chemicum (iii. 634–648) much is said about red and white colours. Compare the Alchemist, ii. 1:—

'*Subtle.* I mean to tinct C in sand-heat tomorrow,

And give him imbibition.

Mammon.   Of *white oil*?

Subtle. No, sir, of *red.*'

No doubt, too, *water* is here used in the sense of the Lat. *aqua*, to denote any substance that is in a liquid state.

l. 808. *Cered pokets.* Tyrwhitt reads **Sered** *pokettes*, and includes this phrase in his short ' List of Phrases not understood ; ' and indeed, it has never been explained. But there is little difficulty about it. *Poket* is the diminutive of *poke*, a bag, and means a little bag. *Cered* (Lat. *ceratus*) means waxed. Thus Cotgrave has—' *Ciré*, m. *-ée*, f. waxed, *seared;* dressed, covered, closed, or mingled, with wax.' In many MSS. the word is spelt *sered*, but this makes no difference, since Cotgrave has ' seared ' in this very place. So we find both ' cere-cloth ' and ' scar-cloth.' It is obvious that bags or cases prepared or closed with wax would be useful for many of the alchemist's purposes ; see **Theat.** Chem. iii. 13. There was a special process in alchemy called *ceration*, but this has nothing to do with it; it means the reduction of any material to the consistency of soft wax ; **Theat.** Chem. ii. 442.

Sal peter, Lat. *sal petræ*, or rock-salt, also called *nitre*, is nitrate of potassa. A recipe for preparing it is given in Theat. Chem. iii. 195.

Vitriole, i.e. sulphuric acid. See ' vitrioli præparatio ; ' Theat. Chem. iii. 95.

l. 810. *Sal tartre*, salt of tartar, i.e. carbonate of potash; so called from its having been formerly prepared from cream of tartar.

Sal preparate, common salt prepared in a certain manner. See the section—' quod ualeat sal commune, et quomodo præparetur ; ' Theat. Chem. ii. 433, 435.

l. 812. *Maad*, i.e. prepared, mixed. *Oile of tartre*, oil of tartar. See the section—' quomodo præparatur tartarum, ut oleum fiat ex illo, quo calces soluuntur ; ' Theat. Chem. ii. 436; and again—' ad faciendum oleum de Tartaro ; ' id. iii. 303. To scan l. 813, remember to pronounce *tartre* as in French, and to accent *alum* on the latter syllable.

Of tártr' | alúm | glas bérm | wort ánd | argoíle ‖

l. 814. *Resalgar*, realgar, red orpiment, or the red sulphuret of arsenic; symbol (As S₂); found native in some parts of Europe, and of a brilliant red colour. *Resalgar* is a corruption of the old Latin name, *risigallum*. The word is explained by Thynne in his Anim-adversions, ed. Furnivall, p. 36—' This *resalgar* is that whiche by some is called Ratesbane, a kynde of poysone named Arsenicke, whiche the chimicall philosophers call their venome or poysone.'

Enbibing, imbibition ; see this term used in the quotation from The Alchemist, in the note to l. 805. It means absorption ; cf. Theat. Chem. iii. 132, l. 27.

l. 816. *Citrinacioun.* This also is explained by Thynne, who says (p. 38)—' Citrinatione is bothe a coolor [colour] and parte of the philo-phers stoone.' He then proceeds to quote from a Tractatus Avicennæ, cap. 7, and from Arnoldus de Nova Villa, lib. i. cap. 5. It was supposed that when the materials for making the philosopher's stone

had been brought into a state very favourable to the ultimate success
of the experiment, they would assume the colour of a citron; or, as
Thynne says, Arnold speaks of 'this citrinatione, perfecte digestione, or
the coolor provinge the philosophers stoone broughte almoste to the
heighte of his perfectione.' So in the Alchemist, iii, 2 :—

> 'How's the moon now? eight, nine, ten days hence
> He will be silver potate; then three days
> Before he *citronise*. Some fifteen days,
> The magisterium will be perfected.'

l. 817. *Fermentacioun*, fermentation. This term is also noticed by
Speght (p. 33), who says—'fermentacione ys a peculier terme of
Alchymye, deduced from the bakers fermente or levyne;' &c. See
Theat. Chem. ii. 115, 175.

l. 820. *Foure spirites*. Chaucer enumerates these below. I have
already mentioned them in the note to l. 778; see also note to l. 798.
Tyrwhitt refers us to Gower's Confessio Amantis, bk. iv, where we
find a passage very much to the point. I quote it from Chalmers
edition, correcting the spelling. Cf. Pauli's edition, ii. 84.

> 'And also with gret diligence
> Thei fonde thilke experience,
> Which cleped is Alconomye,
> Wherof the siluer multiplye
> They made, and eek the gold also.
> And, for to telle how it is so,
> Of bodies seuen in special,
> With foure spirites ioynt withal,
> Stant the substance of this matere.
> The bodies, whiche I speke of here
> Of the planetes ben begonne.
> The gold is titled to the sonne;
> The mone of siluer hath his part;
> And iron, that stant vpon Mart;
> The leed vpon Saturne groweth;
> And Iupiter the bras bestoweth;
> The copper set is to Venus;
> And to his part Mercurius
> Hath the quick-siluer, as it falleth,
> The whiche, after the boke it calleth,
> Is first of thilke foure named
> Of spirites, whiche ben proclamed.
> And the spirit which is seconde
> In sal armoniak is fonde.
> The thridde spirit sulphur is.
> The fourthe, sewend after this,

     Arsenicum by name is hote.
     With blowing and with fyres hote
     In these thinges whiche I saye
     Thei worchen by diuerse waye.'

He further explains that gold and silver are the two 'extremities,' and
the other metals agree with one or other of them more or less, so as to
be capable of transmutation into one of them. For this purpose, the
alchemist must go through the processes of distillation, congelation,
solution, descension, sublimation, calcination, and fixation, after which
he will obtain the perfect elixir of the philosopher's stone. He adds
that there are really three philosopher's stones, one vegetable, capable
of healing diseases ; another animal, capable of assisting each of the
five senses of man ; and the third mineral, capable of transforming
the baser metals into silver and gold.

     'It maketh multiplicacioun
     Of golde, and the fixacioun
     It causeth, and of his habite
     He doth the werk to be perfite
     Of thilke elixir, which men calle
     Alkonomye, as is befalle
     To hem that whylom were wyse.
     But now it stant al otherwyse.
     They speken faste of thilke stone,
     But how to make it now wot none,
     After the trewe experience.
     And natheles gret diligence
     They setten vp[on] thilke dede,
     And spillen more then thei spede.
     For alway thei fynden a lette
     Which bringeth in pouerte and dette
     To him that riche were tofore.
     The losse is had, the lucre is lore.
     To gette a pound they spenden fyue.
     I not how suche a craft shal thryue
     In the manere as it is vsed.
     It were better be refused
     Than for to werchen vpon wene [*expectation*]
     In thing which stant not as thei wene.'

It is easy to see how the various metals were made to answer to
the seven planets. *Gold*, the chief of metals and yellow, of course
answered to the *sun*, and similarly *silver*, to the paler moon. *Mercury*,
the swiftest planet, must be the shifty *quicksilver*; Saturn, the slowest,
of cold and dull influence, must be *lead*. The etymology of *copper*
suggested the connection with the *Cyprian* Venus. This left but two

metals, iron and tin, to be adjusted; iron was suggestive of Mars, the god of war, leaving tin to Jupiter. The notion of thus naming the metals is attributed to Geber; see Thomson, Hist. of Chemistry, i. 117.

Quicksilver, be it observed, is still called *mercury;* and nitrate of *silver* is still *lunar* caustic. Gold and silver are constantly termed *sol* and *luna* in the old treatises on alchemy. See further allusions in Chaucer's House of Fame, iii. 341-397, as pointed out in my Pref. to Chaucer's Astrolabie, p. lxvi.

l. 834. 'Whosoever pleases to utter (i.e. display) his folly.'

l. 838. *Ascance,* possibly, perhaps. See Glossary.

l. 846. *Al conne he,* whether he know. The use of *al* at the beginning of a sentence containing a supposition is common in Chaucer; see Prol. 734. Cf. *al be,* Prol. 297; Kn. Tale, 313. And see l. 861.

l. 848. *Bothe two,* both learned and unlearned alike.

l. 861. 'To raise a fiend, though he look never so rough,' i.e. forbidding, cross.

l. 874. *It is to seken euer,* it is always to seek, i.e. never found. In Skelton's Why Come Ye Nat to Court, l. 314, the phrase 'they are to seke' means 'they are at a loss;' this latter is the commoner use.

l. 875. *Temps,* tense. The editors explain it by 'time.' If Chaucer had *meant* time, it is reasonable to suppose that he would have *said* so. Surely it is better to take 'that futur temps' in the special sense of 'that future tense.' The allusion is to the phrase 'to seken' in the last line, which is not an infinitive mood but a gerund, and often used as a future tense, as Chaucer very well knew. Compare the A.S. version of Matt. xi. 3—'eart þu þe to cumenne eart'—with the Lat. 'Tu es qui *uenturus* es.'

l. 878. *Bitter swete,* i.e. a fatal, though alluring, pursuit. An example of oxymoron; cf. 'insaniens sapientia,' Horat. Carm. i. 34; 'strenua inertia,' Epist. i. xi. 28.

l. 879. *Nadde they but,* if they only should have (*or,* were to have). *Nadde* is for *ne hadde,* past tense subjunctive.

l. 880. *Inne,* within; A.S. *innan;* see l. 881. *A nyght,* for *on nyght,* in the night. Perhaps it should be *nyghte* (with final *e*), and *lyghte* in l. 881.

l. 881. *Bak,* cloth; any rough sort of covering for the back. So in most MSS.; altered in E. to *brat,* but unnecessarily. That the word *bak* was used in the sense of garment is quite certain from two other passages which I shall cite. That it meant originally a covering for the back, will appear from a third one.

(1) In William of Palerne, ed. Skeat, l. 2096, we have—

'Than brayde he brayn-wod & alle his *bakkes* rente,

His berde, and his bright fax for bale he to-twight[e].'

I.e. then he became brain-mad, and tare all his clothes; he plucked asunder, for sorrow, his beard and his bright hair. Note that it is used here in all seriousness.

(2) In Piers the Plowman, B. x. 362, men are blamed for hoarding up clothes, and mention is made of 'owre *bakkes* that moth-eten be,' i.e. of our garments that are moth-eaten for want of use. Here, in one MS., the gloss 'panni' is written above; in another MS., the reading is 'bakclothis.'

(3) In Piers the Plowman, A. xi. 184, we are reminded of the duty of providing bread and clothing for the poor:—

'Dowel it hatte [*is called*]
To breke beggeris bred and *bakken* hem with *clothis.*'

Pronounce the words *And a* rapidly, in the time of one syllable.

l. 907. *To-breketh*, bursts in pieces. *Go*, gone. This must have been a very common result; the old directions about 'luting' and hermetically sealing the vessels employed are so strict, that every care seems to have been (unwittingly) taken to secure an explosion; see note to l. 766 above. So in the Alchemist, iv. 3.

'*Face.* O, sir, we are defeated! all the works
Are flown *in fumo*, every glass is burst:
Furnace, and all rent down! as if a bolt
Of thunder had been driven through the house.
Retorts, receivers, pelicans, bolt-heads,
All struck in shivers!'

l. 921. *Chit*, short for *chideth*; so also *halt* for *holdeth.*

l. 922. *Som seyde*, i.e. one said; note that *som* is here singular, as in Kn. Tale, 2173. Hence the use of *the thridde*, i.e. the third, in l. 925.

l. 929. *So theech*, for *so thee ich*, so may I thrive. See Pard. Tale, C. 947.

l. 933. *Eft-sone*, for the future; lit. soon afterwards.

l. 934. 'I am quite sure that the pot was cracked.'

l. 962. The reading *shyneth* is of course the right one. In the margin of MS. E. is written 'Non teneas aurum,' &c. This proves that Tyrwhitt's note is quite correct. He says—'This is taken from the Parabolæ of Alanus de Insulis, who died in 1294; see Leyser, *Hist. Po. Med. Ævi*, p. 1074.

"Non teneas aurum totum quod splendet ut aurum,
Nec pulchrum pomum quodlibet esse bonum."'

Shakespeare has—'All that glisters is not gold;' Merch. of Venice, ii. 7. 65. Hazlitt's English Proverbs has—'All is not gold that glisters (Heywood). See Chaucer, Chan. Yeom. Prol.; Roxburghe Ballads, ed. Collier, p. 102; Udall's *Royster Doyster*, 1566, where we read: All things that shineth is not by and by pure golde (Act v. sc. 1). Fronti nulla fides, Juvenal, Sat. ii. 8. The French say, Tout ce qui luict n'est

pas or. Non è oro tutto quel che luce; *Ital.* No es todo or lo que
reluce; *Span.*' So in German—' Est ist nicht Alles Gold was glänzt ;'
and again—'Rothe Aepfel sind auch faul.' See Ida v. Düringsfeld's
Sprichwörter, i. 53, 107. Cf. Chaucer's House of Fame, i. 272.

l. 972. *Pars secunda.* This is where the Tale begins. Even now, the
Yeoman has some more to say by way of preface, and only makes a
real start at l. 1012.

l. 975. *Alisaundre*, Alexandria. *And othere three*, and three more as well.

l. 999. *I mente*, I intended; as in l. 1051 below. 'But my intention
was to correct that which is amiss.'

The reading *I-ment*, as a past participle, adopted by Mr. Wright,
is incorrect, as shewn by Mr. Cromie's Ryme-Index. Cf. Nonne Pr.
Tale, 603; Sq. Tale, F. 108. See note to G. 534, above.

l. 1005. *By yow*, with reference to you canons. See *By* in Eastwood
and Wright's Bible Wordbook.

l. 1012. *Annueleer.* So called, as Tyrwhitt explains, 'from their being
employed solely in singing *annuals* or anniversary masses for the dead,
without any cure of souls. See the Stat. 36 Edw. III. c. viii, where the
Chappelleins Parochiels are distinguished from others *chantanz annuales,
et a cure des almes nient entendantz.* They were both to receive yearly
stipends, but the former was allowed to take six marks, the latter only
five. Compare Stat. 2 Hen. V. St. 2. c. 2, where the stipend of the
Chapellein Parochiel is raised to eight marks, and that of the *Chapellein
annueler* (he is so named in the statute) to seven.'

l. 1015. That is, to the lady of the house where he lodged.

l. 1018. *Spending siluer*, money to spend, ready money. The phrase
occurs in Piers the Plowman, B. xi. 278.

l. 1025. *A certeyn*, a certain sum, a stated sum. Cf. l. 776.

l. 1027. *At my day*, on the day agreed upon, on the third day.

l. 1029. *Another day*, another time, on the next occasion.

l. 1030. *Him took*, handed over to him; so in ll. 1034, 1112.

l. 1055. 'In some measure to requite your kindness.' See note to Sq.
Tale, F. 471, and cf. l. 1151.

l. 1059. *Seen at ye*, see evidently; lit. see at eye.

l. 1066. 'Proffered service stinketh' is among Heywood's Proverbs.
Ray remarks on it—' Merx ultronea putet, *apud* Hieronymum. Erasmus
saith, Quin uulgo etiam in ore est, ultro delatum obsequium plerumque
ingratum esse. So that it seems this proverb is in use among the
Dutch too. In French, Merchandise offerte est à demi vendue. Ware
that is proffered is sold for half the worth, or at half the price.' The
German is—'Angebotene Hülfe hat keinen Lohn;' see Ida v. Düringsfeld's Sprichwörter, i. 86.

l. 1096. *Algates*, at any rate. Observe the context.

l. 1103. *That we it hadde*, that we might have it. *Hadde* is here the subjunctive.   **Perhaps** *haue* (present) would be better, but it lacks authority.

l. 1126. *Mortifye,* mortify; a technical term.   See note to l. 1431.

l. 1151. 'To blind the priest with.'   See note to l. 1055.

l. 1185. *Seint Gyles,* saint Giles; a corrupted form of Ægidius.   His day is Sept. 1; see Chambers' Book of Days, ii. 296; Legenda Aurea, cap. cxxx.

ll. 1204, 1205.   The rime is given by *tyme* (two syllables, from A.S. *tíma*) riming with *by me.*   The same rime occurs at least six times in Gower's Confessio Amantis (ed. Chalmers, bk. ii. p. 60, col. 2; bk. iii. p. 76. col. 2; also pp. 103, 105, 120, 157):—

> 'Haue feigned semblant oftë tymë
> To hem that **passen al day by me.**'
> 'And hindred me ful oftë tymë
> When thei no causë wistë by me;' &c., &c.

In all six places, Mr. Chalmers prints *byme* as **one word!**   See *hy the* (l. 1295); *sey ye* (l. 1375).

On referring to Prof. Child's Observations on the Language of Gower, I find *seven* references given for this rime, as occurring in the edition by Dr. **Pauli.**   The references are—i. 227, 309. 370; ii. 41, 114, 277; iii. 369.   Dr. Pauli also prints *byme* as one word.

l. 1210. **Scan** the line by pronouncing the words *or a* rapidly.   The last foot contains the words—or a pannë.

l. 1238, 1239. MS. E. omits these two lines: the other MSS. retain them.

l. 1244. *Halwes* is in the genitive plural.   'And the blessing of Æll the saints may **ye** have, Sir Canon!'

l. 1245. 'And may I have their malison,' i.e. their curse.

l. 1283. 'Why do you **wish** it to be better than well?'   Answering nearly to—'what would you have better?'

l. 1292. A rather lax line.   *Is ther* is to be pronounced rapidly, in **the** time of one syllable, and *her-inne* is of three syllables.

l. 1299. Pronounce *simple* nearly as in French, and   remember the final *e* in *tonge* (A.S. *tunge*).

l. 1313. *His ape,* his dupe.   See Prol. 706.   **The** simile is evidently taken from **the** fact that showmen used to carry apes about with them much as organ-**boys** do   at the present day, the apes being secured by a string.   Thus, 'to make a man one's ape' is to lead him **about** at will.   The **word** *apewarde* occurs in Piers the Powman, B. v. 540. To *lead apes* means to lead about a train of dupes.   In the Prioress's Prologue, B. 1630, **I have** explained *ape* by 'fool,' following former editors.   It now occurs to me that the word 'dupe' expresses the meaning still better.   (This **is** corrected in the second edition.)

l. 1319. *Heyne,* wretch.   This word has never before been properly explained.   It is not in Tyrwhitt's Glossary.   Dr. Morris considers it as another form of *hyne*, a peasant, or hind, but leaves the phonetic difference of vowel unaccounted for. It occurs in Skelton's Bowge of Courte, l. 327 :—

> 'It is great scorne to see suche an *hayne*
> As thou arte, one that cam but yesterdaye,
> With vs olde seruauntes suche maysters to playe.'

Here Mr. Dyce also explains it by *hind*, or servant, whereas the context requires the opposite meaning of a despised *master*. Halliwell gives— '*Heyne*, a miser, a worthless person;' in which sense it occurs in Udall. Cf. Lowl. Sc. *hain*, to hedge in, preserve, spare; Low G. *heinen*, to hedge in, spare, save; Icel. *hegna*.

l. 1320. 'This priest being meanwhile unaware of his false practice.' See l. **1324.**

l. **1342.** Alluding to the proverb—'As fain as a fowl [i.e. bird] of a fair morrow;' given by Hazlitt in the form—'As glad as fowl of a fair day.' See Piers the Plowman, B. x. 153 : Kn. Tale, 1579.

l. 1348. *To stonde in grace;* cf. Prol. 88.

l. 1354. *By our;* pronounced *By'r*, as spelt in Shakespeare, Mid. Nt. Dr. iii. 1. 14.

l. 1362. *Nere*, for *ne were;* meaning 'were it not for.'

l. 1381. *Sy*, saw. The scribes also use the form *sey* or *seigh*, as in Kn. Tale, 208; Franklin's Tale, F. 850, in both of which places it rimes with *heigh* (high). Of these spellings *sey* (riming with *hey*) is to be preferred in most cases. See note to Group B, l. 1 (Prioresses Tale. &c.).

l. 1388. This line begins with a large capital C in the Ellesmere MS., shewing that the Tale itself is at an end, and the rest is the Yeoman's application of it.

l. 1389. 'There is strife between men and gold to that degree, that there is scarcely any (gold) left.'

l. 1408. Alluding to the proverb—'Burnt bairns fear fire.' This occurs among the Proverbs of Hendyng, in the form—'Brend child fur dredeth.' So in the Romaunt of the Rose, l. 1820—'Brent child of fyr hath moche drede.' The German is—'Ein gebranntes Kind fürchtet das Feuer;' see Ida v. Düringsfeld's Sprichwörter, i. 531.

l. 1410. Alluding to the proverb—'Better late than never;' in French 'Il vaut mieux tard que jamais.' The German is—'Besser spät als nie;' see Ida v. Düringsfeld's Sprichwörter, i. 204.

l. 1411. In Hazlitt's Proverbs—'Never is a long term.'

l. 1413. *Bayard* was a colloquial name for a horse; see Piers Plowman, B. iv. 53, 124; vi. 196; and 'As bold as blind Bayard' was a common proverb. See also Chaucer's Troil. and Cress. i. 218.

l. 1416. 'As to turn aside from an obstacle in the road.'

l. 1419. Compare this with the Man of Lawes Tale, B. 552.

l. 1422. *Rape and renne*, seize and plunder. The phrase is of

Scandinavian **origin**. *Rape* is preserved in the Swedish *raffa*, to seize, allied to M. E. *rape*, signifying ' haste'; cf. Icel. *rifsa*, to plunder, Icel. *rífa*, **to rive**, to grasp. *Renne* is not connected with A. S. *rennan*, to run, but with Icel. *ræna*, **to rob**, *rán*, seizure, plunder. The collocation of words is seen in the Icel. *rifsi ok ránum*, with pilfering and plundering, Fornmanna Sögur, i. 119; *rán ok rifs*, plunder and robbery, id. ii. 119, vi. 42, vii. 363 (s. v. *rán* and *rifs* in Cleasby and Vigfusson's Icelandic Dictionary). Hence the Cleveland form of the phrase is 'to rap and reeve,' sometimes 'to rap and ree;' see *Rap* in Atkinson's Cleveland Glossary. **Mr.** Atkinson remarks that ' heo rupten, heo ræfden' in Layamon, ii. 16, first text, is equivalent to ' hii rupten, hii refden' in the second; whilst the Ancren Riwle gives the form *arepen and arechen*, with the various readings *rapen and rinen*, *ropen and rinen*. Ihre quotes the English '*rap and ran*, per fas et nefas ad se pertrahere.' Mr. Wedgwood remarks that in *rap and ran*, to get by hook or crook, to seize whatever one can lay hands on, the word *rap* is joined with the synonymous [verb connected with the] Icel. *rán*, rapine. Palsgrave has—'*I rap or rende*, je rapine.' Coles (Eng. Dict. ed. 1684) has '*rap an[d] ren*, snatch and catch.' The phrase is still in use in the (corrupted) form *to rape and rend*, or (in Cleveland) *to rap and ree*.

l. 1428. Arnoldus de Villa Nova was a French physician, theologian, astrologer, and alchemist; born about A.D. 1235, died A.D. 1314. Tyrwhitt refers us to Fabricius, *Bibl. Med. Æt.*, in v. Arnaldus Villano-**vanus**. In a tract printed in Theatrum Chemicum, iii. 285, we have a reference to the same saying—'Et hoc est illud quod magni philosophi scripserunt, quod lapis noster fit ex Mercurio et sulphure præparatis et separatis, et de hoc opere et substantia dicit Magister Arnoldus in tractatu suo parabolice, nisi **granum** frumentum in terra cadens mortuum fuerit, &c. Intelligens pro grano mortuo in terra, Mercurium mortuum cum salepetræ et vitriolo Romano, et cum sulphure, et ibi mortificatur, et ibi sublimatur cum igne, et sic multum fructus adfert, et hic est **lapis** major omnibus, quem philosophi quæsiverunt, et inventum **absconderunt**.' The whole process is described, but it is quite unintelligible **to me**. It is clear that two circumstances stand very much in the way of **our** being able to follow out such processes; these **are** (1) that **the same** substance was frequently denoted by six or seven different names; **and** (2) that one name (such as sulphur) denoted five or six different things (such **as** sulphuric acid, orpiment, sulphuret of arsenic, &c.)

l. 1429. *Rosarie*, i.e. Rosarium Philosophorum, the name of a treatise **on alchemy** by Arnoldus de Villa Nova; Theat. Chem. iv. 514.

l. 1431. The word *mortification* seems to have been loosely used to denote any change due to chemical action. Phillips explains *Mortify*

by—'Among chymists, to change the outward form or shape of a mixt
body ; as when quicksilver, or any other metal, is dissolved in an acid
menstruum.'

l. 1432. 'Unless it be with the knowledge (i.e. aid) of his brother.'
The 'brother' of Mercury was sulphur or brimstone (see l. 1439). The
dictum itself is, I suppose, as worthless as it is obscure.

l. 1434. *Hermes*, i.e. Hermes Trismegistus, fabled to have been the
inventor of alchemy. Several books written by the New Platonists
in the fourth century were ascribed to him. Tyrwhitt notes that
a treatise *under his name* may be found in the Theatrum Chemicum,
vol. iv. See Fabricius, Bibliotheca Græca, lib. i. c. 10 ; and Smith's
Classical Dictionary. The name is preserved in the phrase 'to seal
hermetically.'

Mr. Furnivall printed, for the Early Eng. Text Society, a tract called
The Book of Quinte Essence, 'a tretice in Englisch breuely drawe out
of the book of quintis essenciis in latyn, that *hermys* the prophete
and kyng of Egipt, after the flood of Noe, fadir of philosophris,
hadde by reuelacioun of an aungil of god to him sende.'

l. 1438. *Dragoun*, dragon. Here, of course, it means mercury, or
some compound containing it. In certain processes, the solid residuum
was also called *draco* or *draco qui comedit caudam suam*. This *draco*
and the *cauda draconis* are frequently mentioned in the old treatises ;
see Theatrum Chemicum, iii. 29, 36, &c. The terms may have been
derived from astrology, since 'dragon's head' and 'dragon's tail' were
common terms in that science. Chaucer mentions the latter in his
Astrolabie, ii. 4. 22. And see the remarks on 'Draco' in Theat.
Chem. ii. 456.

l. 1440. *Sol and luna*, gold and silver. The alchemists called *sol* (gold)
the father, and *luna* (silver) the mother of the elixir or philosopher's
stone. See Theat. Chem. iii. 9, 24, 25 ; iv. 528. Similarly, sulphur was
said to be the father of minerals, and mercury the mother. Id, iii. 7.

l. 1447. *Secre*, secret of secrets. Tyrwhitt notes—'Chaucer refers to
a treatise entitled *Secreta Secretorum*, which was supposed to contain the
sum of Aristotle's instructions to Alexander. See Fabricius, Bibliotheca
Græca, vol. ii. p. 167. It was very popular in the middle ages.
Ægidius de Columnâ, a famous divine and bishop, about the latter
end of the 13th century, built upon it his book De Regimine Principum,
of which our Occleve made a free translation in English verse, and
addressed it to Henry V. while Prince of Wales. A part of Lydgate's
translation of the Secreta Secretorum is printed in Ashmole's Theatrum
Chemicum Britannicum, p. 397. He did not translate more than about
half of it, being prevented by death. See MS. Harl. 2251, and Tanner,
Bibl. Brit. s.v. Lydgate. The greatest part of the viith Book of Gower's
Confessio Amantis [see note to l. 820] is taken from this supposed

work of Aristotle.' In the Theatrum **Chemicum, iii.** 14, I find an allusion to the philosopher's stone ending with these words—' Et Aristoteles ad Alexandrum Regem dicit in **libro de** secretis secretorum, capitulo penultimo: O Alexander, accipe lapidem mineralem, vegetabilem, **et** animalem, et separa elementa.' See Warton, Hist. Eng. Poetry, sect. 19 ; iii. 19 (ed. 1871), or ii. 230 (ed. 1840).

l. **1450.** Tyrwhitt says—' The book alluded to **is** printed in the Theatrum Chemicum, vol. v. p. 219 [p. 191, ed. 1660], under this title, Senioris Zadith fil. Hamuelis tabula Chemica. The story which follows of Plato and his disciples is there told, p. 249 [p. 224, ed. 1660], with some variations, of Solomon. " Dixit Salomon rex, Recipe lapidem qui dicitur Thitarios (*sic*) . . . Dixit sapiens, Assigna mihi illum. . . . Dixit, Est corpus magnesiæ. . . . Dixit, Quid est magnesia ? . . . Respondit, Magnesia est aqua, composita," &c.' The name of Plato occurs thrice *only a few lines below*, which explains Chaucer's mistake. We find ' Titan Magnesia' in Ashmole's Theat. Chem. p. 275 ; cf. pp. 42, 447.

l. 1457. *Ignotum per ignotius*, lit. an unknown thing through a thing **more** unknown ; i.e. an explanation of a hard matter by means of a **term that is** harder still.

l. **1460.** The theory that all things were made of the four elements, earth, air, fire, and water, was the foundation on which all alchemy was **built** ; and it was the obstinacy with which this idea was held that **rendered** progress in science almost impossible. The words were used **in the** widest sense ; thus air meant any vapour or gas ; water, any liquid ; earth, any solid sediment ; and fire, any amount of heat. Hence also the theory of the four complexions of men. See Gower, Conf. Amant. **bk.** vii ; Theat. Chem. iii. 82 ; iv. 533, 537.

l. 1461. *Rote* represents the Lat. *radix*. A similar use of it occurs in Theat. Chem. ii. 463, where we read that the philosopher's stone ' est *radix*, de quo omnes sapientes tractauerunt.'

l. 1469. ' Except where it pleases His Deity to inspire mankind, and again, to forbid whomsoever it pleases Him.'

l. 1479. *terme of his lyue*, during the whole term of his life.

l. 1481. *Bote of his bale*, a remedy for his evil, help out of his trouble.

NOTES TO THE MANCIPLE'S PROLOGUE (GROUP H).

Line 1. *Wite ye*, **know ye.** The singular is *I wot*, A. S. *ic wát*, Mœso-Goth. *ik wait ;* the plural is *we witen* or *we wite*, A. S. *we witon*, Mœso-Goth. *weis witum*. See l. 82, where the right form occurs.

l. 2. *Bob-up-and-down.* **This** place is here described as being ' under the Blee,' i.e. under Blean Forest. It is also between Boughton-under-Blean (see Group G, l. 556) and Canterbury. This situation suits very

well with Harbledown, and it has generally been supposed that Harbledown is here intended. Harbledown is spelt *Herbaldoun* in the account
of Queen Isabella's journey to Canterbury (see Furnivall's Temporary
Preface, p. 124, l. 18 ; p. 127, l. 21), and *Helbadonne* in the account of
King John's journey (id. p. 131, l. 1). However, Mr. J. M. Cowper, in
a letter to the *Athenæum*, Dec. 26, 1868, p. 886, says that there still
exists a place called Up-and-down Field, in the parish of Thannington,
which would suit the position equally well, and he believes it to be the
place really meant. If so, the old road must have taken a somewhat
different direction from the present one, and there are reasons for
supposing that such may have been the case.

The break here between the Canon's Yeoman's and the Manciple's
Tales answers to the break between the first and second parts of
Lydgate's Storie of Thebes. At the end of Part I, Lydgate mentions
the descent down the hill (i.e. Boughton hill), and at the beginning of
Part II, he says that the pilgrims had 'passed the thorp of Boughton-
on-the-blee.'

l. 5. *Dun is in the myre*, a proverbial saying originally used in an old
rural sport. *Dun* means a dun horse, or, like *Bayard*, a horse in general.
The game is described in Brand's Popular Antiquities, 4to. ii. 289 ; and
in Gifford's notes to Ben Jonson, vol. vii. p. 283. The latter explanation is quoted by Nares, whom see. Briefly, the game was of this kind.
A large log of wood is brought into the midst of a kitchen or large
room. The cry is raised that 'Dun is in the mire,' i.e. that the cart-
horse is stuck in the mud. Two of the company attempt to drag it
along ; if they fail, another comes to help, and so on, till Dun is
extricated.

There are frequent allusions to it ; see Romeo and Juliet, i. 4. 41 ;
Beaumont and Fletcher's Woman-hater, iv. 3 ; Hudibras, pt. iii.
c. iii. l. 110.

In the present passage it means—' we are all at a standstill ; ' or,
' let us make an effort to move on.' Mr. Hazlitt, in his Proverbial
Phrases, quotes a line—' And all gooth bacward, and *don is in the myr*.'

l. 12. *Do him come forth*, make him come forward. Cf. Group B,
1888, 1889 (Prioress's Enn-link).

l. 14. *A botel hay*, a bottle of hay ; similarly, we have *a barel ale*,
Monk's Prol. B. 3083. And see l. 24 below. A bottle of hay was
a small bundle of hay, less than a truss, as explained in my note
to The Two Noble Kinsmen, v. 2. 45.

l. 16. *By the morwe*, in the morning. There is no need to explain
away the phrase, or to say that it means in the afternoon, as Tyrwhitt
does. The Canon's Yeoman's tale is the first told on the third day,
and the Manciple's is only the second. The Cook seems to have taken
too much to drink over night, and to have had something more before

starting. **The fresh air has** kept him awake **for a** while at first, but he is now very drowsy indeed.

Tyrwhitt well remarks that there is no allusion here to the unfinished Cook's Tale in Group A. This seems to shew that the Manciple's Prologue was written before the Cook's Tale was begun. See my Preface to the Prioresses Tale, p. xv. Note that the Cook is here excused; l. 29.

l. 23. 'I know not why, but I would rather go to sleep than have **the** best gallon of wine in Cheapside.' *Me wer leuer slepe*, lit. it would be dearer to me to sleep. Cf. l. 14.

l. **24.** *Thau* constitutes the first foot; *beste* is dissyllabic.

l. 29. *As now*, for the present; a common phrase.

l. 33. *Not wel disposed*, indisposed in health.

l. 42. *Fan*, the fan or vane **or** board of the quintain. The quintain, as is well known, consisted of a cross-bar turning on a pivot at the top of a post. At one end of the cross-bar was the fan or board, sometimes painted to look like a shield, and at the other was a club **or bag of sand.** The jouster at the fan **had to strike the** shield, and at the same time to avoid the stroke given by the swinging bag. The Cook was hardly in a condition for this; his eye and hand were alike unsteady, and his figure did not suggest that he possessed the requisite agility. See *Quintain* in **Nares**, and Strutt's Sports and Pastimes, bk. iii. c. 1; As You Like It, i. 2. 263, on which see Mr. Wright's note (Clar. Press Series).

l. **44.** *Wyn ape*, ape-wine, **or** ape's wine. Tyrwhitt rightly considers this the same as the *vin de singe* in the Calendrier des Bergers, sign. l. ii. **b.**, where the author speaks of the different effects produced by wine upon different men, according to their temperaments. 'The Cholerick, he says, *a vin de lyon; cest a dire, quant a bien beu, veult tanser, noyser, et battre.* The Sanguine *a vin de singe; quant a plus beu, tant est plus joyeux.* In the same manner, the Phlegmatic is said to have *vin de mouton*, and the Melancholick *vin de porceau.*'

Tyrwhitt adds—'I find the same four animals applied to illustrate **the effects** of wine in a little Rabbinical tradition, which I shall transcribe **here** from Fabricius, Cod. Pseudepig. Veteris Testamenti, **vol. i. p. 275.** "Vineas plantanti Noacho Satanam se junxisse memorant, **qui, dum** Noa vites plantaret, mactaverit apud illas *ovem, leonem, simiam,* et *suem:* Quod principio potûs vini homo sit instar *ovis,* vinum sumptum efficiat ex homine *leonem,* largius haustum mutet eum in saltantem *simiam,* ad ebrietatem infusum transformet illum in pollutam et prostratam *suem.*" See also Gesta Romanorum, c. 159, **where** a story of the same purport is quoted from Josephus, *in libro de casu rerum naturalium.*'

Warton (Hist. E. P. ed. **1871**, i. 283) gives a slight sketch of this chapter in the Gesta, referring to Tyrwhitt's note, and explaining it

in the words—' when a man begins to drink, he is meek and ignorant as
the lamb, then becomes bold as the lion, his courage is soon transformed
into the foolishness of the ape, and at last he wallows in the mire
like a sow.'

Barclay, in his Ship of Fools, ed. Jamieson, i. 96, speaking of
drunken men, says—

'Some *sowe-dronke*, swaloyng mete without mesure.'
And again—

'Some are *Ape-dronke*, full of laughter and of toyes.'

The following interesting explanation by Lacroix is much to the
same effect :—

' In Germany and in France it was the custom, at the public entries of
kings, princes, and persons of rank, to offer them the wines made in the
district, and commonly sold in the town. At Langres, for instance,
these wines were put into four pewter vessels called *cimaises*, which are
still to be seen. They were called the *lion, monkey, sheep*, and *pig*
wines—symbolic names, which expressed the different degrees or
phases of drunkenness which they were supposed to be capable of
producing : the lion, courage ; the monkey, cunning ; the sheep, good
temper ; the pig, bestiality.'—P. Lacroix ; Manners, Customs, and Dress
during the Middle Ages, 1874, p. 508.

A note in Bell's edition quotes an illustrative passage from a song in
Lyly's play of Mother Bombie, printed in the Songs from the Drama-
tists, ed. Bell, p. 56 :—

'O the dear blood of grapes
Turns us to antic shapes,
Now to show tricks *like apes*,
Now *lion-like* to roar ; ' &c.

The idea here intended is precisely that expressed by Barclay. The
Cook, being very dull and ill-humoured, is ironically termed ape drunk,
as if he were 'full of laughter and of toyes,' and ready to play even with
a straw. The satire was too much for the Cook, who became excited,
and fell from his horse in his attempts to oppose the Manciple.

l. 50. *Chyuache*, feat of horsemanship, exploit. See Prol. 85 for the
serious use of the word, where *in chiuachie* means on an (equestrian)
expedition.

l. 51. 'Alas ! he did not stick to his ladle !' He should have been in
a kitchen, basting meat, not out of doors, on the back of a horse.

l. 57. *Dominacioun*, dominion. See note to G. 352 (Prioresses Tale,
&c.) Cf. ' the righteous shall have *domination* over them in the morning ; ' Ps. xlix. 14, Prayer-book Version. An early example of the
word is in A Balade sent to King Richard, third stanza—' Uertue hath
now no *dominacioun*'—printed at the end of Chaucer's works ; ed. 1561,
fol. cccxxxv, back See Chaucer's Minor Poems, xiv. 16.

l. 62. *Fneseth*, blows, puffs; of which the reading *sneseth* is a poor corruption, though occurring in all the modern editions. Dr. Strat-mann gives—'*Fneosen*, sternuere; *fnese*, Tale of Beryn, ed. Furnivall. l. 42.' This instance is not a very clear one, and perhaps the reading (in Beryn) should really be *sneze*. To *fnese* does not mean to sneeze, but to breathe hard.

I have no doubt that the word *neesings* in Job xli. 18, meaning not 'sneezings' but 'hard breathings,' is due to the word *fnesynge*, by which Wyclif translates the Latin *sternutatio*. In Jer. viii. 16 Wyclif represents the snorting of horses by *fnesting*. Cf. A.S. *fnœst*, a puff, a blast, *fnœstiað*, the windpipe; *fneosung*, a hard breathing. Grimm's law helps us to a further illustration; for, as the English *f* is a Greek *p*, a cognate word is at once seen in the common Greek verb πνέω, I breathe or blow (*not* I sneeze). For further examples, see *fnast*, Owl and Nightingale, 44; *fnaste*, Havelok, 548; *fnasted* (pt. tense), Gawaine and the Grene Knight, 1702; *fnast*, Alliterative Troybrook, ed. Panton and Donaldson, 168, 878.

l. 72. To *reclaim* a hawk is to bring it back to the hawker's hand; this was generally effected by holding out a *lure*, or something tempting to eat. Here the Host means that some day the Cook will hold out a bait to, or lay a snare for, the Manciple, and get him into his power; for example, he might examine the details of the Manciple's accounts with an inconvenient precision, and perhaps the amounts charged, if tested, would not appear to be strictly honest. The Manciple replies in all good humour, that such a proceeding might certainly bring him into trouble. See Prol. 570-586.

l. 76. Read *mauncipl'*, and pronounce *were a* rapidly.

l. 83. 'Yea, of an excellent vintage.'

l. 90. *Pouped*, blown; see Nonne Prestes Tale, 578. Here 'blown upon this horn' is a jocular phrase for 'taken a drink out of this gourd.'

NOTES TO THE PARSON'S PROLOGUE (GROUP I).

Line 1. *Maunciple*, manciple; see Group H. The connection between this Group and the preceding is, in reality, very slight. The best solution seems to be to suppose that the word *maunciple* here was merely inserted provisionally. When the Manciple told his tale, it was still morning; see Group H, l. 16, and the note. The Pilgrims had but a very little way to go, however. Perhaps we may suppose that they halted on the road, having a shorter day's work before them than on the previous days, and then other tales might have been introduced; so that the time wore away till the afternoon came. It is clear, from

made, to be the last on the outward journey. Whatever difficulties
exist in the arrangement of the tales may fairly be considered as due to
the fact that the final revision was never made.

l. 4. *Nyne and twenty.* In my Preface to Chaucer's Astrolabie, p. lxiii,
I have explained this passage fully. In that treatise, part ii. sections
41-43, Chaucer explains the method of taking altitudes. He here says
that the sun was 29° high, and in ll. 6-9 he says that his height was to
his shadow in the proportion of 6 to 11. This comes to the same thing,
since the angle whose tangent is $\frac{6}{11}$ is very nearly 29°. Chaucer would
know this, as I have shewn, by simple inspection of an astrolabe, without
calculation.

l. 5. *Foure,* four p.m. The MSS. have *Ten,* but the necessity of the
correction is undoubted. This was proved by Mr. Brae, in his edition
of Chaucer's Astrolabe, pp. 71-74. We have merely to remember that
ten p.m. would be *after sunset,* to see that some alteration must be
made. Now the altitude of the sun was 29°, and the day of the year
was about April 20 (Pref. to Prioresses Tale, p. xiii); and these data
require that the time of day should be about 4 p.m. Tyrwhitt notes
that some MSS. actually have the reading *Foure,* and this gives us
authority for the change. Mr. Brae suggests that the reading *Ten* was
very likely a gloss upon *Foure;* since *four* o'clock is the *tenth* hour of the
day, reckoning from 6 a.m. The whole matter is thus accounted for.

l. 10. *The mones exaltacioun,* the moon's exaltation. I have discussed
this passage in my Preface to Chaucer's Astrolabie, p. lxiii. My
explanation is that Chaucer uses *exaltation* here (as in several other
passages) in its ordinary astrological sense. The 'exaltation' of a
planet is that sign in which it was believed to exert its greatest
influence; and, in accordance with this, the old tables call Taurus
the 'exaltation of the Moon,' and Libra the 'exaltation of Saturn.'
These results, founded on no reasons, had to be remembered by sheer
effort of memory, if remembered at all. I have no doubt, accordingly,
that Chaucer (or his scribes) have made a mistake here, and that
the reading should be 'Saturnes,' as proposed by Tyrwhitt. The
sentence then means—'Therewith Saturn's exaltation, I mean Libra,
kept on continually ascending above the horizon.' This would be
quite right, as the sign of Libra was actually ascending at the time
supposed. The phrase 'I mene Libra' may be paralleled by the
phrase 'I mene Venus;' Kn. Tale, 1358; see also Group B, 1860,
2141. *Alwey,* continually, is common in Chaucer; see Clerkes Tale,
E. 458, 810. *Gan ascende,* did ascend, is the opposite to *gan descende;*
Clerkes Tale, E 392. It is somewhat remarkable that the astrologers
also divided each sign into three equal parts of ten degrees each, called
'faces;' mentioned in Chaucer's Astrolabie, ii. 4. 38, and in l. 50 of the
Squieres Tale. According to their arrangement, the first 10 degrees of

Libra was called the 'face of the moon,' or 'mones face.' This suggests that Chaucer may, at the moment, have confused *face* with *exaltation*, thus giving us, as the portion of the zodiac intended, the first ten degrees of Libra.

I doubt **if the** phrase is worth further discussion. For further information see my Preface to Chaucer's Astrolabie; and, for an ingenious theory, offered in explanation of the whole passage, see Mr. Brae's edition of the same, p. 74.

l. 16. This means that the Parson's Tale was meant to be the last one **on the** outward journey. Unfortunately, there lack a great many more tales than one, as the matter really stands.

l. 26. 'Unpack your wallet, and let us **see** what is in it.' In other words, tell us a story, **and** let us see what it is like.

l. 32. See 1 Tim. i. 4, iv. 7 ; 2 Tim. iv. 4.

l. 42. *Southren.* In my Essay on Alliterative Poetry, printed **in** vol. iii. of the Percy Folio MS., ed. Hales and Furnivall, I have shewn that nearly all the alliterative poems are in the Northern or West-Midland **dialect**, as opposed to the East-Midland dialect of Chaucer, which approaches the Southern dialect. Still, it is the Parson *himself*, not Chaucer, who says he is a Southerner; and perhaps the poet meant, naturally enough, to tell us that he was a *Kentish* man. The dialect of Kent was properly Southern. Many Southern forms occur in Gower.

l. 43. *Rom, ram, ruf* are of course nonsense words, chosen to represent alliteration, because they all alike begin with *r*. In most alliterative poetry, the number of words in a line beginning with a common letter is, as Chaucer suggests, *three*.

The word *geste* here means no more than 'tell a story,' without reference to the form of the story. Properly, the *gesta* **were** in prose ; see note to Group B, 2123. It is, however, worth noting that one very long alliterative poem on the siege of Troy, edited by Panton and Donaldson (Early English Text Society), bears the title of ' *Gest* Hystoriale.' The number of distinctively Northern words in it is **very** considerable.

I think that this line has been forced by some out of its true meaning, and **made to convey** a sneer against alliterative poetry which was by no means **intended.** Neither Chaucer himself nor his amiable parson would have **spoken** slightingly of other men's labours. The introduction of the words **rom,** *ram, ruf* conveys no more than a perfectly good-humoured **allusion. That** this **is the** true view is clear from the very next line, **where the** Parson declares that 'he holds rime **but** little better.'

The most interesting **question** is—why should Chaucer allude to alliterative poetry *at all*? The answer is, in my view, that he distinctly wished **to** recognise the curious work of his contemporary William whose **Vision of Piers** the Plowman had, by this time, passed, as it were, **into a second** edition, having **been** extremely **popular in London,** **and especially** amongst the **lower** classes. The author was *not* a **Southerner, but** his poem had come to London, together **with himself, before** A.D. 1377.

l. 57. *Textuel,* literally exact in giving the **text.** The next line means —'I only gather (and **give** you) the general meaning.' Most quotations at this period were very inexact, and Chaucer himself was no more exact than others.

l. 67. *Hadde the wordes.* Tyrwhitt says—'This is **a** French phrase. It is applied **to the** Speaker of the Commons in Rot. Parl. **51** Edw. III. n. **87.** "Mons. Thomas de Hungerford, Chivaler, qi *avoit les paroles* pur les **Communes d'Angleterre en** cest Parlement," &c.' It means— was the spokesman.

ADDITIONAL NOTE ON THE NINE-SYLLABLE LINE.

In my Preface to the Prioress's Tale, 1st ed. p. lxiii., 2nd ed. p. lxiv., I give some examples of lines in **which** the first foot consists of a single syllable. In the present volume, we may note similar **lines,** viz. B. 404, 497, G. 341. As lines of this description are somewhat rare in modern English poetry, I may point out that there **are** twelve such lines in Tennyson's Vision of Sin, l. **14–25.** See further in my Preface to Chaucer's Legend of Good **Women.**

ADDITIONAL NOTE ON THE SECOND NUN'S TALE.

Besides the Legenda Aurea (see p. xxxii), Chaucer **also** consulted the Lives **of Valerian** and Tiburtius, in the Acta Sanctorum (April 14). See Dr. Kölbing's **paper in the** Englische Studien, i. 215; and see the note to l. 369, on **p. 176** above. Cf. **Cockayne's** *Shrine,* p. 149.

GLOSSARIAL INDEX.

B = Group B.   C = Group C.   G = Group G.   H = Group H.   I = Group I.

The following are the principal contractions used :—

A.S. = Anglo-Saxon (i.e. Old English words in Bosworth's or Grein's Dictionaries).
Dan. = Danish (Ferrall and Repp).
Du. = Dutch (Tauchnitz edition).
E. = English.
E.E. = Early English (A.D. 1100–1250).
F. = French (Brachet).
G. = German.
Gk. = Greek.
Icel. = Icelandic (Cleasby and Vigfusson).
Ital. = Italian (Meadows).

Lat. = Latin.
M.E. = Middle English (A.D. 1250–1485).
M.H.G. = Middle High German.
Mœso-Goth. or Goth. = Mœso-Gothic.
O.F. = Old French (Burguy, Roquefort).
Prompt.Parv. = Promptorium Parvulorum, ed. Way (Camden Society).
Sp. = Spanish (Meadows).
Sw. = Swedish (Tauchnitz edition).
W. = Welsh (Spurrell).

Also the following : *v.* = verb *in the infinitive mood*; *pr. s.* or *pt. s.* means the *third* person singular of the present or past tense, except when 1 *p.* or 2 *p.* (*first* person or *second* person) is added; *pr. pl.* or *pt. pl.* means, likewise, the *third* person plural of the present or past tense ; *imp. s.* means the *second* person singular of the imperative mood. Other contractions, such as *s.* for substantive, *pp.* for past participle, will be readily understood. In the references, when the letter is absent before a number, supply the letter last mentioned. The references are to the *Group* and the *line*.

'Gloss. I.' means the Glossary to Dr. Morris's edition of the Prologue, Knightes Tale, &c. ; 'Gloss. II.' means the Glossary to the Prioresses Tale, &c. ; both in the Clarendon Press Series.

A.

A, *for* on, *prep.* in, during; *a nyght*, in the night, by night, G 880; *a dayes*, lit. on days, i. e. a-days, 1396. A.S. *on*, E.E. *an, a.*

Abasshed, *pp.* ashamed, disconcerted, B 568. O. Fr. *esbahir*, to frighten ; cf. Ital. *baire*, to astonish (given by Diez), whence Ital. *s-baire* (Diez): possibly from the interjection *bah!* of astonishment.

Abhominable, *adj.* abominable, C 471, 631. Lat. *abominor*, I deprecate an omen ; from *ab* and *omen.*

Abit, *pr. s.* (*for* abideth), abides, G 1175. A.S. *ábidan* from *bidan*, to wait.

Ablucions, *s. pl.* ablutions, washings, G 856.

Abought, *pp.* redeemed, atoned for, C 503. See Abye.

P 2

Abusion, *s.* guile, imposture, deceit, B 214. ' *Abusion,* f. an abusing, an error, fallacy, imposture, guile, deceit;' Cotgrave's French Dict.

Abye, *v.* to suffer for, pay (dearly) for, C 756, G 694; *pp.* Abought, atoned for, C 503. A.S. *âbycgan,* to pay for; from *bycgan,* to buy, See *Aboughte* in Gloss. I.

Accident, *s.* any property or quality of a thing, not essential to its existence; the outward appearance, C 539. See the note. (Lat. *cadere.*)

Accorde, *pr. s. subj.* may agree, G 638; *pp.* Accorded, agreed, B 238. Fr. *accorder,* Lat. *accordare,* from *cor,* the heart.

Adoun, *adv.* down, G 1113, I 72; at the bottom, G 779. A.S. *of-dúne,* lit. off the down or hill; from *dún,* a hill, a *down.*

Aduersarie, *s.* enemy, G 1476. O. Fr. *adversarie* (Burguy), Lat. *aduersarius;* from Lat. *ad,* to, and *uertere,* to turn.

Aduertence, *s.* mental attention, consideration of a matter in hand, G 467. The sense is brought out in Chaucer's Troilus and Cressida, iv. 698, where Cressida is in a state of abstraction—' Her *aduertence* is alwey elleswhere.' From Lat. *uertere.*

Aduocat, *s.* advocate, intercessor, G 68. Lat. *aduocare,* from *uox,* voice.

Affray, *s.* fear, terror, B 1137. See Gloss. II.

Affrayed, *pp.* afraid, frightened, B 563.

After, *prep.* according to, G 25; in expectation of, for, B 467. A.S. *after;* see Gloss. II.

Agast, *adj.* amazed, terrified, B 677. See Gloss. I. and II.

Agayn, *prep.* against, B 580, C 427, G 1415; near, G 1279; opposite to, to meet, B 391;

towards, to meet, B 399, G 1342. A.S. *ongeán,* towards, against.

Agayns, *prep.* before, in presence of, C 743. Formed from A.S. *ongeán,* with addition of (adverbial) suffix -*es.* This M.E. *agayns* is now corrupted to *against.*

Agaynward, *adv.* back again, B 441.

Agon, *pp.* gone away, C 810; *pp.* as *adv.* Agoon, ago, 436. A.S. *ágán,* pp. of verb *ágán,* to go by, pass by, which is equivalent to G. *ergehen.*

Agryse, *v.* to shudder, to be seized with horror, B 614. A.S. *ágrísan,* to fear; cf. A.S. *gríslíc,* grisly, horrible.

Al, *adj.* all; *al a,* the whole of, G 996; *at al,* at all, wholly, C 633. A.S. *eall,* Goth. *alls,* all.

Al, *conj.* whether, G 846; although, 861, C 449, 451. Al so = as, B 396, H 80.

Albificacioun, *s.* albification, whitening, rendering of a white colour, G 805. Lat. *albificationem;* from *albus,* white, and *facere,* to make.

Alderfirst, *adv.* first of all, G 423. A.S. *alra, ealra,* gen. pl. of *eall,* all, which became M. E. *aller, alder,* and *alther.* (Gloss. I. II.)

Alembykes, *s. pl.* alembics, G 774. ' *Alambique,* a limbeck, a stillatory,' i.e. a vessel used in distilling, a retort; Cotgrave's French Dict. From Span. *alambique,* borrowed from Arabic *al-ambik,* which again seems to have been borrowed from Gk. ἄμβιξ, a cup, used by Dioscorides to mean the cap of a still.

Ale-stake, *s.* a stake projecting from an ale-house by way of a sign, C 321. See the note.

Algate, *adv.* at any rate, C 292, G 318, 904. See below.

Algates, *adv.* all the same, nevertheless, at any rate (lit. by all ways, by all means), B 520, G 1096. Here *gate* means a way. Cf. Icel. *gata*, a path, road; G. *gasse*, a street. From the root of *get*, rather than of *go*.

Alkaly, *s.* alkali, G 810. Arabic *al-qali*, the ashes of the plant glass-wort (*Salicornia*), which abounds in soda.

Alkamistre, *s.* alchemist, G 1204. *Alchemy* is Arabic *al-kimiá*, where *al* is the Arabic article, and the sb. is borrowed from the Gk. χημεία, chemistry, equivalent to χυμεία, χύμευσις, a mingling, from χέω, to pour. (Etym. of the Gk. word somewhat uncertain.)

Alle and some, collectively and individually, one and all, B 263, C 336.

Alliaunce, *s.* alliance, C 605. (Gloss. I. II.)

Allye, *s.* ally, G 292, 297.

Almes-dede, *s.* alms-deed, alms-doing, B 1156.

Almesse, *s.* alms, B 168. A. S. *ælmesse*, borrowed from Lat. *eleemosyna*, which from Gk. ἐλεημοσύνη, pity, a bounty; from ἐλεεῖν, to have pity.

Al-so, *conj.* as, B 396, H 80. A. S. *eall-swá*.

Alum, *s.* alum, G 813. O. F. *alum*, (Roquefort), Lat. *alumen*.

Alwey, *adv.* continually, unceasingly, regularly, I 11.

Am, *in phr.* it am I = it is I, B 1109.

Amalgaming, *s.* the formation of an amalgam, G 771. An *amalgam* is a pasty mixture of mercury with other substances (properly with a metal). The derivation is from Gk. μάλαγμα, an emollient, from μαλάσσειν, to soften.

Amased, *pp.* amazed, G 935.

Amis, *adv.* wrongly, C 642. (Gloss. II.)

Amonges, *prep.* amongst, G 608. (Gloss. II.)

Amounteth, *pr. s.* amounteth to, signifies, means, B 569. (Gloss. II.)

Amy, *s.* friend, C 318. F. *ami*, Lat. *amicus*.

An, lit. one, a; *an eighte busshels*, a quantity equal to eight bushels, C 771. A. S. *án*.

And, *conj.* if, G 145, 602, 1371.

Angle, *s.* angle (a technical term in astrology), B 304. (See note.) Lat. *angulus*.

Annexed, *pp.* attached, C 482.

Annueler, *s.* a priest who received *annuals* (see the note), a chaplain, G 1012.

Anon, *adv.* immediately, forthwith, B 326, C 864, 881. A. S. *on án*, lit. in one; i. e. in one minute.

Anon-ryght, *adv.* immediately, G 1141.

Anoyeth, *pres. s. impers.* it annoys, vexes, G 1036; *imp. pl.* Anoyeth, injure ye. (Gloss. II.)

Apayd, *pp.* pleased; *yuel apayd*, ill pleased, dissatisfied, G 921, 1049. (Gloss. II.)

Ape, *s.* a dupe (see the note), G 1313.

Apertening, *pres. pt.* appertaining, G 785. O. F. *apartenir*, Lat. *ad* and *pertinere*.

Apese, *v.* to appease, pacify, H 98. F. *apaiser*, derived from O. F. *pais*, peace; Lat. *pacem*, acc. of *pax*, peace.

Apostelles, *s. pl.* apostles, G 1002.

Apposed, *pt. s.* questioned, G 363. See the note.

Argoile, *s.* mod. E. *argol*, G 813. *Argol* is the crust adhering to the inside of a wine-cask.

Argumenten, *pr. pl.* argue, B 212.

Arist, *pr. s.* (contr. from ariseth) arises, B 265. A. S. *árisan*.

Armeth, *imp.* 2 *p. pl.* arm, G 385.

Armoniak, *adj.* ammoniac; applied to *bole*, G 790, and *sal*, 798. In l. 790, it is a corruption of Lat. *armeniacum*, i.e. Armenian, belonging to Armenia. See notes.

Armure, *s.* armour, B 936, G 385. F. *armure*, O.F. *armëure*, contr. from Lat. *armatura*.

Arrayed, *pp.* arranged, ordered, B 252. O.F. *arraier*, from *arroi*, order; which from sb. *roi*, from a Scandinavian source. Cf Swed. *reda*, to prepare; Goth. *garaidjan*, to make ready. (Gloss. I. II.)

Arsenik, *s.* arsenic, G 778. Lat. *arsenicum*, Gk. ἀρσενικόν, a name occurring in Dioscorides, 5. 121. It signifies *male*, from the Gk. ἄρσην, a male.

Artow, *contr. for* art thou, B 308, C 552, 718, G 424, etc.

Aryght, *adv.* aright, rightly, G 1418.

As, *expletive, expressing a wish; as haue*, may He have, B 1061; *as lat*, i. e. pray let, 859.

As ferforth as, *adv.* as far as, G 1087.

As now, i.e. just now, B 740; on the present occasion, G 944; for the present, with the matter on hand, G 1019.

As swythe, *adv.* as quickly as possible, G 1030, 1194. 1294. M.E. *swythe*, quickly; from A.S. *swið*, strong, severe.

Ascaunce, *adv.* perhaps, G 838. Tyrwhitt (note to C. T., l. 7327) refers us to the present passage, to Tro. and Cress., i. 285, 292, and to Lydgate. It clearly means perchance, perhaps. The etymology was discussed, ineffectively, in Notes and Queries, 4 S. xi. 251, 346, 471; xii. 12, 99, 157, 217, 278. The difficulty has arisen from confusion with the modern *askance*, with which it may have nothing to do. The present word is related rather

to some form in Old French; and, since the publication of vol. vi. of Godefroy's O. F. Dictionary, I can now solve the word entirely. The fact is, it is a hybrid compound, made up of E. *as*, and O.F. *quanses* or *qanses* (with *qu* or *q* pronounced as *k*), signifying 'as if.' The E. *as* is, accordingly, redundant, and merely added by way of partial explanation. The M. E. *askances* means 'as if' in other passages, but here means, 'as if it were,' i. e. 'possibly,' 'perhaps'; as said above. Sometimes the final *s* is dropped, as here; see examples of *Askance* or *Askances* in the New E. Dictionary; noting, that the 'O.Du. *quantsis*' there mentioned seems to be the O. F. word borrowed. The examples in Godefroy make the sense 'as if' quite certain. He refers us to Gaston Paris, in *Romania*, xviii. 152; to Foerster's edition of *Cliges*, 4553. and the note; and to *Partonope*, ed. Crapelet, l. 4495.

Ascencioun, *s.* ascension, rising up, G 778.

Ascende, *v.* to ascend, rise (a term in astrology), I 11.

Ascendent, *s.* ascendant, B 302. The 'ascendant' is that degree of the ecliptic which is rising above the horizon at the time of observing a horoscope, and calculating a nativity.

A-sonder, *adv.* asunder, apart, B 1157. A. S. *on-sundron*, separately, from *sundor*, separate.

Aspye, *s.* spy, C 755. From O. F. *espier*, to espy, a word borrowed from O. H. G. *spehon*, to look at, cognate with Lat. *spicere* (in *conspicere*), Skt. *spaç*.

Assay, *s.* trial, G 1249, 1338. F. *essai*, a trial; from Lat. *exagium*.

Assembled, *pp.* united, G 50. F. *assembler*, Lat. *assimulare*, to collect, from Lat. *simul*, together.

Assent, *s.* consent, conspiracy, C 758.

Assentedest, *pt. s.* 2 *p.* consentedest, didst pay heed, G 233.

Asshes, *s. pl.* ashes, G 807. A. S. *asce, æsce,* a cinder.

Assoile, *pr. s.* 1 *p.* I absolve, pardon, C 387, 913. O. F. *assoldre,* Lat. *absoluere.*

Asterte, *v.* to escape, C 414; *pt. s.* Asterted, escaped, B 437; *pt. s. subj.* Asterte, might (*or* could) escape, 475. Cf. E. *start,* Du. *storten,* to precipitate, rush; G. *stürzen.*

At, *prep.* from, of (*used with* axed), G 542, 621.

'Blithe would I battle for the right
To ask one question *at* the sprite.'
　　　　Scott, *Marmion,* iii. 29.

Atake, *v.* to overtake, G 556, 585. Cf. Icel. *taka,* to take; the prefix is probably A. S. *on,* Icel. *á.* Cf. Icel. *átak,* a touching.

Atazir, *s.* evil influence, B 305. See note, p. 126.

Atones, *adv.* at once, B 670. (Gloss. II.)

Atte. *contr. for* at the; as in *atte fan,* H 42; *atte hasard,* C 608; *atte fulle,* at the full, in completeness, B 203; *atte laste,* at the last, B 506, C 844, G 683.

Atwinne, *adv.* apart, G 1170. Modified from *on tweónum,* in two parts, where *tweónum* is dat. pl. of A. S. *tweón,* double, twin, by the influence of Icel. *twinnr,* in pairs.

Atwo, *adv.* in two, in twain, B 600, 697, C 677, 936, G 528. For *on two.*

Auantage, *s.* convenience, profit; *to don his auantage,* to suit his own interests, B 729; advantage, G 731. O. F. *avantage,* profit, from prep. *avant,* before, which from Lat. *ab ante.*

Auantage, *s. as adj.* advantageous, B 146.

Auaunced, *pp.* advanced, C 410. O. F. *avancer,* from *avant.*

Auctoritee, *s.* authority, C 387. O. F. *auctoriteit,* Lat. *auctoritatem.*

Auenture, *s.* chance, adventure, B 465; peril, B 1151, G 946; *pl.* Auentures, accidents, C 934. O. F. *aventure,* from *venir,* Lat. *uenire.*

Aught, *adv.* by any chance, in any way, B 1034; at all, G 597.

Aungeles, *s. pl.* angels, B 642.

Auow, *s.* vow, B 334, C 695. See note to C 695.

Auowe, *v.* to avow, own publicly, proclaim, G 642. O. F. *avouer, avoer;* from Lat. *ad* and *uouere.*

Auter, *s.* altar, B 451. O. F. *auter* (commonly *autel*), Lat. *altare.*

Auys, *s.* opinion, I 54. F. *avis;* from *à* and *vis,* Lat. *uisum,* a thing seen, an opinion; from *uideri,* to seem.

Auyse us, *v. refl.* consider with ourselves, B 664; *imp. pl.* Auyseth, consider ye, C 583; *pp.* Auysed, well advised, C 690; Auysed me, taken counsel with myself, considered the matter, G 572. See above.

Awake, *v.* to wake, H 7. (Gloss. II.)

Aweye, *adv.* away, from home, B 593; astray, 609. A. S. *onweg;* see Gloss. to Sweet's A. S. Reader.

Axe, *imp. s.* ask thou, C 667; 1 *p. s. pres.* Axe, I ask, G 426; 2 *p. pl. pres.* ask ye, G 460; *pr. s.* Axeth, asks, B 878; *pt. s.* Axed, G 357; 1 *p. s. pt.* Axed, G 542; *pt. pl.* 2 *p.* Axed, ye asked, 430. A. S. *ácsian.*

Axinge, *s.* questioning, question, G 423. See above.

Ay, *adv.* aye, ever, for ever, B 296. Icel. *ei.*

B.

Bak, *s.* cloth for the back, cloak, coarse mantle, **G** 881. See the note.

Balaunce, *s.* balance, **G** 611. *Leye in balaunce,* lay in the balance, i. e. advance as a pledge.

Bale, *s.* misfortune, sorrow, **G** 1481. A.S. *bealo,* torment, wickedness; Goth. *balwyan,* to torment.

Bar, *pt. s.* bore, carried about, B 476 (cf. the name *Christopher*), G 221, 1264. See Ber.

Barbre, *adj.* barbarian, B 281. Lat. *barbarus,* Gk. βάρβαρος.

Baronage, *s.* company of barons, retinue of lords, B 329. The more usual O F. form is (the contracted) *barnage;* both from **O.F.** *baron,* a man. (Gloss. I.)

Baskettes, *s. pl.* baskets, C 445. Dr. Murray finds that the Celtic origin usually assigned to this word **is wrong.**

Bataille, *s.* battle, **G** 386. F. *bataille,* Low Lat. *batalia,* neut. pl. signifying combats.

Baudy, *adj.* dirty, G 635. W. *bawaidd,* dirty, *baw,* dirt.

Bayte, *v.* to bait, feed, **eat,** B 466. Icel. *beita,* to feed, to make to bite; the causal of *bita,* to bite.

Be. See Ben.

Beautee, *s.* beauty, B 162. **O.F.** *biaute, beltet,* from Lat. acc. *bellitatem;* from Lat. *bellus,* fair.

Bechen, *adj.* beechen, made of beech, G 1160. A.S. *bécen,* beechen, *béce, bóc,* a beech; cf. Lat. *fagus.*

Bede, *v.* to offer, proffer, G 1065; **1** *p. pl. pt.* Bede, we bade, we directed, I 65. A.S. *beódan,* to offer, *bid;* Goth. *biudan,* to bid.

Bee, *s.* a bee, G 195. A.S. *beó.*

An Old Sanskrit *bha* (meaning bee) is recorded in Böhtlingk and Roth's Skt. Dictionary.

Beech, *s.* beech-wood, G 928. See Bechen.

Bekke, *pr. s.* 1 *pr.* I nod, C 396. F. *becquer;* Cotgrave.

Bel amy, i. e. good friend, fair friend, C 318. See note. O.F. *bel,* fair, *ami,* friend.

Belle, *s.* bell, 662, **664. A.S.** *belle.*

Ben, *v.* to be, B 227; *pr. pl.* Ben, are, 238; *pr. s. subj.* may be, is, G 1293; Be as be may, let it be as it may, G 935; *imp. pl.* Beth, be ye, B 229, C 683, G 937; *pp.* Be, been, G 262. A.S. *beón,* to be; cf. Lat. *fore,* Skt. *bhú.*

Ber, *pt. s.* bore, B 722. A.S. *beran,* pt. t. *ic bær.* See Bar.

Berth hir on hond, beareth false witness against her, falsely affirms concerning her, B 620. See the note.

Berie, *v.* to bury, C 884; *pp.* Beryed, 405. A.S. *byrgan,* to bury.

Berm, *s.* barm, i. e. yeast, G 813. A.S. *beorma,* barm, leaven, yeast, froth.

Berne, *s. dat.* a barn, C 397. The proper form of the nom. is *bern,* from A.S. *bern,* contr. from *berern* or *bere-ern,* i. e. a place for corn; from *bere,* barley, corn, and *ærn,* a place for stowing.

Beste, *s.* beast, i. e. an animal without reason, brute animal, G 288; *pl.* Bestes, cattle, C 361, 365. O. F. *beste,* Lat. *bestia.*

Besydes, *adv.* on one side, G 1416.

Bet, *adj. comp.* better, B 311, 1091, G 1410. A.S. *bet,* better, from a base *bat,* signifying good; cf. Goth. *batiza,* better.

Bet, *adv.* better, G 1283, 1344; hence *go bet,* go more quickly,

go **as** fast **as** you can, C 667.
See the note.

Beth. See **Be**.

Betten, *pt. pl.* kindled, G. 518.
A.S. *bétan,* to kindle; lit. to
mend, from base *bat,* good. See
Bet; and Beete in Gloss. I.

Beye, *v.* to buy, C 845, G 637.
A.S. *byegan.*

Bible, *s.* book, G 857. Gk. βιβ-
λίον, a little book, βιβλὸς, a book.

Bicched bones, *s. pl.* dice (lit.
evil *or* **accursed** bones), C 656.
See the note.

Biclappe, **ger.** to clasp, grasp,
ensnare, G 9. Allied to A.S.
beclippan, to beclip, embrace.
The A.S. *clappan* is to move, to
palpitate; the Icel. *klappa* is to
stroke; also to clap the hands.

Bidde, *pp.* bidden, commanded, B
440. Here **han** *bidde* = have
bidden; *bidde* is not the *pt. pl.,*
for that takes the form *bede.* See
Bede. A.S. *beódan;* pt. t. *ic
bedd,* pl. *we budon;* pp. *boden;*
cf. G. *bieten,* to offer.

Biddinge, *pres. part.* praying, G
140. A.S. *biddan,* to pray; cf.
G. *bitten,* to beseech.

Bifalle, *pr. s. subj.* may befal, I
68; *pp.* befallen, B 726. A.S.
befeallan, to happen; from *feallan,* to fall.

Biforn, *prep.* before, B 997, C
665; in front of, G 679; before
(in point of time), 763. A.S.
beforan.

Biforn, *adv.* before, B 704.

Biforn-hond, *adv.* before-hand, G
1317.

Bigonne, *pt. s.* **2** *p.* didst begin,
G 442; *pp.* 428. Prefix *bi,* and
A.S. *ginnan,* pt. t. *gann* (2 p.
gunne), pp. *gunnen.*

Bigyled, *pp.* beguiled, G 985,
1385. O.F. *guile,* guile, from a
Teutonic or Scandinavian source;
cf. Icel. *vél,* an artifice, *wile.*

Bihete, *pr. s.* **1** *p.* I promise, G
707. Prefix *be* and A.S. *hátan,*
to command, promise.

Biholde, *pp.* beheld, G 179. A.S.
behealdan, pp. *behealden.*

Bihynde, *adv.* behind, i.e. to
come, future, G 1271. A.S.
behindan.

Biknowe, *v.* to confess, acknow-
ledge, B 886. Lit. to *be-know.*

Bileue, *s.* faith, belief, G 63. Cf.
A.S. *geleáfa,* **creed**; with prefix
ge instead of *bi.*

Bileueth, *imp. pl.* **believe ye,** G
1047. Cf. A.S. *geleáfan,* **to**
believe; with prefix *ge* for *bi.*

Bireue, *v.* to take away, G 482.
A.S. *bereáfian,* to take away,
rob, **bereave.**

Bisie, *v.* tó trouble, busy; *bisie
me,* employ myself, G 758. A.S.
bysgian, to occupy, from *bysgu,*
occupation, employment.

Bisinesse, *s.* busy endeavour, G
24. See **Businesse.**

Bistad, *pp.* hard bestead, greatly
imperilled, B 649. Lit. placed;
from A.S. *stede,* a place, *stead.*

Bitook, *pt. s.* delivered, gave, com-
mitted (to the charge of), G 541.
Formed from *took,* with prefix *bi-*.
See Took.

Bitter, *adj.* bitter; *bitter swete,* G
878. See the note. A.S. *biter,*
bitter; from *bítan,* to bite.

Bitwixen, *prep.* betwixt, between,
C 832. A.S. *betweox, betwix.*

Bitymes, *adv.* betimes, early, soon,
G 1008.

Bityde, *v.* to happen, C 900, G
400. Prefix *bi,* and A.S. *tidan,*
to happen; from *tíd,* time.

Biwreyen, *v.* to betray, G 150;
Biwreye, C 823, G 147; *pp. s.*
2 *p.* Biwreyest, disclosest, B 773.
See Gloss. II.

Bladdre, *s.* bladder, G 439. A.S.
blǽddre; from A.S. *bláwan,* to
blow, puff out.

Blake, *adj. pl.* black, G. 557. A.S. *blæc.*

Blakeberyed, a, a-blackberrying, i. e. a-wandering at will, astray, C 406. See the note.

Blent, *pr. s.* blinds, G 1391; *pp.* Blent, blinded, deceived, 1077. A.S. *blendian*, to make blind (3 p. s. pr. *blent*, he blinds); from *blind*, blind.

Blered, *adj.* bleared, G 730. See the note. Probably only another form of *blur*. Cf. Bavarian *plerr*, a mist before the eyes (Wedgwood).

Blesseth hir, *pr. s.* crosses herself, B 449.

Blinne, *v.* to stop, cease, G 1171. A.S. *blinnan*, to cease; contr. from *bi*, prefix, and *linnan*, to cease.

Blisful, *adj.* blessed, B 845; happy, merry, 403. A.S. *blis*, joy; cf. *blithe.*

Blowe, *pp.* blown, filled out with wind, G 440. A.S. *bláwan*, to blow; cf. Lat. *flare.*

Blundreth, *pr. s.* runs heedlessly, G 1414; I *p. pl. pr.* Blundren, we fall into confusion, we confuse ourselves, become mazed, 670. From Icel. *blunda*, to doze, *blundr*, a doze; connected with A.S. *blendan*, to blend, confuse, and *blind*, blind.

Blynde, *adj. pl.* blind, G 658. A.S. *blind.* See above.

Blynde with, *ger.* to blind (the priest) with, G 1151.

Blythe, *adj.* blithe, joyful, B 1154. A.S. *blíðe*, glad, *bliss*, joy.

Bodies, *s. pl.* bodies, metallic bodies (metals) answering to the celestial bodies (planets), G 820, 825.

Boist, *s.* box, C 307. O. F. *boiste* (Fr. *boîte*), Low Lat. accus. *boxida, buxida*, from Gk. πυξίδα, accus. of πυξίς, a box, a *pyx*; properly a box made of boxwood; Gk. πύξος, Lat. *buxus*, the box-tree.

Bole armoniak, Armenian clay, G 790. See the note.

Boles, *gen. sing.* bull's, G 797.

Bolle, *s.* a bowl, often a wooden bowl, G 1210. A.S. *bolla.*

Bond, *pt. s.* bound, B 634. A.S. *bindan*, to bind; pt. t. *ic band.*

Bone, *s.* petition, prayer, G 234, 356. Not from A.S. *bén*, a prayer, but from the cognate Scandinavian form; Icel. *bón*, a prayer. Now spelt *boon.*

Boras, *s.* borax, G 790. 'Borax, biborate of soda; a salt formed by a combination of boracic acid with soda. Fr. *borax*, Span. *borrax*, Arabic *búraq*, nitre, saltpeter; from Arab. *baraqa*, to shine;' Webster. But rather borrowed from Pers. *búrah*, borax.

Bord, *s.* table, B 430; board, i. e. meals, G 1017. A.S. *bord*, a board, a table.

Bost, *s.* boast, B 401, C 764; pride, swelling, G 441. Probably of Celtic origin, as we find not only W. *bost*, a boast, *bostio*, to boast, but also Gaelic *bòsd*, a boast, vain-glory, *bosdail*, boasting, *bòsdair*, a boaster.

Bote, *s.* relief, G 1481. E. *boot*, A.S. *bót*, a remedy; from the base *bat*, good. See Bet.

Botel, *s.* bottle (of hay), H 14; *pl.* Botels, bottles, C 871.

Botme, *s. dat.* bottom, G 1321. A.S. *botm*, dat. *botme*; cognate with Lat. *fundus*, Gk. πυθμήν.

Bothe, *adj.* both, B 221.

Boughte, *pt. s.* bought; *boughte agayn*, redeemed, C 766. See Beye.

Bounden, *pp.* bound, B 270. A.S. *bindan*, pp. *bunden.*

Bourde, *s.* jest, H 81. O.F. *bourde*, a jest, pleasantry; supposed to be a contraction of *bohort*, a mock tournament, knightly exercise, from *horde*, a

barrier, the lists. The prefix *bo-* is explained from O.F. *bot,* a blow, stroke. (But this etymology is now given up.)

Bourde, *pr. s.* 1 *p.* I jest, C 778. See above.

Boweth, *imp. pl.* 2 *p.* bow ye, C 909. A.S. *búgan,* to bow, bend; cf. Lat. *fugare,* to turn to flight; Skt. *bhuj,* to bend.

Brak, *pt. s.* broke, B 288. A.S. *brecan,* pt. t. *bræc.*

Brast, *pt. s.* burst, B 697; *pl.* Braste, 671. A.S. *berstan,* to burst; pt. t. *ic bærst.* Either the *r* was transposed in course of time, or this form was brought about by Danish influence. Cf. Icel. *bresta,* to burst; pt. t. *brast.* (Gloss. I.)

Brede, *s.* breadth, G 1228. A.S. *brǽdo,* breadth; from *brád,* broad.

Breech, *s.* breeches, C 948. A.S. *bréc,* breeches, brogues, pl. of *bróc,* a brogue; the form *brogue* is Celtic; cf. Gaelic *briogais,* breeches, *bróg,* a shoe. The A.S. *bróc* seems to be cognate with the Celtic.

Breke, *v.* to break, C 936; *breke his day,* fail to pay at the appointed time, G 1040; *imp. s.* Brek, interrupt, 1 24. A.S. *brecan.*

Brennen, *v.* to burn, G 313; Brenne, G 1192; *pr. pl.* Brennen, B 964; *pr. s. subj.* Brenne, may burn, G 1423; *imp. s.* Brenne, G 515; *pt. s.* Brende, burnt, B 289; *pp.* Brent, burnt, G 759, 1197, 1407; *pres. pt.* Brenning, G 118, 802; Brenninge, G 114. Icel. *brenna,* to burn; cf. A.S. *byrnan, beornan,* Goth. *brinnan,* Ger. *brennen.*

Breyde, *pt. s.* drew, B 837. A.S. *gebregdan* or *bregdan,* to pull, to draw a sword; also to weave,

braid ; cf. Icel. *bregða,* to draw, to braid. See **Abreyde** in Gloss. I.

Brid, *s.* bird, G 1342. A.S. *brid,* the young of birds.

Brimstoon, *s.* brimstone, sulphur, G 798, 824, 1439. Lit. burning-stone ; cf. Icel. *brenni-steinn,* sulphur; from *brenna,* to burn, and *steinn,* a stone.

Broches, *s. pl.* brooches, C 908. (Gloss. II.)

Brode, *adv.* broadly, wide awake, G 1420.

Brother, *gen. sing.* brother's, G 1432.

Bulle, *s.* papal bull, C 909; *pl.* Bulles, 336. Lat. *bulla,* the leaden ball, with a stamp on it, affixed to a document.

Buriels, *s. pl.* burial-places, i.e. the Catacombs, G 186. Originally *buriels* was the *singular* form of the sb. (see the note).

Businesse, *s.* business, industry, G 5. See **Bisinesse.**

But, *conj.* except, unless, B 431, C 741, G 221, 984; But-if, unless, B 636. A.S. *bútan, búte,* except ; from prefix *bi,* and *útan, úte,* out.

By, *prep.* about, concerning, with respect to, G 1035, 1438. A.S. *bi,* by.

By, *v.* to buy; *go by,* go to buy, G 1294. See **Beye.**

Byiaped, *pp.* tricked, G 1385. See **Iape.**

C.

Cacche, *v.* to catch, G 11. O.Fr. *cachier,* Low Lat. *captiare,* from Lat. *captare,* to take captive. Its doublet is *chase.*

Caityf, *s.* caitiff, wretch, C 728. O.Fr. *caitif* (F. *chétif*), from Lat. *captiuus,* a captive.

Cake, *s.* loaf (lit. a cake), C 322. Icel. and Swed. *kaka,* Dan. *kage.*

Calcening, *s.* calcination, G 771. From Lat. *calx.*

Calcinacioun, *s.* calcination; *of c.,* for calcining, G 804.

Can, *pr. s.* knows, G 600, 620, 1091. A.S. *cann* (1 and 3 p.), from *cunnan,* to know.

Canevas, *s.* canvas, G 939. F. *canevas;* cf. Ital. *canavaccio.* The derivation is from Lat. *cannabis,* Gk. κάνναβις, hemp.

Canon, *s.* the 'Canon,' the title of a book by Avicenna, C 890. See the note.

Canstow, *contr. for* canst thou, B 632, C 521.

Capel, *s.* horse, nag, H 64. From Lat. *caballus,* a nag; cf. W. *ceffyl,* a horse.

Capitayn, *s.* captain, C 582.

Capouns, *s. pl.* capons, C 856.

Cardiacle, *s.* pain about the heart, C 313. Cotgrave gives *Cardiaque,* as an adj., one meaning being 'wrung at the heart.' The deriv. is from Gk. καρδία, the heart.

Care, *s.* anxiety, trouble, B 514; *pl.* Cares, G 347. A.S. *caru,* care, anxiety; *not* Lat. *cura.* See Cure.

Carieden, *pt. pl.* carried, G 1219. (Gloss. II.)

Carl, *s.* churl, country fellow, C 717. A.S. *carl,* Icel. *karl,* a man, male. The A.S. also had *ceorl,* whence E. *churl.*

Carolinge, *s. dat.* carolling, singing, song, G 1345. (Gloss. I.)

Caryinge, *s.* carrying, C 875.

Cas, *s.* circumstance, case, condition, B 305, 311, 983. F. *cas.* Lat. *casus.*

Caste, *pt. s.* threw, H 48; cast up, B 508; imagined, contrived, devised, B 406, 584, 805; *pl.* exhaled, emitted, G 244; *pr. pl.* Casten, cast about, debate, B 212; *pr. s.* Casteth, considers, G 1414; *refl.* casts himself, devotes him-

self, G 738; *pp.* Cast, planned, devised, C 880. Scandinavian; Icel. *kasta,* to throw. (Gloss. II.)

Catel, *s.* property, chattels, C 594. (Gloss. II.)

Cause, *s.* reason, B 252.

Cementing, *s.* cementing, hermetically sealing, G 817. From Lat. *caementum,* cement.

Cered, *pp. as adj.* waxed, G 808. See the note. Cf. Lat. *ceratum,* a salve whose chief compound is wax, *cera.* See *cérat* in Brachet's Fr. Etym. Dict.

Ceriously, *adv.* minutely, with full details (see note), B 185. The word is glossed by *ceriose* in the Ellesmere MS., and Ducange has '*Seriose,* fuse, minutatim, articulatim.' From Lat. *series,* order.

Certein, *adj.* a certain quantity of; *certein gold,* a stated sum of money, B 242; *certein tresor,* a quantity of treasure, B 442; *as sb.,* Certeyn, a certain sum, a fixed quantity, G 776, 1024.

Certes, *adv.* certainly, G 1478. (Gloss. II.)

Cesse, *v.* to cease, B 1066; *pt. s.* Cessede, G 124; Cessed, 538. F. *cesser,* Lat. *cessare.*

Chaffare, *s.* chaffer, traffic, G 1421; Chaffar, merchandise, B 138. For *chap-fare;* from A.S. *ceáp,* purchase, *fær,* proceedings. (Gloss. I.)

Chaffare, *ger.* to trade, barter, deal, traffic, B 139. See above.

Chalk-stoon, *s.* a piece of chalk, G 1207.

Chambre, *s.* chamber, B 167. F. *chambre,* Lat. *camera.*

Chanon, *s.* canon, G 573 (see the note); Chanoun, 972.

Chapmen, *s. pl.* traders, merchants, B 135. See Chaffare.

Chapmanhode, *s.* trade, barter, B 143.

Charge, *s.* burden, weight, importance ; *of that no charge*, for that no matter, it is of no importance, G 749. The original sense is a burden, load ; F. *charger*, to load, from Low Lat. *carricare*, to load.

Chaunce, *s.* 'chance,' a technical term in the game of hazard, C 653 ; luck, G 593. O. Fr. *cheaunce*, Lat. *cadentia*, that which falls out, from *cadere*, to fall (used in dice-playing).

Chees, *imp. s.* choose, G 458 ; *pt. s.* chose, G 38. See Chese.

Cherche, *s.* a church, G 546.

Chere, *s.* cheer, i. e. mien, G 1233 ; entertainment, B 180. O. Fr. *chere*, Low Lat. *cara*, the face.

Cherl, *s.* churl, C 289. A. S. *ceorl* ; see Carl.

Chese, *v.* to choose, B 227 ; *imp. s.* Chees, choose, G 458 ; *pt. s.* Chees, chose, G 38. A. S. *ceósan* ; pt. t. *ic ceás.*

Cheue, *in phr.* yuel mot he cheue = ill may he end, *or* ill may he thrive, G 1225. F. *chevir*, to compass, manage, from *chef*, Lat. *caput.*

Chit, *pr. s.* chides (contr. from *chideth*), G 921. A. S. *cídan*, to chide.

Chiteren, *v.* to chatter, prattle, G 1397.

Chiuache, *s.* feat of horsemanship, H 50. O. Fr. *cheuauchie*, *chevauchee*, an expedition on horseback, from vb. *chevaucher*, *chevalcher*, to ride a horse ; which from *cheval*, a horse, Lat. *caballus.*

Chiualrye, *s.* chivalry, company of knights, B 235. Cf. E. *cavalry*, from the same source, viz. Fr. *cheval*, a horse, Lat. *caballus.*

Cink, *num.* cinque, five, C 653. Fr. *cinq*, Lat. *quinque.*

Citee, *s.* city, B 289.

Citrinacioun, *s.* citronising, the

turning to the colour of citron, a process in alchemy, G 816. See note.

Clappe, *pr. pl.* prattle, chatter, G 965. A. S. *clappan*, to clap together, make a noise by clapping. (Gloss. II.)

Clause, *s.* sentence, B 251.

Cleernes, *s.* clearness, brightness, glory, G 403. O. Fr. *cler*, Lat. *clarus* ; with A. S. suffix *-ness.*

Clene, *adv.* clean, entirely, G 625, 1425. The A. S. adv. *cláne* has the same sense.

Clepe, 1 *p. pl. pres.* we call, name, G 827 ; *pr. pl.* call, B 191, G 2 ; *pr. s.* call, C 675 (here *clepeth* is sing. rather than plural ; see Men), also *pp.* Clept, named, G 863. A. S. *clipian*, *cleopian*, to call. (Gloss. I.)

Clergial, *adj.* clerkly, learned, G 752.

Clerkes, *s. pl.* learned men, B 480.

Cley, *s.* clay, G 807. A. S. *clág.*

Clinke, *v.* to ring, sound, clink, tingle, C 664. Cf. Icel. *klingja*, Swed. *klinga*, Dan. *klinge*, to tingle, ring ; also Du. *klinken*, to tingle. The word is probably of A. S. origin, as shewn by the Dutch form.

Cloistre, *s.* cloister, G 43.

Clokke, *s. dat.* clock, I 5.

Cloos, *adj.* close, secret, G 1369.

Clote-leef, *s.* a leaf of the burdock or Clote-bur (see note), G 577. A. S. *cláte*, a burdock ; cf. G. *klette*, a bur, burdock ; Mid. Du. *kladde*, a bur.

Clowt, *s.* a cloth, C 736 ; *pl.* Cloutes, cloths, portions of a garment, rags, 348. A. S. *clút*, a little cloth.

Coagulat, *pp.* coagulated, clotted, G 811. Lat. *coagulatus.*

Cofre, *s.* coffer, money-box, G 836. O. Fr. *cofre*, *cofin*, Lat. *cophinus*, Gk. *κόφινος*, a basket.

Cokes, *s. pl.* cooks, C 538. **A. S.** *côc*, but borrowed from **Lat.** *coquus.*

Cokkes, *a corruption of* Goddes, H 9, I 29.

Colde, *v.* to grow cold, B 879.

Coles, *s. pl.* coals, G 1114. **A. S.** *col*, coal.

Comaundour, *s.* commander, B 495.

Combust, *pp.* burnt, G 811. **Lat.** *combustus*, burnt; from a form *burere; cf. *bustum.*

Come, *v.* to come; *Come therby*, come by it, acquire it, G 1395; *pr. s.* Comth, comes, B 407, 603, C 781; *pt. pl.* Come, came, G 1220; Comen, B 145; *pp.* Comen, B 260; ben comen = are come, 1130. **A. S.** *cuman.*

Come, *s.* coming, G 343. **A. S.** *cyme*, a coming; from *cuman*, to come.

Commune, *v.* to commune, converse, G 982. **O. Fr.** *communier*, **Lat.** *communicare.*

Commune, *adj.* general, common, B 155. **O. Fr.** *commun*, **Lat.** *communis.*

Companye, *s.* company, B 134, (Gloss. II.)

Compas, *s.* enclosure, continent; *tryne compas*, the threefold world, containing earth, sea, and heaven, G 45. **O. Fr.** *compas*, measure; from **Lat.** *cum* and *passus*, a step.

Conceit, *s.* idea, G 1214.

Conclude, *v.* to include, put together, G 429; to attain to a successful result, 773; I *p. s. pr.* I draw the conclusion, 1472. **Lat.** *concludere.*

Conclusioun, *s.* result, successful end of an experiment, G 672.

Confiture, *s.* composition, C 862. **Fr.** *confiture*, a mixture, preserve, from *confire*, to preserve, pickle; **Lat.** *conficere*, in late sense of to 'make up' a medicine; from *facere.*

Confort, *s.* comfort, G 32. **O. Fr.** *conforter*, **Lat.** *confortare*, to strengthen; from *fortis*, strong.

Confounde, *v.* to bring to confusion, B 362; *pp.* Confounded, overwhelmed with sin, destroyed in soul, G 137. **Cf.** the phrase— 'Let me never be *confounded*;' in Latin—' ne *confundar* in aeternum.'

Confus, *pp. as adj.* put to confusion, convicted of folly, G 463. **O. Fr.** *confondre*, to confound; *pp.* **confus**; **Lat.** *confundere*, *pp. confusus*; from *fundere*, to pour.

Conioyninge, *s.* conjoining, conjunction, G 95. **O. Fr.** *conjoindre*, **Lat.** *coniungere*, to join together.

Conne, *pr. pl.* I *p.* we can, are able, B 483; *pr. s. subj.* he may know; *al conne he*, whether he may know, G 846. **A. S.** *cunnan*, to know, has pr. pl. *cunnon*; pr. s. subj. *cunne.*

Conning, *s.* skill, B 1099, G 653, 1087. **A. S.** *cunning*, experience; from *cunnan*, to know.

Conquereden, *pt. pl.* conquered, B 542. **O. Fr.** *conquerre*, to conquer, acquire; from *querre*, **Lat.** *quaerere*, to seek.

Conseil, *s.* council, B 204; counsel, 425; secrecy, 777; a secret, 561, C 819, G 145, 192. **Fr.** *conseil*, **Lat.** *concilium.*

Conserued, *pp.* kept, G 387.

Considereth, *imp. pl.* 2 *p.* consider, G 1388.

Constable, *s.* constable, governor, B 512. **O. Fr.** *conestable*, Low **Lat.** *conestabulus*, a corruption of *comestabulus*, a word formed by uniting *comes stabuli* (count of the stable) into one word.

Constablesse, *s.* constable's wife, B 539. See above.

Contenaunce, *s.* pretence, appearance, G 1264. **O. Fr.** *contenance*, countenance, from *contenir*, **Lat.**

continere, **to** contain; from Lat. *tenere*, to hold.

Contrarie, *adj.* contrary; *in contrarie*, in contradiction, G 1477.

Contree, *s.* country, B 434. F. *contree*, from Lat. *contrata*, the country over against one, from *contra*, against. (Gloss. I.)

Coper, *s.* copper, G 829. Late Lat. *cuprum*, copper; from *Cyprium æs*, brass of Cyprus.

Corn, *s.* a grain, C 863. A.S. *corn*, a grain; cognate with Lat. *granum*. Thus *corn* and *grain* are doublets.

Corniculere, *s.* registrar, secretary, G 369. See the note. Lat. *cornicularius*, a registrar, clerk to a magistrate; from *corniculum*, a horn-shaped ornament; from *cornu*, a horn.

Corny, *adj.* applied to ale, strong of the corn or malt, C 315, 456. See Corn.

Corones, *s. pl.* crowns, G 221, 226. Lat. *corona*.

Corosif, *adj.* corrosive, G 853.

Corpus bones, *an intentionally nonsensical oath, composed of* 'corpus domini,' the Lord's body, and 'bones,' C 314. See the note.

Correccioun, *s.* correction, I 60.

Cors, *s.* body, C 304, H 67; corpse, C 665. O. Fr. *cors*, Lat. *corpus*.

Couchen, *ger.* to lay, G 1152; *pt. s.* Couched, laid, placed, 1157; *pp.* Couched, laid, 1182, 1200. O. Fr. *couchier*, *colcher*, to place, Lat. *collocare*; from *locus*, a place.

Coude, *pr. s.* could, G 291. A.S. *cúðe*, pt. t. of *cunnan*, to know, be able.

Coueityse, *s.* covetousness, C 424. O. Fr. *coveitise*, *covoitise*, Low Lat. *cupiditia*, from *cupidus*, desirous; which from *cupere*, to wish for.

Couent, *s.* convent, G 1007. O. Fr. *covent*, Lat. *conuentus*, a coming together; from *uenire*, to come.

Counterfete, *v.* to imitate, C 447; *pp.* Counterfeted, imitated, B 746, 793. (Gloss. II.)

Cours, *s.* course, B 704; life on earth, G 387. F. *cours*, Lat. *cursus*; from *currere*, to run.

Cradel, *s.* cradle, G 122. A.S. *cradel*; perhaps of Celtic origin. Cf. Irish *craidhal*, W. *cryd*, a cradle, Gaelic *creathall*, a cradle; allied to Gk. *κραδάειν*, to shake.

Crafty, *adj.* skilful, clever, G 1290 A.S. *cræft*, knowledge, skill.

Crased, *pp.* cracked, G 934. The O. F. only has *escraser*, to break, but this is formed as if from *craser*. It is of Scandinavian origin; cf. Swed. *sld i kras*, to dash in pieces.

Creance, *s.* belief, object of faith, B 340; Creaunce, creed, 915. O. F. *creance*, from *croire*, to believe, Lat. *credere*.

Creatour, *s.* Creator, C 901.

Crede, *s.* creed, belief, G 1047.

Cristal, *adj.* crystal, C 347. O. F. *cristal*, from Lat. *crystallum*, Gk. *κρύσταλλος*, ice, crystal; from *κρύος*, frost.

Cristen, *adj.* Christian, B 222.

Cristendom, *s.* the Christian religion, B 351; Christianity, G 447.

Cristenly, *adv.* in a Christian manner, B 1122.

Cristianitee, *s.* company of Christians, B 544.

Cristned, *pp.* baptised, B 226, 355, G 352.

Crommes, *s. pl.* crumbs, G 60. A.S. *cruma*, a crumb, a fragment.

Crone, *s.* crone, hag, B 432. Apparently of Celtic origin; cf. Gaelic *crìonna*, prudent, penurious, old, ancient; *crìon*, little, mean, *crìon*, to wither, decay blast. Or rather, it answers to Picard *carone*, F. *charogne*, our *carrion*.

Croper, *s.* crupper, G 566. Cf. F. *croupière*. From O. F. *crope*, *crupe* (F. *croupe*), the rump of an animal; apparently of Scandinavian origin; cf. Icel. *kryppa*, a hump, hunch; Icel. *kroppr*, a hump; Dan. *krop*, the trunk of the body. See Croppe in Gloss. I.

Croslet, *s.* a crucible, G 1147; *also* Crosselet, 1117; *pl.* Croslets, 793. A diminutive of *cross*, apparently intended as a sort of translation of Lat. *crucibulum*. But the latter is *not* derived (as might be supposed) from Lat. *crux*, a cross. See *Crucible* in Webster and Wedgwood.

Croude, *v.* to push, B 801; *pr. s.* 2 *p.* Crowdest, dost press, dost push, 296 (see note to l. 299). A. S. *crúdan* (not found).

Crowding, *s.* pressure, motive power, B 299. See the note.

Croweth, *pr. s. refl.*; him croweth = crows, C 362. A.S. *cráwan*, to crow, croak.

Croys, *s.* cross, B 450, 844, C 532. O. F. *crois*, Lat. *crucem*, acc. of *crux*.

Cucurbites, *s. pl.* cucurbites, G 794. 'Cucurbite, a chemical vessel originally made in the shape of a gourd, but sometimes shallow, with a wide mouth, and used in distillation;' Webster. From Lat. *cucurbita*, a gourd.

Cure, *s.* care, endeavour, B 188; honest cure = care for honourable things, C 557; in cure = in her care, in her power, B 230. Fr. *cure*, Lat. *cura*, care.

Cursednesse, *s.* wickedness, C 400, 498, 638, G 1101. A.S. *cursian*, to curse; *curs*, a curse.

Curteisye, *s.* courtesy, B 166. O. F. *curteisie*; from O. F. *cort*,

a court, Lat. *cohortem*, acc. of *cohors*. (Gloss. II.)

Cut, *s.* a lot, C 793. W. *cwtws*, a lot; originally the *short* straw, from *cwta*, short. (Gloss. I.)

D.

Dagger, *s.* dagger, C 830. From the root *dag*, which appears in *dagges* = pierces, and *daggande* = piercing, Morte Arthur, ed. Brock (E. E. T. S.), 2102, 3749. Of Celtic origin; cf. Breton *dagi*, to pierce, *dag*, a dagger.

Daliaunce, *s.* playful demeanour, G 592. (Gloss. I. and II.)

Dame, *s.* mother, C 684. F. *dame*, Lat. *domina*, lady.

Dampnable, *adj.* damnable, C 472.

Dampnacioun, *s.* damnation, C 500.

Dampned, *pp.* condemned, B 1110, G 310. O. F. *dampner*, Lat. *damnare*, to condemn.

Dar, *pr. s.* 1 *p.* I dare, B 273, G 214; *pr. s.* Dar, G 312; 2 *p.* Darst, B 860; *pt. s.* Dorste, durst, B 753, G 532. A.S. *ic dearr*, I dare, *he dearr*, he dare; *pt. t. ic dorste*.

Daswen, *pt. pl.* daze, are dazed, are dazzled, H 31. Cf. Icel. *dasask* (i. e. *dasa-sk*), to become weary; *dasaðr*, exhausted; cf. also Swed. *dasa*, to be idle; E. *doze*.

Date, *s.* a date, term, period, G 1411. F. *date*, Lat. *datum*, a thing given.

Day, *s.* day; also, an appointed day for the payment of a sum of money, G 1040. A.S. *dæg*.

Debaat, *s.* strife, G 1389. F. *débat*, from vb. *débattre*, which 'from *battre*, Lat. *batuere*, to beat.

Deed, *pp. as adj.* dead, B 209, G 64, 204.

Deedly, *adv.* deadly, morta'ly, G 476.

Dees, *s. pl.* dice, C 467, 623. (Gloss. II.)

Defame, *s.* dishonour, C 612.

Defamed, *pp.* defamed, slandered, C 415. F. *diffamer*, Lat. *diffamare*, to defame.

Defaute, *s.* fault, sin, C 370; a defect, G 954. (Gloss. II.)

Defenden, *v.* to forbid, C 590; *ger.* Defende, G 1470; *pp.* Defended, forbidden, C 510. F. *défendre*, Lat. *defendere*.

Deknes, *s. pl.* deacons, G 547. Lat. *diaconus*.

Del, *s.* part; *euery del*, every whit, entirely, G 1269. A.S. *dǽl*, a part.

Delices, *s. pl.* delights, pleasures, C 547, G 3. F. *délices*, Lat. *deliciæ*.

Delte, *pt. s.* dealt, G 1074. The inf. is *delen*, from A.S. *dǽlan*, to divide, from *dǽl*, a part.

Delyt, *s.* delight, B 1135, G 1070. O.F. *delit, deleit*; from Lat. *delectare*, to delight. The modern spelling *delight* is due to an absurd supposed connection with *light*.

Demaunde, *s.* demand, question, B 472; Demande, G 430. O.F. *demande*, from Lat. *de* and *mandare*.

Deme, *v.* to suppose, B 1038; to judge, conclude, 1091; to give a verdict, G 595; *pr. s.* Demeth, fancies, 689; *imp. pl.* Demeth, suppose ye, 993. A.S. *dēman*, to judge, from *dóm*, judgment.

Departed, *pt. s.* parted, B 1158; divided, C 812, 814. O.F. *desparter*, Lat. *dispartire*, from *dis* and *partire*; which from *pars*, a part.

Departing, *s.* departure, B 260; Departinge, 293.

Depe, *s.* the deep, the sea, B 455.

VOL. III.

A.S. *deóp*, deep water, neut. sb.; from *deóp*, adj. deep.

Depper, *adv. comp.* deeper, more deeply, B 630, G 250.

Dere, *adj.* (*voc.*) dear, D 447, G 257, 321. The noun is also *dere*; the final *e* is due to the A.S. form; A.S. *deóre, dýre*, dear.

Dere, *adv.* dearly; *to dere*, too dearly, C 293.

Derkest, *adj. superl.* darkest, B 304. A.S. *deorc*, dark.

Descensories, *s. pl.* G 792. 'Descensories, vessels used in chemistry for extracting oils *per descensum*;' Tyrwhitt. From Lat. *descendere*, to descend.

Desolaat, *adj.* deserted, alone; *holden desolaat*, shunned, C 598. Lat. *desolatus*, from *desolare*, to waste, make lonely; from *de* and *solus*, alone.

Despit, *s.* spite, B 391; vexation, dishonour, 699. O.F. *despit* (F. *dépit*), Lat. *despectus*, a looking down upon; from *de*, down, and *specere*, to look. (Gloss. I.)

Despitously, *adv.* despitefully, maliciously, B 605.

Desport, *s.* amusement, sport, G 592. O.F. *desport*; from Lat. prefix *dis* and *portare*, to carry. Similarly to *divert* is from Lat. *uertere*, to turn.

Destourbe, *v.* to disturb; *destourbe of*, to disturb in, C 340. O.F. *destorber*, from Lat. prefix *dis* and *turbare*, to confuse; from *turba*, a crowd.

Deue, *adj. pl.* deaf, G 286. The sing. is *deef*. From A.S. *deáf*.

Deuyse, *v.* to relate, tell, B 154, 349, 613, G 266. (Gloss. II.)

Deye, *v.* to die, B 525, 592; Deyen, G 472; *pr. s.* Deyeth, dies, G 1436; *pt. s.* Deyde, died, C 580, G 138. Scandinavian: Icel. *deyja*, to die, Swed. *dö*, Dan. *döe*.

Deyntee, *adj.* dainty, C 520; *as sb.*,

Q

special or peculiar pleasure, B 139; *s. pl.* Deyntees, dainties, 419. O. F. *daintie*, agreeableness; from Lat. acc. *dignitatem*, worthiness.

Digne, *adj.* worthy, honoured, C 695; suitable, B 778. F. *digne*, Lat. *dignus*, worthy.

Dilatacioun, *s.* diffuseness, B 232. Formed like a French sb. from Lat. acc. *dilatationem*, which from *dilatare*, to make broad, from *latus*, broad.

Disclaundered, *pp.* slandered, B 674. From O. F. prefix *des*, Lat. *dis*, and F. *esclandre*, formerly *escandle*, from Lat. *scandalum*, which from Gk. σκάνδαλον.

Discouere, *v* to reveal, G 1465; 2 *p. s. pr.* Discouerest, revealest, 696; *pp.* Discouered, revealed, 1468. O. F. *descovrir*, from Lat. prefixes *dis* and *con*, and *operire*, to hide.

Disese, *s.* lack of ease, trouble, distress, misery, B 616, G 747, H 97.

Displesances, *s. pl.* displeasures, annoyances, C 420.

Disport, *s.* pleasure, B 143. See Desport.

Disposed, *pp.* inclined; *wel disposed*, in good health (the converse of *indisposed*), H 33.

Disseuer, *ger.* to part, G 875. From O.F. *sevrer*, Lat. *separare*, to separate.

Dissimuleth, *pr. s.* dissimulates, acts foolishly, G 466. Lat. *dissimulare*, to pretend that a thing is not.

Dissimulinge, *s.* dissembling, G 1073.

Diuerse, *adj. pl.* diverse, B 211.

Doon, *v.* to do, G 166; to cause, as in *doon vs henge*, cause us to be hung, C 790; *do werche*, cause to be wrought or built, G 545; *ger.* Done, to do, B 770, G 932; *for to done*, a fit thing to do, I 62; *pr. s.* 2 *p.* Dost, makest, C 312; *pr. s.* Doth, causes, B 724; *imp. s.* Do, make, H 12; cause, G 32; *do hang*, cause me to be hung, G 1029; *do fecche*, cause to be fetched, B 662; *do wey* = put away, lay aside, G 487; *imp. pl.* Doth, do ye, C 745; *pp.* Doon, B 174; Do, done, G 745, 1155; Doon, completed, 387. A. S. *dón*, to do; originally to place, as in Skt. *dhá*, to place, Gk. τίθημι, I place, Lat. *con-dere*, to put together.

Domb, *adj.* dumb, B 1055; *pl.* Dombe, G 286. A. S. *dumb*.

Dome, *s.* judgment, C 637. A. S. *dóm* (Gloss. II.)

Dominacioun, *s.* domination, dominion, C 560; power, H 57. From Lat. *dominus*, a lord.

Dore, *s.* door, G 1137, 1142, 1217. The word is dissyllabic; A.S. *duru*.

Dorste. See Dar.

Doten, *v.* to grow foolish, act foolishly, G 983. Cf. F. *ra-doter*, to dote: but the F. is borrowed from a Low-German source, which appears in the Du. *dutten*, to take a nap, to mope, from *dut*, a nap, sleep, dotage.

Doublenesse, *s.* duplicity, G 1300.

Doughter, *s.* daughter, B 151. A. S. *dohtor*.

Doute, *s.* doubt, B 777, G 833; *out of doute*, doubtless, B 390, C 822. F. *doute*, doubt, from *douter*, Lat. *dubitare*, to doubt.

Doutelees, *adv.* doubtless, C 492, G 16, 1435; without hesitation, B 226.

Dowue, *s.* dove, pigeon, C 397. Of A. S. origin, though not easily found; cf. Icel. *dúfa*, Swed. *dufva*, Du. *duif*. (Somner's A. S. Dict. gives the form *duua*.)

Dradden, *pt. pl. subj.* should dread, should fear, G 15. See Drede.

Draf, *s.* draff, refuse, chaff, I 35.

A. S. *drabbe*, lees, dregs; Du. *draf*, swill, hog's-wash; Icel. *draf*, draff, husks.

Dragoun, *s.* dragon, G 1435. F. *dragon*, Lat. *draconem*, Gk. δράκοντα.

Drede, *s.* fear, G 204*; doubt, C 507; *it is no drede*, there is no doubt, B 869; *withouten drede*, without doubt, 196. A. S. *drǽd*, dread, fear.

Dreden, *v.* to fear, G 320; *ger. to drede*, to be feared, 437; 2 *p. s. pres. subj.* thou mayest dread, 477. A. S. *drǽdan*, to fear.

Drenchen, *v.* to be drowned. B 455; *pp.* Drenched, G 949. The A. S. *drencan* is properly transitive, meaning, to make to drink, to *drench*.

Drenchyng, *s.* drowning, B 485; Drenching, B 489.

Dresse, *v.* to prepare (himself), get ready, B 1100; address (myself), G 77; *v. refl.* address himself, G 1271; *pt. s. refl.* Dresseth hir, prepares herself, B 265; *pr. pl.* Dressen, prepare themselves, set forward, B 263; Dresse, 416; *pr. pl. refl.* direct themselves, i. e. take their places in order, 416. F. *dresser*; from Lat. *directus*, direct. (See Brachet.)

Dronke, *pp.* drunk, H 17. A. S. *druncen*, pp. of *drincan*, to drink.

Dronkelewe, *adj.* drunken, overcome with drink, C 495. From the A. S. verb *drincan*, to drink.

Dronkenesse, *s.* drunkenness, B 771, C 484. A. S. *druncennes*; from *drincan*, to drink.

Droppe, *s.* drop, 522. A dissyllabic word; A. S. *dropa*, a drop; cf. G. *tropfe*.

Drough, *pt. s.* drew (himself), G 685. A. S. *dragan*, to draw; pt. t. *ic dróg* or *ic dróh*, I drew.

Dryue, *v.* to drive; *dryue the day*

awey, pass the time, C 628. A. S. *drifan*, to drive.

Dulle, *adj. pl.* dull, stupid, B 202. A. S. *dol*, foolish; put for *dwal*, as shewn by A. S. *gedwolgod*, a false god or idol; Goth. *dwals*, foolish; cf. Du. *dol*, mad, G. *toll*, mad.

Dulleth, *pr. s.* makes dull, stupefies, G 1093, 1172.

Dun, *s.* the dun horse, (see note), H 5. A. S. *dun*, dun; of Celtic origin; cf. W. *dwn*, dun, dusky, Gaelic *donn*, brown.

Dure, *v.* to last, B 187, 1078. F. *durer*, Lat. *durare*, to last; from *durus*, hard.

Dwelte, *pt. s.* dwelt, B 134; *pl.* Dwelten, 550. Grein gives an A. S. *dwellan*, to hinder; cf. Icel. *dvelja*, to delay, Swed. *dväljas*, to delay; Sw. *dvala*, torpor, connects the word with A. S. *dwol*, *dol*. See Dulle.

Dye, *v.* to die, B 644; *pt s.* Dyde, died, C 658. See Deye.

E.

Eek, *adv.* moreover, also, B 140, 444. A. S. *éc*, *eác*, eke, also.

Eet, *pt. s.* ate. C 510. (Gloss. II.)

Effect; *in effect*, in fact, in reality, G 511.

Eft, *adv.* again, B 792, G 1263. A. S. *eft*, again, back; cf. A. S. *æft*, again, allied to *after*.

Eftsone, *adv.* soon after, G 1288; soon after this, H 65; hereafter, G 933; again, B 909. From A. S. *eft*, *æft*, again, and *sóna*, soon.

Eggement, *s.* instigation, incitement, B 842. A hybrid word; the suffix *-ment* is French, but the first part is from A. S. *eggian*, to excite, from a root *ag*, cognate with the Indo-European root *ak*, sharp.

Egremoin, s. agrimony, G 800. Lat. *agremonia, argemonia,* Gk. ἀργεμώνη; so called, apparently, because supposed to cure a white spot in the eye. Gk. ἄργεμα; which from ἀργός, white. (Webster.)

Eighte, *num.* eight, C 771. A dissyllabic word; A. S. *eahta,* eight; cognate with Lat. *octo,* Gk. ὀκτώ.

Eleccioun, s. choice, 'election' (a technical term), B 312. See note, p. 126.

Elementes, s. *pl.* elements, G 1460.

Elf, s. fairy, B 754. A. S. *elf, ælf,* an elf, a genius; Icel. *álfr.*

Elles, *adv.* otherwise, G 1131, 1377, B 644; *elles god forbede,* God forbid it should be otherwise, G 1046. A. S. *elles.*

Elleswher, *adv.* elsewhere, G 1130.

Elixir, s. elixir, G 863. Arabic *el iksír,* the philosopher's stone.

Eluish, *adj.* lit. elvish, implike, mysterious; but used in the sense of foolish, G 751, 842. Cf. Icel. *álfalegr,* silly, from *álfr,* an elf, fairy.

Embassàdour, s. ambassador, C 603.

Embassadrye, s. embassy, negociation, B 233.

Empoisoning, s. poisoning, C 891.

Empoysoner, s. poisoner, C 894. (Gloss. II.)

Emprise, s. enterprise, B 348; Empryse, G 605. O. F. *emprise,* an enterprise; from the verb *prendre,* Lat. *prehendere,* to take, with prefix *em- = in.*

Empte, *v.* to empty, make empty, G 741; Empten, 1404. A. S. *ge-æmtigian,* to disengage from. A. S. *æmtig,* vacant, at leisure; from *æmta,* leisure.

Enbibing, s. imbibition, absorption, G 814.

Encense, *v.* to offer incense, G 395, 413. F. *encenser,* from sb. *encens,* Lat. *incensum* (used by Isidore of Seville), incense; which from Lat. *incendere,* to burn.

Encorporing, s. incorporation, G 815. From Lat. *corpus,* body.

Encrees, s. increase, B 237, G 18. See below.

Encresse, *v.* to increase, B 1068. O. F. *encroistre,* to increase, from Lat. *increscere,* which from *crescere,* to grow.

Ende, s. end, result, B 481. A dissyllabic word; A. S. *ende,* end.

Endeles, *adj.* endless, B 951.

Endetted, *pp.* indebted, G 734. O F. *s'endeter,* to be indebted; from O. F. *dete* (F. *dette*), a debt, Lat. *debita,* from *debere,* to owe.

Endyten, *v.* to indite, write, B 781; Endyte, G 80. O. F. *enditier,* to instruct, from *ditier,* to write a work; Lat. *dictare,* to dictate; from *dicere,* to say.

Engyn, s. genius, skill, G 339. F. *engin,* Lat. *ingenium,* skill.

Enluting, s. securing with 'lute,' daubing with clay, &c., so as to exclude air, G 766. F. *luter,* to secure with 'lute,' from Lat. *lutum,* clay.

Enquere, *v.* inquire, search into, B 692. O. F. *enquerrer,* to inquire into; O. F. *querre,* to seek; Lat. *quaerere,* to seek.

Enqueringe, s. inquiry, B 888.

Ensamples, s. *pl.* examples, C 435. O. F. *ensample* (Roquefort); from Lat. *exemplum.*

Entencioun, s. intention, intent, C 408.

Entente, s. will, B 824; intention, B 857, G 998; design, C 432; plan, B 147, 206; endeavour, G 6. O. F. *entente,* intent;

from *entendre*, to intend, **Lat.** *intendere*.

Entringe, *pr. part.* entering, I 12. F. *entrer*, Lat. *intrare*, to enter.

Envoluped, *pp.* wrapped **up**, enveloped, involved, C 942. **O. F.** *envoluper*, to envelope, **cover**; derived (says Brachet) **from a** radical *velop*, of **unknown** origin. Perhaps this **radical** is the same as appears in **the M. E.** verb to *wlappe*, used **by** Wyclif for to *wrap*; and cf. **E.** *wrap*.

Er, *adv.* before, B 420, G 1273; *prep.* before, C 892; Er that, before that, **G** 375. A. S. *ǽr*, before, formerly.

Erme, *v.* to grieve, to feel sad, **C** 312. See the note. A. S. *yrman*, to afflict, grieve, make unhappy, from *earm*, poor, miserable; cf. **Icel. armr**, Goth. *arms*, G. *arm*, poor.

Erst, *adv.* first; *at erst*, at first, G 151, 264; *long erst er*, long first before, C 662. Superlative of *er*. See **Er.**

Eschue, *v.* to eschew, avoid, shun, G 4. O. F. *escheveir*, *eschiver*, **to** avoid (F. *eschiver*); from O. H. G. *skiuhan*, to avoid. From the same root we have A. S. *sceóh*, shy, and E. **skew** and *shy*.

Ese, *s.* pleasure, G 746; ease, relief, H 25. F. *aise*.

Espye, *v.* to espy, perceive, G 291; to enquire about, B 180; *pp.* Espyed, observed, 324. O. F. **espier**, from O. H. G. *spehen*, to spy (G. *spähen*).

Est, **s.** East, B 297, 493; Eastwards, 949, **C** 396; A. S. *eást*. (Gloss. II.)

Estaat, *s.* rank, B 973, C 597, **G** 1388. O. F. *estat*, Lat. *status*; from *stare*, to stand.

Euangyles, *s. pl.* gospels, B 666. Lat. *euangelium*, Gk. εὐαγγελίον, signifying (1) a reward for good tidings; (2) glad tidings; from εὖ, well, good, and ἄγγελλος, a messenger; from ἀγγέλλω, I announce.

Eue, *s.* evening, **G** 375. **A. S.** *ǽfen*, evening.

Euen, *adv.* evenly, exactly, G 1200.

Euerich, *pron.* every one, all, B 531, 626, C. 768; either of the two, B 1004. For *ever-each*; M. E. *euer*, and *iche*, **each.**

Euerichon, **every one**, B 330, G 1365; Euerichoon, G 960, I 15; *pl.* Euerichone, all of them, B 429, 678. For *ever-each-one*; M. E. *euer*, ever, *iche*, each, *oon*, **one.**

Euermo, *adv.* evermore, always, B 1076. See **Mo.**

Exaltacioun, *s.* exaltation (a **term** in astrology); see **the** note, I 10. From Lat. *exaltare*, to exalt; from *ex*, out, and *altus*, high.

Expert, *adj.* skilful in performing an experiment, experienced, G 1251. Lat. *expertus*, pp. of *experior*, to try.

Expoune, *v.* to explain, G 86. Lat. *exponere*, to expose; from *ex*, out, and *ponere*, to put.

Extenden, *pr. pl.* are extended, B 461. Lat. *extendere*.

Ey, *interj.* eh! what! C 782. Dan. *ei*, eh! Icel. *hei*, eh!

Ey, *s.* egg, G 806. A. S. *æg*, an egg; cf. Icel. *egg*, Swed. *ägg*, Dan. *æg*; also Du. *ei*, G. *ei*.

Eyleth, *pr. s.* aileth, H 16. A. S. *eglan*, to molest, afflict; from *egl*, that which pricks, a thistle, also an '*ail*,' or beard of corn; from the same root as *eggian*, to incite. See **Eggement.**

Eyre, *s.* air, gas, G 767. F. *air*, **Lat.** *aer*, air.

F.

Fable, *s.* fable, story, I 31. F. *fable*, Lat. *fabula*.

Fader, s. father, B 274, G 1434; *gen.* Fader, *in phr.* fader kin = father's race, ancestry, G 829. A.S *fæder*, gen. *fæder*.

Faille, s. fail, doubt, B 201. F. *faillir*, Lat. *fallere*.

Falle, v. to happen, H 40; *pt. s.* Fil, fell, C 804, G 204, 1198; Fel, befell, B 141; *pp.* Falle, B 303. A.S. *feallan*, pt. t. *ic feóll*, pp. *feallen*.

False get, cheating contrivance, G 1277. See Get.

Falshede, s. falsehood, G 979, 1274. O.F. *fals*, Lat. *falsus*, false; with M.E. suffix *-heed*, A.S. *hád*.

Faltren, *pr. pl.* falter, fail, B 772. (Etym. doubtful.)

Fan, s. vane, quintain, H 42. A.S. *fan, fann*, a fan.

Fantome, s. a phantom, delusion, B 1037. F. *fantôme*, O.F. *fantosme*, Lat. *phantasma*, Gk. φάντασμα, an appearance, φαντάζω, make to appear; from φαίνω, I shew.

Fare, s. business, goings on, B 569. A.S. *faru*, a journey, hence, proceedings; from *faran*, to travel. See below.

Fare, *pr. s.* 1 p. I go, G 733; *pr. pl.* 1 p. Faren, we fare, live, **662**; 2 p. Fare, ye fare, ye succeed, 1417; *pr. s.* Fareth, it turns out, 966; *imp. pl.* Fareth well = fare ye well, B 1159; *pp.* Fare, gone, B 512. A.S. *faran*, to go, to fare. (Gloss. I. and II.)

Farewel, *interj.* farewell! it is all over, G 907, 1380; *used ironically*, 1384.

Faste, *adv.* quickly, G 245; *as faste*, very quickly, 1235. A.S. *fæst*, firm; adv. *fæste*, firmly, *also* quickly.

Faste, *pt. s.* fasted; *pres. part.* Fastinge, C 363. A.S. *fæsten*, fasting; *fæstung*, the season of Lent.

Fayn, *adj.* glad, H 92; *adv.* gladly, willingly, B 173, 222. A.S. *fægn*, fain, glad; Icel. *feginn*.

Fecchen, v. to fetch, G 411; *pt. s.* Fette, fetched, 548, 1365; *pp.* Fet, B 667. A.S. *feccan*; pt. t. *ic feahte*, pp. *gefetod*.

Feelede, *pt. s.* felt, G 521. A.S. *félian*, to feel; pt. t. *ic félode*.

Feend, s. fiend, B 1064, C 844; enemy, B 454; evil spirit, G 861. A.S. *feón*, to hate; whence pres. pt. *feónd*, hating, a fiend; cf. Sanskrit *pi*, to hate.

Feendly, *adj.* fiendlike, devilish, B 751, 783, G 1071.

Fel, *pt. s.* befell, happened, B 141 See Falle.

Felawe, s. companion, H 7; *pl.* Felawes, companions, G 747; comrades, C 696. Icel. *félagi*, a companion; from *fé*, cattle, property; and *lagi*, law, society; applied to one who has a share in a property.

Felonye, s. crime, B 643. Low Lat. *fello, felo*, a traitor, rebel, criminal; O.F. *fel*, cruel (Roquefort). Of uncertain and disputed origin; perhaps allied to Bret. *fall*, Irish *feall*, W. *ffel*, evil, wily.

Femininitee, s. feminine form, B 360.

Fen, s. chapter, or subdivision of Avicenna's book called the Canon, C 890. See the note.

Fende, *s. dat.* fiend, B 780. See Feend.

Fer, *adj.* far, B 508, 658. A.S. *feorr*.

Fered, *pp.* terrified, afraid, G 924. From A.S. *fǽr*, **fear**, sudden danger.

Ferforth, *adv.* far, to such a degree, G 1390; *as ferforth as*, as far as, B 1099; *so ferforth*, to such a degree, 572, G 40. See Fer.

Fermentacioun, *s.* fermenting, G
817. **From** Lat. *fermentum.*

Ferthe, *ord. adj.* fourth, B 823. G
531, 824, 927. A. S. *feórða,*
fourth; from *feówer,* four.

Fest, *s.* fist, C 802; *dat.* Feste,
I 35. A.S. *fýst,* the fist; cf.
Lat. *pugnus.*

Feste, *s.* a feast, festivity, B 418,
I 47; *to feste,* to the feast, at a
feast, B 1007, 1010; *han to
feste,* to invite, 380. Here *feste*
is a sb. throughout, not a verb.
O. F. *feste,* from Lat. *festum.*

Fet, **Fette.** See Fecchen.

Fete, *s. pl. dat.* feet; *to fete,* at his
feet, B 1104. A.S. *fót,* a foot ; ·
pl. *fét,* dat. pl. *fótum.*

Fetys, *adj.* well-made, neat, grace-
ful, C 478. O.F. *faitis* (Lat.
factitius), well-made, neat; from
O. F. *faire,* Lat. *facere.* (Gloss.
I)

Fey, *s.* faith, C 762, H 13, I 23.
O. F. *fei, feid,* faith; Lat. acc.
fidem.

Feyne, *v.* feign, pretend; *feyne vs,*
pretend as regards ourselves, B
351. F. *feindre,* Lat. *fingere.*

Fiers, *adj.* fierce, B 300. O. F.
fier, originally *fiers.* Lat. *ferus,*
fierce. (Not from Lat. *ferox.*)

Figuringe, *s.* similitude, figure, G
96.

Fil. **See Falle.**

Fixe, *pp.* fixed, solidified, G 779.
From Lat. *figere,* to fix.

Flambes, *s. pl.* flames, G 515.
O. F. *flambe,* Lat. *flamma.* The
b is a mere excrescence ; Wedgwood's derivation of *flame* from a
radical *flab* cannot be sustained.

Fleen, I *pl.* fleas, H 17. A. S. *fled,*
pl. *fleán.*

Fleet, *pr. s. (contr. from* fleteth)
floats, B 463. **See** Fleteth.

Flekked, *pp.* spotted, G 565.' A
Low German word ;. O. Friesic
flekka, to spot (Richtofen); cf.

Du. *vlekken,* to spot, *vlek,* a spot ;
also Icel. *flekka,* to stain, *flekkr,*
a spot, stain.

Flemed, *pp.* banished, G 58. **A. S.**
fliman, flýman, to banish.

Flemer, *s.* banisher, driver away, B
460. **See above.**

Fleteth, *pr. s.* floateth, B 901.
A. S. *fleótan,* to float.

Florins, *s. pl.* florins, C 770, 774.
So named from having been first
coined at Florence.

Flour, *s.* flower, B 1090. O. F.
flour, fleur, Lat. *florem,* acc. of
flos.

Flye, *s.* a fly, G 1150. A. S.
fleóge.

Fneseth, *pr. s.* breathes heavily,
puffs, snorts, H 62. See the note.
A. S. *fnéosan,* to puff, *fnastiað,*
the windpipe, *fnæst,* a puff, blast ;
cf. Gk. *πνέω,* I blow.

Folily, *adv.* foolishly, G 428.
From F. *fol,* mad ; see Brachet.

Folwen, *pr. pl.* follow, C 514.
A. S. *folgian.*

Fome. See Foom.

Fond, *pt. s.* found, B 514, 607, C
608, G 185. A. S. *findan,* **to**
find; pt. t. *ic fand,* pp. *funden.*

Fonde, *v.* to endeavour, G 951 ;
to try to persuade, B 347. **A. S.**
fandian, to try, tempt.

Fonge, *v.* to receive, B 377. From
a form *fangan,* appearing in A. S.
in the contracted form *fón,* to
take ; cf. **Du.** *vangen,* G. *fangen,*
to take.

Font-ful water, fontful of water,
B 357.

Fontstoon, *s.* font, B 723.

Foom, *s.* foam, G 564 ; *dat.* Fome,
565. A. S. *fám* (*fám*), foam.

Foot-hot, *adv.* instantly, on the
spot, B 438. See note.

Fostred, *pp.* nurtured, brought
(up), B 275. G 122 ; nurtured in
the faith, G 539. (Gloss. II.)

Foul, *adj.* foul, bad ; *for foul ne*

fayr, by foul means or fair, B 525. A.S. *fúl,* foul.

Founden, *pp.* found, B 612; provided, 243. See Fond.

Foure, *num.* four, B 491, G 1460. A.S. *feówer.* The word is dissyllabic, **being treated as** a *plural* adjective.

Fourneys, *s.* furnace, G 804. F. *fournaise,* from Lat. acc. *fornacem.*

Foyson, *s.* abundance, B 504. O.F. *foison,* from Lat. acc. *fusionem* : which from *fundere,* to pour forth.

For, *conj.* because, B 340, C 440, G 232; in order that, B 478; *prep.* because of, C 504; as being, G 457. A.S. *for.*

Forbede, *imp. sing.* forbid, **may** (He) forbid, G 996; *pr. s.* Forbedeth, forbids, C 643. **A.S.** *forbeódan,* Goth. *faurbiudan.*

Forby, *adv.* past, by, C 668.

Fordoon, *v.* to do for, to destroy, B 369. A.S. *fordón,* to destroy, 'do for'; cf. Lat. *perdere.*

For-dronke, *pp.* very drunk, C 674. **Cf. A.S.** *fordrencan,* to intoxicate. The prefix *for-* is here intensive.

Forgon, *v.* to forgo (**commonly** *misspelt* forego), G 610. **A.S.** *forgón,* to forgo; Goth. *faurgaggan,* to pass by; cf. **G.** *vergehen.* Distinct from A.S. *foregán,* to go before.

Forlete, *v.* to **give up,** C 864. **A.S.** *forlǽtan,* to let go, relinquish; cf. Du. *verlaten,* to abandon, G. *verlassen.*

Fors, *s.* heed; *make no fors,* take no heed, H 68; *no fors,* it is no matter, it is of no consequence, B 285, C 303, G 1019, 1357. 'I gyue no force, I care not for a thing, *Il ne men chault* ;' Palsgrave's French Dict.

Forswering, *s.* perjury, C 657;

s. pl. Forsweringes, 592. A.S. *for-swerian,* to swear falsely.

Forth, *adv.* forth, forward, B 294, C 660. **A.S.** *forð,* forth, thence, forward.

Forthermo, *adv.* moreover, C 594; Forthermore, 357.

Forther ouer, *adv.* furthermore, moreover, C 648.

Forthward, *adv.* forward, B 263.

For-waked, *pp.* tired out with watching, B 596. A.S. prefix *for,* and *wacian,* to watch.

For-why, *conj.* because, C 847.

Forwrapped, *pp.* wrapped up, C 718. A.S. prefix *for,* and M.E. *wrappen,* to wrap, closely related to *wlappen,* to wrap (used by Wyclif). See Enveluped.

Foryeue, *v.* to forgive, B 994; *imp. s.* Foryeue, may (He) forgive, C 904; *imp. pl.* Foryeue, forgive, G 79. A.S. *forgifan,* Goth. *fragiban* ; cf. G. *vergeben.*

Fraught, *pp.* freighted, B 171. For an account of **the** idiom, see the note, p. 122. Cf. Swed. *frakta,* Dan. *fragte,* to freight, load; Swed. *frakt,* Dan. *fragt,* Du. *vracht,* a load, burden.

Fredom, *s.* liberality, bounty, B 168. The A.S. *freó* means both free and bountiful.

Frendes, *s. pl.* friends, B 269. A.S. *freónd,* a friend; pres. part. of a lost verb *freón,* to love; this is shewn by Goth. *frijonds,* a friend, pres. part. of Goth. *frijon,* to love. Cf. Skt. *prí,* to love.

Frete, *pp.* eaten, devoured, B 475. A.S. *fretan,* to devour; contr. from *for-etan,* to eat up; cf. Goth. *fra-itan,* to eat up, from *itan,* **to eat.** Thus *fret* is short for *foreat*; and G. *fressen* = *ver-essen.*

Freyned, *pp.* asked, questioned, G 433. A.S. *frignan,* to ask; Goth. *fraihnan* ; cf. Du. *vragen,* G. *fragen,* Lat. *precari.*

Fructuous, *adj.* fruitful, I 73. Lat. *fructuosus,* fruitful; from *fructus,* fruit.

Fruyt, *s.* result (lit. fruit), B 411. F. *fruit,* Lat. *fructus.*

Fruytesteres, *s. pl. fem.* fruit-sellers, C 478.

Fulfild, *pp.* filled full, B 660; completed, fully performed, I 17. A.S. *fullfyllan,* to fill full, perform, accomplish.

Fumositee, *s.* fumes arising from drunkenness, C 567. From Lat. *fumus,* fume, smoke.

Furlong wey, a furlong's distance, B 557. A.S. *furhlang,* the length of a furrow, a furlong.

Fusible, *adj.* fusible, capable of being fused, G 856. F. *fusible,* from Lat. *fundere,* to pour out.

Fyn, *s.* end, B 424. F. *fin,* Lat. *finis,* end.

Fynally, *adv.* finally, B 1072.

Fynt, *pr. s.* finds, G 218. Contr. for *findeth.*

Fyres, *s. gen.* fire's, G 1408. A.S. *fyr,* Du. *vuur,* G. *feuer,* Dan. *fyr,* Gk. πῦρ.

G.

Galianes, *s. pl.* medicines, C 306. So named after Galen. See the note.

Galle, *s.* gall, G 58, 797. A.S. *gealla;* cf Lat. *fel,* Gk χολή.

Galoun, *s.* gallon, H 24. The forms *galona* and *galo* are found in Low Lat.

Game, *s.* sport, G 703, H 100. A.S. *gamen,* a sport, play.

Gan, *pt. s.* began, G 462; *used as aux.,* did, B 614, I 11. A.S. *ginnan,* to begin; pt. t. *ic gann.*

Ganeth, *pr. s.* yawneth, H 35. A.S. *gānian,* to yawn, gape.

Gat, *pt. s.* obtained, got (for himself), B 647, G 373. A.S. *getan,*

Icel. *geta,* to get. The commoner A.S. form is *gitan,* pt. t. *ic geat.*

Gaude, *s.* trick, course of trickery, C 389.

Gauren, *ger.* to gaze, stare, B 912. (Gloss. II.)

Gaye, *adj.* fine, G 1017. F. *gai,* gay; from O.H.G. *wāhi,* bright, gay. Not O.H.G. *gāch, gā,* G. *jähe,* quick, hasty; from O.H.G. *gān,* to go.

Gentillesse, *s.* kindness, G 1054; condescension, B 853. O.F. *gentillece,* from *gentil,* gentle, noble, Lat. *gentilis,* belonging to a *gens* or family.

Gentilly, *adv.* courteously, B 1093.

Gentils, *s. pl.* gentlefolks, C 323.

Gere, *s.* gear, property, B 800. A.S. *gearwa,* clothing, preparation; *gearwan,* to prepare; from *gearo,* ready, *yare.*

Gerland, *s.* garland, G 27. Provençal *garlanda;* cf. Ital. *ghirlonda,* F. *guirlande.* Etym. doubtful; Mr. Wedgwood fails to explain the Italian form.

Gesse, *v.* to imagine, B 622; I *p. s. pr.* I suppose, 246, 1008, 1143, G 977. Cf. Du. *gissen,* Swed. *gissa,* to guess; Icel. *gizka,* to guess.

Gestes, *s. pl.* gests, tales (Lat. *gesta*), B 1126.

Get, *s.* contrivance, G 1277. Appears in A.S. only in the compound *and-get,* the understanding. From *gitan,* to get.

Gete, 2 *p. s. pr.* ye get, ye obtain, H 102. See Gat.

Giltlees, *adj.* guiltless, B 643; **Giltelees,** 1062, 1073.

Gin, *s.* snare, contrivance, G 1165. Contracted from F. *engin,* a machine.

Giternes, *s. pl.* guitars, C 466. O.F. *guiterne,* also *guiterre, guitare,* Lat. *cithara,* Gk. κιθάρα, a stringed instrument.

Glade, *v.* to gladden, G 598. **A. S.** *glæd*, glad.

Gleyre, *s.* white (of an egg), G 806. ' *Gleyre* of eyryne [i. e. *eggs*] or other lyke, *glarea* ;' Prompt. Parv. F. *glaire* (which in Ital. is *chiara*), the white of an egg ; corrupted from *claire*, from Lat. *clarus*, clear.

Glose, *v.* to flatter, I 45. F. *glo·e*, a gloss, from Lat. *glossa*, Gk. γλῶσσα, the tongue ; also an explanation. (Gloss. II.)

Glotonyes, *s. pl.* excesses, C 514. From O. F. *gloton*, (F. *glouton*), a glutton ; Lat. *glutonem* ; cf. Lat. *glutire*, to swallow.

Glyde, *v.* to glide, ascend, G 402. A. S. *glidan*.

Gode, *adj. voc.* good, B 1111.

Gold, *s.* gold, G 826; *allusion to proverb—*'all is not gold that glisters,' 962. A. S. *gold*.

Goldsmith, *s.* goldsmith, G 1333.

Golet, *s.* throat, gullet, C 543. Dimin. of O. F. *gole*, the throat, Lat. *gula*.

Gon, *v.* to go, B 282 ; Goon, 373 ; to go on, proceed, G 563 ; *pr. s.* Goth, goes, B 385, 704, 728 ; 2 *p.* Goost, goest, G 56 ; 2 *p. pl. pr.* Go, ye walk, go on foot, C 748; *pp.* Go, gone, B 1006, G 907. A. S. *gán*, Goth. *gaggan*.

Gonne, *pt. pl.* began, C 323 ; *pt. pl.* began, G 376 ; did, 517, 1192. See **Gan.**

Good, *s.* goods, property, wealth, G 831, 868, 949, 1289. A. S. *gód*, pl. *gód*, goods, wealth ; neut. adj. as sb., like Lat. *bona*.

Goodlich, *adj.* kind, bountiful, G 1053. A. S. *gódlic*, kind, lit. good-like.

Good-man, *s.* master of the house, C 361.

Goon, *v.* to go ; *let it goon*, let it go, neglect it, G 1475. And see **Gon.**

Goot, *s.* a goat, G 886. A. S. *gát* ; cognate with Lat. *haedus*.

Gost, *s.* spirit, B 404, 803 ; ghost (ironically), H 55 ; the Holy Ghost, G 328. A.S. *gást*, breath ; cf. G. *geist*, Du. *geest*.

Gostly, *adv.* spiritually, mystically, G 109. A. S. *gástlice*, spiritually, adv. from *gást-lic*, ghost-like.

Gouernance, *s.* government, B 289 ; Gouernaunce, C 600. From O. F. *governer*, Lat. *gubernare*, to direct, steer.

Gourde, *s. dat.* gourd, H 82. F. *gourde*, from Lat. *cucurbita*.

Grace, *s.* favour, G 1348; *hir grace*, her favour (i.e. that of the blessed Virgin), B 980 ; pardon, B 647 ; *harde grace*, hardihood of demeanour, boldness, G 665, 1189. F. *grace*, Lat. *gratia*.

Gracelees, *adj.* void of grace, unfavoured by God, G 1078.

Grame, *s.* anger, grief, G 1403. A.S. *grama*, rage, from *gram*, furious, fierce, cruel ; cf. *grim*, fury, also as adj. severe. Cf. also O. H. G. *gram*, angry.

Grant mercy, much thanks, G 1380 ; Graunt mercy, 1156. F. *grand merci*, great thanks. In English corrupted to *gramercy*.

Graunte, *pr s. 1 p.* I agree, consent, C 327. O.F. *granter*, to grant. (Gloss. II.)

Gree, *s.* favour, B 25. F. *gré*, inclination ; from Lat. *gratus*, pleasing.

Grene, *s.* green, greenness, living evidence, G 90.

Grenehede, *s.* greenness, wantonness, B 163.

Grette, *pt. s.* greeted, B 1051, C 714. A. S. *grétan*, pt. t. *ic grette*.

Grisly, *adj.* horrible, grewsome, C 473. A S. *grislic*, hideous, *agrisan*, to shu·lder at.

Grope, *pr. pl. 1 p.* we grope, G

679; *imp. s.* Grope, 1236. A.S. *grápian*, to lay hold of; from *gráp*, a grasp. Cf. *grip, gripe, grasp, grab.*

Grotes, *s. pl.* groats, fourpenny pieces, C 376. Du. *groot*, the name of a coin, originally of large size; from *groot*, great. First used in Bremen, where they superseded smaller coins.

Grounden, *pp.* ground, G 760. A.S. *grindan*, to grind; pt. t. *ic grand*; pp. *grunden.*

Grys, *s.* gray, G 559. F. *gris*, O.H.G. *gris*, gray-haired; cf. G. *greis*, a gray-haired man.

Gyde, *imp. s.* may (He) guide, B 245. O.F. *guider*, another form of *guier*. See Gye.

Gyde, *s.* guide, ruler, G 45.

Gye, *ger.* to guide, regulate, I 13; *imp. s.* do thou guide, O.F. *guier*, to guide, Ital. *guidare*; from O. Sax. *witan*, to observe; cf. O.H.G. *wizan*, to observe, whence G. *weisen.*

Gyse, *s.* guise, wise, way; *in his gyse*, as he was wont, B 790.

H.

Habundantly, *adv.* abundantly, B 870. From O.F. *habonder*, Low Lat. *habundare*, to abound, written for Lat. *abundare*; from *ab* and *unda*, a wave.

Hakeney, *s.* hack-horse, hackney, G 559. Cf. F. *haquenée*, a nag, Span. *hacanea*, a nag; said to be spelt *facanea* in Old Spanish, and to have a shorter form *faca* (Webster, Diez.).

Halkes, *s. pl.* corners, hiding-places, G 311. Cf. Mid. Eng. *hale*, a recess, Owl and Nightingale, l. 2; A.S. *heal*, an angle, a corner; probably from the verb *helan*, to hide. Cf. A.S. *hule*, a cottage, cabin; *heolstor*, a cavern.

Hals, *s.* neck, G 1029. A.S. *heals*, Icel. *háls*, G. *hals.*

Halt, *pr. s.* holds (*put for* holdeth), B 807; considers, G 921.

Halwed, *pt. s.* consecrated, hallowed, G 551. A.S. *hálgian*, to hallow; from *hálig*, holy.

Halwes, *s. pl.* saints (lit. holy ones), B 1060; *gen. pl.* of (all) saints, G 1244. A.S. *hálig*, holy.

Hamer, *s.* hammer, G 1339. A.S. *hamor.*

Han, *v.* to keep, retain, C 725; to take away, 727; to obtain, G 234; to possess (cf. 'to have and to hold'), B 208; *pr. pl.* Han, have, B 142. A.S. *habban*, to have.

Hap, *s.* luck, G 1209. W. *hap*, luck, Icel. *happ*, luck, chance.

Happeth, *pr. s.* it chances, G 649; *pt. s.* Happede, happened, C 606, 885. See above.

Harrow, *interj.* alas! C 288. See the note.

Hasard, *s.* the game of hazard, C 591, 681. O.F. *asart* (with excrescent *t*), Provençal *azar*, Span. *azar*, from Arabic *al-zár*, the die, which from Pers. *zár*, a die.

Hasardour, *s.* gamester, C 596; *pl.* Hasardours, 613, 618.

Hasardrye, *s.* gaming, playing at hazard, C 590, 599, 897.

Hasteth, *imp. pl. refl.* hasten, make haste, I 72. O.F. *haster*, to hasten; from G. *hast*, haste; cf. Icel. *hastarligr*, hasty.

Hastou, *for* hast thou, B 676.

Haunteth, *pr. s.* practises, C 547; *pt. pl.* Haunteden, practised, 464. F. *hanter*, to haunt; of uncertain origin.

Hauteyn, *adj.* loud, C 330. F. *hautain*, haughty, from *haut*, O.F. *halt*, Lat. *altus*, high.

Hawe, *s.* haw, yard, enclosure, C 855. A.S. *haga*, a hedge, a garden.

He, *used for* it, G 867, 868.

Heed, *s.* head, H 19; *pl.* Hedes, heads, G 398. A.S. *heáfod*, M.E. *heued*, contr. to *heed*. (Gloss. II.)

Heeld, *pt. s.* held, esteemed, C 625. A.S. *healdan*, pt. t. *ic heóld*.

Heer and ther, *phr.* now here, now there; never long in one place, G 1174. A.S. *hér*.

Heer, *s.* hair, G 812. A.S. *hǽr*, Du. and G. *haar*.

Helpeth, *imp. pl.* help ye, G 1328. A.S. *helpan*.

Helplees, *adj.* helpless, B 303.

Hem, *pron.* them, B 140; *dat.* to them, G 539, 540. A.S. *hig*, nom. they; gen. *heora, hira*; dat. *heom, him*; acc. *hig*.

Hem-self, *pron. pl. nom.* themselves, B 145.

Heng, *pt. s.* hung, G 574. A.S. *hón*, to hang; pt. t. *ic heng*.

Henne, *adv.* hence, C 687. A.S. *heonan, henan*, hence.

Hente, *v.* to seize, C 710; *pt. s.* Hente, seized, caught, G 370, 1325; caught away, B 1144; raised, lifted, G 205; *pr. s. subj.* may seize, G 7; *pp.* Hent, caught, 12. A.S. *hentan*, to seize.

Her, *pron. poss.* their, B 137, 138, 140, 221, 373, C 892, G 363, 1387. A.S. *heora, hira*, of them; gen. pl. of *hé*, he.

Herafterward, *adj.* hereafter, G 1168.

Herbergage, *s.* lodging, abode, B 147. O. F. *herbergage* (Roquefort); from O. H. G. *heriberga*, a camp, an army-shelter; from O. H. G. *heri*, an army, and *bergan*, to hide, shelter.

Herbergeours, *s. pl.* harbingers, providers of lodging, B 997. See above. Hence the modern *harbinger*, with excrescent (inserted) *n.*

Her-biforn, *adv.* here-before, B 613.

Herde, *s.* shepherd, G 192. A.S. *hyrde*, a guardian of a herd, from *heord*, a herd.

Here, *v.* to hear, B 182; *pp.* Herd, heard, 613, G 372. A.S. *héran, híran*, to hear; pp. *gehíred*. Cf. Du. *hooren*, G. *hören*.

Here, *pers. pron.* her, B 460. A.S. *hire*, of her, gen. sing. of *heó*, she.

Herieth, *pr. s.* praiseth, B 1155; *pl.* Herien, G 47; *pp.* Heried, B 872. A.S. *herian*, to praise; from *here*, fame.

Her-inne, *adv.* herein, G 1292. A.S. *hér*, here; and the adv. suffix *innan*, within.

Herknen, *v.* to hearken, listen to, G 691; Herkne, 1006; 1 *p. s. pr.* Herkne, I hear, 261; *imp. pl.* Herkneth, hearken ye, C 454. A.S. *heorcnian*, to listen to; from *híran*, to hear.

Hernes, *s. pl.* corners, G 658. A.S. *hyrne*, a corner; from *horn*, a horn, a corner, cognate with Lat. *cornu*, whence our *corner*.

Herte, *s.* heart, B 167, 1056, G 870; *pl.* Hertes, hearts, B 1066. A dissyllabic word; A.S. *heorte*, pl. *heortan*; cf. Gk. καρδία.

Herte-blood, heart's-blood, C 902. Here *herte* is the gen. sing. of the *feminine* substantive *herte*; the A. S. *heorte* makes *heortan* in the genitive, not *heortes*.

Her-to, *adv.* for this purpose, B 243.

Heste, *s.* command, B 382, C 490, 641; *dat.* B 1013; *pl.* Hestes, commands, B 284, C 640. A.S. *hǽs*, a command, with added *t*.

Hete, *pr. s.* 1 *p.* I promise, B 334, 1132. A.S. *hátan*, to command, to promise; cf. G. *heissen*, to bid.

Hete, *s.* heat, G 1408. A.S. *hǽto*,

hátu, heat; Du. *hitte,* G. *hitze*; shewing that *hete* is disyllabic.

Hethen, *adj.* heathen, B 904. A.S. *hǽðen,* of or belonging to a heath; *hǽð,* a heath; cf. Icel. *heiðinn,* a heathen, *heiðr,* heath, G. *heide,* masc. a heathen, fem. a heath. Cf. *pagan* from Lat. *pagus.*

Hethenesse, *s.* heathen lands, B 1112. A.S. *hǽðennes,* heathenism. See above.

Heuene, *gen.* heaven's, of heaven, G 542. A.S. *heofone,* fem. ; gen. *heofonan*; we also find *heofon,* masc.; gen. *heofnes.*

Hewe, *s. dat.* hue, colour, B 137, G 728; pretence, C 421. A.S. *hiw,* hue; dat. *hiwe.*

Hey, *s.* hay, H 14. A.S. *hig*; Du. *hooi,* G. *heu.*

Hey, *adj.* high, B 162, 252; severe, 795; *def.* Heye, C 633. A.S. *heáh*; Icel. *hár,* Du. *hoog,* G. *hoch.*

Hey and low, in, in high and low things, i. e. in all respects, wholly, B 993.

Heyer, *adj. comp.* higher, C 597.

Heyne, *s.* a worthless person, G 1319. The true sense is ' miser '; it is so used by Udall, in his Apophthegmes (1564), bk. i. § 22, and § 106: ' *haines* and niggardes '; ' a niggard or *hain.*' Of Scand. origin; cf. Icel. *hegna,* to hedge in, Swed. *hägna,* to fence, guard, protect, Low G. *hegenen,* to hedge, protect, spare, save, (Lübben); Lowl. Sc. *hain,* to hedge in, preserve, save money, be penurious (Jamieson).

Heyr, *s.* heir, B 766. O. F. *heir* (F. *hoir*), from Lat. acc. *haeredem.*

Heyre, *adj.* hair, made of hair, C 736; *as sb.* a hair shirt, sackcloth, G 133. A.S. *hǽra,* cloth made of hair, sackcloth ; from *hǽr,* hair ; also *hǽren,* adj. hairy.

Hir, *pron. pers.* her, B 162. The A.S. acc. is *hí*; *hire* is the gen. and dat. form.

Hir, *pron. poss.* her, B 164. From A.S. *hire,* gen. case of pers. pron. *heó,* she.

Hires, *poss. pron.* hers, B 227.

Hold, *s.* fort, castle, B 507. A.S. *heold,* a fort; from *healdan,* to hold, keep.

Holde, *pr. s.* 1 *p.* I consider, deem, G 739; *pp.* Holden, considered, kept, made to be, C 598. A.S. *healdan,* pt. t. *ic heóld,* pp. *healden.*

Hole, *adj. pl.* whole, hale; *hole and sounde,* safe and sound, B 1150. A.S. *hál,* whole; pl. *hále.* E. *whole* is misspelt ; it is the A.S. *hál,* and should be *hole.* The form *hale* is dialectal; from O. Northumbrian *hál.* The Gr. ὅλος is from a totally different root, and goes with Lat. *solidus,* E. *solid.* See Hool.

Holwe, *adj.* hollow, G 1265. The root appears in A.S. *hol,* hollow, *holu,* a hole; cf. A.S. *holh,* a hollow, a cavern. The Swedish has the longer form *hålig,* hollow.

Hom, *s.* home, homewards, B 385. A.S. *hám*; G. *heim.*

Homicyde, *s.* manslaughter, murder, C 644. Lat. *homicidium*; from *homo,* a man, and *caedere,* to kill.

Honde, *s. dat.* hand, G 13; *on honde,* in hand, B 348; *pl.* Hondes, hands, C 398, G 189; A.S. *hond, hand*; gen. and dat. *honde, hande.*

Honest, *adj.* honourable, seemly, decent, C 328; *pl.* l'oneste, H 75 ; Lat. *honestus,* honourable ; from *honor,* honour.

Honestly, *adv.* honourably, G 549.

Honge, *v.* to hang, C 790. See Doon; also Heng.

Hool, *adj. sing.* whole, perfect, G III, 117; well, C 357. A.S. *hál.* See Hole, the pl. form.

Hoom, *s.* home, homewards, B 173, 603. A.S. *hám.*

Hoom-cominge, *s.* home-coming, B 765.

Hoor, *adj.* hoary, gray, C 743. A.S. *hár*, hoary; Icel. *hárr.*

Hoot, *adj.* hot, G 887. A.S. *hát*, hot, Du. *heet*, G. *heiss.*

Hope, *s.* hope, expectation, G 870. The word is dissyllabic. A.S. *kopa*, hope; cf. G. *hoffen*, to hope.

Hord, *s.* hoard, treasure, C 775. From the same root as *herd.*

Horn, *s.* horn (musical instrument), H 90. A.S. *horn*; cf. Lat. *cornu.*

Hose, *s.* hose, old stocking, G 726. A.S. *hose*, hose, breeches, covering.

Hostelrye, *s.* hostelry, G 589. From O.F. *hostel* (our *hotel*); which from Lat. *hospitale* (our *hospital*); from Lat. *hospidem* (our *host*).

Hous, *s.* house (a technical term), B 304. See note to l. 302.

Housbond, *s.* husband, B 863; *pl.* Housbondes, 272. Commonly derived (wrongly) from *house* and *band*, whereas it is the A.S. *húsbonda*, Icel. *húsbondi*, contr. from *hús buandi*, the inhabitant of a house, from *búa*, to inhabit. The sense is therefore that of ‘occupier (i.e. master) of a house.’ The word is, accordingly, wholly unconnected with *band* or *bond* or *bind*; but connected with Dan. *bonde*, a peasant; and again with our *boor* (a word borrowed from the Du. *boer*), and with the last syllable in *neighbour.*

Humblesse, *s.* humility, B 165. From Lat. *humilis*, humble.

Hurlest, *pr. s.* 2 *pr.* dost hurl, dost whirl, B 297. Etym. difficult; but it can be proved to be a doublet (and an abbreviation) of the old word *hurtle*, to dash, clash; the frequentative of *hurt*; from F. *heurter*, to dash.

Hye, *v.* to hasten, G 1084; *me hye*, hurry myself, make haste, 1151; Hy the, hasten thyself, be quick, 1295. A.S. *higan, higian*, to hasten; cf. Lat. *citus*, quick.

Hye, *s.* haste; *in hye*, in haste, B 209. Extremely common in Barbour's Bruce. See above.

Hyghte, *pt. s.* was called (apparently used in a present sense, i.e. is called), I 51; was called, G 119, 550. A.S. *hátan*, to be named, *ic hátte*, I was called. (Gloss. I. and II.)

Hyghte, *s. dat.* height, I 4. A.S. *heiðo*; Icel. *hæð*, Du. *hoogte*, height.

Hyne, *s.* hind, peasant, C 688. A.S. *hina*, a domestic, a servant; whence modern E. *hind*, by adding an excrescent *d.*

I (*for* I *and* J).

Ialous, *adj.* jealous, C 367. O.F. *jalous*, Lat. *zelosus*, full of zeal. Thus *jealous* is a doublet of *zealous.*

Ialousye, *s.* jealousy, C 366.

Ianglest, *pr. s.* 2 *p.* chatterest, B 774. O.F. *jangler*, to chatter; from a Teutonic source; cf. Du. *janken*, to howl, Du. *jangelen*, to importune.

Iape, *s.* a trick, G 1312; a jest, H 84; *pl.* Japes, jests, C 319, 394. Probably allied to F. *gaber*, to mock, Icel. *gabba*, to deceive; cf. E. *jabber.*

Iape, *ger.* to jest, H 4.

Iay, *s.* a jay, B 774; *pl.* Iayes, G 1397. F. *geai*, formerly *gai*; so named from its *gay* colours. Cf. Span. *gayo*, a jay; O. Span. *gayo*, gay.

Ignotum, *s.* an unknown thing (see note), G 1457. Lat. *ignotum,* an unknown thing; comp. *ignotius,* a less known thing. From *noscere,* to know, formerly *gnoscere,* and cognate with our *know.*

Impresse, *pr. pl.* force themselves (upon), make an impression (upon), G 1071. From Lat. *imprimere,* to press upon ; from *premere,* to press.

Ile, *s.* isle, B 545. F. *île,* O. F. *isle,* Lat. *insula,* an island.

Ilke, *adj.* same, G 80, 1366 ; very, 501. A. S. *ylc,* same.

In, *s.* inn, lodging, B 1097. A. S. *inn,* an inn, house.

Induracioun, *s.* hardening, G 855. From Lat. *durus,* hard.

In-fere, *adv.* together, B 328. Cf. A. S. *fær,* an expedition; whence M. E. *in fere,* upon an expedition, on a journey ; hence, together.

Infortunat, *adj.* unfortunate, inauspicious, B 302. Lat. *in,* prefix, and *fortunatus,* fortunate.

Ingot, *s.* an ingot, a mould for pouring metal into, G 1206, 1209, 1223; *pl.* Ingottes, G 818. From *in,* in, and A. S. *geótan,* to pour ; cf. Du. *ingieten,* to pour in ; G. *einguss,* a pouring in, from *giessen,* to pour.

Inne, *adv.* within, G 880. A. S. *innan,* within ; from prep. *in.*

Intellect, *s.* understanding, G 339. Lat. *intellectus.*

Iolitee, *s.* joviality, C 780. From F. *joli,* pleasant, from a Scandinavian source ; Icel. *jól,* E. *Yule,* a great feast held in midwinter.

Ioyned, *pp.* joined, G 95. F. *joindre,* to join, Lat. *iungere;* Skt. *yuj,* to join.

Ire, *s.* anger, C 657. Lat. *ira.*

Iuge, *s.* judge, B 814, G 462 ; *pl.* Iuges, C 291. F. *juge,* Lat. acc. *iudicem.*

Iugement, *s.* judgment, opinion, B 1038 ; judgment, 688.

Iupartye, *s.* jeopardy, hasard, G 743. O. F. *jeu parti,* Lat. *iocus partitus,* a divided game, a game in which sides were taken. See note.

Iusten, *v.* to joust, H 42. O. F. *jouster* (F. *jouter*), to joust ; derived by Brachet from a Low Lat. *iuxtare,* to approach, from *iuxta,* near. Cf. E. *jostle.*

Iustise, *s.* a judge, B 665, C 289, G 497; the administration of justice, C 587. The O. F. *justice* meant (1) justice, and (2) the administrator of justice ; and this double use of the word is retained in English.

Iuyse, *s.* justice, judgment, B 795. The word is *ju-ys-e,* in three syllables ; Roquefort gives the O. F. sb. *juise,* formed, by loss of *d,* from Lat. *iudicium,* judgment.

K.

Kepe, *pr. s.* 1 *p.* I care; *I kepe han,* I care to have, G 1368 ; *pt. pl.* Kepte, regarded, tended, B 269 ; *imp. pl.* Kepeth, keep ye, B 764, G 226. A.S. *cépan,* to keep ; *pt. t. ic cépte.*

Kepe, *s.* heed; *tak kepe,* take heed, C 352, 360.

Kerchef, *s.* kerchief, B 837. From O. F. *couvrir,* to cover, and *chef,* the head ; it meant, originally, a covering for the head. Cf. *curfew,* from O. F. *couvrir,* and *feu,* fire.

Key, *s.* key (*pronounced* kay), G 1219. A. S. *cǽg,* also *cǽge,* a key.

Kin, *s.* kindred, race, G 829. A. S. *cynn,* a kin, lineage.

Kin, *adj.* kind ; *som kin,* of some kind, B 1137. A.S. *cynn,* akin, fit.

Kiste, *pt. s.* kissed, B 385; *pl.* Kiste, C 968; *pp.* Kist, *in phr.* been they kist = they have kissed each other, B 1074. A.S. *cyss*, a kiss; *cyssan*, to kiss; cf. G. *küssen*.

Kitte, *pt. s.* cut, B 600. M.E. *cutten*, to cut; a Celtic word. Cf. Welsh *cwta*, short, *cwtan*, *cytio*, to shorten; Gaelic *cutaich*, to curtail, *cutach*, docked; *cut*, a bob-tail. (No; Scandinavian.)

Knaue, *s.* boy, servant-lad, B 474, C 666; *as adj.* male, B 722. A.S. *cnapa*, *cnafa*, a boy, G. *knabe*, Icel. *knapi*, a servant-lad.

Knitte, *ger.* to knit, I 47; Knittest thee, *pr. s.* 2 *p. refl.* knittest thyself, joinest thyself, art in conjunction, B 307; see note on p. 127. A.S. *cnyttan*, to knit; from *cnott*, a knot, cognate with Lat. *nodus* (for *gnodus*).

Knowestow, knowest thou, B 367; *pp.* Knowe, known, 890, 955. A.S. *cnáwan*; cf. Lat. *noscere* (for *gnoscere*).

Knowleching, *s.* knowledge, G 1432. In the verb to *knowlechen*, the suffix is the common A.S. suffix -*lǽcan*; in the sb. *knowleche* (our *knowledge*), the suffix is the related noun-suffix -*lác*, which appears also in *wed-lock*.

Knyght, *s.* knight, servant (of God), G 353. A.S. *cniht*, a servant; cf. G. *knecht*.

Kynde, *s. dat.* nature, G 41, 659; race, lineage, 121. A.S. *cynd*, nature. The final *e* is due to the fact that in all three passages it is a dative case.

Kythe, *pr. s. subj.* may shew, B 636; *pp.* Kythed, shewn, G 1054. A.S. *cýðan*, to make known; from *cúð*, known, which is the p. p. of *cunnan*, to know.

L.

Laas, *s.* lace, band, G 574. O.F. *las*, *laz* (F. *lacs*), from Lat. *laqueus*, a noose. Our *lasso* is from the O. Spanish form of the same word. (Gloss. I.)

Labour, *s.* endeavour, B 381. O.F. *labour*, Lat. acc. *laborem*.

Ladde, *pt. s.* led, B 976, G 370, 374; brought, B 442; *pp.* Lad, 646. A.S. *lǽdan*, pt. t. *ic lædde*; connected with A.S. *líðan*, to travel.

Ladel, *s.* ladle, H 51. The A.S. *hlædel* meant the handle of a windlass for drawing water; from *hladan*, to lade, draw.

Ladyes, *s. pl.* ladies, B 254. Pron. *laadee-ez*, as a trisyllable. A.S. *hláfdige*, a lady.

Lafte, *pt. s.* 1 *p.* I left, C 762; *pp.* Laft, G 883, 1321. A.S. *lǽfan*, to leave; Icel. *leifa*.

Lakketh, *pr. s.* lacks, G 498. Cf. Icel. *lakr*, deficient.

Lampe, *s.* lamina, thin plate, G 764. F. *lame*, a thin plate; Lat. *lamina*. The insertion of excrescent *p* occurs after *m* in other words in Chaucer; as in *solempne*, *dampne*, *empty*, *nempnen*.

Lampes, *s. pl.* lamps, G 802.

Lappe, *s.* skirt or lappet of a garment, G 12. A.S. *læppa*, a lap, border, hem; Du. *lap*, a remnant, shred.

Lasse, *adj.* less, C 602. A.S. *læs*, less; also *læssa*.

Lat, *imp.* permit, let, G 164; lat take = let us take, 1254. A.S. *lǽtan*, to allow, let; Du. *laten*, G. *lassen*.

Late, *adj.* late; *bet than neuer is late*, G 1410. A.S. *læt*, slow.

Latoun, *s.* a kind of brass, C 351. See the note. O.F. *laton* (F. *laiton*), from Low Lat. acc. *latonem*.

Latyn, s. Latin, B 519.

Lay, s. religious belief, faith, creed, B 376, 572. O. F. *lei* (F. *loi*), from Lat. acc. *legem*.

Leche, s. physician, C 916, G 56. A. S. *læce*, a physician; *lácnian*, to heal; Goth. *lekeis*, *leikeis*, a physician.

Lede, v. to govern, B 434; *pr. s. subj.* may bring, 357. A.S. *lǽdan*. See Ladde.

Leden, *adj.* leaden, G 728.

Leed, s. lead, G 406, 828. A. S. *leád*, lead; *leáden*, leaden; Du. *lood*, lead.

Leef, adj. dear, precious, G 1467; *yow so leef* = so dear to you, so desired by you, C 760. A. S. *leóf*, dear; G. *lieb*. The *pl.* is *lene*, voc. sing. *leue*. See Leue.

Leek, s. leek, i. e. thing of small value, G 795. · A. S. *leác*, a herb; whence gar-*lick*.

Lees, s. leash, G 19. F. *laisse*, from Lat. *laxa*, used to mean a loose rope, fem. of *laxus*, loose.

Leet, *pt. s.* let, caused (to be), B 959; let, G 190; *imp. s.* let, C 731. See Lat.

Lemman, s. (leof- or lef-man) lover; lit. dear man, B 917. A. S. *leóf*, dear, *man*, a human being of either sex. Similarly *Lammas* answers to A. S. *hláfmæsse*.

Lene, *ger.* to lend, G 1024, 1037; *imp. s.* lend, 1026. A.S. *lǽnan*, to lend; from *lán*, a loan. The addition of excrescent *d* appears also in *sound* (F. *son*), *hind* (A. S. *híne*), &c.

Lenger, adj. *comp.* longer, B 262; *adv.* longer, B 374. A.S. *lang*, long; comp. *lengra*, longer.

Leos, s. *pl.* people, G 103, 106; Gk. λεώς. See the note.

Leoun, s. lion, B 475. G 178. O. F. *leon*; from Lat. acc. *leonem*.

Lepe, *pr. pl.* leap, G 915. A. S.

hleápan, to leap, run; Du. *loopen*, to run (whence *e-lope*, *interloper*); cf. G. *laufen*, to run.

Lere, *ger.* to learn, B 181, 630, C 325, G 838, 1056, 1349; *v.*, C 578; *pres. s. subj.* may learn, G 607. Chaucer uses the word wrongly; the A. S. *lǽran*, like G. *lehren*, meant to *teach*. (Gloss. II.) See below. ·

Lerne, *ger.* to teach, G 844; Lerned of, taught by, G 748. Chaucer uses the word wrongly, and so does mod. prov. English. The A.S. *leornian* meant to *learn*, like mod. G. *lernen*. See above.

Lerninge, s. instruction, G 184.

Lese, v. to lose, G 229, 745, 833; *ger.* G 321; 1 *p. s. pres. subj.* I may lose, B 225. A.S. *leósan*, to lose; Goth. *fra-liusan*.

Lesing, s. lie, G 479; *pl.* Lesinges, lies, C 591. A.S. *leásung*, a falsehood; from A. S. *leás*, adj. meaning (1) loose, (2) false.

Leste, *adj. superl.* least, B 1012.

Leste, *pr. s. subj. impers.* it may please, B 742; *pt. s. subj.* it might please, I 36. A.S. *lystan*, to choose, gen. used impersonally; from *lust*, wish, desire, pleasure.

Let, *pt. s.* caused, permitted, B 373. See Lat.

Lete, v. to forsake, B 325; *ger.* 331; to leave, 986; *v.* to let out, lose, G 406, 523; 1 *p. s. pr.* I let, permit, B 321, 410, 1119; *imp. pl.* let go, give up, G 1049. A.S. *lǽtan*, Du. *laten*, G. *lassen*.

Lette, v. to hinder, delay; *used intrans.* to cause delay, B 1117. A. S. *lettan*, to hinder; Du. *letten*; Icel. *letja*, to hold back. From A. S. *læt*, late.

Letterure, s. literature, book-lore, G 846. O. F. *letreúre*, Lat. *literatura*.

Lettres, s. *pl.* letters, B 736. The M. E. *lettres*, like Lat. *literae*, often means a *letter*, in the singular.

Letuarie, *s.* electuary, C 307. Late Lat. *electuarium.* (Gloss. I.)

Leue, *v.* to give up, leave, let alone, G 714; *ger.* to forsake, 287; *imp. pl.* Leueth, leave ye, C 659. A.S. *léfan,* to leave, give up; Icel. *leifa.*

Leue, *pr. s.* 1 *p.* I believe, G 213; 2 *p.* Leuestow, believest thou, 212. A.S. *lýfan,* Du. *ge-looven,* G. *g-lauben,* E. *be-lieve.*

Leue, *s.* leave, permission, C 848, G 373. A.S. *leáf,* leave.

Leue, *adj. voc.* dear, C 731; beloved, G 257; *pl.* lief, dear, 383. The nom. sing. is *leef.* See Leef.

Leueful, *adj.* permissible, praise-worthy, allowable, G 5, I 41. It has nearly the sense of *lawful,* but is totally unconnected with *law* etymologically; it is for *leave-ful;* from A.S. *leáf,* leave.

Leuer, *adj. comp.* rather; *me were leuer,* it would be dearer to me, I had rather, C 615, H 23; *adv.* G 1376, H 78. Comparative of *leef.* See Leef.

Lewed, *adj.* ignorant, B 315, C 392, G 497, 647, 787. A.S. *lǽwed,* lay, a layman.

Lewedly, *adv.* ignorantly, ill, G 430, H 59. See above.

Leye, *v.* to lay a wager, bet, G 596; 1 *p. pl. pr.* we lay out, we expend, 783; *pt. pl.* Leyden forth, brought forward, B 213; *pp.* Leyd, laid, G 441. A.S. *lecgan,* pt. t. *ic legde,* pp. *geled.*

Lia, *put for* Lat. Lia, i.e. Leah in the book of Genesis, G 96. See the note.

Licour, *s.* juice, C 452. O.F. *liqeur,* from Lat. acc. *liquorem,* l quor, juice.

Lieges, *s. pl.* subjects, B 240. F. *lige,* from O.H.G. *ledic* (G.

ledig), free. A *liege* lord was a *free* lord; in course of time his subjects were called *lieges,* no doubt from confusion with Lat. *ligare,* to bind.

Liftinge, *s.* lifting, H 67.

Lige, *adj.* liege, C 337. See Lieges.

Ligeaunce, *s.* allegiance, B 895. See above.

Likerous, *adj.* gluttonous, dainty, greedy, C 540. From O.F. *lecher, lichier,* to lick up, be glut-tonous, borrowed from O.H.G. *lechon,* M.H.G. *lechen* (G. *lecken*), to lick. The *k* is due to remem-brance of A.S. *liccera,* a glutton, from the same root.

Lilie, *s.* lily, G 87. Lat. *lilium.*

Linage, *s.* lineage, kindred, B 999. O.F. *linage,* kindred; from Lat. *linea,* a line.

List, *pr. s. impers.* it pleases (him), B 520, 701, 766, G 234, I 69; *pers.* is pleased, pleases, chooses, B 477, G 30, 271; Listeth, pleases, 834; *pt. s. impers.* Liste, it pleased, 1048, G 1313. *List* is the contr. form of *listeth.* A.S. *lystan,* to please.

Litarge, *s.* litharge, G 775. 'Li-tharge, protoxide of lead, pro-duced by exposing melted lead to a current of air. It generally contains more or less red lead;' Webster. Lat. *lithargyrus,* Gk. λιθάργυρος, scum of silver, from λίθος, a stone (hard scum), and ἄργυρος, silver. (Gloss. I.)

Lofte, *s.* (*dat.*) the air; hence *on lofte,* in the air, aloft, B 277. A.S. *lyft,* air; cf. G. *luft.*

Loketh, *imp. pl.* look ye, behold, G 1329; search ye, C 578. A.S. *lócian,* to look.

Lomb, *s.* lamb, B 459, 617. A.S. *lamb,* a lamb; Du. *lam,* G. *lamm.*

Londe, *s.* (*dat.*) land, B 522, G

950. A.S. *lond, land*; the M.E. nom. case is also *lond*.

Long, *prep.*; the phrase *wher-on .. long = long on wher*, along of what, G 930; Long on, along of, because of, G 922. A.S. *gelang*, along of, because of.

Loos, *s.* praise, G 1368. O.F. *los, lox*, praise; a mere adaptation of Lat. nom. *laus*, praise.

Lordings, *s. pl.* sirs, B 573, C 329, I 15.

Lore, *s.* teaching, instruction, B 342, G 414; learning, B 761; study, G 842. A.S. *lár*, teaching, lore.

Lorn, *pp.* lost, B 774, 843. A.S. *loren*, lost; pp. of *leósan*, to lose; cf. G. *verloren*, pp. of *verlieren*.

Losten, *pt. pl.* lost, G 398.

Lotinge, *pres. part.* lurking, G 186. (See the note.) A.S. *lútian*, to lurk; as in Sweet's A.S. Reader, p. 9, l. 41; from A.S. *lútan*, to bow, bend down.

Loues, *s. pl.* loaves, B 503. A.S. *hláf*; pl. *hláfas*.

Lough, *pt. s.* laughed, C 476, 961. A.S. *hlihhan*, to laugh; pt. t. *ic hlóh*.

Lucre, *s.* profit, G. 1402. Lat. *lucrum*, gain.

Lulleth, *pr. s.* lulls, soothes, B 839. Cf. Swedish *lulla*, to hum, to lull; *lulla till sömns*, to lull to sleep.

Luna, *s.* the Moon, G 826; a name for silver, 1440. Lat. *luna*.

Lunarie, *s.* lunary, moon-wort, G 800. See the note.

Lure, *s.* a hawk's lure, the bait by which a hawk was tempted to return to the fowler's hand, H 72. F. *leurre*, a decoy; from Middle H. German *luoder*, a decoy.

Lust, *s.* will, pleasure, desire, wish, B 188, 762, G 1398; *pl.* Lustes,

desires, C 833. A.S. *lust*, pleasure, will.

Luste, *pt. s. impers.* it pleased, G 1235; *pers.* was pleased, desired, 1344. See List.

Lustier, *adj. comp.* more joyous, G 1345.

Lusty, *adj.* pleasant, G 1402; lusty, H 41. Formed from A.S. *lust*, pleasure; cf. Du. *lustig*, merry.

Lutes, *s. pl.* lutes, B 466. A word of Arabic origin; see Webster.

Lyghte, *imp. s.* illumine, G 71. A.S. *gelíhtan*, to lighten; from *leóht*, light.

Lyghte, *pt. s.* alighted, dismounted, B 786, 1104. A.S. *líhtan*, to alight from a horse.

Lyghtly, *adv.* easily, G 1400, H 8, 77. A.S. *líht*, light (not heavy).

Lyking, *s.* pleasure, C 455. A.S. *licung*, pleasure; from *lician*, to like.

Lym, *s.* lime, G 806, 910. A.S. *lim*, lime; Du. *lijm*, G. *leim*.

Lymaille, *s.* filings of any metal, G 853, 1162, 1197; Lymail, 1164, 1267, 1269. From Lat. *limare*, to file; *lima*, a file.

Lymes, *s. pl.* limbs, B 461, 772. A.S. *lim*, Icel. *limr*, a limb.

Lyt, *adj.* little, G 567; *as sb.*, a little, B 352. A.S. *lýt*, little, few; also used as a sb.

Lyte, *adv.* little, in a small degree, G 632, 699. Formed from A.S. *lýt*, little, by adding the adverbial suffix *-e*.

Lyth, *pr. s.* lieth, i.e. he lies, B 634. A.S. *licgan*, to lie; pr. s. *hé ligð*, or *lið*.

Lyues, *s. pl. gen.* souls', lives', G 56. A.S. *líf*, life.

Lyuestow, *for* lyuest thou, i.e. livest thou, C 719. A.S. *lifian*, to live; from *líf*, life.

Lyuinge, *s.* manner of life, C 847; state of life, G 322.

M.

Maad, *pp.* made, G 1459.

Magestee, *s.* majesty, B 1082. O. F. *maiestee*, Lat. acc. *majestatem*; cf. *magnus*, great.

Magnesia, *s.* magnesia, G 1455. Lat. *magnesia*, so called because found in Magnesia, in Thessaly. The word *magnet* has its name from the same source.

Maistres, *s. pl.* masters, B 141. O. F. *maistre*, Lat. acc. *magistrum*; cf. *magnus*, great.

Maistrie, *s.* a masterly operation (*un coup de maître*), G 1060. O. F. *maistrie*, from *maistre*, a master.

Make, *s.* mate, wife, B 700; husband, G 224. A. S. *maca*, Icel. *maki*, a mate.

Makestow, i. e. makest thou, B 371; *pp.* Maked, G 484. (Chaucer also has *Maad*, q. v.) A. S. *macian*, to make; pp. *macod*. From the same root as *machine* (Gk. μηχάνη).

Male, *s.* bag, wallet, C 920, G 566, I 26. O. F. *male* (F. *malle*), a budget; from O. H. G. *malaha*, a leathern bag. Cf. E. *mail* in *mail-bag*.

Malisoun, *s.* curse, G 1245. O. F. *malison*; from Lat. acc. *maledictionem*; so also *benison* is a doublet of *benediction*.

Malliable, *adj.* malleable, such as can be worked by the hammer, G 1130. From Lat. *malleus*, a hammer, *mallet*.

Maner, *s.* manner, sort, G 424; *maner pley*, kind of game, C 627; *maner chaunce*, kind of luck, G 527; *maner latyn*, kind of Latin, B 519; Manere, G 45, 142. O. F. *maniere*, manner; from Lat. *manus*, the hand.

Mannish, *adj.* man-like, i. e. unwomanly, B 782. Cp. A. S. *mennise*, human.

Manslaughtre, *s.* murder, C 593. A. S. *sleán*, to slay, kill.

Marie, *interj.* marry, i. e. by St. Mary, G 1062.

Mark, *s.* a piece of money, of the value of 13*s.* 4*d.* in England, G 1026; *pl.* Mark, i. e. marks, C 390. See note to C 390.

Mars (the planet), G 827.

Mary, *s.* marrow, C 542. A. S. *mearh*, marrow. (Gloss. I.)

Mased, *pp.* bewildered, B 526, 678. (Gloss. I.)

Mat, *adj.* struck dead, defeated utterly, B 935. O. F. *mat*, defeated, languid, feeble, G. *matt*, dull. Borrowed from the game of chess, in which *check-mate* is a corruption of Persian *sháh mat*, the king is dead; Diez.

Matere, *s.* matter, subject, affair, B 322, 411, 581; *pl.* Materes, materials (of a solid character), G 776; *gen. pl.* Matires, of the materials, 770. O. F. *matiere*, *matere*, Lat. *materia*.

Maumettrye, *s.* Mahometanism, B 236. *Maumet* is a corruption of Mahomet or Muhammed.

Maunciple, *s.* manciple, H 25, 69, 103, I 1. From Lat. *manceps*, a purchaser, contractor; from *manus*, the hand, and *capere*, to take. (Gloss. I.)

Mawe, *s.* maw, B 486. A. S. *maga*, the stomach. (Gloss. II.)

May, 1 *p. s. pr.* I can, B 231, 1070; Maystow, mayest thou. G 336. A. S. *magan*, to be able; pr. t. *ic mæg*; pt. t. *ic mihte*; Icel. *mega*, G. *mögen*.

May, *s.* maiden, B 851. A. S. *mǽg*, a kinsman; also, a son; also, a daughter.

Maydenhede, *s.* maidenhood, G 126. A. S. *mægdenhád*.

Medle, *v.* to medd'e, take part in, G 1184; *imp. pl.* Medleth, G 1424. O.F. *medler,* given by Burguy as another form of *mesler,* which is the Low Lat. *misculare,* to mix; from Lat. *miscere,* to mix.

Meel, *s.* meal, B 466. A.S. *mǽl,* a time, a portion; also, a meal.

Memorie, *s.* memory, G 339. From Lat. *memoria.*

Men, *s. pl.* men, people, folks; *often put for* Man, one, *with a verb in the* singular, C 675, G 392; *gen.* Mennes, men's, B 202.

Mene, *pr. s.* 1 *p.* l mean, speak of, B 641, G 1424, I I I; Menestow, meanest thou, G 309; 1 *p. s. pt.* Mente, intended, 999, 1051; *pt. s.* B 327. A.S. *mǽnan,* to have in mind; cf. G. *meinen,* to intend.

Mene, *adj.* mean, intermediate, B 546, G 1262. O.F. *meien, moien* (F. *moyen*), from Lat. *medianus;* which from Lat. *medius,* middle.

Menes, *s. pl.* means, B 480. See above.

Mercurie, Mercury, the planet, G 827.

Mercurie, *s.* mercury, i. e. quicksilver, G 772, 774, 827, 1431, 1438.

Meschance, *s.* misfortune, B 602, 610; Meschaunce, 896, 914; with meschaunce = with ill luck (to him), H 11. O.F. *meschaance,* a mishap; from Lat. *minus,* less, i. e. badly, and *cadentia,* hap; from Lat. *cadere,* to fall, happen.

Mescheef, *s.* tribulation, trouble, H 76; misfortune, G 1378; Meschief, 713, 1072. O.F. *meschief;* from Lat. *minus,* less, badly; and *caput,* the head.

Message, *s.* errand, B 1087: also, messenger, B 144, 333. F. *message,* Low Lat. *missaticum,* a message, *missaticus,* a messenger; from *mittere,* to send.

Messager, *s.* messenger, B 724,

785. F. *messager;* see above. The *n* is excrescent, as in *passenger,* i. e. *passager.*

Mesurable, *adj.* moderate, C 515. O.F. *mesurable,* Lat. *mensurabilis;* from *metiri,* to measure.

Ministre, *s.* minister, B 168. From Lat. *minus,* less; as *magister* is from *magis,* more.

Mirour, *s.* mirror, B 166, G 668. O.F. *mireor,* a mirror; from Lat. *mirari,* to gaze, wonder at.

Mis, *adj.* amiss, wrong, blameworthy, G 999. Icel. *missa,* a fault; Icel. *missa,* A.S. *missian,* to miss.

Misauenture, *s.* misfortune, B 616. O.F. *mesaventure.* (Note that in most E. words taken from the French the prefix *mis-* is a corruption of O. F. *mes,* Lat. *minus.*) In native words it is the (totally different) A. S. prefix *mis-.*

Misbileue, *s.* belief of trickery, suspicion, G 1213. Here the prefix is probably the A. S. *mis-,* wrong. See above.

Mistriste, *v.* mistrust, C 369. See Misauenture.

Miteyn, *s.* mitten, glove, C 372, 373. F. *mitaine,* explained by some as a *half*-glove, from O.H.G. *mittle,* middle; by others, more probably, as being from a Celtic source. Cf. Gaelic *miotag,* a worsted glove, Irish *mitinigh,* mittens.

Mochel, *adj.* much, G 611, H 54; many, G 673. A.S. *mycel,* much.

Moder, *s.* mother, B 696; *gen.* Modres, mother's, C 729, G 1243. A.S. *módor;* cf Icel. *módir,* G. *mutter,* Lat. *mater,* Gk. μήτηρ, Skt. *mátri.*

Moebles, *s. pl.* movable goods, personal property, G 540. From Lat. *mouere;* cf. F. *meubles,* furniture.

Moeued, *pt. s.* moved, disturbed, B
1136; *pres. pt.* Moeuyng, moving,
295. O. F. *mouvoir*, *movoir*,
from Lat. *mouere*.

Mollificacioun, *s.* mollifying,
softening, G 854. From Lat.
mollis, soft.

Mones, *s. gen.* moon's, I 10. A.S.
móna, gen. *mónan*; hence the
M. E. gen. is often *mone* as well
as *mones*; see Gloss. II.

Moneye, *s.* money, G 1033. O. F.
moneie, from Lat. *moneta*, money,
a mint.

Mo, *adj.* more (in number), B 419,
C 891, G 207, 675, 693, 723,
818; othere mo = others besides,
1001; na mo = no more, none
else, B 695. A.S. *má*, more in
number; chiefly used as the comparative of our *many*; whereas
the word *more* commonly means
greater in size, used as the comp.
of *mickle*, great.

Mooder, *s.* mother, B 276. See
Moder.

Moorning, *s.* mourning, B 621.
A. S. *meornan*, *murnan*, to mourn.

Moot, *pr. s.* must, is to, B 294.
See Mot.

Moralitee, *s.* morality, i. e. a moral
tale, I 38. From Lat. *mores*,
manners.

More and lesse, greater and lesser,
i.e. every one, B 959. See
Mo.

Mortifie, *v.* to mortify; lit. to
kill; used of producing change
by chemical action, G 1431 (see
note to the line); Mortifye, 1126.
From Lat. *mors*, death.

Morwe, *s.* morrow, morn; *by the
morwe*, early in the morning, at
dawn, H 16. A.S. *morgen*,
morning. By change of g to w
we get *morwen*, whence *morwe*
by dropping *n*, which is mod. E.
morrow. Direct contraction, with
loss of *g*, gives *morn*.

Mot, *pr. s.* 1 *p.* I must, I have to,
B 227, 737, C 327, 725; *subj.*
may, G 634, H 80; mot I theen
= may I thrive, C 309; foule
mot thee falle = foully (i. e. ill)
may it happen to thee, H 40; *pt.
s.* 1 *p.* Moste, I must, I ought, B
282; *pt. s.* must, had to, B 886,
G 523; *subj.* might, B 380; vs
moste = it must be for us, i.e. it
should be our resolve, G 946.
A.S. *ic mót*, I may; pt. t. *ic
móste*, I ought to, I *must*.

Motyf, *s.* motive, incitement, B
628. F. *motif*; from *mouvoir*,
to move; Lat. *mouere*.

Mountance, *s.* amount, quantity,
C 863. O. F. *montance*, amount,
value; from *monter*, to mount;
which from *mont*, a mountain;
from Lat. acc. *montem*.

Mow, 2 *p. s. pr. subj.* mayest, G
460; *pl.* Mowe, may, can, G
510, 780, 909; I *p. pr. pl.*
Mowen, we cannot. From A.S.
magan, to be able.

Moysty, *adj.* new (applied to ale),
H 60; Moiste, C 315. O. F.
moiste (F. *moite*); from Lat.
musteus, adj. of *mustum*, new
wine, *must*.

Mullok, *s.* rubbish, refuse, confused heap of materials, G 938,
940. Gower uses *mull* in a
similar sense; see Specimens of
English, ed. Morris and Skeat.
Mullok is a diminutive. It is
connected with *mould*.

Multiplicacioun, *s.* multiplying,
i. e. the art of alchemy, G 849.

Multiplye, *v.* to make gold and
silver by the arts of alchemy, G
669, 731.

Mused, *pt. s.* pondered, considered,
B 1033. F. *muser*, to loiter,
trifle.

Myle, *s. pl.* miles, G 556; cf.
Myles in l. 561 In the former
case the older form is retained;

cf. A. S. *mila*, the plural nom. gen. and acc. of *mil*, fem. sb.

Mynde, *s.* memory, B 527; remembrance, 908, 1127; to mynde = to (my) memory, 788. A. S. *mynd, gemynd,* memory, from *munan, gemunan,* to remember.

Myte, *s.* a mite, thing of no value, G 511, 633, 698, 1421. We also find the form *mint* (Piers Plowman); it is probable that the word *mite* (with long *i* for *in*) is the same word, from the root *min,* small, which appears in Gothic as well as in the Lat. *minor.*

N.

Nadde, *pt. pl.* had not, G 879, H 51. For *ne hadde.*

Naked, *pp. as adj.* destitute, void, weak, G 486. A. S. *nacod,* naked, a pp. form. The verb *to nake,* to lay bare, is used by Chaucer in his translation of Boethius.

Nam, *pt. s.* took, G. 1297. A. S. *niman,* to take; *pt. t. ic nam;* cf. G. *nehmen,* to take.

Namely, *adv.* especially, B 563, C 402.

Na mo, i. e. no more, none else, B 695; Namo, G 543. See Mo.

Namore, *adv.* no more, never again, B 1112, C 962, G 651, 1266.

Nappeth, *pr. s.* naps, slumbers, nods, H 8. A. S. *hnæppian,* to slumber.

Nart, *for* ne art, i. e. art not, G 499.

Nas, *for* ne was, i. e. was not, B 159, 209, 292, 938.

Nat, *adv.* not, H 23; Nat but, only, C 403. Cf. prov. E. *nobbut* (i. e. not but), only.

Nat, *for* ne at, i. e. nor at (see note, p. 6), B 290. So also Chaucer has *nin* for *ne in* ; see Gloss. II.

Natheles, *adv.* nevertheless, none

the less, B 621, C 813, G 717. A. S. *ná,* not, *þý,* on that account, instrumental case of *se, seó, þæt.* Thus it means—'not less on that account.'

Naught, *adv.* not, not so, G 269. From *aught,* with *ne* prefixed; E. *not* is the same word.

Nay, *adv.* no (*answering a simple question*), B 740; nay, G 1339. Cf. Icel. *nei,* nay; the A. S. *ná* is our *no.*

Nayles, *s. pl.* nails, C 288, 651. See note to C 651.

Ne, *adv.* not; *ne doth,* do ye not, C 745; *conj.* nor, C 619. A. S. *ne,* not.

Necessarie, *adj.* necessary, H 95. From Lat. *necessarius.*

Nede, *s. dat.* need, necessity, B 658; *pl.* Nedes, necessary things, business, 174; needs, G 178. A. S. *néad,* need; cognate with G. *noth.*

Nede, *adv.* necessarily, needs, G 1280. Originally a dat. case of the sb. See above.

Nede, *v.* to be necessary, B 871. The A. S. *neádan,* to compel, is usually transitive.

Nedles, *s. gen.* needle's, G 440. A. S. *nǽdl,* a needle; G. *nadel;* cf. Lat. *nere,* to sew.

Neer, *adj.* nearer, G 721. Comparative of *neigh* (A. S. *neáh*), nigh. See below.

Neigh, *prep.* nigh, B 550. A. S. *neáh,* nigh; comp. *neárra,* nigher; superl. *neáhsta, néhsta,* whence E. *next.*

Nekke-boon, *s.* nape of the neck, lit. neck-bone, B 669. A. S. *hnecca,* the neck (whence *nekke* is dissyllabic), and *bán,* bone.

Nempnen, *v.* to name, B 507. A. S. *nemnan,* to name; from *nama,* a name; cf. Lat. *nomen,* a name. The *p* is excrescent; see **Lampe. Empte.**

Nere, *pt. s. subj.* were not (*put for* ne were), B 547, G 1362.

Neuer the neer, *phr.* never the nearer, none the nearer, G 721. See **Neer**.

Neueradel, *adv.* not a bit, C 670. See **Del**.

Neuene, *v.* to name, G 821; *pr. pl. subj.* may name, may mention, 1473. Icel. *nefna*, to name; *nafn*, a name; see **Nempne**.

Nexte, *adj.* next, nearest, B 807, C 870. See **Neigh**.

Nil, 1 *p. s. pr.* I will not, G 1463; *pr. s.* will not, B 972. A. S. *nyllan*, to be unwilling; cf. Lat. *nolle*.

Nis, *for* ne is, is not, B 319, C 861, G 13, 919.

Niste, *pt. s.* knew not, B 384, G 216. A. S. *nytan*, not to know; pt. t. *ic nyste*; from *ne*, not, and *witan*, to know.

Nobledest, *pt. s.* 2 *p.* ennobledest, didst ennoble, G 40. A translation of Dante's *nobilitasti*; see the note.

Nobles, *s. pl.* gold coins worth 6s. 8d.; C 907, G 1365.

Noblesse, *s.* nobility, worthy behaviour, B 185, 248. F. *noblesse*; Low Lat. *nobilitia*; from *nobilis*, noble.

Nobley, *s.* nobility, assembly of nobles, G 449. Cf. O. F. *nobloier*, to look noble.

Nodde, *v.* to nod, H 47. A Low-German word, cognate with O.H.G. *nuoton*, *hnoton*, to shake. The Lat. *nuere*, to nod, shews the root; *nutare* is but a frequentative, so that the *t* in it does not answer to the E. *d*.

Nolde, *for* ne wolde, I would not, I should not desire, G 1334; *pt. pl.* Nolde, would not, 395. See **Nil**.

Noot, *for* ne wot, *pr. s.* 1 *p.* I know not, B 892, 1019, G 1148; Not, B 242, C 816, H 23.

A S. *ic nât*, I know not, from *nytan*, not to know.

Norice, *s.* nurse, G 1. O. F. *norice*, Lat. acc. *nutricem*.

No-thing, *adv.* in no respect, B 576, 971, C 764; not at all, C 404, 433, G 1036.

Notifyed, *pp.* made known, proclaimed, B 256. Lat. *notificare*, to make known; *notus*, known.

Nought, *s.* nothing, C 542, G 1401; in no respect, B 400. See **Naught**.

Nyce, *adj.* foolish, weak, B 1088, G 493, 647, 842, H 69. F. *nice*, Sp. *necio*, Port. *nescio*, or *necio*, Lat. *nescius*, ignorant. See Gloss. II.

Nycetee, *s.* folly, G 463, 495. See above.

Nyghtingale, *s.* nightingale, G 1343. A. S. *nihtegale*, Icel. *nætrgali*, G. *nachtigall*. The *n* is apparently excrescent. The word means *night-singer*; A. S. *galan*, to sing.

O.

O, *num.* one, B 1135, G 340. Shortened from *on* or *oon*; see **Oon**.

Occident, *s.* West, B 297. From Lat. acc. *occidentem*.

Occupieth, *pr. s.* takes up, dwells in, B 424. From Lat. *occupare*.

Of, *prep.* during, B 510; with, G 626. A. S. *of*.

Offreth, *imp. pl.* 2 *p.* offer ye, C 910. A. S. *offrian*, to offer; merely borrowed from Lat. *offerre*.

Of-newe, *adv.* newly, lately, G 1043. Hence E. *anew*.

Ofte, *adv.* often, B 278.

Ones, *adv.* once, B 588, 861, G 768; of one mind, united in design, C 696; at ones = at once, H 10. A. S. *ánes*, ones; gen. case of *án*, one.

Oo, *adj.* one, G 207. See **Oon**.

Ook, *s.* oak, C 765. A. S. *âc,* Icel. *eik,* G. *eiche.*

Oon, *adj.* one, B 271, 334, I 16; one and the same. C 333; that oon = the one, 666. A. S. *án,* Icel. *einn,* Goth. *ains,* Lat. *unus.*

Oppresse, *v.* to put down, G 4. From Lat. *opprimere.*

Or, *adv.* ere, before, G 314; *conj.* B 373. A. S. *âr,* before; another form of *ær,* E. *ere.*

Ordeyned, *pp.* ordained, i. e. prepared, G 1277. O. F. *ordener,* Lat. *ordinare,* to set in order; from *ordo,* order.

Ordinaunce, *s.* ordaining, governance, arrangement, B 763, 805; provision, 250. See above.

Ordre, *s.* order, class, G 995. F. *ordre,* from Lat. acc. *ordinem.*

Organs, *s. pl.* 'organs,' the old equivalent of organ, G 134; see the note. Or it may mean 'musical instruments.' Lat. pl. *organa;* from Gk. ὄργανον, an implement; from ἔργειν, to work.

Orisons, *s. pl.* prayers, B 537, 596. O. F. *orison,* from Lat. acc. *orationem.*

Orpiment, *s.* orpiment, G 759, 774, 823. 'Orpiment, tri-sulphide of arsenic; it occurs in nature as an ore of arsenic, and is usually in combination with realgar, or red sulphuret of arsenic;' Webster. F. *orpiment,* Lat. *auripigmentum;* from *aurum,* gold, and *pigmentum,* a pigment or paint.

Osanne, i. e. Hosannah, B 642. A Hebrew phrase; meaning 'save, we pray.'

Otes, *s. pl.* oats, C 375. A. S. *áta,* Icel. *æti,* oats.

Other ... other, either ... or, B 1136, G 1147. In the first instance, the second *other* is written in the contracted form or (which is short for *other*).

Otheres, *pron. sing.* each other's,

lit. of the other, C 476. A. S. *öðer,* Du. *ander,* Icel. *annar,* Goth. *anthar.* The E. form has lost an *n.*

Othes, *s. pl.* oaths, C 472, 636. A. S. *áð,* Icel. *eiðr,* Goth. *aiths,* an oath.

Ouer, *prep.* over, above (*pron. rapidly*), B 277; ouer her might = to excess, C 468. A. S. *ofer,* Icel. *yfir,* G. *über.*

Oueral, *adv.* everywhere, generally, G 507. Cf. G. *überall.*

Ouerdone, *pp.* overdone, carried to excess, G 645. A. S. *oferdón,* to overdo.

Ouer-greet, *adj.* too great, G 648.

Ouertake, *v.* to overtake, attain to, G 682.

Ought, *s.* anything of value, G 1333. A. S. *á-wiht.*

Oughte, *pt. s.* became; as him oughte = as it became him, B 1097; it was fit, as in hem oughte be = it was fit for them, G 1340; *pt. s. subj.* it would become, *as in* oughte vs = it would become us, it would be our duty, 14; I *p. pt. pl.* Oughten, we ought, 6. A. S. *ágan,* to owe, to own; pr. t. *ic áh,* I own; pt. t. *ic áhte,* I ought.

Ounces, *s. pl.* ounces, G 756. From Lat. *uncia.*

Oures, *poss. pron.* ours, C 786.

Outen, *v.* to come out with, utter, display, exhibit, G 834. A. S. *útian,* to put out, eject; cf. O. H. G. *úzon,* to put out. (A rare word.)

Outrageous, *adj.* violent, excessive, C 650. From F. *outrer.* O. F. *oltrer,* to pass beyond bounds; O. F. *oltre,* Lat. *ultra,* beyond.

Outrely, *adv.* utterly, C 849.

Out-taken, *pp.* excepted (lit. taken out), B 277.

Oversloppe, *s.* upper-garment, **G** 633. See note. Cf. Icel. *yfir-sloppr*, an upper or over garment; cf. E. *slop*, in the compound '*slop*-shop.'

Owen, *adj.* own, B 1058, C 834; *pl.* Oweue, G 1154. A.S. *ágen*, own; from *ágan*, to possess. Cf. Icel. *eiginn*, own, from *eiga*, to possess.

Oweth, *pr. s.* owneth, owns, possesses, C 361. A.S. *ágan*, to possess; Icel. *eiga*.

Owher, *adv.* anywhere, **G** 838. A.S. *áhwǽr*, anywhere.

Oyles, *s. pl.* oils, G 856. From Lat. *oleum*, oil.

P.

Paas, *s.* pace, foot-pace, **G** 575 (see the note); gon a paas = go at a foot pace, C 866. From Lat. *passus*, a step.

Pace, *ger.* to pass; *to pace of* = to pass from, B 205. F. *passer*, Low Lat. *passare*, to pass over. From *pandere*.

Palled, *adj.* enfeebled, languid, **H** 55. It is connected with *pale*, not with W. *pallu*, to fail, **W.** *pall*, loss of energy. See *Appalled* in Murray's Dict.

Palm, *s.* palmbranch, G 240. **Lat.** *palma*.

Panne, *s.* a pan, G 1210. A dissyllabic word. A.S. and Icel. *panna*.

Parauenture, *adv.* peradventure, perhaps, B 190.

Par cas, by chance, B 885.

Parde, *interj.* F. par Dieu, C 672.

Parfay, *interj.* by my faith, verily, B 849. O.F. *par fei*.

Parfit, *adj.* perfect, **G** 353. F. *parfait*, Lat. *perfectus*.

Paritorie, *s.* pellitory, *Parietaria officinalis*, G 581. 'In rural districts an infusion of this plant is

a favourite medicine;' Flowers of the Field, by C. A. Johns. '*Paritoire*, pellitory of the wall;' Cotgrave. From Lat. *paries*, a wall.

Pas, *s.* pace, B 399; *pl.* Pas, paces, movements, 306. See **Paas.**

Passen, *v.* to surpass, outdo, G 857. See **Pace.**

Passing, *adj.* surpassing, excellent, G 614.

Patente, *s.* a letter of privilege, so called because *open* to all men's inspection, C 337. From Lat. *patere*, to lie open.

Paue, *v.* to pave, G 626. From Lat. *pauire*, to ram or beat down earth; cf. Gk. παίειν, to strike.

Payens, *s. pl.* pagans, B 534. F. **paien,** Lat. *paganus*, prop. a villager. See **Hethen.**

Pees, *s.* peace, G 44; in pees = in silence, B **228.** O.F. *pes*, Lat. acc. *pacem*.

Pees, *interj.* peace! hush! B 836, G 951.

Pens, *s. pl.* pence, C 376. (N.B. *Pens* was pronounced with sharp *s*, as in *pens-ive*, not with z, as in the pl. of *pen*.)

Pepeer, *s.* pepper, G 762. From Lat. *piper*, Skt. *pippali*.

Perauenture, *adv.* perhaps, perchance, C 935, H 71. See **Parauenture.**

Percen, *pr. pl.* pierce, G 911. F. *percer*.

Perfit, *adj.* perfect, I 50. See **Parfit.**

Perseueraunce, *s.* continuance, G 443. See below.

Perseuereth, *pr. s.* lasteth, C 497. From Lat. *perseuerare*.

Perseueringe, *s.* perseverance, G 117.

Person, *s.* parson, I 23. From Lat. *persona.*

Peter, *interj.* by St. Peter, G 665. See note, p. 185.

Peyne, s. pain, G 1398; penalty, H 86. F. *peine,* Lat. *poena.*

Peyne, *pr. s.* **1** *p. refl.* I peyne me =I take pains, C 330, 395; *pr. s. refl.* Peyneth hir, endeavours, B 320.

Peytrel, s. properly, **the breast-plate of a horse in armour ;** heie used for the breast-plate of a horse's harness, G 564. Cf. O. F. *poitral* (Roquefort), Fr. *poitrail,* Lat. *pectorale;* from Lat. *pectus,* the breast.

Philosophre, s. philosopher, G 490; *pl.* Philosophres, 1427.

Pinchen, *ger.* to find fault, H 74. F. *pincer,* O. F. *pinser* (for *picer*), from a Low German source; cf. Old Dutch *pitsen,* to pinch ; **G.** *pfetzen,* **to cut** ; O. H. G. *pfezzen,* to pinch ; Diez.

Pitee, s. pity, B 292, 660. F. *pitié,* O. F. *pited,* **Lat.** acc. *pietatem.* (Gloss. II.)

Pitous, *adj.* pitiful, sad, B 449.

Pitously, *adv* piteously, B 1059, C 298.

Plages, *s. pl.* regions, B 543. From Lat. *plaga,* a region. Used twice by Chaucer in his Treatise on the Astrolabe (ed. **Skeat,** i. 5. **7;** ii. 31. 10) to signify 'quarters of the compass.'

Plantayn, s. plantain, G 581. F. *plantain,* from Lat. acc. *plantaginem.* Cf. **Romeo** and Juliet, **i. 2.** 52—' Your plantain-leaf is excellent for that.' The A. S. name **was** *wegbræde,* lit. way-broad (*not* way-bread) ; see *weg-bræde,* in Gloss. to Cockayne's Leechdoms.

Plat, *adv.* bluntly, flatly, openly, plainly, B 886, C 648. F. *plat,* flat ; from O. **H. G.;** G. *platt.*

Playn, *adv.* plainly, clearly, B 990. F. *plain,* Lat. *planus.* See **Pleyn.**

Plesance, s. pleasure, will, delight, B 149, 276, 762, 1140. F.

plaisance; from Lat. *placere,* to please.

Pleyn, *adj.* plain, clear, B 324. F. *plain,* **Lat.** *planus.* See **Playn.**

Pleyn, *adv.* plainly, clearly, B 886, G 360. See above.

Pleyn, *adj.* full, G 346. F. *plein,* Lat. *plenus.*

Pleyne, *v.* to complain, lament, B 1067, C 512. F. *plaindre,* Lat. *plangere.*

Pleyntes, *s. pl.* complaints, lamentations, B 1068. O. F. *plainte,* Lat *planctus,* a lament.

Plyght, *pp.* pledged, plighted, C 702. A.S. *plihtan,* to pledge ; pp. *gepliht ; pliht,* a pledge ; G. *pflicht,* a duty.

Plyte, s. plight, state, G 952. O. F. *pliste, plyte,* state, condition; Roquefort.

Point, s.; in point = on the point, ready (to), B 331, 910. F. *point,* Lat. *punctum.*

Pokets, *s. pl.* pockets, i. e. little bags, G 808. A.S. *pocca,* a poke, bag ; **perhaps** Celtic; cf. Gaelic *poca,* a bag, a pocket, Icel. *poki,* a bag.

Pokkes, *s. pl.* pocks, pustules, **C** 358. A. S. *poc,* Du. *pok,* a pock, pustule. *Small pox* is a corrupt form of ' the small pocks.'

Polcat, s. polecat, C 855.

Policye, s. public business, C 600. From Gk. πόλις, a state, city; whence πολιτεία, administration, Latinised as *politia,* and thence adopted into French.

Pomely, *adj.* dapple ; in the compound *pomely gris,* i. e. dapple-grey, G 559 ; cf. Prologue, 616. Cotgrave has—' *Gris pommelé,* a dapple gray.' Also—' *Pommelé,*' daple, or dapled ; also round, or plump as an apple.' And again —' *Pommeler,* to grow round, or plump like **an apple;** also, to daple.' *Dapple*, by the way, is from the verb to *dab*, and Wedgwood well remarks,—'The resemblance of *dapple-gray* to O. N. *apalgrár*, or *apple-gray*, Fr. *gris pommelé*, is accidental.'

Porphurie, *s.* porphyry, i. e. a slab of porphyry used as a mortar, G 775. From Lat. *porphyrites*, Gk. πορφυρίτης, like purple; from πορφύρα, purple.

Pose, *s.* a cold in the head, H 62. A. S. *gepose*, a stuffing or cold in the head.

Potage, *s.* broth, C 368. (Gloss. II.)

Pothecarie, *s.* apothecary, C 852.

Poudre, *s.* powder, G 760; *pl.* Poudres, **807**. F. *poudre*, O. F. *poldre*, Lat. acc. *puluerem*, dust.

Pouert, *s.* poverty, C 441. O. F. *poverte*, Lat. *paupertatem*.

Pound, *s. pl.* pounds, G 1364. A. S. *pund*, a pound; pl. *pund*. So we say,—'a five-*pound* note.'

Pouped, *pp.* blown, H 90. An imitative word. See Gloss. I.

Pouren, 1 *p. s. pr.* we pore, gaze steadily, G 670.

Pourest, *adj. superl.* poorest, C 449. O. F. *povre*, Lat. *pauper*.

Poynt, *s.* a stop, G 1480. See **Point**.

Predicacioun, *s.* preaching, sermon, C 345, 407. From **Lat.** *praedicare*, to preach.

Preef, *s.* the test, H 75; a test, proof, G 968, 1379. Cf. F. *prouver*, Lat. *probare*, to prove. See **Preue**.

Prees, *s.* press, throng, B 393, 646, 677. F. *presse*; from Lat. *premere*, to press.

Prefectes, *s. pl.* prefects, G 369. Lat. *praefectus*.

Preue, *v.* to prove, i. e. bide the test, G 645; to prove to be right, to succeed when tested, 1212; *pp.* Preued, tested, 1336.

Cf. F. *prouver*, Lat. *probare*, to test. But it is not certain that *prove* is a French word; we find also **A. S.** *prófian*, Icel. *prófa*, G. *prüfen*, to prove, try. 'For þeof he bið to *prófianne*, he is to be held to be a thief;' Laws of Ine (A. D. 689–728); cap. x.

Preyde, *pt. s.* prayed, besought, B 391. O. F. *preier*, Lat. *precari*, to pray.

Preyere, *s.* prayer, G 256; Preyer, H 6. O. F. *priere*, *preere*.

Priked, *pp.* spurred, G 561. A. S. *priccian*, to prick, goad; Du. *prikken*.

Priuee, *adj.* privy, private, secret, B 204, C 675; Priuy, G 1452. F. *privé*, Lat. *priuatus*.

Priuetee, *s.* secret counsel, secrecy, B 548, G 1052, 1138; Priuyte, G 701.

Profre, 2 *p. s. pr. subj.* mayst proffer, mayst offer, G 489. F. *proférer*, Lat. *proferre*, to bring forward.

Prolle, *pr. pl.* 2 *p.* ye prowl, prowl about, search widely, G 1412. See *Prollyn*, and *Prollynge*, in Prompt. Parv. The origin of it is doubtful.

Propre, *adj.* fine, handsome, C 309. F. *propre*, proper; Lat. *proprius*.

Prose, *s.* prose, I 46. F. *prose*, Lat. *prosa*.

Protestacioun, *s.* protest, I 59.

Prow, *s.* profit, advantage, C 300, G 609. O. F. *prou*, *prod*, gain, advantage; the source appears in Lat. *prod-est*, it is advantageous.

Prye, *v.* to pry, look, peer, G 668. Origin unknown. Perhaps it is merely a peculiar use of F. *prier*, to pray; also, to beseech, beg.

Pryme, *s.* prime; used in Chaucer, apparently, to signify 9 A.M., C 662. (Gloss. II.)

Pulpet, s. pulpit, C 391. Lat. *pulpitum.*

Purchasen, ger. to purchace, **acquire,** G 1405; *imp. s.* Purchace, may (He) provide, B 873. F. *pourchasser,* to hunt after, acquire.

Purged, pp. absolved, cleansed (by baptism), G 181. Lat. *purgare,* to purify.

Purpos, s. purpose, **design,** B 170. F. *propos,* Lat. *propositum.* The verb to *purpose* is both *proposer* and *purposer* in Old French.

Purses, s. pl. purses, G 1404. **F.** *bourse,* Gk. βύρσα, a skin.

Purveiance, s. equipment, B 247; providence, 483. F. *pourvoir* (O. F. *porvoir*), to purvey or provide; Lat. *prouidere.*

Pye, s. magpie, G 565. **F. *pie,*** Lat. *pica.*

Pyne, s. suffering, B 1080. **A.S.** *pin,* pain; Icel. *pina,* to torment.

Q.

Quelle, v. to kill, C 854; *imp. s.* may (he) **kill,** G 705. M.E. *cullen,* Icel. *kolla,* to hit on the head, to harm, from *kollr,* head, top, gives E. *kill;* but *quell* is the A.S. *cwellan.*

Quene, s. queen, G 1089; Queene, B 161. A.S. *cwen,* Gk. γυνή, a woman. It is remarkable that Chaucer makes it a dissyllabic word; see also Gloss. II.

Queynte, adj. pl. strange, G 752. O.F. *cointe,* instructed, Lat. *cognitus,* known; but it seems to have been influenced by Lat. *comptus,* trimmed.

Quike, ger. to make alive, quicken, G 481. A.S. *cwiccan,* to make alive; cf. Icel. *kvikna,* to revive; from A.S. *cwic,* Icel. *kvikr,* alive; related to Lat. *uiuus.*

Quik-siluer, s. quicksilver, i.e. lively silver, G 822. **A.S.** *cwic,* alive.

Quyte, v. to repay (lit. quit), G 736, 1025; Quyten, 1027; Quyte with = to repay ... with, 1055; to satisfy, pay in full, B 354; Quyte hir whyle = requite her time or trouble, lit. repay her time, i.e. her occupation, pains, trouble, B 584; **I** *p. s. pr.* I requite, C 420; *pp.* Quit, freed, G 66, 448. O.F. *quiter* (F. **quitter**), Lat. *quietare,* to quiet, satisfy; from *quies,* rest.

R.

Rad, pp. read, G 211. See **Rede.**

Rammish, adj. ramlike, strongscented, G 887. Cf. Icel. *ramr,* strong, fetid; which is probably closely related to A.S. *ramm,* a ram.

Rancour, s. rancour, ill-feeling, H 97. O.F. *rancor, rancuer, rancure* (F. *rancune*); from Lat. acc. *rancorem,* a rankling.

Rape, v. to snatch up; *rape and renne,* seize and plunder, G 1422. See the note. The Icel. *hrapa* means to rush, to hurry; the proper word to use in this phrase would rather have been *rive;* but there was probably a confusion here with the common Lat. verb *rapere.* Similarly the Icel. verb *ræna,* to rob, to plunder, has been turned into *renne,* as if from A.S. *rennan,* to run. Thus *rape and renne* (as if from Lat. *rapere,* and A.S. *rennan*) has been substituted for the original Icel. *hrapa* (or *rifsa*) ok *ræna.* See **Renne.**

Rather, adv. sooner, earlier (in point of time), B 225, 335, C 643. A.S. *hraðe,* soon; *hraðor,* sooner.

Rattes, s. pl. rats, C 854. A.S. *ræt.*

Raue, I *p. pl. pres.* we rave, we speak madly, G 959. Etym. doubtful. Roquefort gives an

O. F. *raver*, to run about. Cf. Lat. *rabere*, to be mad; from which, however, the F. has *enrager*.

Recche, 1 *p. s. pres.* I reck, G 489. A. S. *récan*, Icel. *rækja*, O. Flemish *roeken*. See **Rekke.**

Recchelees, *adj.* careless, indifferent (lit. reckless), B 229. A. S. *recceleás*; cf. Du. *roekeloos.*

Receit, *s.* receipt, i. e. recipe for making a mixture, G 1355, 1366. *Receit* is from Lat. pp. *receptus*; *recipe* is the Lat. imperative singular from the same verb, viz. *recipere.*

Receyued, *pp.* accepted (as congenial), acceptable, B 307. F. *recevoir*, Lat. *recipere.*

Reclayme, *v.* to reclaim, as a hawk by a lure, i. e. check, H 72. From Lat. *re*, back, and *clamare*, to call.

Recomandeth, *pr. s. refl.* commends (herself), B 278; *ger.* Recomende, to commend, commit, G 544. Lat. *re*, back; *con*, with; *mandare*, to hand over.

Rede, *v.* to read, G 206; 1 *p. s. pr.* I read, B 1095, C 508; I advise, C 793, 941, G 502, 1008, 1475; *pp.* Rad, read, G 211. A. S. *rǽdan*, to read, to advise; cf. G. *rathen*, to advise.

Rede, *adj.* as *sb.* red, i. e. the blood, B 356; *as sb.* red wine, C 526, 562; *pl.* Rede, red, G 1095. A. S. *reád*, red; Icel. *rauðr*, G. *roth*. The indef. form is *reed*, q. v.; *rede* is def. or plural.

Redily, *adv.* quickly, C 667. A. S. *rád, rǽd*, ready.

Reed, *s.* counsel, advice, C 744. A. S. *rǽd*; cf. G. *rath.*

Reed, *adj.* red, ruddy, B 452, H 20. See **Rede.**

Reednesse, *s.* redness, G 1097, 1100. See above.

Refut, *s.* place of refuge, refuge, B 546, 852, G 75. Cf. O. F. *refui,*

refuge; Lat. *refugium.* It is not easy to account for the *t*; but cf. F. *fuite*, flight, from Lat. pp. *fugitus.*

Regne, *s.* kingdom, realm, B 389, 392, 735; *pl.* Regnes, kingdoms, 181. F. *règne*, Lat. *regnum.*

Regneth, *pr. s.* reigneth, has dominion, B 776. From Lat. *regnare.*

Reherse, *v.* to rehearse, recount, G 786. O. F. *rehercer*, to repeat, lit. to harrow over again; from *herce*, Lat. acc. *herpicem*, a harrow (Varro). See Gloss. I.

Rehersaille, *s.* rehearsal, enumeration, G 852. See above.

Rekeninges, *s. pl.* reckonings, H 74. A. S. *recnan*, to reckon.

Rekke, *pr. s.* 1 *p.* I reck, care, C 405; *imp. s.* reck, care, G 698; *pr. s.* Rekketh, accounts, cares, 632. See **Recche.**

Rekne, *ger.* to reckon, B 158. A. S. *recnan*, to reckon; G. *rechnen.*

Relees, *s.* relaxation, ceasing; *out of relees*, without ceasing, G 46. O. F. *reles, relais*, relaxation; from the verb *relesser* (F. *relaisser*), which is the Lat. *relaxare*, to relax; from *laxus*, loose.

Relente, *v.* to melt, G 1278. From prefix *re-*, again; and Lat. *lentare*, to bend; from Lat. *lentus*, pliant.

Relesse, *v.* to relieve, relax, B 1069. O. F. *relesser* (F. *relaisser*), to relax; Lat. *relaxare*, to relax; from *laxus*, lax, loose.

Releued, *pp.* relieved, made rich again, G 872. Lat. *releuare*, to lift up again.

Remenant, *s.* remnant, remainder, G 1004. From Lat. *manere*, to remain.

Remeueth, *imp. pl.* 2 *p.* remove ye, G 1008. From Lat. *mouere*, to move.

Renegat, s. renegade, apostate, B 932. Low Lat. *renegatus,* one who has abjured his faith; from *negare,* to deny. See below.

Reneye, v. to renounce, abjure, B 376, G 268, 448, 459; 1 p. s. pr. subj. I (may) renounce, 464; pt. pl. 1 p. we abjured, B 340; pp. Reneyed, 915. Lat. *renegare,* to adjure, renounce, deny; from *negare,* to deny. Shakespeare uses the Lat. form *renege,* King Lear, ii. 2. 84; Ant. and Cleop. i. 1. 8.

Renne, ger. to run, C 796. G 1415; pr. s. Renneth, runs, 905. A.S. *rennan, yrnan,* to run; Icel. *renna,* G. *rennen.*

Renno, v. to ransack, plunder; *but only in the phrase* rape and renne, seize and plunder, G 1422. See the note. Icel. *ræna,* to plunder; *rán,* plunder; which appears in E. *ransack.* The word has been turned into *renne,* which properly means *to run.* See above; and see Rape.

Rente, s. rent, toll, B 1142. F. *rente,* from F. *rendre,* Lat. *reddere,* to restore, render.

Repaireth, pr. s. returns, B 967. O. F. *repairier* = Ital. *ripatriare,* to return to one's native country; from Lat. *patria,* native country.

Replet, adj. full, replete, C 489. Lat. *repletus.*

Repreuable, adj. reprehensible, C 632. See below.

Repreue, v. to reprove, H 70; pr. s. Repreueth, I 33. From Lat. *reprobare;* whence O. F. *reprover,* to reprove.

Repreue, s. reproof, shame, C 595. See above.

Resalgar, s. realgar, G 814. 'Realgar, a combination of sulphur and arsenic, of a brilliant red colour as existing in nature; red orpiment;' Webster. F.

realgar, answering to an O. F. *resalgar,* Low Lat. *risigallum.*

Respyt, s. respite, delay (of death), G 543. O. F. *respit,* (F. *répit*), Lat. *respectus,* a respect, regard, looking back. Hence *respite* and *respect* are doublets.

Restelees, adj. restless, C 728. A. S. *rest,* rest, repose. Distinct from F. *reste,* rest; *rester,* to remain, Lat. *restare.*

Reue, ger. to take away, G 376. A. S. *reáfian,* to rob; whence E. *be-reave.*

Rewe, v. to suffer for, do penance for, G 997; imp. s. have pity; B 853; pr. s. 2 p. Rewest, hast pity, 854. A. S. *hreówian,* to grieve; from *hreów,* grief.

Rewful, adj. sorrowful, sad, B 854. See above.

Rewthe, s. pity, ruth, B 529, 654, 689; as adj. pitiful, 1052. Formed from the verb *to rewe* (see above); but the A. S. sb. is *hreów,* grief. Still, the Icel. has *hryggð.*

Rewthelees, adj. pitiless, B 863.

Reyse, ger. to raise, G 861. Icel. *reisa,* to raise; the A. S. is *rǽran,* whence E. *rear.*

Ribaudye, s. ribaldry, ribald jesting, C 324. O. F. *ribald,* Low Lat. *ribaldus,* a ribald, a worthless fellow.

Riden, pt. pl. rode, C 968. See Rydinge.

Ringes, s. pl. rings, C 908. A. S. *hring,* Icel. *hringr;* cognate with Lat. *circus,* whence E. *circle.*

Rist, pr. s. contr. riseth, rises, B 864.

Rit, pr. s. rides (contr. from *rideth*), G 608, H 79.

Roialtee, s. royalty, B 418. From F. *roi,* Lat. *rex;* Skt. *rájá,* a king.

Roialler, adj. comp. royaller, more royal, B 402.

Rolleth, pr. s. rolls, turns over, C 838. O. F. *roler* (F. *rouler*);

Lat. *rotulare*, to turn round; from *rota*, a wheel.

Rom, ram, ruf; nonsense words, to imitate alliteration (see note), I 43.

Rombled, *pt. s.* rummaged, fumbled, G 1322. Cf. Du. *rommelen*, to rumble, buzz; also, to mix up, disarrange; Dan. *rumle*, to rumble, to roll. See Gloss. II.

Romen, *v.* to roam, B 558. Cf. O. F. *romieu*, *romien*, *romier*, Ital. *romeo* (Dante), a pilgrim to Rome. Hence *romen* =to go to Rome; the connection with E. *roam* is doubtful.

Rong, *pt. s.* rang, C 662. A. S. *hringan*, to ring.

Rose-reed, *adj.* red as a rose, G 254. (Trisyllabic.)

Rote, *s.* root; an astrological term for the epoch of a nativity, B 314 (see note): the radix, the fundamental principle, G 1461; root, source, B 358, G 1069, 1301. Icel. *rót*, Swed. *rot* (Scandinavian).

Rote, *in phr.* by rote, i.e. by heart, C 332. O. F. *rote*, F. *route*; allied to F. *routine*, O.F. *rotine*. 'Par *rotine*, by rote;' Cotgrave. See Route.

Roten, *pp.* rotten, G 17, 228. A.S. *rotian*, to rot, putrefy, pp. *gerotod*. The form *rotten* is Scandinavian; Icel. *rotinn*, rotten, pp. of *rotna*, to rot.

Round, *adv.* roundly, fully, melodiously, C 331. F. *rond*, O.F. *roond*, Lat. *rotundus*. Cf. Lat. ' ore rotundo.'

Route, *s.* troop, throng, company, B 387, 650, 776. F. *route*, from Lat. *rupta*, a broken (band); from *rumpere*, to break. Cf. G. *rotte*, a troop; O. Flemish *rote*.

Route, *v.* to assemble in a company, B 540. See above.

Row, *adj.* rough, angry, forbidding,

G 861. A. S. *ruh*, rough, rugged, hairy; Du. *ruw*, rough, rugged.

Rownen, *v.* to whisper, G 894. A. S. *rúnian*, to whisper; from *rún*, a rune, a magic character, a mystery; O. Flemish *ruunen*, to whisper. Hence *round*, to whisper, in Shakespeare.

Rubifying, *s.* rubefaction, reddening, G 797.

Rydinge, *pres. pt.* riding, G 623. A. S. *rídan*, Icel. *ríða*, to ride; pt. t. *ic rád*, pl. *we riden*; pp. *riden*.

Ryghtwisnesse, *s.* righteousness, C 637. A. S. *rihtwis*, righteous; Icel. *rétviss*. *Righteous* is a corrupt spelling of *rightwise*.

Rym, *s.* rime (commonly misspelt *rhyme*), I 44. The spelling *rhyme*, or *rhime* (with *h* inserted from ignorance) is not older than A. D. 1550. A. S. *rim*, Icel. *ríma*, G. *reim*, Du. *rijm*, Dan. *riim*, Swed. *rim*, F. *rime*.

Ryme, *v.* to rime, to speak in verse, G 1093. See above.

Ryotoures, *s. pl.* rioters, roysterers, C 661. Roquefort gives *rioter*, to dispute; *riote*, noise, combat; *faire riote*, to grumble, dispute; *rios*, a dispute, debate. The suggested connection with Du. *ravotten*, to romp, is unlikely.

Ryue, *v.* to rive, pierce, C 828 Icel. *rifa*, Dan. *rive*, to rive, tear; cf. Icel. *hrifa*, to catch, grapple.

S.

Sad, *adj.* sober, calm, settled, G 397; *pl.* Sadde, discreet, B 135. A. S. *sæd*, sated, satiated (hence, settled, firm).

Sadel, *s.* saddle, H 52. A. S. *sadel*.

Sadly, *adv.* in a settled manner, i. e. deeply, unstintingly, B 743. See Sad.

Saffron **with, to** tinge with
saffron, to colour, C 345. F.
safran; from the Arab. *za'farún*,
saffron.

Sal armoniak, s. sal ammoniac, G
798, 824. Lat. *sal armeniacum*,
Armenian salt. '*Sal ammoniac*,
chloride of ammonium, a salt of
a sharp, acrid taste ; ... also called
hydrochlorate, or muriate of am-
monia'; Webster. The word
armoniac certainly answers to the
Lat. *Armen'acum* in the old
treatises. Nevertheless the right
spelling is, perhaps, *ammoniac*;
'ἀμμωνιακόν, τό, sal ammoniac,
rock-salt, Dioscorides'; Liddell
and Scott.

Sal peter, s. saltpetre, G 808.
Lat. *sal petræ*, rock-salt ; 'so
called because it exudes from
rocks or walls ; nitrate of potassa ;
—called also nitre ' ; Webster.

Sal preparat, s. prepared salt, G
810. See the note.

Sal tartre, s. salt of tartar, G 810.
'*Salt of tartar*, carbonate of
potash ; ... at first prepared from
cream of tartar '; Webster.

Salueth, *pr.* s. saluteth, B 731.
F. *saluer*, Lat. *salutare*.

Sans, *prep.* without, B 501. **F.**
sans, O. F. **sens**, Lat. *sine.*

Sapience, s. wisdom, G 101, 111 ;
pl. Sapiences, kinds of intelligence
(see note), 338. From Lat.
sapere, to know.

Satins, s. *pl.* satins, B 137. F.
satin, Low Lat. *setinus*, adj. from
Lat. **seta**, silk ; whence also F.
soie.

Sauacioun, s. salvation, B 283, H
58.

Saue, *prep.* save, **except,** B 217, G
1355. F. *sauf*; from Lat. *saluus.*

Saue, *imp.* s. 3 *p.* **save,** may (he)
save, G 1361 ; *pt. s.* 2 *p.* Sauedst,
savedst, B 639; Saveth, *imp. pl.*

save ye, 229. O. F. *sauer*, Lat.
saluare, to keep.

Sauf, *adj.* safe, B 343, G 950. F.
sauf, Lat. *saluus.*

Sauour, s. savour, smell, G 887.
F. *saveur*, Lat. acc. *saporem.*

Sawe, s. discourse (lit. saw, **or**
saying), G 691 ; saw, saying,
1441. A. S *sagu*, a saying.

Scabbe, s, scab, a disease of sheep,
C 358. A. S. *scæb, sceab.*

Scaped, *pp.* escaped, B 1151.
O. F. *escaper*, said to be from
Low Lat. *excappare*, to get out
of one's cloak, to flee. See
Brachet, s. v. *échapper.*

Scarsete, s. scarcity, G 1393.
O. F. *escharsete*, sparingness, fru-
gality ; from O. F. *eschars*, or
escars, Low Lat. *excarpsus*, pp.
of *excarpere = excerpere*, to select.

Scatered, *pp.* scattered, G 914.
A. S. *scateran*, to scatter ; cf.
sceddan, to separate.

Sclaundre, *pr. s.* 1 *p.* I slander, G
993 ; 2 *p.* Sclaundrest, 695. F.
esclandre; from Lat. *scandalum*;
whence also *scandal*. Slander
and scandal are doublets.

Scorpioun, s. scorpion, B 414.
Lat. acc. *scorpionem.*

Secre, *adj.* secret, G 178, 643.
O. F. *secroi*, **secreit**; Lat. *secretum.*

Secre of **secrees,** secret of secrets.
Lat. Secreta Secretorum (the name
of a book), G 1447.

Secrenesse, s. secrecy, B 773.

See, *imp.* s. 3 *p.* may (He) behold,
or protect, B 156, C 715. See
note to the latter passage, p. 162.
See Seen.

Seel, s. seal, B 882, C 337. O. F.
seel; from Lat. *sigillum.*

Seen, *v.* to see. B 182. A. S. *seón*,
to see. See See, and Sey.

Seistow, *for* sayest thou, G 260.
See Seye.

Seken, *ger.* to seek, i. e. a matter

for search, G 874. A.S. *sécan*, to seek; ger. *tó sécenne*.

Seled, *pp.* sealed, B 736. See Seel.

Sely, *adj.* blessed, holy, B 682; innocent, C 292; silly, simple, G 1076. A.S. *sǽlig*, happy.

Sendeth, *imp.* 2 *p. pl.* send ye, C 614; *pt. s. subj.* Sente, would send, B 1091. A.S. *sendan*.

Sentence, *s.* judgment, **order, I 17**; verdict, G 366; Sentens, general meaning, I 58. **From** Lat. *sententia*.

Sepulture, *s.* sepulchre, **C 558.** Lat. *sepultura*, burial.

Sergeants, *s. pl.* sergeants, G 361. F. *sergent*, Lat. *seruientem*, pres. pt. of *seruire*, to serve.

Sermone, *ger.* to preach, speak, C **879.** From Lat. *sermo*, a discourse.

Seruage, *s.* servitude, thraldom, bondage, B 368. F. *servage*; from F. *serf*, Lat. *seruus*.

Seruisable, *adj.* serviceable, useful, G 1014.

Sesoun, *s.* season, G 1343. O.F. *seson*, Lat. *sationem*, a sowingtime.

Sette, *pt. s.* set, B 1053; *refl.* set herself, i. e. sat, 329; sette her on knees = cast herself on her knees, 638; *pl. refl.* Sette hem, seated themselves, C 775; Setten hem **adoun**, set themselves, G 396; *pp.* Set, set, placed, put. B 440. A.S. *settan*, to place; from *sittan*, to sit.

Seurtee, *s.* security, surety, B 243, C 937. O.F. *seurte*, Lat. acc. *securitatem*.

Sey, *pt. s.* saw, B 583, 615, 809, 1051, 1128, C 961, G 355, 402; 1 *p.* I saw, G 589; 2 *p.* Sey, thou sawest, B 848; 2 *p. pl.* Sey, ye saw, G 1106; *pt. pl.* Seye, saw, B 218; Seyen, G 110; *pp.* Seyn, **seen**, B 172, 624. A.S. *seún*, to see.

Seye, *ger.* to say, **tell**, i. e. to be told, B **706**; 1 *p. s. pr.* Sey, I say, 1139; *pt. pl.* Seyden, said, B 211; **2 *p.*** Seydestow, saidst thou, G 334. A.S. *secgan*, pt. t. *ic sægde*.

Shadwe, *s.* shadow, I 7. A.S. *sceado*.

Shal, *pr. s.* is to, must, B 268, 665; 1 *p.* I am to (go), G 303; **2 *p.*** Shaltow, *for* shalt thou, G 257. A.S. *ic sceal.* See **Sholde.**

Shames, *s. gen.* of shame; *shames deth*, death of shame. i. e. shameful death, B **819.** A.S. *scamu*, shame.

Shap, *s.* shape, form, G 44. A.S. *gesceapu*, shape; from *scippan*, to create.

Shapen, *v.* to devise, invent, B 210; *pp.* disposed (themselves), 142; prepared, **249**; appointed, 253; planned, 951. A.S. *scippan*, to create, plan.

Shauing, *s.* a thin slice, G 1239. A.S. *scafan*, to shave, scrape.

Sheene, *adj.* showy, fair, B 692. A. S. *scéne, scíne*, beautiful, fair; from *scéawian*, to **show.** Cf. G. *schön*, fair.

Shetten, *v.* to shut, enclose; *gonne shetten*, did enclose, G 517; *pt. s.* Shette, shut, 1142; *pt. pl.* Shette, 1218; *pp.* Shet, shut, B 1056, G 1137. A.S. *scyttan*, to lock up, pt. t. *ic scyttode*.

Shete, *s.* a sheet, G 779; *pl.* Shetes, 536. A.S. *scedt.*

Shifte, *v.* to apportion, assign, G 278. A.S. *sciftan, scyftan*, to appoint, divide; Icel. *skipta*, to divide, distribute.

Sholde, *pt. s.* had to, **was** to, G 1382, I 65. A.S. *ic scolde, sceolde*, pt. t. of *sculan*. The pres. t. is *ic sceal*. See **Shal, Shul.**

Shoop, *pt. s.* formed, shaped, G

1222; shoop him = purposed, intended, C 874. See Shapen.

Showuing, *s.* shoving, pushing, H 53. A. S. *scúfan,* to push, shove.

Shrewe, *adj.* evil, wicked, 995; as *sb.,* evil one, 917; an ill-tempered (male) **person,** C 496; *pl.* Shrewes, wicked **men,** rascals, 835, G 746. '*Schrewe,* pravus;' Prompt. Parv.

Shul, *pr. pl.* **shall,** may, C 733; 1 *p.* I must, I have to, B 351; 2 *p. pr. pl.* Shullen, ye shall, G 241; *pt. s.* 1 *p.* Shulde, I should, I ought to, B 247. See Shal.

Siker, *adj.* sure, G 934; certain, **1047**; safe, 864. O. Friesic *sikur, siker;* O. Saxon (Heliand) *sikor;* Du. *zeker;* O. H. G. *sihhur,* G. *sicher.*

Sikernesse, *s.* security, safety, B 425.

Siluer, *s.* silver, G 826. A. S. *seolfor.*

Similitude, *s.* comparison; *hence,* proposition, **statement,** G 431. Lat. *similitudo.*

Sin, *conj.* since, B 282, 1115, G 495, 504; *adv.* since, B 157. Contr. from A. S. *siððan,* since; from *sið,* time. See Sithen.

Singuler, *adj.* a single, G 997. Lat. *singularis.*

Sith, *conj.* since, B 484, 814, G 1472; *adv.* afterwards, C 869. See below.

Sithen, *adv.* afterwards, B 1121. A. S. *siððan,* afterwards; for *sið ðám,* since then; where *sið* is from the adj. *sið,* late; which from *sið,* a time. See below.

Sithe, *s. pl.* **times;** *ofte sithe,* many times, G 1031. A. S. *sið,* a time. See Sythe.

Skilful, *adj.* discerning, B 1038, G 329. Icel. *skil,* discernment; *skilja,* to separate.

Skilfully, *adv.* reasonably, with good reason, G 320. (The M. E.

skile often means a **reason**; see Gloss. II).

Slee, *v.* to slay, G 896; **Sle,** 168; **Sleen,** C 846; *ger.* Sleen, G 481; *pr. s.* Sleeth, slays, C 676, 754; *pr. pl.* Sleen, they slay, B 964; *pt. s.* Slow, slew, B 627, 664, 894. A. S. *sleán,* pt. t. *slóh,* pp. *slagen,* to strike, slay.

Sleighte, *s. dat.* craft, skill, G 867; *pl.* Sleightes, devices, 773, 976. Icel. *slægð,* slyness; *slægr,* sly.

Sleue, *s.* sleeve, G 1224, 1231. A. S. *sléf,* a sleeve.

Slewthe, *s.* sloth, B 530; **Slouthe,** G 258. A. S. *sláwð,* sloth; from *sláw,* slow.

Slit, *p. s.* slides (contr. from *slideth*), G 682. A. S. *slidan.* See Slyding.

Slogardye, *s.* sloth, sluggishness, G 17. '*Slugge,* deses, seguis;' Prompt. Parv.

Slough, *s.* mud, mire, H 64. A. S. *slóh,* a slough, hollow place.

Slouthe, *s.* sloth, G 258. See Slewthe.

Slow, *pt. s.* slew, B 627, 664, 894. See Slee.

Sluttish, *adj.* slovenly, G 636. Cf. **Du.** *slodder,* a sloven; *sloddering,* slovenly; *slodderen,* **to** hang loosely about.

Slyding, *adj.* unstable, slippery, G 732. See Slit.

Smart, *adj.* brisk (said of a fire), G 768. The word *smart,* sb., is properly used of a *sudden* pain.

Smert, *s.* smart, pain, G 712. Du. *smart* (O. Du. *smert*), painfulness; cf. G. *schmerz.*

Smerte, 1 *p. pl. pres. subj.* may smart, may suffer, G 871. Cf. Du. *smarten,* to give pain.

Smot, *pt. s.* smote, struck, B 669; Smoot, C 677. A. S. *smítan,* to smite; pt. t. *ic smát.*

Snare, *s.* snare, B 571, H 77. Icel. *snara,* a twisted cord, a snare; Swed. *snara*, a snare; cf. Icel. *snara*, to twist tightly.

Snow-whyte, *adj.* white as snow, G 254.

Socour, *s.* succour, help, B 664. O. F. *socors*, help; from Lat. *succurrere*.

Sodeyn, *adj.* sudden, B 421. O. F. *sodain*, Lat. *subitaneus*, sudden; from *subitus*, sudden, which from *subire*; from *sub*, under, and *ire*, to go.

Softe, *adj.* gentle, slow, B 399; *adv.* softly, tenderly, 275. A. S. *sóft*, G. *sanft*, soft, mild.

Softely, *adv.* gently, quietly, G 408.

Soiourned, *pp.* sojourned, dwelt, B 148, 536. O. F. *soiorner*, to dwell; from Lat. *sub*, and *diurnare*, to delay, formed from *diurnus*, daily; which from *dies*, a day.

Sol, Sol (the sun), G 826. Lat. *sol*.

Solempne, *adj.* magnificent, illustrious, B 387. O. F. '*solempne*, célèbre, de grande reputation, illustre;' Roquefort. Lat. *solennis*.

Solempnely, *adv.* with pomp, solemnly, B 317, 399, 691, G 272.

Som, *pron. indef.* one, a certain man, G 922; som shrewe is = some one (at least) is wicked, 995. A. S. *som, sum*, some.

Someres, *s. gen.* summer's, B 554. A. S. *sumer*.

Somme, *s.* sum, G 1364; *pl.* Sommes, 675. F. *somme*, Lat. *summa*.

Somtym, *adv.* sometimes, G 949.

Sond, *s.* sand, B 509. A. S. *sond*, sand.

Sonde, *s.* sending, message, B 388, 1049; dispensation of providence, visitation, 760, 826; trial, 902; message (or messenger), G 525.

A. S. *sand*, a message, sending, mission; also, a messenger; *sendan*, to send.

Sone, *adv.* soon, B 769, C 609.

Sonne, *s.* sun, G 52. A. S. *sunne*, Icel. *sunna*, G. *sonne*; all feminine.

Sooth, *adj.* true; used as *adv.* truly, C 636. A. S. *sóð*, true; cognate with Gk. *ἐτεός* (Curtius).

Sorwe, *s.* sorrow, grief, B 264, 1035. A. S. *sorg*, sorrow.

Sory, *adj.* ill, C 876; miserable, H 55. A. S. *sárig*, sore, wounded; from A. S. *sár*, a sore; not from *sorh*, sorrow.

Sote, *adj. def.* sweet, G 91, 229, 247, 251. Icel. *sætr*, Du. *zoet*, Goth. *suts*, sweet. Cf. A. S. *swéte*, sweet.

Soth, *adj.* true, B 169, 842. See Sooth.

Soth, *s.* true, B 1072, C 370; Sothe, G 662 (see note). A. S. *sóð*, truth; from *sóð*, true.

Sother, *adj. comp.* truer, G 214. See Sooth.

Sothfastnesse, *s.* truth, G 335, 1451, I 33. A. S. *sóðfæstnes*, veracity.

Sotilte, *s.* craft, skill, lit. subtlety, G 1371. From O. F. *subtiliteit*, which from Lat. acc. *subtilitatem*.

Sotted, *adj.* besotted, befooled, G 1341. O. F. *sot*, foolish; Low Lat. *sottus*; of uncertain origin.

Souereyn, *adj.* sovereign, chief, B 276, 1089; as *sb.*, master, G 590. O. F. *soverain*, Low Lat. *superanus*, one who is above; from *super*, above.

Soughte, *pt. s. subj.* should search, were to search, were to examine, C 488. A. S. *sécan*, to seek; pt. t. *ic sóhte*.

Soun, *s.* sound, B 563. F. *son*, Lat. acc. *sonum*.

Southren, *adj.* Southern, I 42. A. S. *súð*, south; *súðerne*, southern.

Sowdan, *s.* Sultan, B 177. F. *soudan*, O. F. *soldan*, Low **Lat.** *soldanus*; from Turkish *sultán*.

Sowdanesse, *s.* Sultaness, B 358, 958.

Sowed, *pp.* sewn, G 571. **A.S.** *siwian, suwan,* **to sew, stitch;** Goth. *siujan.*

Sowen, *v.* to sow, I 35. A.S. *sáwan,* to sow seed.

Sowled, *pp.* endued with a soul, G 329. A.S. *sáwul,* soul, life.

Space, *s.* opportunity, I 64. From Lat. *spatium.*

Spede, *subj. s.* may prosper, B 259; *pp.* Sped, prospered, accomplished, G 357. A.S. *spédan,* to succeed; *spéd,* success, speed.

Speedful, *adj.* advantageous, B 727.

Spekestow, speakest thou, G 473.

Spending-siluer, *s.* silver to spend, money in hand, G 1018.

Spicerye, *s.* mixture of spices, B 136, C 544. O. F. *espisce, espece,* spice; from a peculiar use of the Lat. *species,* a kind.

Spille, *v.* to perish, die, B 587, 815, 910; I *p. s. pr. subj.* may I die, 285; *pp.* Spilt, killed, 857. A. S. *spillan,* to destroy.

Spirites, *s. pl.* the (four) spirits in alchemy, G **820. See** note.

Spitte, *pr. s.* I *p.* I spit, C 421. A. S. *spittan,* Icel. *spýta;* from the same root as Lat. *spuere.*

Spoke, *pp.* spoken, G 689. A.S. *sprecan,* to speak; **at a later** period altered to *specan.* The *r* is still retained in Du. *spreken,* G. *sprechen.*

Spones, *s. pl.* spoons, C 908. A.S. *spón,* a chip of wood.

Spouted, *pp.* spouted, vomited, B 487. A Low German word; cf. Du. *spuiten,* to spout, to squirt.

Spreynd, *pp.* sprinkled, B 422. The infin. is *springen* (see Gloss. II.); from A.S. *sprengan,* **to**

make to spring, to scatter, *pp.* *sprenged;* cf. Du. *sprengen,* to sprinkle.

Squames, *s. pl.* scales, G 759. Lat. *squama,* a scale, a small layer.

Stal, *pt. s. refl.* stole away, secretly retreated, C 610. A.S. *stelan,* **to steal ; pt. t.** *ic stæl.*

Stampe, *pr. pl.* stamp, bray in **a** mortar, C 538. Icel. *stampa,* to push with the foot ; Swed. *stampa,* to pound, **beat.**

Stant, *pr. s.* standeth *(contracted form),* B 618, 651, 1055, G 173, H 1. A.S. *standan;* pr. *s. he stent.* From the same root as Lat. *stare,* Skt. *sthá,* **to stand.** See Stonde.

Starf, *pt. s.* **died,** B 283, 633. A.S. *steorfan,* **to die ;** pt. t. *ic stærf, stearf;* cf. Du. *sterven,* to die; G. *sterben.*

Stere, *s.* (1) pilot, helmsman, B 448; (2) rudder, 833. (1) A.S. *steóra,* **a** steersman, pilot ; (2) Icel. *stýri,* a helm, rudder; A.S. *steorn,* a rudder.

Sterelees, *adj.* rudderless, B 439. See above.

Sterlinges, *s. pl.* pence of sterling money, C 907. *Sterling* is a corruption of *Esterling,* an Easterling; a name given to German traders, whose money was of excellent quality.

Sterres, *s. pl.* stars, B 192. A.S. *steorra;* cf. Lat. *stella* (i. e. *sterula*), a little star; Skt. *tára* (for *stára*), a star.

Sterte, *v.* to start, pass away, B 335; *pr. pl.* start, rise quickly, C 705. Cf. Du. *storten,* to plunge, fall, rush; G. *stürzen,* to dash.

Sterue, *v.* to die, C 865 ; die of famine, 451 ; I *p. pl. pr. subj.* may die, G 420. See Starf.

Stiked, *pt. s.* stuck, B 509; *pp.* stabbed, 430; a stiked swyn = a stuck pig. C 556. A. S. *stician*, to stab, pierce.

Stikke, *s.* stick, G 1265, 1271. A.S. *sticca*.

Stillatorie, *s.* still, **vessel ùsed in** distillation, G 580. From Lat. *stilla*, a drop ; whence *stillare*, to fall in drops, distil.

Stinte, *v.* to leave off, desist, **cease** to speak, B 953; to cease, G 883 ; *pr. s. subj.* may cease, B 413 ; *imp. s.* leave off, cease, G 927. A. S. *stintan*, to be blunt.

Stire, *v.* to stir, move, C 346. A. S. *styrian*.

Stonde, *v.* to stand, B 1050; *ger.* G 203; *pr. s.* Stondeth, stands, C 645; *pt. pl.* Stode, stood, B 176; Stoden, 678; *imp. pl.* Stondeth, stand ye, G 1205. See Stant.

Stoor, *s.* store, farm-stock, C 365. From O. F. *estorer*, to furnish ; from a Lat. *staurare*, seen in comp. *instaurare*, to repair, and *restaurare*, to re-store.

Storie, *s.* story, legend, G 86. A doublet of *history*.

Storuen, *pt. pl.* died, C 888. **See** Starf.

Stounde, *s.* hour, short time, B 1021. A. S. *stund*, **a** space of time.

Stoupe, *ger.* to stoop, G 1311; *imp. pl.* Stoupeth, stoop ye, 1327. A. S. *stúpian*, Orosius, vi. 24 ; cf. Swed. *stupa*, to fall.

Straw, *interj.* a straw! G 925. A.S. *streáw*, Icel. *strá*. See Stree.

Strayte, *s.* strait, B 464. O. F. *estreit*, narrow ; Lat. *strictus*. *Strait* and *strict* are doublets.

Stree, *s.* straw, B 701. O. Friesic *stre*, *stree*, straw. See Straw.

Strenger, *adj. comp.* stronger, C 825. A. S. *strang*, strong ; comp. *strengra*.

Strogelest, *pr. s.* 2 *p.* strugglest, C

829. '*Strogolyn, strobelyn*, or *toggyn*, collector ;' Prompt. Parv.

Stronde, *s.* strand, shore, B 825. A. S. *strand*, Du. *strand*, a shore.

Style, *s.* stile, gate to climb over, C 712. A. S. *stígel*, dimin. of *stíg*, a path; from *stígan*, to climb. Du. *stijl*, a style ; *stijgen*, to climb.

Styward, *s.* steward, B 914. A. S. *stíge*, a sty, pen for cattle, **and** *weard*, a keeper; cf. Icel. *stívarðr*, from *stía*, **a** sty; but the Icel. word seems to have been borrowed from English.

Subieccioun, *s.* subjection, obedience, B 270.

Sublymed, *pp.* sublimed, sublimated, G 774. Lat. *sublimare*, to raise; from *sublimis*, exalted. '*Sublimate*, to bring by heat into the state of vapour, which, on cooling, returns again to the solid state;' Webster.

Sublyming, *s.* sublimation, G 770.

Sublymatories, *s. pl.* vessels for sublimation, G 793. See Sublymed.

Substaunce, *s.* the essential part of a thing, the thing itself, C 539. See the note. Lat. *substantia*.

Subtilte, *s.* skill, craft, G 844; Subtilitee, subtlety, craft, secret knowledge, 620. See Sotilte.

Suburbes, *s. pl.* suburbs, G 657. From Lat. *sub*, and *urbs*, a town.

Successour, *s.* successor, follower, B 421. From Lat. *succedere*.

Suffisant, *adj.* able, sufficient, B 243, C 932. F. *suffisant*, pres. pt. of *suffire*, Lat. *sufficere*.

Superfluitee, *s.* superfluity, excess, C 471, 528. Lat. *super*, beyond, *fluere*, to flow.

Surplys, *s.* surplice, G 558. F. *surplis*, Low Lat. *superpellicium*, from *super*, over, *pellicium*, a coat of fur ; from *pellis*, a skin.

Susteene, v. to sustain, uphold, preserve, B 160. Lat. *sustinere.*

Suster, s. sister, G 333. A. S. *sweostor, swustor*; cf. G. *schwester,* Lat. *soror* (for *sos-or*).

Swap, *imp. s.* strike off, **G 366.** Cf. *swoop, sweep.*

Swatte, *pt. s.* **sweated, G 560.** See **Swete.**

Sweigh, s. sway, motion, B 296. Cf. Icel. *sveigja*, **to** sway; Du. *zwaai*, a turn, **swing**; Du. *zwaaijen*, to **swing.**

Swerd, s. sword, G 168. A. S. *sweord*, **Du.** *zwaard.*

Swering, s. swearing, C 631. A. S. **swerian**, to swear.

Swete, *ger.* to sweat, G 522; **v.** 579; *pt. s.* **Swatte**, 560. A. S. *swátan*; from *swát*, sweat.

Swete, *adj.* sweet, H 42. A. S. *swéte.* See **Sote.**

Swich, *adj.* such, B 146, G 719, **1402.** A. S. *swylc*, Goth. *swaleiks*, lit. so-like.

Swink, s. labour, G 730. A. S. *swinc*, toil.

Swinke, v. to labour, G 669; *ger.* to labour, toil, C 874; *pr. pl.* gain by labour, work for, G 21. A. S. *swincan*, to toil.

Swolwe, v. to swallow, H 36. A. S. *swelgan.*

Sworen, *pt. pl.* swore, B 344; *pp.* Sworn, i. e. sworn to do it, G 681. A. S. *swerian*, **to swear**; pt. t. *ic swór.*

Swote, s. *dat.* sweat, G 578. **A. S.** *swát.*

Swowned, *pt. s.* swooned, B 1058. **Cf. A. S.** *swindan*, to languish; pt. t. *ic swand*, pp. *swunden.*

Swythe, adv. quickly, B 730, C 796; as swythe = as quickly **as** possible, B 637, G 936, 1426. A. S. *swíð*, strong, great; *swíðe*, greatly, very; Goth. *swinths*, Icel. *svinnr*, strong.

Sy, *pt. s.* saw, G **1381.** See **Seye.**

Syketh, *p. s.* sigheth, sighs, B 985; *pt. s.* Syghte, sighed, 1035. A. S. *sícan*, to sigh.

Sythe, s. *pl.* times, B 733, 1155. A. S. *síð*, a time, Icel. *sinni*, Goth. *sinth.*

Syve, s. sieve, G 940. **A. S.** *sife,* Du. *zeef, zift*, a sieve.

T.

Table, s. board; at table = at board, i. e. entertained as a lodger, G 1015. F. *table*, Lat. *tabula.*

Tabyde, *contr.* for to abide, B 797.

Tacord, *for* **to accord,** i. e. to agreement, H 98.

Take, v. to give, deliver over, present, G 223; 2 *p. s. pr.* Takestow, i. e. takest thou, 435; *imp. pl.* **Taketh**, take ye, H 41; *pp.* Take, taken, B 769, G 605. Icel. *taka*; cf. Goth. *tekan.*

Talent, s. desire, appetite, C 540. Cotgrave gives 'will, desire, appetite,' as meanings of F. *talent.* From **Lat.** *talentum.*

Talking, s. discourse, **G 684.** Of Scand. origin.

Tamenden, *ger.* **to** amend, B 462.

Tanoyen, (*for* **to** anoyen) *v.* to annoy, to injure, B 492.

Tarien, v. to tarry, B 983. O. F. *targier*, to delay; from Lat. *tardare.* See Gloss. II.

Tartre, s. tartar, G 813. F. *tartre*, Low Lat. *tartarum.* 'An acid concrete salt, deposited from wines when perfectly fermented; . . . when in the crude state, it **is** much **used as** a flux in the assaying of **ores**;' Webster.

Tassoille, *contr. for* to assoille, i. e. to absolve, C 930.

Taste, *imp. s.* feel, G 503. See the note.

Tauernor, *s.* innkeeper, C 685. From Lat. *taberna.*

Teche, *v.* to teach, G 343. A.S. *tǽcan,* to shew, point out; cf. E. *token*; Gk. δείκνυναι, to shew.

Telle, *ger.* to tell, relate, B 408. A S. *tellan,* to count, tell; G. *zählen, erzählen.*

Tempred, *pp.* tempered, G 926. To *temper* is to adjust or moderate the heat at which a thing is melted. **Lat.** *temperare.*

Temps, *s.* tense; *futur temps,* future tense, futurity, time to come, G 875. **See the note.**

Tenspyre, *for* to enspire, i. e. to inspire, G 1470.

Terme, *s.* term; *in terme,* in set terms or phrases, C 311; *pl.* Termes, set terms, pedantic expressions, G 1398; *terme of his lyue,* all his life-time, 1479.

Terve, Terued; see **Torned.**

Testes, *s. pl.* vessels for assaying metals (Tyrwhitt), G 818. A vessel called a 'testa' is figured in Theatrum Chemicum, iii. 326. See *Test* in Wedgwood or Webster.

Textuel, *adj.* literal, keeping strictly to the letter of the text, I 57. Lat. *textum, textus* (from *texere*), a weaving; also, a composition, a subject for discourse.

Teyne, *s.* a thin plate of metal, G 1225, 1229; *pl.* Teynes, 1332, 1337. Lat. *tænia,* Gk. ταινία, a band, fillet, riband, strip; from τείνειν, to stretch; Skt. *tan,* to stretch.

Than, than; *er than,* sooner than, before, G 899.

Tharray, *for* the array, B 393.

Thassemblee, *contr. from* the assemblee, the assembly, B 403.

That, *conj.* as, as well as, B 1036; *rel. pron.* = with reference to whom, G 236. That oon, the

one, B 551. A.S. *þæt,* neut. of def. art.; cf. Sanskrit *tad.*

Thee, *v.* to thrive, prosper, G 641. A.S. *þeón,* to prosper, flourish, G. *gedeihen.* See below.

Theech, *contr. from* thee ich, i. e. may I thrive, C 947, G 929. See above.

Theffect, *for* the effect, result, B 893, G 1261.

Theme, *s.* text, thesis of a sermon, C 333. Lat. *thema,* Gk. θέμα, a subject for discussion; from τίθημι, I lay down; cf. Skt. *dhá,* to place, put.

Themperour, *for* the emperour, B 248; Themperoures, the emperor's, 151.

Thende, *contr. for* the ende, the end, B 423, 965, G 1266.

Thennes, *adv.* thence, B 308, 510, 1043; *used as sb.,* the place that, G 66. From A.S. *þanon,* thence.

Thentencioun, *for* the entencioun, i. e. the intention, G 1443.

Thentent, *for* the entent, purpose, end, G 1306.

Ther, *adv.* where, B 307, 308, 576, 602, 634; when, 474; whither, at which, 469; whereas, G 724. A.S. *þær.*

Ther-aboute, *adv.* thereupon, therein, G 832.

Ther-biforn, *adv.* beforehand, before the event, B 197, C 624.

Ther-oute, *adv.* outside there, G 1136.

Therto, *adv.* there-to, moreover, B 135. *Ther* (A.S. *þǽre*) is the dat. fem. sing. of the def. article; understand a fem. sb., such as *sacu,* sake; and we have *tó þǽre sace,* in addition to that matter.

Thewes, *s. pl.* virtues, good qualities, G 101. A.S. *þeaw,* manner, quality; from *þeón,* to flourish. See Thee.

Thexcellent, *put for* the excellent, B 150.

Thider, *adv.* thither, B 144, C 749. A. S. *ðider.*

Thilke, *demon. pron.* that, B 190, 365, C 364 ; that very, that same, C 753, G 197 ; that sort of, I 50. A. S. *þylc* ; from *þý,* instrumental case of *se, seó, þæt,* and *l1c,* like ; cf. Lat. *talis.*

Thing, *s. pl.* possessions, G 540. A. S. *þing,* a thing, neut. sb.; pl. *þing* (unchanged).

Thingot, *for* the ingot, G 1233, 1314. See **Ingottes.**

Thinketh, *impers.; me thinketh,* it seems to me, G 308. A. S. *me þyncð,* it seems to me ; G. *mir dünkt* ; slightly different from *þencan,* to think, G. *denken.*

Thinne, *adj. pl.* thin, poor, scanty, limited, G 741. A. S. *þyn,* thin ; *þenian,* to stretch ; cf. Skt. *tan,* to stretch.

Tho, *adv.* then, G 205, 424, 487, 692. A. S. *þá,* then.

Thonketh, *imp. 2 p. pl.* thank ye, B 1113. A.S. *þancian,* Icel. *þakka,* G. *danken.*

Thoughte, *pt. s. impers.* it seemed, B 146 ; Thoughte hem, it seemed to them, C 475. See **Thinketh.**

Thral, *s.* servant, G 196. A. S. *þræl,* Icel. *þræll.*

Thraldom, *s.* bondage, slavery, B 286, 338. See above.

Threpe, I *p. pl. pres.* we call, assert to be, G 826. 'Threap, v.n. to maintain or insist pertinaciously ; to repeat or reiterate obstinately. A. S. *þreápian,* to afflict, chide ;' Atkinson's Cleveland Glossary.

Threting, *s.* threatening, menace, G 698. A.S. *þreátung,* an urging, correction.

Thridde, *adj. ord.* third, C 836, G 823, 925. A. S. *þridda,* third ; from *þreó,* three.

Thrift, *s.* success, prosperity in

moneymaking, G 739, 1425. Icel. *þrift,* profit.

Thrifty, *adj.* cheap, profitable to the buyer, B 138. See above.

Thropes, *s. gen.* village's, I 12. A.S. *þorp,* Icel. *þorp,* G. *dorf,* Goth. *thaurp* ; cognate with Lat. *turba,* a crowd.

Throwe, *s.* a short space of time, B 953 ; time, G 941. A.S. *þráh, þrág,* a short space of time, period.

Thryue, *ger.* to thrive, prosper, G 1411. Icel. *þrífa-sk,* to thrive, where the final *sk.* is reflexive, meaning 'self.' See **Thrift.**

Thurgh, *prep.* through, by, G 325. A.S. *þurh,* G. *durch.*

Thurgh-out, *prep.* throughout, all through, B 256, 464 ; quite through, C 655.

Til, *prep.* to, G 306. Icel. *til,* to.

Tin, *s.* tin, G 829. A.S. *tin,* prob. a shortened form of an Old British word ; cf. Irish *stan,* Gael. *staoin,* Welsh *ystaen* ; whence Lat. *stannum.*

Tirannye, *s.* tyranny, cruelty, B 165. From Lat. *tyrannus,* Gk. *τύραννος,* a tyrant.

To, *prep.* to (used after its case), G 1449. A. S. *tó.*

To, *adv.* too, G 644 ; overmuch, G 1423; To dere, too dearly, C 293 ; To and fro, all ways, H 53.

To-bete, *v.* to beat severely, G 405. See the note. A.S. *tó-,* prefix, = G. *zer-,* Goth. and Lat. *dis-,* meaning, in twain, apart ; and *beátan,* to beat ; whence A. S. *tó-beátan,* to beat to pieces.

Tobreketh, *pr. s.* breaks in twain, breaks asunder, G 907. A. S. *tó-brecan,* to break in pieces, or in twain. See above.

Togidres, *adv.* together, C 702, G 960. A. S. *tógædre.*

Tohewe, *pp.* hewn in twain. hewn in pieces, B 430, 437. A. S. *tó-heawan*, to hew·in twain. See Tobete.

Tokening, *s.* token, proof, G 1153. A. S. *tácen*, a token. See Teche.

Tombesteres, *s. pl. fem.* dancing girls, lit. female tumblers, C 477. A. S. *tumbian*, to tumble, dance; *tumbere*, a tumbler; *tumbestre*, a dancing girl. See the note.

Tonge, *s.* tongue, B 899, C 398. A. S. *tunge*, G. *zunge*, Lat. *lingua* (for *dingua*). Hence *tonge* is a dissyllabic word.

Took, *pt. s.* took, had, B 192; gave, handed over, G 1030, 1034, 1365, H 91. See Take.

To-rente, *pt. pl.* rent asunder, C 709. A. S. *tó-*, in twain, and *rendan*, to rend; the comp. *to-renda* occurs in O. Friesic.

Torment, *s.* torment, suffering, B 845. From Lat. *tormentum.*

Tormentour, *s.* tormentor, i. e. executioner, B 818, G 527, 532; *pl.* Tormentoures, 373; Tormentours, 376. See above.

Torn, *s.* turn, C 815. See below.

Torne, *v.* to turn, G 1403.

Torned (so in most MSS.); Terued (E.), *pp.* flayed, G 1171; Terve (E.), *imp. s.* 3 *p.* flay, G 1274. Low G. *tarven.*

Tortuous, *adj.* oblique, a technical term in astrology, used of the six of the zodiacal signs which ascend most obliquely, B 302. Lat. *tortuosus*, twisted; from *torquere*, to twist.

To-swinke, *pr. pl.* labour greatly, C 519. Prefix *tó-*, in twain (intensive), and *swincan*, to toil.

To-tere, *pr. pl.* rend, tear in pieces, C 474; *pp.* To-tore, torn in pieces. A. S. *tó-teran*, to tear in twain. See To-bete.

Traitorye, *s.* treachery, B 781.

From O. F. *traitor*, a traitor; Lat. acc. *traditorem*, from *tradere*, to hand over.

Trappe, *s.* trap, G 11. A. S. *trappe*, a trap; hence *trappe* is dissyllabic.

Tresor, *s.* treasure, B 442, C 779. O. F. *tresor*, Lat. *thesaurus*, Gk. θησαυρός; from τίθημι, I lay up in store.

Trete, *pr. pl.* discourse, treat, C 630. F. *traiter*, Lat. *tractare*, to handle.

Tretee, *s.* treaty, C 619. F. *traité*, Lat. *tractatus.* See above.

Tretys, *s.* treaty, B 233. Another form of the above.

Trewe, *adj. pl.* true, B 135; used as *sb.*=the faithful, 456. A. S. *treówe*, Icel. *trúr*, G. *treu.*

Trowthe, *s.* troth, truth, B 527. A. S. *treówð.*

Treye, *num.* 'tray,' three, C 653. O. F. *trei, treis*, Lat. *tres.*

Triacle, *s.* a sovereign remedy, B 479, C 314. O. F. *triacle*, Low Lat. *theriacum*, Gk. θηριακόν, a remedy against the wounds made by wild beasts; from θήρ, a wild beast.

Triste, *pr. s.* 1 *p.* I trust, B 832. Icel. *treysta*, to trust.

Troden, *pp.* stepped, C 712. A. S. *tredan*, to tread.

Trompe, *s.* trumpet, B 705. F. *trompe*, a trumpet; from Icel. *trumba*, a pipe, a trumpet.

Trone, *s.* throne (of God), heaven, C 842. F. *trône*, O. F. *trone*, Lat. *thronus*, Gk. θρόνος, a seat, chair.

Trouthe, *s.* truth, G 238. A. S. *treówð.*

Trowe, *ger.* to trust, believe, G 378; 1 *p. s. pr.* I suppose, believe, imagine, B 288, 400, 1074, C 689, G 667, H 44; *pr. pl.* Trowe, suppose, believe, B 222; 2 *p.* ye believe, G 171; suppose,

Imagine ye, C 439. A.S. *treów-ian*, Icel. *trúa*, to believe, think to be *true*.

Trusteth, *imp. pl. 2 p.* trust ye, believe ye, B 1048, G 229, 889, I 42. Icel. *traust*, sb. trust, *treysta-sk*, to trust in.

Tryne compas, the threefold world, containing earth, sea, and heaven, G 45. Lat. *trinus*, three-fold, from *tres*, three.

Twenty deuel weye, a, in the manner of twenty devils, in all sorts of evil ways, G 782.

Tweye, *num. adj.* two, twain, C 817, 824, 828, G 677. A.S. *twegen*, twain, used in masc. and neuter; *twá*, two, in the feminine.

Tweyfold, *adj.* twofold, double, G 566.

Twinne, *v.* to separate, B 517; *ger.* to depart (from), C 430; 2 *p. pr. pl.* ye depart, lit. ye part company, G 182. From the root *two*, A.S. *twá*; cf. E. *be-tween*.

Twyes, *adv.* twice, B 1058. A.S. *twywa*, *tuwa*; but the M.E. *twyes* is formed from A.S. *twý*, double, with adverbial suffix -*es*.

Tyde, *s.* a certain portion of time, an hour, B 510, 798; see note to B 798; time of day, 1134. A.S. *tíd*, Icel. *tíð*, G. *zeit*, a time.

Tyden, *v.* to befal, B 337. A.S. *tídan*, to happen; from *tíd*, time.

Tyding, *s.* tidings, news, B 726. Icel. *tíðindi*, news, tidings; from *tíð*, time.

Tyme, *s.* time, G 1204. The word is dissyllabic, riming with *by me*; see the note. A.S. *tíma*, Icel. *tími*.

V (*for* U *and* V).

Valerian, *s.* valerian, G 800. Lat. *ualeriana*.

Variaunt, *adj.* varying, changing, changeable, fickle, G 1175. From Lat. *uariare*, to vary, *uarius*, different.

Venim, *s.* venom, poison, B 891, C 421. O.F. *venim*, Lat. *uene-num*.

Venquisshed, *pp.* vanquished, B 291. From O.F. *venquis*, pp. of *vencre*, to conquer. Lat. *uin-cere*.

Verdegrees, *s.* verdigris, G 791. Derived (see the note) from O.F. *vert de Grece*, green of Greece.

Vermin, *s.* vermin, C 858. From Lat. *uermis*.

Verray, *adj.* very, true, B 167, C 576, G 165. O.F. *verai* (F. *vrai*), Lat. acc. *ueracem*; from Lat. *uerus*, true.

Veyn, *adj.* vain, empty, power-less, silly, G 497. F. *vain*, Lat. *uanus*.

Viage, *s.* voyage, B 259, 300, 312. O.F. *veiage*, from Lat. *uiaticum*, lit. provisions for a journey, then a journey, in Fortu-natus (Brachet).

Vicary, *s.* a vicar, I 22. From Lat. *uicarius*, a deputy; from Lat. *uicis*, change.

Vilanye, *s.* discourtesy, C 740; licentiousness, G 231. O.F. *vilanie*, from *vilain*, a farm-labourer; from Lat. *uilla*, a farm.

Violes, *s. pl.* vials, phials, G 793. F. *phiale*, Lat. *phiala*, a sort of saucer, Gk. φιάλη. Cotgrave has—'*Phiole*, f. a violl, or small glass bottle.'

Virago, *s.* virago, cruel woman, B 359. Direct from Lat. *uirago*.

Vitaille, *s.* victuals, B 443, 499. O.F. *vitaille*, Lat. *uictualia*, victuals; from *uiuere*, to live.

Vitailled, *pp.* victualled, provisioned, B 869. See above.

Vitriole, *s.* vitriol, G 808. F.

vitriol, Lat. *vitriolum*; from *vi-trum*, glass. Cotgrave has—'*Vitriol*, m. vitrioll, copperose.'

Vnbokel, *imp. s.* unbuckle, undo, C 945, I 26. The prefix *un-* is here not the common negative prefix, but cognate with G. *ent-*; cf. *entbinden*, to unbind. *Bokel* is O. F. *bocle* (F. *boucle*), Lat. *bucula*, boss of a shield.

Vndernom, *pt. s.* perceived, G 243. A.S. *underniman*, to perceive, pt. t. *undernam*; cf. G. *unternehmen*. From A. S. *niman*, to take.

Vnderpyghte, *pt. s.* stuffed, filled underneath, B 789. *Pyghte* is *pitched*, pt. t. of M. E. *picche*, to pitch, place, set.

Vnderstondeth, *pr. pl.* understand, C 646; *imp. pl.* understand, know, G 1165; *pp.* Vnderstonde, understood, B 520. From A. S. *standan*, to stand.

Vnfeyned, *pp.* unfeigned, true, G 434. From Lat. *fingere*.

Vnkyndenesse, *s.* unkindness, B 1057. From A. S. *cynd*, nature. *Unkindness* is *unnaturalness*, what is contrary to natural feeling.

Vnnethe, *adv.* hardly, scarcely, B 1050, G 563; Vnnethes (with adverbial suffix *-es*), G 1390. A.S. *un-*, not, *eððe*, easily; from *eð*, **easy.**

Vnsely, *adj.* unhappy, G 468. See Sely.

Vnslekked, *adj.* unslacked, G 806. To *slack* is to deprive lime of cohesion by combining it with water. A.S. *slacian*, to slacken, relax; *sleac*, slack.

Vnthriftily, *adv.* poorly, G 893. See Thrift.

Vntrewthe, *s.* untruth, B 687.

Vnwar, *adj.* unexpected, B 427. A.S. *wær*, wary, cautious; cf. Lat. *uereor*, I fear.

Vnweldy, *adj.* unwieldy, difficult

to move, H 55. A.S. *wealdan*, to control.

Vnwemmed, *pp.* unspotted, G 137, 225. A. S. *wem*, Icel. *vamm*, Goth. *wamm*, spot, blemish.

Vnwit, *s.* want of wit, G 1085. A. S. *gewitt*, knowledge.

Vnwiting, *pr. part.* unknowing, G 1320. A.S. *witan*, to know, G. *wissen*.

Vouche-sauf, *v.* to vouchsafe, grant, B 1083; 2 *p. pr. pl.* ye vouchsafe, G 1246, I 52. Here *vouche* is the verb, and *sauf* the adjective; it means to 'call (it) safe.'

Voydeth, *imp. pl.* send away, G 1136. O. F. *voide* (F. *vide*), void; from Lat. *uiduus.*

Voys, *s.* voice, rumour, B 155, C 531. O. F. *vois* (F. *voix*), Lat. acc. *uocem*, a voice; cf. Skt. *vach*, to speak.

Vp, *prep.* on, upon, B 795, 884. A. S. *up.*

Vp so doun, upside down, G 625. See the note.

Vp-caste, *pt. s.* cast up, B 906. Icel. *kasta*, to throw.

Vpryght, *adv.* upright, C 674.

Vsage, *s.* usage, custom, C 899. F. *usage*; from Lat. *uti*, to use.

Vse, *pr. pl.* 2 *p.* ye use, G 1409. *pp.* Vsed, accustomed, 666. F, *user*; Lat. *uti*, to use.

Utter, *adj.* outer, outward, G 498. A.S. *út*, out; *úttera*, *útera*, outer.

W.

Wafereres, *s. pl.* makers of *gaufres* or wafer-cakes, confectioners, C 479. From an O. F. form *waufre*, commonly spelt *gaufre*; which from O. Low G. Cf. Du. *wafel*, a wafer.

Walke, *pr. s. subj.* 2 *p.* thou

mayest walk, B 784. A.S. *wealc-an*, to roll; also, to walk.

Wan, *adj.* wan, pale, G 728. A.S. *wann*, wan; sometimes, dark, dusky.

Wan, *pt. s.* won, G 33. **A.S.** *winnan*, pt. t. *ic wann*, pp. *wun-nen*.

War, *adj.* aware, G 13, 1079; be war = beware, **take** heed, take warning, 737. **A.S.** *wær*, wary, cautious.

Ware, *pres. s. subj.* (or *imp.*), may (he) warn, cause you to be ware, C 905. **Cf. A.S.** *warian*, to guard; *wær*, **wary.** See Ch. Prol. 662; and cf. Gloss. I.

Ware, *s.* merchandise, B 140. A.S. *ware*, merchandise.

Warente, *v.* to warrant, protect, C 338. O.F. *warantir*, to guard, warrant; from O.H.G. *werjan*, *warjan*, to protect.

Warice, *v.* to heal, cure, C 906. Formed from **O.F.** *warir, garir* (**F.** *guérir*), to preserve; from O.H.G. *warjan*, to protect.

Warye, 1 *p. s. pr.* I curse, B 372. A.S. *wergian*, to curse; *werg*, accursed; *wearh*, an accursed wretch.

Wasshe, *pp.* washed, C 353. A.S. *wæscan, wascan*; pt. t. *wosc*, pp. *wæscen*. See **Wesh**.

Wast, *s.* waste, B 593. A.S. *wéste*, waste, deserted; *wésten*, a wilderness.

Wawe, *s.* a wave, B 508; *pl.* **Wawes**, 468. A.S. *wǽg*, a wave.

Wayke, *adj.* weak, B 932. A.S. *wác*, weak; Icel. *vákr, veikr*.

Wayte, *v.* to expect, B 467; Wayten, 264; *pr. s.* **Wayteth**, watches, 593. O.F. *waiter, guaiter*; from O.H.G. *wahtan*, to watch. Cf. F. *guetter*.

We, *pron.* apparently used as acc. = us, G 315. But see the note.

Weep, *pt. s.* wept, B 606, 1052, G 371. A.S. *wépan*, to weep; pt. t. *weóp*. See **Wepen**.

Weex, *pt. s.* waxed, grew, G 513. See **Wex**.

Wel, *adv.* well, i. e. well placed, happily or luckily situated, B 308. A.S. *wel*.

Wele, *s.* prosperity, B 175. **A.S.** *wela*, weal.

Welful, *adj.* full of weal, blessed, B 451. See above.

Welked, *pp.* withered, C 738. A.S. *wealwian*, to roll up, dry, wither, shrivel. Cf. G. *welken*, to wither. [The form is English; *not borrowed* from German.]

Welle, *s.* well, source, B 323. **A.S.** *wælla*, Icel. *vella*, a well; the more usual form is A.S. *well*.

Wemmelees, *adj.* stainless, G 47. A.S. *wem*, Icel. *vamm*, Goth. *wamm*, a spot, blemish.

Wende, *ger.* to go, to wend, B 142, 253, 265: *pr. pl.* **Wende**, go, 1157; 2 *p.* ye wend, travel, C 927; **Wente** him, *pt. s.* turned himself, i. e. went his way, G 1110; *pp.* Went, gone; *ben went*, are gone, B 173; *is went*, is gone, G 534 (see note). A.S. *wendan*, G. *wenden*, to turn.

Wenen, *v.* to ween, suppose, G 675; Wene, 1088; *pr. s.* **Weneth**, imagines, C 569; *pr. pl.* Wenen, suppose, 349; *pt. s. subj.* Wende, would have thought, C 782. A.S. *wénan*, Icel. *væna*, Goth. *wenjan*, G. *wähnen*, to imagine; from A.S. *wén*, Icel. *van*, Goth. *wens*, G. *wahn*, expectation, hope.

Wepen, *pr. pl.* weep, B 820; *pt. s.* Wepte, wept, 267; Weep, 606, 1052, G 371. See **Weep**.

Werche, *v.* to work, do, make, perform, B 566, G 14, 1155, 1477. A.S. *weorcan*, to work. See **Werkes**.

Were, *pt. s. subj.* should be, might

be, G 581 ; Were it, **whether it
were**, i.e. either, B 143 ; **Were,
2 p. s. pres. indic.** wast, B 366 ;
pt. pl. Weren, were, G 1340.
N.B. The A.S. *wére* is the 2 p.
pr. indic. as well as subj. ; **the
forms** *wast, wert,* are later ; hence
Chaucer's use of *were* in B 366 **is
quite** correct, and it need not **be
taken as** an instance of the subjunctive mood. From A.S. *wesan,*
to be ; cf. Skt. *vas,* to dwell.

Wered, *pt. s.* wore, G 558. A.S.
werian, to wear ; pt. t. *werode.*
Originally a *weak* verb. Cf. Icel.
verja, Goth. *wasjan,* to put on
clothing ; Lat. *uestis,* clothing.

Werieth, *pr. s.* wearies, G 1304.
A.S. *wérian,* to weary.

Werkes, *s. pl.* works, B 478. G
64. A.S. *weorc,* Icel. *verk,* Gk.
ἔργον.

Werking, *s.* work, mode of operation, G 1367 ; Werkinge, action,
116.

Wesh, *pt. s.* washed, B 453. See
Wasshe.

Wete, *s.* wet, perspiration, G 1187.
A.S. *wǽta,* wetness, moisture.

Wex, *s.* wax, G 1164, 1268. **A.S.**
wex, weax, wæx.

Wexe, *v.* to wax, become, G 837 ;
Wexen, 877 ; *pr. pl.* Wexen, become, 1095 ; I *p.* we become,
869 ; I *p. s. pr. subj.* Wexe, may
I become, 1374 ; *pt. s.* Wex, became, B 563, 568. A.S. *weaxan,*
Icel. *vaxa,* Goth. *wahsjan,* G.
wachsen, to grow.

Weye, *s.* way, B 385, G 1374 ;
manner, wise, B 590, G 676.
A.S. *weg,* way, road.

Weyed, *pt. s.* weighed, G 1298.
A.S. *wegan,* to weigh, Icel. *vega,*
Lat. *uehere.*

Weylawey, *interj.* well away! alas!
B 370, 632, 810. A.S. *wá la
wá,* lit. woe! lo! woe!

Weyue, *v.* to forsake, G 276 ; *pr.*

pl. Weyuen, waive, set aside, I
33 ; *pp.* Weyued, removed, swung
aside, B 308. O.F. *weiver,
guesver,* **guever,** to waive.
'*Guesver,* to waive, refuse, abandon, give over, also, to surrender,
give back, resign, redeliver ;' Cotgrave.

What, why, B **232, 374, 703,** G
754. A.S. *hwæt.*

What so, whatsoever, G 711, 965.

Whelpes, *s. pl.* dogs, G 60. A.S.
hwelp.

Whennes, *adv.* whence, C 335, G
247 ; of whennes = from whence,
G 432, 433. A.S. *hwanon.*

Wher, **adv.** wherever, C 748, G
727 ; **Wher-as**, where that, where,
B 647, 1131, C 466, H 49.

Wher-on ; *long wher-on,* i.e. along
of what, because of what, G 930.

Wher-so, **adv.** whether, B 294.

Whete, *s.* wheat, I 36. A.S.
hwǽte, wheat.

Which, *pron.* what sort of, G 731 ;
pl. Whiche, which, B 553. A.S.
hwylc, Goth. *hwa-leiks,* (i.e. who-
like), Lat. *qualis.*

Whider, *adv.* whither, G 303.
A.S. *hwider.*

Why, *adv.* for what reason? why?
I 35. A.S. *hwi,* instrumental case
of *hwá,* who.

Whyle, *s.* time, B 370, 546 ; *s. pl.*
Whyles, times ; in the mene whyles
= during the mean while, 668.
A.S. *hwil,* Goth. *hweila,* a time.

Whyl-er, *adv.* formerly, G 1328.
A.S. *hwil,* **a time** ; and *ǽr,* formerly.

Whylom, *adv.* formerly, B 134, C
463. A.S. *hwilum,* dat. pl. of
hwil, a time.

Whyls, *adv.* while, G 1137. A.S.
hwiles, gen. sing. of *hwil,* a time.

Whyte, *adj.* white ; *used as sb.*
white wine, C 526, 562. A.S.
hwit, white ; Icel. *hvitr,* Goth.
hweits, G. *weiss.*

Whytnesse, *s.* whiteness, G 89.

Widwe, *s.* widow, C 450. A.S. *widwe, wuduwe.*

Wight, *s.* wight, man, B **656**. See Wyght.

Wike, *s.* week, C 362. A.S. *wice, wuce, wucu,* a week; Icel. *vika,* a week.

Wikke, *adj.* wicked, G 524. Cf. A.S. *wicca,* a wizard, *wicce,* a witch.

Wilfully, *adv.* willingly, of free will, by choice, C **441**. ' *Wylfulle,* voluntarius, spontaneus;' Prompt. Parv.

Winne, *ger.* to get gain, C 461. A.S. *winnan.*

Wisly, *adv.* certainly, B 1061. Cf. Icel. *viss,* sure; Du. *gewis,* G. *gewiss,* certain; from the root of *witan,* to know.

Wite, *v.* to know, wit, G 621, 1333; *pr.pl.* 2 *p.* know ye, H 1, 82; *pt.s. subj.* should know, knew, C 370; (if he) knew, C 513; *pp.* Wist, known, B 1072, G 282. A.S. *witan,* Icel. *vita,* G. *wissen,* Skt. *vid,* to know. See Wost.

With, *prep.* by, B 475, G 1437.

Withholde, *pp.* detained, G 345. A.S. *wið,* against, and *healdan,* to hold.

Withseye, *v.* to renounce, G 447, 457. A.S. *wið,* against, and *secgan,* to say.

Witnes, *imp. s.* let (it) bear witness, G 277. A.S. *witnes,* knowledge.

Wittes, *s.pl.* understandings, senses, B 202. A.S. *wit, gewit,* mind, understanding.

Wo, *adj.* sad, B 757. A.S. *wá,* woe, sb.; but sometimes used as an adjective.

Wol, *pr. s.* permits, H 28; *wol adoun,* is about to set, I 72: *pr. pl.* Wole, will, B 468; Wol, G 84; Woltow, wilt thou, G 307, 464; *pt. s.* Wolde, wished, B

698; *pt.pl.* would, B 144. A.S. *willan,* to will, wish; pres. t. *ic wile,* pt. t. *ic wolde.*

Wolle, *s.* wool, C 448, 910. A.S. *wull,* wool, Icel. *ull;* but also dissyllabic, as shewn by Goth. *wulla,* wool, G. *wolle.*

Wombe, *s.* the belly, C 522, 533. A.S. *wamb,* Goth. *wamba.*

Wommanhede, *s.* womanhood, B 851, G 1346.

Wonder, *s. as adj.* wondrous, wonderful, B 1045, C 891, G 308. A.S. *wunder.*

Wonder. *s. as adv.* wondrously, G 751; greatly, 1035; very, H 94.

Wone, *ger.* to dwell, inhabit, G 38; *v.* 332; *pr. s.* Woneth, dwelleth, 311. A.S. *wunian,* to dwell; G. *wohnen.*

Wood, *adj.* mad, C 287, G 450, 576, 869, 1377. A.S. *wód,* Goth. *wods,* Icel. *óðr,* mad.

Woodeth, *pr. s.* plays the madman, acts madly, G 467. A.S. *wódian, wédan,* to rage, G. *wüthen.*

Woodnesse, *s.* madness, C 496. A.S. *wódnes.*

Wook, *pt. s.* was awake, B 497; awoke, 8c6. A.S. *wacan,* pt. t. *ic wóc,* pp. *wacen.*

Wordes, *s. pl.* words; *hadde the wordes,* was spokesman (see note), I 67. A.S. *word.*

Worm, *s.* snake (lit. worm), C 355. A.S. *wyrma, wurm,* Icel. *ormr,* G. *wurm,* Lat. *uermis.*

Wort, *s.* unfermented beer, wort, G 813. Somner's A.S. Dict. has *wert,* unfermented beer.

Wost, 2 *p. s. pr.* knowest, C 824, G 653. A.S. *witan,* to know, has strong pt. t. used as present, viz. *ic wát, þu wást, he wát,* I wot, thou wost (wottest), he wot (*not* wots). See Wite.

Wostow, *for* wost thou, i. e. knowest thou, G 265, 444, 469. See above.

Wot, *pr. s.* knows, B 195, 436, 439, 962, G 723. See Wost.

Woxen, *pp.* grown, waxed, G 379, 381. See Wex.

Woweth, *pr. s.* wooes, B 589. A. S. *wógan,* to woo ; prob. orig. to bend ; cf. A. S. *wóg, wóh,* bent.

Wrak, *s.* wreck, B 513. O. Fries. *wrak,* injured ; Du. *wrak,* broken, also a wreck ; Icel. *reki,* a thing drifted ashore.

Wraw, *adj.* savage, fierce, angry, H 46. Apparently merely a corruption of *wroth* (A. S. *wráð*), i. e. wrathful; cf. Icel. *reiðr,* Dan. and Sw. *vred,* wrathful, angry. See other examples of *wraw* in Stratmann.

Wrecchednesse, *s.* a miserable matter, folly, I 34. From A. S. *wræc,* wretched.

Wreche, *s.* vengeance, B 679. A. S. *wracu,* vengeance.

Wreke, *v.* to avenge, C 857. A. S. *wrecan,* to avenge, punish.

Wrenches, *s. pl.* frauds, stratagems, tricks, G 1081. A. S. *wrence,* deceit, stratagem.

Writen, *pp.* written, B 195. See Wroot.

Wrong, *pt. s.* wrung, B 606. A. S. *wringan,* to wring, strain.

Wroot, *pt. s.* wrote, B 725, 890, G 83. A. S. *writan,* to write ; pt. t. *wrát,* pp. *writen* ; Icel. *ríta,* to write.

Wroth, *adj.* wroth, angry, H 46. A. S. *wráð,* angry ; *wráð,* wrath, anger ; Icel. *reiðr,* angry, *reiði,* anger.

Wrought, *pp.* made, G 326. A. S. *weorcan,* to work ; pt. t. *ic worhte,* I worked, I wrought.

Wyde-wher, *adv.* widely, everywhere, B 136.

Wyf, *s.* mistress of a household, G 1015. A. S. *wíf,* G. *weib,* a woman.

Wyght, *s.* wight, man, B 139, 203, G 215, 404. H 26. A. S. *wiht, wuht,* Goth. *waiht,* G. *wicht* ; Eng. *wight* and *whit.*

Wyghte, *s.* weight, G 73. A. S. *wiht,* weight.

Wyn ape, lit. ape-wine, H 44. See the note.

Wynde, *v.* to wind about, twist and turn, G 980. A. S. *windan,* Icel. *vinda,* G. *winden.*

Wyse, *s. (dat.)* wise, manner, way, B 153. A. S. *wise,* a way ; G. *weise* ; F. *guise* is from O. H. G. ; *wise* and *guise* are doublets.

Wyse, *adj. pl.* as *sb.* wise men, G 1067. A. S. *wís,* wise ; from *witan,* to know.

Wyte, *s.* blame, G 953. A. S. *wíte,* a punishment, fine, blame; cf. *wítan,* to punish; Icel. *víta,* to fine, mulct.

Wyues, *s. pl.* wives, women, B 273, C 910. See Wyf.

Y.

Yaf, *pt. s.* gave, B 939, 975, C 460, 887, G 223 ; *pt. pl.* Yaueu, gave, G 415. See Yeue.

Yblessed, *pp.* blessed, H 99. A. S. *blédsian,* to consecrate ; from *blód,* blood. The prefix *y-* answers to A. S. prefix *ge-*.

Yboren, *pp.* born, C 704. A. S. *beran,* to bear; pp. *boren, geboren.*

Ybounde, *pp.* bound, G 347. A. S. *bindan,* to bind ; pp. *bunden, gebunden.*

Ybrend, *pp.* burnt, G 318. A. S. *bærnan,* pp. *bærned.* See Brenne.

Ycaried, *pp.* carried, C 791. O. F. *carier,* to carry ; *char,* a car.

Ycast, *pp.* cast, thrown, G 939. See Caste.

Yclad, *pp.* clothed, G 133. A. S. *gecladed,* clothed.

Ycleped, *pp.* called, H 2, G 129; Yclept, G 772. See Clepe.

Ycome, *pp.* come, B 755. A. S. *cuman,* to come; pp. *cumen, gecumen.*

Ycoruen, *pp.* cut, G 533. A. S. *ceorfan,* to cut; pp. *corfen, gecorfen.*

Ycouered, *pp.* covered, G 764. From O. F. *covrir,* to cover; from Lat. *co-operire.*

Ycoyned, *pp.* coined, C 770. F. *coin,* Lat. *cuneus,* a wedge; hence, a coin.

Ycrammed, *pp.* crammed, C 348. A. S. *crammian,* to cram; pp. *gecrammed;* cf. Du. *krammen,* to fasten with cramps or clamps.

Ycristned, *pp.* baptized, B 240. A. S. *cristnian,* to baptize.

Ydelly, *adv.* idly, C 446. A. S. *ídel,* idle, vain; *ídellíce,* vainly.

Ydo, *pp.* done, i.e. finished, done with, G 739, 850, 866, 899; Ydoon, fought, lit. accomplished, 386. A. S. *gedón,* pp. of *dón,* to do.

Ydoles, *s. pl.* idols, G 269, 285, 298. From Gk. εἴδωλον, an idol.

Ydrawe, *pp.* drawn, taken, G 1440. A. S. *dragan,* to drag, draw; pp. *gedragen.*

Ye, *adv.* yea, verily, B 417, G 471, 599, **1061**; *ye or nay,* yea or **nay,** 212. A. S. *ge, geá,* G. *ja.*

Yë, *s. (pronounced as long e in* meet, *followed by* e *obscure),* eye, B 280; at yë=at eye, to sight, evidently, G 964, 1059; *pl.* Yën, eyes, B 552, 661, G 190, 498, **504,** 1418. A. S. *eáge,* pl. *eágan;* cf. E. *eyne.*

Yede, *pt. s.* went, G 1141, 1281. A. S. *eóde,* Goth. *iddja,* I went; from the root *i,* to go; cf. Skt. *i,* to go; Lat. *ire,* to go.

Yeer, *s. pl.* years, B 499, G 720,

978; Yeres, H 463. A. S. *geár,* Icel. *ár,* Goth. *jer,* G. *jahr;* the A. S. pl. is also *geár.*

Yeman, *s.* yeoman, servant, G 562, 587. Cf. O. Fries. *gaman,* a villager; from *ga,* a village; cf. Goth. *gawi,* G. *gau,* a district. Note esp. *gäuman,* a peasant, pl. *gäuleute,* in Schmeller's Bavarian Dict., col. 855.

Yerne, *adv.* briskly, glibly, C 398. A. S. *georn,* eager; **georne,** eagerly.

Yet, *adv.* moreover, **G 622.** A. S. *git,* yet, still.

Yeue, *v.* to give, G 390, I 64; *ger.* to give, for giving, C 402, G 990; *imp. s.* give, G 1193; 3 *p.* may (He) give, B 284, 602, H 15; *pp.* Yeuen, given, B 333, 444, C 449, 779, 922, G 470, 480. A. S. *gifan,* pt. t. *gæf, geaf,* pp. *gifen;* Icel. *gefa,* Goth. *gifan,* G. *geben,* to give.

Yeuing, *s.* giving; *wyn-yeuing,* wine-giving, the giving of wine, C 587.

Yfallen, *pp.* fallen, turned out, happened, C 938, G 61, 1043; having **come** upon, having befallen, C **496.** A. S. *feallan,* to fall; pp. *gefeallen.*

Yfere, *adv.* together, B 394, G 380. Cf. A. S. *geféra,* a travelling companion; from A. S. *faran,* to go. *From fér*

Yfet, *pp.* fetched, G 1116. A. S. *fetian,* pp. *gefetod.*

Yfounde, *pp.* found, 1152. A. S. *findan,* to find; pp. *funden, gefunden.*

Yglosed, *pp.* flattered, H 34. Formed from F. sb. *glose,* a gloss, comment; from Lat. *glossa,* Gk. γλῶσσα, the tongue, &c.

Ygo, *pp.* gone, B 599; Ygon, G 183. A. S. *gán,* to go; pp. *gegán.*

Ygraunted, *pp.* granted, C 388.

Yhent, *pp.* seized, caught, C 868, G 536. A. S. *hentan*, to sieze.

Yhid, *pp.* hid, G 317. A. S. *hýdan*, to hide; pp. *gehýded*.

Yholde, *pp.* held, considered, C 602. A. S. *healdan*, to hold, pp. *gehealden*.

Yif, *imp. s.* give, grant, B 462, 562, G 65. See Yiue.

Yifte, *s.* gift, G 275; *pl.* Yiftes, C 295. A. S. *gift*.

Yit, *adv.* yet, still, B 634. A. S. *git*.

Yknowe, *pp.* known, B 314. A. S. *cnáwan*, to know; pp. *gecnáwen*.

Ylent, *pp.* lent, G 1406. A. S. *lǽnan*, to lend, give; pp. *gelǽned*.

Yliche, **adv.** alike, equally, G 1202. A. S. *gelíce*, adv.; cf. G. *gleich*. See Ylyke.

Ylost, *pp.* lost, G 722. A. S. *leósan*, to lose; pp. *loren*, lorn. Here used as a *weak* verb.

Ylyke, *adv.* alike, equally, G 850. See Yliche. •

Ymaad, *pp.* made, caused, B 693, G 868, 1149; Ymaked, made, C 545. A. S. *macian*, to make; pp. *macod*, *gemacod*.

Ymette, *pp.* met, B 1115. A. S. *métan*, to meet; pp. *gemét*.

Ynow, *adj.* enough, sufficient, G 1018; *pl.* Ynow, B 255. A. S. *genōg*, sufficient, Goth. *ganohs*.

Ynow, *adv.* enough, G 864, 945.

Yore, *adv.* of old, formerly, B 174, 272. A. S. *geára*, formerly; from *geár*, a year.

Youres, *pron. poss.* yours, C 672,

Cf. A. S. *pycan*, to pick, pull (Lye).

Ypocras, Hippocrates; *hence* a kind of cordial, C 306. See the note.

Ypocrisye, *s.* hypocrisy, C 410.

Yput, *pp.* put, G 762.

Yren, *adj.* iron, G 759; *s.* iron, 827. A. S. *íren, ísen*, iron; G. *eisen*.

Yrent, *pp.* rent, torn, B 844. A. S. *rendan*, to rend.

Y-schette, *pp.* shut, B 560. A. S. *scittan, scyttan*, to lock up (Somner); cf. A. S. *sceótan*, to shoot; Icel. *skjóta*, to shoot, also to shoot a bolt, *shut*.

Ysent, *pp.* sent, B 1041.

Yset, *pp.* seated (lit. set, put), C 392. A. S. *settan*, to set; pp. *geset*.

Yshape, *pp.* shaped, formed, H 43; Yshapen, shaped, i. e. contrived, G 1080. A. S. *scippan*, to shape, make; pp. *scapen*, *gescapen*.

Yshriuen, *pp.* shriven, C 380. A. S. *scrífan*, to shrive; pp. *gescrifen*.

Yslawe, *pp.* slain, B 484, C 856; Yslayn, slain, B 605, 848, C 673. A. S. *sleán*, to strike; pp. *geslagen*; whence *yslayn*, by change of *g* into *y*, and *yslawe* (for *yslawen*) by change of *g* into *w*.

Ystonge, *pp.* stung, C 355. A. S. *stingan*, pt. t. *ic stang*, pp. *stungen*, *gestungen*.

Ysweped, *pp.* swept, G 938. A. S. *swápan*, to sweep; pt. t. *sweóp*, pp. *swápen*. But here it is a *weak* verb, as at present.

Yuel, *adj.* evil, ill, C 408; *adv.* evilly, ill, G 921. (Pron. nearly in *one* syllable.) A.S. *yfel*, Goth. *ubils*, G. *übel*, evil, bad; A.S. *yfele*, evilly.

Ywedded, *pp.* wedded, G 128. A.S. *weddian*, to pledge; pp. *weddod*, *geweddod*; from *wed*, a pledge.

Ywis, *adv.* certainly, C 327, G 263, 439, 617, 689, 823, 1107, 1359. A. S. *gewis*, Du. *gewis*, G. *gewiss*, adv. certainly. From the root of *witan*, to know.

Ywriten, *pp.* written, B 191, G 210. A. S. *writan*, to write; pt. t. *wrát*, pp. *gewriten*.

INDEX OF PROPER NAMES, &c.

N.B. Many of the names are commented upon in the Notes.

Achilles, B 198.

Adam, C 505, 508,

Alisaundre, Alexandria, 975.

Alkaron, the Korán, B 332.

Alla, Ælla, B 578, 604, 610, 659.

Almachius, G 421, 435, 468, 487; Almache, 362, 431.

Ambrose, seint, G 271.

Anne, St. Anna, B 641, G 70.

Apia, Via, i.e. Via Appia, the Appian way, G 172.

Arnold of the newe toun, Arnoldus de Villa Nova, G 1428. See Theatrum Chemicum, iv. 514.

Attila, C 579.

Auicen, Avicenna, C 889.

Bachus, Bacchus. H 99.

Bayard, a horse's name, G 1413. (So called from his bay colour.)

Bernard, St. Bernard, G 30.

Blee, i.e. Blean, H 3.

Bob-vp-and-down (see note), H 2.

Boughton vnder Blee, G 556. See note.

Briton, adj. British, Welsh, B 666.

Cananee, adj. Canaanite, G 59.

Catoun, Cato (Dionysius Cato), G 688. See the note.

Caunterbury, Canterbury, G 624, H 3.

Cecilie, St. Cecilia, G 28, 85, &c.; Cecile, G 92, 94, &c.; lyf of seint Cecile, 554.

Chepe, Cheapside, C 564, 569, H 24.

Corinthe, Corinth, C 604.

Crist, Christ, B 277, 283, &c.

Custance, Constance, B 151, 226, 264, 319, 431, 438, &c.

Danyel, Daniel, B 473.

Dauid, David, B 935.

Demetrius, C 621.

Donegild, B 695, 778, 896.

Ebrayk, adj. Hebrew, B 489.

Ector, Hector, B 198.

Egypcien Marie, Egyptian Mary, Sta. Maria Ægyptiaca, B 500.

Engelond, England, B 1130, C 921, G 1356.

Ercules, Hercules, B 200.

Eua, Eve, B 368; son of Eue, G

Fishstrete, Fish Street, C 564.
Flaundres, Flanders, C 463.

Galianes, *s. pl.* drinks named after Galen, C 306.
Golias, Goliath, B 934.
Grece, Greece, B 464.
Gyle, St. Giles, St. Ægidius, **G** 1185.

Hanybal, Hannibal, B 290.
Hayles, the Abbey of Hailes, Gloucestershire, C 652.
Hermengild, Hermengild, B 533, 539, 597, **625;** *gen.* Hermengildes, 595.
Hermes, Hermes Trismegistus, G 1434.

Ieremye, Jeremiah, C 635.
Ierusalem, Jerusalem, I 51.
Iesu, Jesus, B 538.
Iewes, Jews, C 475.
Iohn Baptist, C 491.
Iohn, St. John, B 1019, C 752.
Ionas, Jonah, B 486.
Itayle, Italy, B 441.
Iubaltar, Gibraltar, B 947.
Iudas, Judas, G 1003.
Iudith, Judith, B 939.
Iulius, Julius Cæsar, B 199, 400.
Iupiter, Jupiter, G 364; the planet, 828.

Lacidomie, Lacedæmon, C 605.
Lamuel, Lemuel, C 584.
Lepe, a town in Spain, C 563, 570.
Lia, Leah, G 96, 98.
Libra, a sign of the zodiac, I 11.
Londoun, London, H 11; London, G 1012.
Lucan, B 401.

Mahoun, Mahomet, B **224, 340;** Makomete, **333;** *gen.* Makometes, 336.
Marie, St. Mary the Egyptian, B 500.
Marrok, Morocco, B 465.

Mars, B 301, 305.
Marye, Mary, B 841.
Mathew, St. Matthew, C 634.
Mauricius, Maurice, B 723; Maurice, B 1063, 1121; *gen.* Maurices, B 1127.
Maximus, G 338; Maxime, 377.
May, *s.* May, G 1343.

Niniuee, Nineveh, B 487; Niniue, G 974.
Northumberlond, Northumberland, B 508, 578.

Olofernus. Holophernes, B 940.
Osanne, Hosannah, **G 69.**

Paradys, *s.* Paradise, C 506, 509, G 227.
Parthes, Parthia (*or*, the Parthians), C 622.
Paul, St. Paul, C 521, I 32; Paulus, C 523.
Pirrus, Pyrrhus, B 288.
Plato, G **1448,** 1453, 1460.
Pompei, Pompey, B 199.

Rochel, Rochelle, C 571.
Romayn, *adj.* Roman, B 954; *pl.* Romayns, the Roman people, **291,** 394, G 121; Romayn gestes, **the** *gesta Romanorum,* B 1126.
Rome, B 142, 290, G 975.
Romeward, to, towards Rome, B 968.
Ronyan, St. Ronan, C 310; Ronyon, **320.** See the note.
Rosarie, *s.* Rosarium (name of a book), **G 1429.**

Salomon, Solomon, G 961.
Sampson, Samson, B 201; Sampsoun, C 554, 572.
Samuel, C 585.
Sathan, Satan, B 582, 634.
Saturnus, Saturn (the planet), G 828.
Scottes, *s. pl.* the Scots, B 580.
Semyram, Semiramis, B 359.

INDEX TO THE PRINCIPAL SUBJECTS
EXPLAINED IN THE NOTES.

The more difficult *words* are explained in the Glossary; but some are further commented on in the Notes. These are entered in the following Index, and are distinguished by being printed in *italics*. The numbers refer to the pages.

THE END.

CHAUCER.

The Complete Works of Geoffrey Chaucer. Edited, from numerous Manuscripts. In Six Volumes, demy **8vo**, with Portrait and Facsimiles. 4*l.* 16*s.*, or 16*s.* each volume.

Chaucerian and other Pieces, being a Supplementary **Volume** to the Above. Edited from numerous Manuscripts. 8vo, **18***s.*

The Prologue to the Canterbury Tales. (School **Edition.**) Extra fcap. 8vo, 1*s.*

The Prologue, The Knightes Tale, The Nonne Preestes Tale; from **the** Canterbury Tales. **Edited by R.** Morris, LL.D. **A** New Edition, with Collations **and Additional** Notes. Extra fcap. 8vo, **2***s.* 6*d.*

The Prioresses Tale, **Sir** *Thopas, The Monkes Tale, The* **Clerkes Tale**, *The Squieres* **Tale**, &c. *Fifth Edition.* Extra fcap. **8vo, 4***s.* **6***d.*

Minor Poems. Second Edition. Crown 8vo, **10***s.* 6*d.*

The Hous of Fame. Crown 8vo, paper boards, 2*s.*

The Legend of Good Women. **Crown** 8vo, **6***s.*

The Student's Chaucer. Being a complete Edition **of his** Works, edited from numerous MSS., **with** Introduction and Glossary. In one vol., crown 8vo, cloth, **7***s.* 6*d.*

The Oxford Chaucer. On India Paper, cloth **extra, 9***s.* **6***d.*

The **Vision** *of* **William** *concerning Piers the Plowman,* in three Parallel Texts; **together** with Richard the Redeless. By William Langland **(about** 1362–1399 A.D.). Edited from numerous Manuscripts, **with** Preface, Notes, and **a** Glossary. 2 vols. 8vo, 1*l.* 11*s.* 6*d.*

The Vision of William concerning Piers the Plowman, by William Langland. **Edited** with Notes. *Sixth Edition.* Extra fcap. 8vo, 4*s.* 6*d.*

Gamelyn, The Tale of. Edited, with Notes, Glossary, &c. *Second Edition, Revised.* Extra fcap. 8vo, stiff covers, 1*s.* 6*d.*

26/11/97

Clarendon Press Series.

❖❖

ENGLISH LANGUAGE AND LITERATURE . . pp. 1-6
HISTORY AND GEOGRAPHY . . . . p. 6
MATHEMATICS AND PHYSICAL SCIENCE . . p. 7
MISCELLANEOUS . . . . p. 8

❖❖

The English Language and Literature.

HELPS TO THE STUDY OF THE LANGUAGE

1. DICTIONARIES.

A NEW ENGLISH DICTIONARY, ON HISTORICAL PRIN-CIPLES: founded mainly on the materials collected by the Philological Society. Imperial 4to.

PRESENT STATE OF THE WORK.

			£	s.	d.
Vol. I. {A / B} Edited by Dr. MURRAY. . . . . Half-morocco	2	12	6
Vol. II. C Edited by Dr. MURRAY. . . . . Half-morocco	2	12	6
Vol. III. {D / E} Edited by Dr. MURRAY / Edited by HENRY BRADLEY } . . . Half-morocco	2	12	6

Vol. IV. ⎰ F Edited by HENRY BRADLEY {F-Field . . . . 0 7 6 / Field-Frankish . . . 0 12 6}

(*The remainder of the Letter* F *will be published on Jan.* 1, 1898.)

⎱ G Edited by HENRY BRADLEY. *In the Press.*

Vol. V. **H-K** Edited by Dr. MURRAY. *In the Press.*

Bosworth and **Toller.** *An Anglo-Saxon Dictionary*, based on the MS. Collections of the late JOSEPH BOSWORTH, D.D. Edited and enlarged by Prof. T. N. TOLLER, M.A. Parts I-III, A-SAR. . . . [4to, 15s. each.
Part IV, Section I, SAR—SWÍÐRIAN. . . . . [4to, 8s. 6d.

Mayhew and **Skeat.** *A Concise Dictionary of Middle English*, from A.D. 1150 to 1580. By A. L. MAYHEW, M.A., and W. W. SKEAT, Litt.D.
[Crown 8vo, half-roan, 7s. 6d.

Skeat. *A Concise Etymological Dictionary of the English Language.* By W. W. SKEAT, Litt.D. *Sixth Edition.* . . [Crown 8vo, 5s. 6d.

2. GRAMMARS, READING BOOKS, &c.

Earle. *The Philology of the English Tongue.* By J. EARLE, M.A.,
   Fifth Edition. .   .   .   .   .   .   [Extra fcap. **8vo**, 8s. 6d.
——— *A Book for the Beginner in Anglo-Saxon.* By J. EARLE, M.A.,
   Third Edition. .   .   .   .   [Extra fcap. 8vo, 2s. 6d.
Mayhew. *Synopsis of Old-English Phonology.* By A. L. MAYHEW,
   M.A. .   .   .   .   .   [Extra fcap. 8vo, bevelled boards, 8s. **6d.**
Morris and **Skeat.** *Specimens of Early English*—
   Part I. From Old English Homilies to King Horn (A.D. 1150 to A.D. 1300).
     By R. MORRIS, LL.D. *Second Edition.* .   .   [Extra fcap. 8vo, 9s.
   Part II. From Robert of Gloucester to Gower (A.D. 1298 to A.D. 1393). By R.
     MORRIS, LL.D., and W. W. SKEAT, Litt.D. *Third Edition.* [7s. 6d.
Skeat. *Specimens of English Literature,* from the 'Ploughmans
   Crede' to the 'Shepheardes Calender.' .   .   [Extra fcap. 8vo, 7s. 6d.
——— *The Principles of English Etymology*—
   First Series. The Native Element. *Second Edition.* [Crown 8vo, 10s. 6d.
   Second Series. The Foreign Element. .   .   [Crown 8vo, 10s. 6d.
——— *A Primer of English Etymology.* [Extra fcap. 8vo, *stiff covers,* 1s. 6d.
——— *Twelve Facsimiles of Old-English Manuscripts.* [4to, 7s. 6d.
Sweet. *A New English Grammar, Logical and Historical.* **Part I.**
   Introduction, Phonology, and Accidence. .   .   [Crown 8vo, 10s. 6d.
——— *A **Short** Historical English Grammar.* [Extra fcap. 8vo, 4s. **6d.**
——— *A Primer of Historical English Grammar.* [Extra fcap. 8vo, 2s.
——— *History of English Sounds from the Earliest Period.* With full
   Word-Lists. .   .   .   .   [8vo, 14s.
——— ***First** Steps in Anglo-Saxon.* .   . [Extra fcap. 8vo. **2s. 6d.**
——— *An Anglo-Saxon Primer, with Grammar, Notes, and Glossary.*
   Eighth Edition. .   .   .   .   .   [Extra fcap. 8vo, 2s. 6d.
——— *An Anglo-Saxon Reader.* In Prose and Verse. With Gram-
   matical Introduction, Notes, **and Glossary.** *Seventh Edition, Revised and*
   Enlarged. .   .   .   .   .   .   [Crown 8vo, 9s. 6d.
——— *A Second Anglo-Saxon **Reader**.* .   . [Extra fcap. 4s. 6d.
——— *Old English Reading Primers*—
   I. *Selected Homilies of Ælfric.* .   . [Extra fcap. 8vo, *stiff covers,* 2s.
   II. *Extracts from Alfred's Orosius.* [Extra fcap. 8vo, *stiff covers,* 2s.
——— *First Middle English Primer, with Grammar and Glossary.*
   Second Edition. .   .   .   .   .   [Extra fcap. 8vo, 2s. 6d.
——— *Second Middle English Primer.* Extracts from Chaucer, with
   Grammar and Glossary. .   .   .   [Extra fcap. 8vo, 2s. 6d.
——— *A Primer of Spoken English.* .   . [Extra fcap. 8vo, 3s. 6d.
——— *A Primer of Phonetics.* .   .   [Extra fcap. 8vo, 3s. **6d.**
——— *A Manual of Current Shorthand, Orthographic and Phonetic.*
           [Crown 8vo, 4s. 6d.
Tancock. *An Elementary English Grammar and Exercise Book.*
   By O. W. TANCOCK, M.A. *Third Edition.* .   . [Extra fcap. 8vo, 1s. 6d.
——— *An English Grammar and Reading Book,* for Lower Forms
   in Classical Schools. By O. W. TANCOCK, M.A. *Fourth Edition.* [3s. 6d.

A SERIES OF ENGLISH CLASSICS.

(CHRONOLOGICALLY ARRANGED.)

Chaucer. I. *The Prologue to the Canterbury Tales.* (*School Edition.*) Edited by W. W. SKEAT, Litt.D.   .   .   [Extra fcap. 8vo, *stiff covers*, **1s.**

—— II. *The Prologue; The Knightes Tale; The Nonne Prestes Tale.* Edited by R. MORRIS, LL.D. *A New Edition, with Collations and Additional Notes,* by W. W. SKEAT, Litt.D. . . [Extra fcap. 8vo, **2s.** 6d.

—— III. *The Prioresses Tale; Sir Thopas; The Monkes Tale; The Clerkes Tale; The Squieres Tale, &c.* Edited by W. W. SKEAT, Litt.D. *Sixth Edition.* . . . . [Extra fcap. 8vo, 4s. 6d.

—— IV. *The Tale of the Man of Lawe; The Pardoneres Tale; The Second Nonnes Tale; The Chanouns Yemannes Tale.* By the same Editor. *New Edition, Revised.* . . . . [Extra fcap. 8vo, 4s. 6d.

—— V. *Minor Poems.* By the same Editor. [Crown 8vo, 10s. 6d.

—— VI. *The Legend of Good Women.* By the same Editor.
[Crown 8vo, 6s.

—— VII. *The Hous of Fame.* By the same Editor. [Crown 8vo, 2s.

Langland. *The Vision of William concerning Piers the Plowman,* by WILLIAM LANGLAND. Edited by W. W. SKEAT, Litt.D. *Sixth Edition.*
[Extra fcap. 8vo, 4s. 6d.

Gamelyn, The Tale of. Edited by W. W. SKEAT, Litt.D.
[Extra fcap. 8vo, *stiff covers*, 1s. 6d.

Wycliffe. *The New Testament in English,* according to the Version by JOHN WYCLIFFE, about A.D. 1380, and Revised by JOHN PURVEY, about A.D. 1388. With Introduction and Glossary by W. W. SKEAT, Litt.D.
[Extra fcap. 8vo, 6s.

—— *The Books of Job, Psalms, Proverbs, Ecclesiastes, and the Song of Solomon:* according to the Wycliffite Version made by NICHOLAS DE HEREFORD, about A.D. 1381, and Revised by JOHN PURVEY, about A.D. 1388. With Introduction and Glossary by W.W.SKEAT, Litt.D. [Extra fcap. 8vo, 3s. 6d.

Minot. *The Poems of Laurence Minot.* Edited, with Introduction and Notes, by JOSEPH HALL, **M.A.** *Second Edition.* [Extra fcap. 8vo, 4s. 6d.

Spenser. *The Faery Queene.* Books I and II. Edited by G. W. KITCHIN, D.D., with Glossary by A. L. MAYHEW, M.A.
[Extra fcap. 8vo, 2s. 6d. each.

Hooker. *Ecclesiastical Polity,* **Book I.** Edited by R. W. CHURCH, M.A., late Dean of St. Paul's. . . . . . [Extra fcap. 8vo, 2s.

Marlowe and **Greene.** MARLOWE'S *Tragical History of Dr. Faustus,* and GREENE'S *Honourable History of Friar Bacon and Friar Bungay.* Edited by A. W. WARD, Litt.D. *New and Enlarged Edition.* [Crown 8vo, 6s. 6d.

Marlowe. *Edward II.* Edited by O. W. TANCOCK, M.A. *Second Edition.* . . . . . [Extra fcap. 8vo. *Paper covers,* 2s.; *cloth,* 3s.

Shakespeare. Select Plays. Edited by W. G. CLARK, **M.A.**, and
W. ALDIS WRIGHT, D.C.L. . . . . [Extra fcap. 8vo, *stiff covers.*
   The Merchant of Venice. **1s.**   *Macbeth.* **1s. 6d.**
   Richard the Second. 1s. **6d.**   *Hamlet.* **2s.**

Edited by **W. ALDIS** WRIGHT, **D.C.L.**
   The Tempest. 1s. 6d.   *Coriolanus.* **2s. 6d.**
   As You Like It. 1s. 6d.   *Richard the **Third.* 2s. 6d.**
   A Midsummer Night's Dream. **1s. 6d.** *Henry the Fifth.* 2s.
   Twelfth Night. 1s. 6d.   *King John.* 1s. 6d.
   Julius Caesar. 2s.   *King Lear.* 1s. 6d.
   Henry the Eighth. 2s.   *Much Ado About Nothing.* 1s. 6d.
      Henry the Fourth, Part I. 2s.

Shakespeare as a Dramatic Artist; *a popular Illustration of the
Principles of Scientific Criticism.* By R. G. MOULTON, M.A. [Cr. 8vo, 7s. 6d.
Bacon. *Advancement of Learning.* Edited by W. ALDIS WRIGHT,
D.C.L. *Third Edition.* . . . . . [Extra fcap. 8vo, 4s. 6d.
————— *The Essays.* Edited, with Introduction and Illustrative Notes,
by S. H. REYNOLDS, **M.A.** . . . . [Demy 8vo, *half-bound,* 12s. 6d.
Milton. I. *Areopagitica.* With Introduction and Notes. By JOHN
W. HALES, M.A. *Third Edition.* . . . . [Extra fcap. 8vo, 3s.
————— II. *Poems.* Edited by **R. C. BROWNE,** M.A. In two
Volumes. *New Edition.* . . . . [Extra fcap. 8vo, 6s. 6d.
   Sold separately, Vol. I. 4s., Vol. **II.** 3s.
   In paper covers, *Lycidas,* 3d. *Comus,* 6d.
By OLIVER ELTON, B.A.
  Lycidas, 6d. *L'Allegro,* 4d. *Il Penseroso,* 4d. *Comus,* 1s.
————— III. *Paradise Lost.* Book I. Edited with Notes, by H. C.
BEECHING, M.A. . . [Extra fcap. 8vo, 1s. 6d. *In Parchment,* 3s. 6d.
————— IV. *Paradise Lost.* Book II. Edited by E. K. CHAMBERS,
B.A. . . . . [Extra fcap. 8vo, 1s. 6d. Books I and II together, 2s. 6d.
————— V. *Samson Agonistes.* Edited, with Introduction and Notes,
by JOHN CHURTON COLLINS, M.A. . . [Extra fcap. 8vo, *stiff covers,* 1s.
Milton's Prosody. By ROBERT BRIDGES. [Extra fcap. 8vo, 1s. 6d.
Bunyan. I. *The Pilgrim's Progress, Grace Abounding, Relation of
the Imprisonment of Mr. John Bunyan.* Edited by E. VÉNABLES, M.A.
    [Extra fcap. 8vo, 3s. 6d. *In Parchment,* 4s. 6d.
————— II. *The Holy War, and the Heavenly Footman.* Edited by MABEL
PEACOCK. . . . . [Extra fcap. 8vo, 3s. 6d.
Clarendon. I. *History of the Rebellion.* Book VI. Edited, with Intro-
duction and Notes, by T. ARNOLD, M.A. *Second Edition.* [Crown 8vo, 5s.
————— II. *Selections.* Edited by G. BOYLE, M.A., Dean of Salisbury.
    [Crown 8vo, 7s. 6d.
Dryden. *Select Poems.* (*Stanzas on the Death of Oliver Cromwell;
Astræa Redux; Annus Mirabilis; Absalom and Achitophel; Religio Laici;
The Hind and the Panther.*) Edited by W. D. CHRISTIE, M.A. *Fifth Edition.*
Revised by C. H. FIRTH, M.A. . . . . [Extra fcap. 8vo, 3s. 6d.
————— *Essay of Dramatic Poesy.* Edited, with Notes, by T. ARNOLD,
M.A. *Second Edition.* . . . . . . [Extra fcap. 8vo, 3s. 6d.
Locke. *Conduct of the Understanding.* Edited, with Introduction,
Notes, &c., by T. FOWLER, D.D. *Third Edition.* . [Extra fcap. 8vo, 2s. 6d.

Addison. *Selections from Papers in the 'Spectator.'* By T. ARNOLD, M.A. *Sixteenth Thousand.* .   [Extra fcap. 8vo, 4s. 6d. *In Parchment*, 6s.

Steele. *Selections from the Tatler, Spectator, and Guardian.* By AUSTIN DOBSON. *Second Edition.* .   .   .   .   [Crown 8vo, 7s. **6d.**

Swift. *Selections from his Works.* Edited, with **Life**, Introductions, and Notes, by Sir HENRY CRAIK, K.C.B. Two Vols.
[Crown 8vo, **cloth** extra, **price 15s.**
Each volume may be had separately, price 7s. **6d.**

Pope. I. *Essay on Man.* Edited by MARK PATTISON, B.D.   *Sixth Edition.* .   .   .   .   [Extra fcap. 8vo, 1s. 6d.

———— II. *Satires and Epistles.* By the same Editor. *Fourth Edition.*
[Extra fcap. 8vo, 2s.

Thomson. *The Seasons,* and *The Castle of Indolence.* Edited by J. LOGIE ROBERTSON, M.A. .   .   .   [Extra fcap. 8vo, 4s. 6d.

———— *The Castle of Indolence.* By the same Editor. [Extra fcap. 8vo, 1s. 6d.

Berkeley. *Selections.* With Introduction and Notes. By A. C. FRASER, LL.D. *Fourth Edition.* .   .   .   .   [Crown 8vo, 8s. 6d.

Johnson. I. *Rasselas.* **Edited,** with Introduction and Notes, by G. BIRKBECK HILL, D.C.L.
[**Extra fcap.** 8vo, *limp*, **2s.**; *Bevelled boards*, 3s. 6d. ; *in Parchment*, 4s. 6d.

———— II. *Rasselas ; Lives of Dryden and Pope.* Edited by ALFRED MILNES, M.A. .   .   .   .   [Extra fcap. 8vo, 4s. 6d.
Lives of Dryden and Pope. .   . [*Stiff covers*, 2s. 6d.

———— III. *Life of Milton.* Edited, with Notes, &c., by C. H. FIRTH, M.A. .   .   . [Extra fcap. 8vo, *stiff covers*, 1s. 6d. ; *cloth*, 2s. 6d.

———— IV. *Vanity of Human Wishes.* With Notes, by E. J. PAYNE, M.A. .   .   .   .   [*Paper covers*, 4d.

Gray. *Selected Poems.* Edited by EDMUND GOSSE, M.A.
[*In Parchment*, 3s.

———— *The same,* together with Supplementary Notes for Schools. By FOSTER WATSON, M.A. .   .   .   [Extra fcap. 8vo, *stiff covers*, 1s. 6d.

———— *Elegy, and Ode on Eton College.* .   .   [*Paper covers*, 2d.

Goldsmith. *Selected Poems.* Edited, with Introduction and Notes, by AUSTIN DOBSON. .   .   [Extra fcap. 8vo, 3s. 6d. *In Parchment*, 4s. 6d.

———— *The Traveller.* Edited by G. B. HILL, D.C.L. [*Stiff covers*, 1s.

———— *The Deserted Village.* .   .   .   .   [*Paper covers*, 2d.

Cowper. I. *The Didactic Poems of* 1782, with Selections from the Minor Pieces, A.D. 1779-1783. Edited by H. T. GRIFFITH, B.A.
[Extra fcap. 8vo, 3s.

———— II. *The Task, with Tirocinium,* and Selections from the Minor Poems, A.D. 1784-1799. By the same Editor.   [Extra fcap. 8vo, 3s.

Burke. I. *Thoughts on the Present Discontents ; the two Speeches on America.* Edited by E. J. PAYNE, M.A. .   . [Extra fcap. 8vo, 4s. 6d.

———— II. *Reflections on the French Revolution.* By the same Editor. *Second Edition.* .   .   .   .   [Extra fcap. 8vo, 5s.

———— III. *Four Letters on the Proposals for Peace with the Regicide Directory of France.* By the same Editor.   [Extra fcap. 8vo, 5s.

Burns. *Selected Poems.* Edited by J. LOGIE ROBERTSON, M.A.
[Crown 8vo, 6s.

Keats. *The Odes of Keats.* With Notes and Analyses and a Memoir, by ARTHUR C. DOWNER, M.A. With Four Illustrations.
[Extra fcap. 8vo, 3s. 6d. net.

―――― *Hyperion*, Book I. With Notes, by W. T. ARNOLD, B.A. 4d.

Byron. *Childe Harold.* With Introduction and Notes, by H. F. TOZER, M.A.   .   .   .   .   [Extra fcap. 8vo, 3s. 6d. *In Parchment*, 5s.

Shelley. *Adonais.* With Introduction and Notes. By W. M. ROSSETTI.   .   .   .   .   [Crown 8vo, 5s.

Scott. *Lady of the Lake.* Edited, with Preface and Notes, by W. MINTO, M.A. With Map.   .   .   .   [Extra fcap. 8vo, 3s. 6d.

―――― *Lay of the Last Minstrel.* Edited by W. MINTO, M.A. With Map.   .   .   . [Extra fcap. 8vo, *stiff covers*, 2s. *In Parchment*, 3s. 6d.

―――― *Lay of the Last Minstrel.* Introduction and Canto I, with Preface and Notes, by W. MINTO, M.A.   .   .   .   . [*Paper covers*, 6d.

―――― *Lord of the Isles.* Edited, with Introduction and Notes, by THOMAS BAYNE.   .   .   .   . [Extra fcap. 8vo, 3s. 6d.

―――― *Marmion.* By the same Editor.   . [Extra fcap. 8vo, 3s. 6d.

Campbell. *Gertrude of Wyoming.* Edited, with Introduction and Notes, by H. MACAULAY FITZGIBBON, M.A. *Second Edition.* [Extra fcap. 8vo, 1s.

Wordsworth. *The White Doe of Rylstone.* Edited by WILLIAM KNIGHT, LL.D., University of St. Andrews.   . [Extra fcap. 8vo, 2s. 6d.

Typical Selections *from the best English Writers. Second Edition.* In Two Volumes.   .   .   .   .   .   [Extra fcap. 8vo, 3s. 6d. each.

GEOGRAPHY, &c.

Greswell. *History of the Dominion of Canada.* By W. PARR GRESWELL, M.A.   .   .   .   .   .   .   [Crown 8vo, 7s. 6d.

―――― *Geography of the Dominion of Canada and Newfoundland.* By the same Author.   .   .   .   .   .   .   [Crown 8vo, 6s.

―――― *Geography of Africa South of the Zambesi.* By the same Author.   .   .   .   .   .   .   [Crown 8vo, 7s. 6d.

Hughes (Alfred). *Geography for Schools.* Part I, *Practical Geography.* With Diagrams.   .   .   .   .   .   [Extra fcap. 8vo, 2s. 6d.

Lucas. *Historical Geography of the British Colonies.* By C. P. LUCAS, B.A.

    Introduction. With Eight Maps.   .   .   .   . [Crown 8vo, 4s. 6d.

    Vol. I. *The Mediterranean and Eastern Colonies (exclusive of India).* With Eleven Maps.   .   .   .   . [5s.

    Vol. II. *The West Indian Colonies.* With Twelve Maps.   . [7s 6d.

    Vol. III. *West Africa.* With Five Maps.   .   .   . [7s. 6d.

    Vol. IV. *South and East Africa.* Historical and Geographical. With Eleven Maps.   .   .   .   . [9s. 6d.

      Also Vol. IV in two Parts—
    Part I. *Historical.* 6s. 6d.   Part II. *Geographical.* 3s. 6d.

MATHEMATICS AND PHYSICAL SCIENCE.

Aldis. *A Text Book of Algebra (with Answers to the Examples).* By W. STEADMAN ALDIS, M.A. . . . . . . [Crown 8vo, 7s. 6d.

Emtage. *An Introduction to the Mathematical Theory of Electricity and Magnetism.* By W. T. A. EMTAGE, M.A. . . [Crown 8vo, 7s. 6d.

Fisher. *Class-Book of Chemistry.* By W. W. FISHER, M.A., F.C.S. *Fourth Edition.* . . . . [Crown 8vo, 4s. 6d.

Fock. *An Introduction to Chemical Crystallography.* By ANDREAS FOCK, Ph.D. Translated and Edited by W. J. POPE. With a Preface by N. STORY-MASKELYNE, M.A., F.R.S. . . . . [Crown 8vo, 5s.

Hamilton and **Ball.** *Book-keeping.* By Sir R. G. C. HAMILTON, K.C.B., and JOHN BALL. *New and Enlarged Edition.* [Extra fcap. 8vo, 2s.
*** *Ruled Exercise Books adapted to the above may be had,* price 1s. 6d.;
also, *adapted to the Preliminary Course only,* price 4d.

Harcourt and **Madan.** *Exercises in Practical Chemistry.* By A. G. VERNON HARCOURT, M.A., and H. G. MADAN, M.A. *Fifth Edition.* Revised by H. G. MADAN, M.A. . . . . . [Crown 8vo, 10s. 6d.

Hensley. *Figures made Easy: a first Arithmetic Book.* By LEWIS HENSLEY, M.A. . . . . . . [Crown 8vo, 6d. *Answers,* 1s.

———— *The Scholar's Arithmetic.* By the same Author.
[Crown 8vo, 2s. 6d. *Answers,* 1s. 6d.

———— *The Scholar's Algebra.* An Introductory work on Algebra. By the same Author. . . . . [Crown 8vo, 2s. 6d.

Nixon. *Euclid Revised.* Containing the essentials of the Elements of Plane Geometry as given by Euclid in his First Six Books. Edited by R. C. J. NIXON, M.A. *Third Edition.* . . . . . . [Crown 8vo, 6s.
*** May likewise be had in parts as follows—
Book I, 1s. Books I, II, 1s. 6d. Books I-IV, 3s. Books V, VI, 3s. 6d.

———— *Geometry in Space.* Containing parts of Euclid's Eleventh and Twelfth Books. By the same Author. . . . [Crown 8vo, 3s. 6d.

———— *Elementary Plane Trigonometry; that is, Plane Trigonometry without Imaginaries.* By the same Author. . . . [Crown 8vo, 7s. 6d.

Russell. *An Elementary Treatise on Pure Geometry.* By J. WELLESLEY RUSSELL, M.A. . . . . [Crown 8vo, 10s. 6d.

Selby. *Elementary Mechanics of Solids and Fluids.* By A. L. SELBY, M.A. . . . . [Crown 8vo, 7s. 6d.

Williamson. *Chemistry for Students.* By A. W. WILLIAMSON, Phil. Doc., F.R.S. . . . . [Extra fcap. 8vo, 8s. 6d.

Woollcombe. *Practical Work in General Physics.* By W. G. WOOLL-COMBE, M.A., B.Sc. . . . . [Crown 8vo, 2s.

———— *Practical Work in Heat.* By the same Author.
[Crown 8vo, 2s.

———— *Practical Work in Light and Sound.* By the same Author.
[Crown 8vo, 2s.

———— *Practical Work in Electricity and Magnetism.* By the same Author. *In Preparation.*

MISCELLANEOUS.

Fowler. *The Elements of Deductive and Inductive Logic.* By T. FOWLER, D.D. . . . . [Extra fcap. 8vo, 7s. 6d.

Also, separately—

The Elements of Deductive Logic, designed mainly for the use of Junior Students in the Universities. With a Collection of Examples.
[Extra fcap. 8vo, 3s. 6d.

The Elements of Inductive Logic, designed mainly for the use of Students in the Universities. *Sixth Edition.* . . . [Extra fcap. 8vo, 6s.

Music.—Farmer. *Hymns and Chorales for Schools and Colleges.* Edited by JOHN FARMER, Organist of Balliol College. . . . . [5s.
☞ *Hymns without the Tunes,* 2s.

Hullah. *The Cultivation of the Speaking Voice.* By JOHN HULLAH.
[Extra fcap. 8vo, 2s. 6d.

Maclaren. *A System of Physical Education: Theoretical and Practical.* By ARCHIBALD MACLAREN. *New Edition,* re-edited and enlarged by WALLACE MACLAREN, M.A., Ph.D. . . . . [Crown 8vo, 8s. 6d. net.

Troutbeck and **Dale.** *A Music Primer for Schools.* By J. TROUTBECK, D.D., and R. F. DALE, M.A., B.Mus. . . . [Crown 8vo, 1s. 6d.

Tyrwhitt. *Handbook of Pictorial Art.* With Illustrations, and a chapter on Perspective by A. MACDONALD. By R. ST. J. TYRWHITT, M.A. *Second Edition.* . . . . [8vo, *half-morocco,* 18s.

Upcott. *An Introduction to Greek Sculpture.* By L. E. UPCOTT, M.A. . . . . [Crown 8vo, 4s. 6d.

Helps to the Study of the Bible, taken from the *Oxford Bible for Teachers.* New, Enlarged and Illustrated Edition. Pearl 16mo, stiff covers, 1s. *net.* Large Paper Edition, Long Primer 8vo, cloth boards, 5s.

Helps to the Study of the Book of Common Prayer. Being a Companion to Church Worship. By W. R. W. STEPHENS, B.D.
[Crown 8vo, 3s. 6d.

Old Testament History for Schools. By T. H. STOKOE, D.D.
Part I. From the Creation to the Settlement in Palestine. (*Second Edition.*)
Part II. From the Settlement to the Disruption of the Kingdom.
Part III. From the Disruption to the Return from Captivity. *Completing the work.* [Extra fcap. 8vo, 2s. 6d. each Part.

Notes on the Gospel of St. Luke, for Junior Classes. By E. J. MOORE SMITH, Lady Principal of the Ladies' College, Durban, Natal.
[Extra fcap. 8vo, *stiff covers,* 1s. 6d.

Oxford

AT THE CLARENDON PRESS

London, Edinburgh, and New York

HENRY FROWDE, M.A.

www.ingramcontent.com/pod-product-compliance
Lightning Source LLC
Chambersburg PA
CBHW021116270326
41929CB00009B/906